The Idealist

THE IDEALIST

WENDELL WILLKIE'S WARTIME
QUEST TO BUILD ONE WORLD

SAMUEL ZIPP

THE BELKNAP PRESS OF
HARVARD UNIVERSITY PRESS

Cambridge, Massachusetts

London, England

2020

First printing

Library of Congress Cataloging-in-Publication Data
is available from loc.gov

ISBN: 978-0-674-73751-8 (cloth)

For Ilona

The earth to be spann'd, connected by network,

. . .

The oceans to be cross'd, the distant brought near,

The lands to be welded together.

—Walt Whitman, "Passage to India," 1871

CONTENTS

Introduction   1

CHAPTER 1   Taking Flight
ELWOOD, PUERTO RICO, PARIS   15

CHAPTER 2   Power and the Presidency
AKRON, NEW YORK, KHARTOUM   33

CHAPTER 3   Egypt Is Saved
LONDON, CAIRO, ALEXANDRIA   53

CHAPTER 4   A Great Social Laboratory
ANKARA   78

CHAPTER 5   The Imperial Dilemma
BEIRUT AND JERUSALEM   89

CHAPTER 6   How East and West Will Meet
BAGHDAD   113

CHAPTER 7   First Flight
TEHRAN   126

CHAPTER 8   Working with Russia
KUIBYSHEV, MOSCOW, RZHEV   141

CHAPTER 9   The China Mystique
LANZHOU, CHONGQING, XI'AN   173

CHAPTER 10   A Report to the People
YAKUTSK, WASHINGTON, NEW YORK   207

CHAPTER 11   One World Barnstorming
AMERICA AND THE WORLD   237

CHAPTER 12   The Narrows of 1944
KANSAS CITY, WISCONSIN, RUSHVILLE   270

Conclusion   298

Notes   323
Acknowledgments   377
Index   381

Illustrations follow page 112

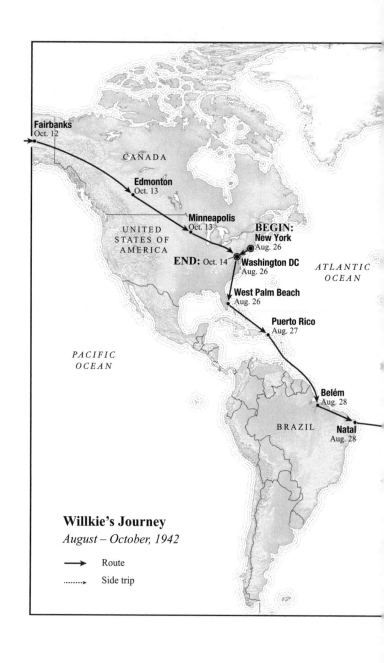

Fairbanks
Oct. 12

CANADA

Edmonton
Oct. 13

Minneapolis
Oct. 13

UNITED
STATES OF
AMERICA

BEGIN:
New York
Aug. 26

END: Oct. 14

Washington DC
Aug. 26

ATLANTIC
OCEAN

West Palm Beach
Aug. 26

Puerto Rico
Aug. 27

PACIFIC
OCEAN

Belém
Aug. 28

BRAZIL

Natal
Aug. 28

Willkie's Journey
August – October, 1942

⟶   Route

·····▸   Side trip

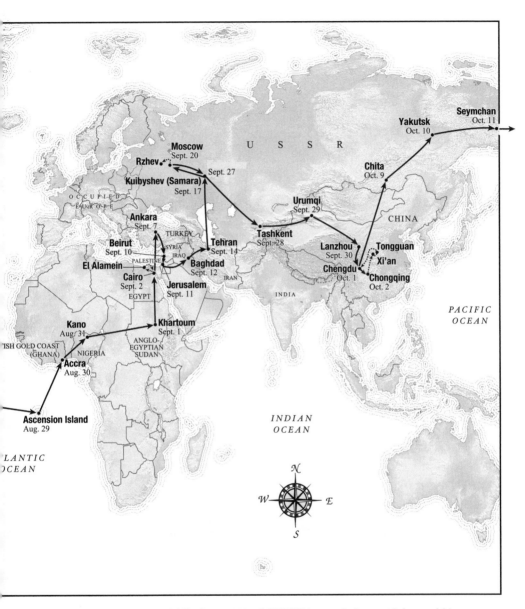

In the late summer and fall of 1942, Wendell Willkie traveled around the world in forty-nine days, leaving from New York on August 26 and returning to Washington, DC, on October 14.

The Idealist

Introduction

Two LIMOUSINES motored out of Manhattan in the rising light of an unseasonably cool August morning in 1942, crossing the East River at Fifty-Ninth Street and winding through the streets of Queens, past row houses and car lots and red brick apartment buildings, slipping loose from morning traffic and out into the suburbs. No barricades lined the route, no American flags fluttered from the cars' hoods, but honks and shouts followed them as they drove into Long Island. Somewhere along the way several police motorcycles pulled alongside the limousines, speeding the travelers toward Mitchel Field, an army airstrip some ten miles beyond the city limits.

The police officers peeled away as the limousines pulled up under one wing of a massive four-engine Consolidated C-87—the transport version of the B-24 Liberator bomber. The plane bore a snub nose, a distinctive double tail, a gently curved fuselage with a single row of square windows, and four propellers on long, high-set wings. This was the *Gulliver*, and the limousines were delivering its cargo.

Out came Gardner "Mike" Cowles Jr., head of the domestic branch of the Office of War Information (OWI) and publisher of the picture magazine *Look* (second only to *Life* in circulation) with his wife, Virginia. Then came Joseph Barnes, the former foreign news editor and Moscow correspondent for the *New York Herald Tribune*, now deputy director of the overseas branch of the OWI, accompanied by his wife, Betty. Finally there

1

was the star of the show: Wendell Lewis Willkie, the 1940 Republican presidential candidate, whose wife, Edith, had also come to see him off. Husky and affable, with a shock of brown hair perpetually falling across his forehead, Willkie looked younger than his fifty years. He held no public position or role in the massive war effort groaning into motion across America. He was not running for office. But he was one of the most famous men in the country, famous enough to draw cheers and stares on a quiet Long Island morning.

A small crowd of military personnel—two full crews led by Major Richard Kight, a lean, soft-spoken Texan—waited to greet the passengers. A gaggle of press usually trailed Willkie, but no reporters or photographers tagged along that morning, and despite the mounting hoopla on the road to the airfield, the send-off was quick and quiet. Just before nine o'clock Kight and his copilot, Captain Alexis Klotz, got the *Gulliver*'s four props going and taxied away to the far end of the runway. A minute or two later the plane roared past, climbing up into the rising sun. It was, Betty Barnes thought, watching from the tarmac below, a "thrilling and auspicious departure."[1]

Theirs was one departure among many in a year when millions would see their loved ones off at airfields and train stations and docksides across the nation, but Willkie and his colleagues were not just crossing the country or even the ocean. They had embarked on the first leg of a 31,000-mile journey around the globe during the darkest and most uncertain days of World War II. They traveled via recently opened and occasionally unscouted air lanes over Africa, the Middle East, the Soviet Union, and China—often well within range of enemy aircraft. Not quite a diplomatic mission, the flight of the *Gulliver* had been authorized by President Franklin Delano Roosevelt and would become something between a fact-finding tour and a propaganda circuit. It would bring Willkie and his companions face-to-face with Soviet factory workers, Siberian peasants, Arab nationalists, Joseph Stalin, Chiang Kai-shek, Charles de Gaulle, and the shah of Iran. The journey would offer the travelers an unparalleled view of the world at war, and glimpses of a possible postwar world unavailable to any other Americans.

Willkie's fame meant that newspaper and magazine readers around the world would follow his progress. Millions tracked his route around a planet that was becoming, as Willkie would later put it, "small and completely interdependent." Interest in Roosevelt's charismatic Republican challenger swept much of the world during the war, beginning with his closely watched travels in the late summer and fall of 1942. Willkie mania crested during the spring and summer of 1943, when his account of his journey, *One World,* raced to the top of the bestseller lists, becoming by some accounts the fastest-selling book ever published in America. In these years Willkie, his book, and the idea of "one world" jump-started an unprecedented challenge to the way Americans looked at the world and their place in it.

As he traveled, Willkie would discover that in countries across Africa, the Middle East, and Asia the war was seen as much more than a struggle against Nazi fascism and Japanese militarism. For many in these regions, it represented a colossal turning point in their history, a moment when the great European empires might finally be forced to relinquish their hold on the globe. The United States, Willkie would realize, was at a crossroads, too. He understood that America would become the next great power—but what kind of power would it choose to become? Here, in the midst of worldwide terror and destruction, he discovered a rare opportunity. The country had a chance to lead the planet to a new era of cooperation—but only if it would truly embrace its own ideals, expanding their reach to the world at large in an effort to end colonialism and colonial thinking. To win a lasting peace, Willkie came to believe, Americans would have to accept a more cooperative relationship with the rest of the planet. And to do so they would have to confront their own history of imperial ambition and racial discrimination.

In time Willkie and his companions would count this journey as the great adventure of their lives. But as they took off that morning they saw the voyage ahead in prosaic terms. They hoped their trip would do some good, both for the war effort and the terms of the eventual peace. Willkie was traveling as a private citizen, on his own initiative, but with the informal backing of his former opponent, President Roosevelt. The two men had agreed on several immediate goals for the trip. Willkie would carry confidential messages to Allied leaders. He would observe the growing war effort firsthand and report back to the president and the American people. He would urge neutral nations and reluctant Allies to commit to the cause. He would demonstrate to the entire world that the United States was united—that, contrary to Axis propaganda, the president and the nominal leader of the opposition party were of one mind when it came to winning the war. The audacious air journey would demonstrate Allied control of what Willkie later called the "ocean of the air," and show how overwhelming American military power meant an inevitable and complete Allied victory.[2]

But as the *Gulliver* touched down in thirteen countries on five continents, and as the fierce and urgent spectacle of a world at war unfurled around them, Willkie began to realize that this trip could become much more than a recruitment drive for the Allied war effort. He started to give himself his own personal, unofficial mission. He began to treat the journey as a form of political barnstorming, like a global version of the old whistle-stop tour, with reporters and photographers waiting on every foreign tarmac. This campaign was not for office but for an idea. If he was lucky, the journey might become one of those rare events that has the chance to reorient the way men and women see their world.

There are moments in time—periods of weeks, months, even years—that disrupt the patterns of regular experience. Some burst in to command full civic attention, when public life is distilled down to a bundle of dilemmas and possibilities around which almost everything appears to revolve. But often we don't notice them as they are happening; they arrive surreptitiously and dissipate almost as imperceptibly. Only later do we mark them as watersheds or turning points, moments when things gathered and then broke one way or another. Sometimes these moments hinge on the words and deeds of a particular person, someone who collects, with concentrated fervor, all the currents of possibility and wary foreboding that confront us. Times like these grab public attention and rend the fabric of the possible, revealing much that was settled as suddenly, expansively at stake. Fixed ideas of national life, distant problems of geopolitics, and day-to-day reality: all can suddenly detach from their moorings. Disparate ideas, fashions, and principles suddenly come together, while once-settled ways of thinking are suddenly up for grabs. Old debates are refreshed and transformed, new vantages opened, possibilities welcomed.

The middle of the twentieth century saw no shortage of transformative moments. We are familiar with many of them; they mark our conventional histories. We recognize World War II as the hinge of the American Century, swinging between the Great Depression and postwar affluence. On one side of the conflict was a world of European nations competing to rule the globe; on the other was the rise of the United States as a dominant power, the beginning of the end of the system of European empires, and the emergence of the "smaller" nations—many of them former colonies—onto the world stage. We know the battles that are said to have turned the tides of war: Midway, El Alamein, Stalingrad, D-Day. And we know the names in the headlines, the world leaders who sit astride this history: Hitler and his plans for world domination, Churchill and de Gaulle standing firm in the face of desperate odds, Stalin willing the Russians to repel the Nazi invaders, Roosevelt cannily guiding a reluctant people toward war and unprecedented world power. We also know to look to the years between 1945 and 1948, when deepening tensions between the Soviet Union and the United States hardened into a cold war that divided the globe for almost a half century.

But some of these moments are not marked in the official chronicles of war, diplomacy, and politics. Some intense but fleeting episodes, tears in the fabric of conventional history, are easily overlooked or forgotten. They slip away with their great promise or danger unfulfilled. They register as failed visions or incomplete transformations. We rarely write histories of failure. We prefer the hard currency of recognized success, the official coin with which we count winners and losers and measure the meaning of what happened. But in concentrating on what is said to have *really happened,* we risk missing what almost happened, and what could happen still. History sometimes works like this. It lurches forward as a shared drama in which sweeping change dawns and just as suddenly subsides, resolving as a shadow of its striking promise. Unrealized ideas and possibilities go back underground, onto those "lower frequencies" the novelist Ralph Ellison discovered, waiting to be recognized and taken up again when another such moment collects and surges into public view.[3]

This book unearths one of those moments, one that has largely disappeared from memory: the sudden emergence of Wendell Willkie onto the world stage between the summer of 1942 and the end of 1944. During this brief, blazing moment, a corporate lawyer and failed presidential candidate conducted a one-man campaign to reintroduce America and the world. Over the course of those two years, Willkie—the most popular American internationalist since his boyhood hero Woodrow Wilson—promised to reshape the country's fundamental understanding of the planet it would soon come to dominate. Americans, he argued, had not only to dispense with the insular form of nationalism many called "isolationism" but also to confront the truly global stakes of the war and make it count for all the world's peoples.

World War II was an unprecedented catastrophe, an organized slaughter greater than any the world had ever seen. Americans have too often avoided grappling with this reality. Comparatively untouched by the war's horrors and lucky enough to have been on the winning side, we have swaddled our memories in "Greatest Generation" bromides about "the Good War," as if the entire gruesome thing—the firebombing of cities, the mass slaughter in the "bloodlands" between Germany and Russia, Hiroshima and Nagasaki, the death camps—amounted to a demonstration of American righteousness. We divide the war into two dominant military "theaters," western Europe and the Pacific islands, that feature starring roles for US forces, effectively erasing the battles and intrigues that played out in the Soviet Union, eastern Europe, Africa, Asia, and the Middle East, where Americans played no more than a supporting role. Sometimes in our endlessly recycled retellings the whole war becomes as simple as the moralistic plot of Steven Spielberg's film *Saving Private Ryan:* all the terror and gore and chaos, rendered indelibly in the film's visceral D-Day sequence, were worth it, we are told, to save the life of one blond farm boy.

But some saw the war as something more than a gory fable about American exceptionalism. They embraced a more expansive and riskier story line than the anodyne triumphalist narratives we know so well. For Willkie and other idealists like him, if the war was to prove worth fighting, worth all the death and terror and privation, it had to deliver a peace worthy of the stakes.[4]

Many Americans were reluctant to sacrifice for another European war, and they mobilized only to punish the Japanese for Pearl Harbor. Once stirred, they saw the war in prosaic terms: go over there, lick the Nazis and the "Japs," and come home. They fought for home and family, for a return to normal life, for revenge, or for the guy next to them in the foxhole. And they embraced vicious stereotypes, seeing the Japanese as less than human. Few soldiers—or civilians, for that matter—bought into, or sometimes even knew of, the lofty war aims of Roosevelt's Four Freedoms, or popular propaganda like Frank Capra's *Why We Fight* films.

In 1941, Roosevelt and Winston Churchill had tried to explain the war as a fight for freedom and self-determination, issuing a joint declaration called the Atlantic Charter. The document, which seemed to pledge the Allies to secure liberty for peoples everywhere, attracted great interest among African Americans and many others abroad, particularly in the colonized zones of the world. The Atlantic Charter, one civil rights leader declared, was something African Americans would "live, work, fight and, if need be, die for." This would prove highly controversial, particularly when Churchill soon disavowed it. But most Americans took less notice, focusing only on the rudimentary goals of winning the war and getting home.[5]

Willkie challenged them to do more. He argued that the peace would have to be won as much as the war. The United States and its allies would have to forge the coming interdependent world order *during* the war, not after. As a young man Willkie had felt cruel disappointment when America abandoned Woodrow Wilson's League of Nations. Hell-bent on getting it right this time, he had a novel if risky strategy: he would show Americans that the nation's fight for freedom against fascism—what he called the "war of liberation"—was no mere abstraction if they understood how the war mattered to people around the world. In many countries, the Atlantic Charter encouraged people to see World War II as their version of the American Revolution, a chance to gain the freedom and self-determination that so many felt set the United States apart. With breezy tales of meeting and greeting the "important and anonymous" foreigners for whom the war held such high stakes, Willkie put flesh and bones on the true *world* nature of World War II. The conflict reached all corners of the globe—everyone could see that. But Willkie showed how its outcome would affect the political and social imaginations of all the world's peoples, even ordinary Americans who had often been content to insulate themselves from world events.[6]

Willkie's journey, which wound through Africa and the Middle East to the Soviet Union and China during the direst months of the war, challenged Americans to see the struggle of ideas that played out behind headlines announcing ground gained and lost, tonnage sunk, cities bombed. The prospects opened by global war gave him the opportunity to reorient mainstream conceptions of the world away from Europe, the center of the imperial system and source of so many American immigrant pasts. His voyage challenged those who rarely or never traveled abroad, who had no connection to the larger world, who did not "think globally"—as the contemporary cliché has it—to discard the familiar and faulty frameworks of exoticism, racism, or paternalism. Willkie asked Americans to see the wider world through the lens of fraternity and cooperation instead. He pushed them to get to know a world made small by the technology of flight and total war, a world in which American independence would require a new form of *interdependence* with the world. Claiming world leadership would force the United States to reckon with global desires for an end to empire and a guarantee of self-determination. And that would require really feeling that the war was a great crucible in which freedom could be forged for all.

When Willkie took off from Mitchel Field that August morning, he was putting himself at the center of a surging popular passion for worldliness, for international connection, and for opening the United States to the rest of the world. He sensed that he could link Americans to millions around the globe through the medium of his magnetic personality. He was not an intellectual wielding a painstakingly argued philosophy of the world, nor was he concerned, like so many thinkers in those years, with diagnosing the ills of "man" or "civilization." He was not a radical seeking to make over society. Neither was he truly a politician.[7]

He had first come to public attention for his work as a lawyer and later as an energy industry executive. A confident capitalist, he began his political life as a Progressive Era Indiana Democrat and ended it as a liberal internationalist Republican in New York City. All along he backed labor and civil rights but championed free enterprise. A populist iconoclast in the world of business, he sought to dispel the hidebound conservatism of his class. He was far more recognizable than any ambassador, but too restless, impractical, and irresponsible, some said, to be a diplomat. He was a wild card in many realms, particularly in foreign relations, where he went out of his way to make the sober affairs of state into fodder for the media. His unruly journey upset the conventional practices of diplomacy just as his popular idea of "one world" unsettled the international order on which diplomacy subsisted. As a journalist for the newsmagazine *Collier's* put it, Willkie "sassed the censors, made formal diplomatic calls in a lounge suit instead of the sacred striped pants and tail coat of tradition. He managed to impart to nearly everything he did an atmosphere of clambake."[8]

Willkie's charisma made him something close to a celebrity. He popped up in the newsreels that ran before the movies, addressed millions over the radio, and grabbed headlines in papers across the country and around the world. He wrote articles for *Life* and the *Saturday Evening Post*. He was photographed with kings, presidents, prime ministers, and premiers, starlets and labor leaders, farmers and factory workers. His journey, his writings, and the widespread acclaim and controversy he attracted all entered the popular consciousness at a level reserved for heads of state and movie stars. At the same time, he could not put his hands on the levers of power; he commanded no armies, organized no great social movement. But as one of the most recognized American political figures of his day, Willkie had the power to shape the common sense by which people lived, to push to make his ideas the frame through which they would confront and understand the events of their time. Roosevelt recognized Willkie's capacity for shaping public opinion, hailing him as "Private Citizen Number One" on the eve of his journey. "My point of view all along, you know," Willkie told the *New Yorker* near the end of his life, "has been to create a state of mind in this country. That's what I've been working toward."[9]

Willkie's brand of power—often written off as crafty public relations—had in truth taken on a subtle but capricious kind of influence by the middle of the twentieth century. At the beginning of the era of mass communications, when for the first time millions consumed the same national and even international radio broadcasts, picture magazines, news wire services, and movies—the "age of broadcasting," we might call it—a personality like Willkie had access to the biggest audience yet assembled in human history. Of course, much like the conventional power conferred by electoral office, money, or force of arms, broadcasting power could be won or lost. In fact, Willkie's influence, his ability to push and pull the levers of impression and belief, was even more precarious. His exertions for interdependent internationalism were subject to the whims of the very mass appeal he had so eagerly cultivated. The popularity of the "one world" idea surged with Willkie's own fame, but he struggled to channel the ebb and flow of acclaim into the concrete gains sought by an officeholder or the leader of a movement with specific goals.[10]

Just under 23 million people had voted for him in the 1940 election, but the constituency he assembled around his vision was broad but never deep. Willkie reached a huge number of people: middle- and upper-middle-class whites, liberals in both parties, and many African Americans, but fewer in the white working class, where distrust of his business background lingered. He was nominally a Republican, but the conservative wing of the party never fully accepted him. He inspired productive debate around the future of the nation, but with his sudden death in 1944 his ideas receded. Willkie's vision of an interconnected world reverberated in the halls of internationalist institutions such as the United Nations, but they mostly entered the subterranean reservoir of ideas, waiting for the next moment when people across the world might find a new faith in global connection and international cooperation.

"The energy that actually shapes the world," George Orwell wrote in 1941, "springs from emotions." If Willkie ever read those lines, he would have agreed. Orwell was talking about those primal political drives—"racial pride, leader-worship, religious belief, love of war"—that propped up the nationalism Willkie sought to undermine. But Willkie hoped to call on rival sentiments—empathy and a shared sense of humanity—made more vivid in a world shrunk by flight and the perils of war. He bet on the idea that the new sense of connection felt amid a catastrophic conflict would offer an antidote to those base emotions that had sparked the war in the first place. These connective feelings might not entirely dispel more sinister urges, but they could be more firmly nestled in the public mind, and could guide progress toward a better world. Orwell would no doubt have found this naive, as did many Willkie skeptics on the left and right. But for a brief, intense stretch of time FDR's Private Citizen Number One rallied the nation's attention and seemed poised to open American minds to the world.[11]

The easy and jocular manner he cultivated was seen as characteristically "American." His forthright air came, he and many others believed, from his unpretentious midwestern roots, so often identified as the wellspring of mainstream national life. But for all his love of America, Willkie did not think his country could go it alone. His travels would convince him that Americans needed to give up some of their sense that they were a people apart, a special people, for the sake of a lasting and just peace. His solution was to conceive of the Americanness he was said to embody—the neighborly folksiness that gave him such sway in the age of broadcasting—as an invitation rather than an impediment to worldly connection. He would make himself a popular medium for global connection, a public diplomat rather than a statesman.

His success in this quixotic endeavor would depend on coaxing Americans to confront the pervasive sway of imperial power and its faithful handmaiden, racism. If our familiar stories of World War II tend to simplify the stakes of the war, it is in large part because they skirt the topics of colonialism and racism. In keeping with the idea of "the Good War," we see a showdown between grand Manichean abstractions: democracy against fascism, freedom versus totalitarianism. For much of the world, however, dragooned into another great global conflict by the European powers, the war gave them a chance to emerge from the shadow of European domination. Called upon to fight alongside the Allies in a war against Nazi racial ideology or Japanese empire, many people experienced the British, French, or Americans as the actual source of racial exclusion on the ground. Civil rights campaigners in the United States and nationalist movements from Latin America to Africa and Asia pressed to make the "war of liberation" their own, demanding inclusion in the freedom and self-determination Roosevelt and Churchill had promised in the Atlantic Charter.

Some prominent Americans, including President Roosevelt, shared Willkie's sense that the imperial powers were to blame for the two great conflagrations of the twentieth century. "Don't think for a moment," Roosevelt remarked to his son Elliott in 1943, "that Americans would be dying in the Pacific tonight, if it had not been for the shortsighted greed of the French and the British and the Dutch." The president did not want to fight a war to preserve European empire. He hoped to corral them into a postwar peace organization that would, in cooperation with the Soviet Union, gradually phase out colonial power. He knew, however, that the Allies *were* fighting to safeguard their empires. Ever the cagey operator, Roosevelt talked about an end to colonialism, but he made whatever deals were necessary to preserve Allied goodwill. His postwar vision came to rest on the "Four Policemen"—the United States, Britain, the Soviet Union, and China (later amended to include France)—taking their places at the head of a world body while the rest of the world looked on as glorified spectators.[12]

Roosevelt was less self-reflective about the nation's power. He assumed that the United States was, in the words of one of his State Department officials, a "non-imperialist nation." American sway in the Western Hemisphere, its rule over the Philippines, Hawai'i, Puerto Rico, and other possessions, appeared benevolent to the president, and to most Americans. These were arrangements made in the spirit of the Monroe Doctrine to keep European despotism at bay. The arc of US empire, Americans told themselves, bent toward freedom. FDR believed the war could bring the full arrival, at long last, of what Thomas Jefferson had called "the empire of liberty": an era in which democracy and economic freedom would spread across the world under American patronage. That this might also herald an era of American world power and domination was all to the good; surely the United States could claim the burdens of world leadership without creating its own kind of imperial dominion.[13]

Willkie and Roosevelt shared a sense that European empire had had its day, and that peace beyond the war would require the United States to compromise and cooperate with the Soviet Union and China. Willkie cultivated a respectful but wary friendship with FDR in the years after the 1940 election, but he was less constrained by politics than the president and less parochial in his passion for an interdependent globe. He was setting off across the whole of a planet unsettled by a rising clamor for freedom encouraged by the Atlantic Charter. He would see firsthand the widespread revulsion at the color line laid down by imperial dominion—and would have an unprecedented chance to make America answerable to that worldly surge of hope.[14]

The trip would unleash in Willkie a renewed swell of feeling for worldliness, refreshing the passions of his youth. Seized by a moral fervor for global freedom that startled many of his friends and acquaintances—allies and adversaries alike—he posed a series of crucial questions to Americans. Would they honor the terms of the Atlantic Charter? Would they recognize their chance to ratify the freedom dreams of the "peoples of the East"? Could they take the lead in making a truly interdependent world, in which a new global body, a successor to the League of Nations, would equitably represent the planet's peoples?

These urgent questions would be shadowed by Willkie's own, often unacknowledged personal dilemmas. Enamored by his own appeal to an ineffable "American" spirit, would he be able to recognize his country's imperial role for what it was? Could he shake himself loose from the assumption that American power was likely to be welcomed wherever it was deployed in the years beyond the war? He went further than most public figures of his stature in asking Americans to navigate between "narrow nationalism" and "international imperialism," but his blind spot for US empire revealed how these forces worked in him and other Americans. His efforts would reveal how many in his vast audience hoped to leave American nationalism and imperialism relatively untroubled at a moment when the country was on the verge of assuming responsibility for the global capitalist system once overseen by the British Empire.

Willkie's travels were an epic air-age adventure, a lost story of global intrigue and media spectacle that captures the very real anxieties of the moment before the war had turned in the Allies' favor, when Americans were struggling to understand a conflict they had hoped to avoid. The Willkie moment also marked the arrival of a new time of global awareness. It echoed and prefigured other episodes of globalization in human history, when barriers and borders suddenly appeared fragile and permeable: the early modern age of "discovery" and conquest; the highwater years of industrial capitalism, global migration, and European empire in the mid-nineteenth century; the inauguration of the American empire at the turn of the twentieth century; and our own post–Cold War, postcolonial age of intense financial acceleration, technological interdependence, environmental crisis, and planetary mobility.[15]

In fact, the term Willkie helped to put into common circulation— "one world"—would become shorthand for the disruptive charge of worldly connection set off by the war. Over the years Willkie's name would fade away, but "one world" would be adopted by world government advocates, anti-imperialists, environmentalists, and even corporate marketers to signify the promise of times in which global shrinkage offered new contacts and new ideas to offset the dangers of war, xenophobia, and racism.

Willkie—his trip, his book, and the phenomenon of his sudden celebrity—was an avatar of a precarious moment almost lost to our own cultural memory, a time when millions stood ready to rethink how they saw the world. His popular internationalism revealed the hopeful mood of a nation wrangling with its emerging power and a fleeting moment when one unique traveler showed the country an alternative possible future. He hoped that his vision of interdependence, of "one world" emerging from the wake of global struggle—as impractical and utopian as it may have seemed—would steer the country away from the rigid binary of the coming Cold War and onto a path of cooperation between great powers and the soon-to-be postcolonial states.

If that picture seems improbable from this distant remove, all the better to return to that moment itself and see what lessons it may impart for the new contest between nationalism and globalism we confront today. Willkie's idealism may appear ill fitted for the rough arena of actual politics, particularly now, when so many of the hopes he championed have been discarded. But his diagnosis of the value of global interdependence has never been more prescient. His warnings about the perils of racially charged "narrow nationalism" have never been more indispensable. As the United States reaches the end of its long turn as the great global power, the quandaries of American exceptionalism he faced remain ours today, and his example may yet offer us undiscovered resources for living in the "one world" he heralded more than three-quarters of a century ago.

CHAPTER I

Taking Flight

Elwood, Puerto Rico, Paris

H OPSCOTCHING DOWN the Eastern Seaboard, the *Gulliver* alighted at Bolling Field in Washington, DC, just before noon. There it picked up Major Grant Mason and Captain Paul Pihl, who had been assigned as liaisons to the Allied military units abroad. Willkie must have pulled some strings to get Pihl detailed to the flight—he was a friend, and his brother-in-law to boot. Mason, recently commissioned in the Air Transport Command, was one of the founders of Pan American Airways. That afternoon, the *Gulliver* followed the coast down to Morrison Field in West Palm Beach, where the travelers spent the night and received their final briefings for the legs ahead—several days of flying that would take them into the Caribbean, over the Equator, and then across the Atlantic to Africa.[1]

Captain Kight was an experienced pilot, but that did little to diminish the dangers of the coming journey. Flight lanes crisscrossed the globe, but air travel, already a symbol of distance-conquering modernity, had not yet become universal in 1942. Regular passenger and mail service had spanned the continental United States for the better part of two decades, and Mason's Pan Am, the US leader in long-distance flight, had established its Clipper service throughout the Americas by the early 1930s. European airlines had gradually united the continent and reached colonies in Africa and Asia during the 1930s, and Pan Am spanned both the Atlantic and the Pacific by the early 1940s. In fact, on the first leg of their journey Kight would follow Pan Am's routes to Africa and land at fields built by the airline. The *Gulliver*'s path was a sign of things to come—the company had pioneered the routes at the behest of the US military, and in a matter of months they would turn them over to Kight's superiors in the Army's Air Transport Command. As the war closed in on the United States in 1940 and 1941, air-age entrepreneurs like Mason and his Pan Am partner, Juan Trippe, had almost realized their ambition of connecting the entire planet by air. Pan Am had put the final links in its global circuit on February 24, 1942, just six months before Willkie took flight. The company advertised its skyways as a new kind of geography, its routes connecting people and places on a planet that had, as Willkie would later put it, "become small" through the technology of flight.[2]

Yet air travel in the early 1940s was more potential than practical, the province of the rich and the daring. Almost everyone crossed the plains and oceans by train and steamer. Planes were speedy once they got up, but air travel was cramped and uncomfortable, and plagued by interminable delays due to weather and equipment problems. It wasn't for the faint of heart, either. Planes of the era were big metal shells that rattled and pitched and hummed in the wind, their propellers blasting away any hope of conversation or calm. Gruesome crashes were frequent enough to keep many terrified of flight. Two of the most famous Americans of the Depression years, the football coach Knute Rockne and the humorist Will Rogers, had died in much-publicized plummets. Even on routine flights many passengers couldn't handle the turbulence, while others found it downright unnatural to be up there bumping along in the wind and clouds. As Ernest Gann, an early commercial pilot, put it: "The airplanes smell of simmering aluminum, disinfectant, feces, leather, and puke . . . the stewardesses, short-tempered and reeking of vomit, come forward as often as they can for what is a breath of comparatively fresh air." It wasn't until the late 1930s and early 1940s that pressurized cabins debuted, allowing planes to get above the chop of lower altitudes. But it took a while for the innovation to spread, and most travelers wouldn't experience that luxury until after the war.

A plane like the *Gulliver*—as sturdy and rugged as it got, a true marvel of modern technology—could reach speeds of almost two hundred miles per hour and climb upward of fifteen thousand feet. But the C-87 needed frequent refueling and hopped from airfield to airfield on any long journey. Only eighteen years had passed since the first around-the-world flight, a 175-day epic undertaken by four US Army Air Service planes, fifteen years since Charles Lindbergh's solo navigation of the Atlantic enraptured the world, and five since Amelia Earhart disappeared over the Pacific. Both Willkie and Roosevelt had campaigned by plane during their contest for the presidency in 1940, but FDR didn't like to fly—all the jostling caused his polio-ravaged legs immense pain. He would become the first American president to leave the country by air in May 1943, when he met Churchill and Stalin at Casablanca. Simply by boarding a plane and setting off into a world at war, Willkie had become an icon of the promises and risks of the air age, assuming the new worldliness that many Americans felt awaited them beyond the war.[3]

In July 1942, at a low ebb in Allied hopes, three American reporters sent Willkie a telegram from the Soviet Union. Maurice Hindus of the *New York Herald Tribune,* Eddy Gilmore of the Associated Press, and Ben Robertson of the newsmagazine *PM* all knew him and had covered his sudden rise to prominence. Trapped in Kuibyshev, the provincial city on the Volga River that the Soviet government had made its wartime capital, they were isolated, bored, and worried about the course of the war. The Red Army was besieged at Stalingrad and Leningrad, Moscow was under threat, and the Soviets, from Stalin on down, had begun to doubt Allied resolve. The three newspapermen remembered how Willkie had been to London in 1941, during the Blitz, and boosted British morale, so they lightheartedly suggested that he get over to the Soviet Union as soon as possible. "Nothing I'd like to do so much," Willkie cabled in return. "My personal regards to each of you."[4]

This was not the first time Willkie had considered another trip abroad. He had hoped for a mission to Asia in early 1941, and he and President Roosevelt had discussed a trip to Australia later that year, just before Pearl Harbor. In the spring of 1942 he had contemplated a trip to colonial India with his friend Walter White, the head of the NAACP. Hoping to confront the imperialism and racism hampering the war effort, White had even written to the president to suggest that Willkie lead an official US delegation to India. FDR seemed on board at first, but he was wary of irking the British and soon backed away.

With this new invitation in hand, Willkie decided to approach Roosevelt from another angle, writing to the president on July 29 that he "would like to take a trip to the Middle East, into Russia, and perhaps China." He left India off, knowing that the president didn't want him to go there, but the initial rumors about the trip suggested he might stop there anyway. Those rumors were enough to set off a flurry of concern among some British officials, who were always leery of having "well-meaning sentimentalists" poking around the empire.[5]

Apart from the sore spot of India, Roosevelt was enthusiastic about the prospect of the trip. The president hoped Willkie would "put some pep talks into the officials of Egypt, Palestine, Syria, Iraq, Iran, and China." He cabled Willkie that he could arrange for him to travel with government support and invited him to meet at the White House to plan the trip. "It is my thought that you could do the Middle East," he wrote, "and that Russia and China could be subject to developments which you and I could talk over." Their discussions convinced him that Willkie's itinerary should include the Soviet Union and China, and soon after he sent a personal message to Stalin seeking permission for the visit and recommending Willkie to the Soviet premier as "heart and soul with my administration in our foreign policy of opposition to Nazism and real friendship with your government." The State Department followed up, working with the Soviets to find a route around India, while General Hap Arnold of the Army Air Forces agreed to lend a plane and crew.[6]

Willkie met Roosevelt twice in August to confer on details. They made the trip official on August 20, just six days prior to his departure. China presented the main delay in planning. The typical route went through off-limits India, over the infamous Himalayan "hump," where American and British pilots were ferrying arms and supplies to the Chinese, but the army flight planners finally came up with an alternative path that went from Moscow over western China. With that settled, the president could write to Chiang Kai-shek to introduce his emissary and secure permission for the visit. Meanwhile, they decided that Cowles and Barnes would join the expedition as representatives of the Office of War Information, and that the army and navy would send their own liaisons. Later Willkie would remember that the president had warned him of the danger he faced: "I've got a very great regard for you, even though we have differed politically in the past. I think you are Private Citizen Number One. And I just want to warn you. I know you've got guts, but remember, you may get to Cairo just as Cairo is falling, and you may get to Russia just at the time of a Russian collapse." Willkie may have exaggerated Roosevelt's words, but his account captured the foreboding surrounding Allied fortunes that summer and fall—and the boost FDR hoped Willkie might provide to Allied morale.[7]

One of Willkie's last meetings with the president was particularly memorable. He and Mike Cowles went up the Hudson River from Manhattan to the Roosevelt family home at Hyde Park. They arrived around noon in a summer downpour, Cowles remembered, only to find that their host was not yet up. FDR's close adviser Harry Hopkins gave them a tour of the house, and the president appeared forty-five minutes later, rolling out in his wheelchair with a characteristic grin. Cowles was amazed. Everyone he knew in New York and Washington was deeply troubled that summer. For months the war news had been dire, and he had expected the commander in chief to betray some of the burden he bore. But FDR nonchalantly wheeled himself over to the bar and announced that they all had to have one of his "famous Old-Fashioneds" with lunch.

Roosevelt ribbed Willkie about the 1940 campaign, and they shared a laugh recalling how the du Pont family, like a host of other business donors, had generously backed the Republican campaign with public contributions, while also funding Roosevelt behind the scenes. After lunch, they went into the study and Roosevelt sat down to draft a personal letter to Stalin. When he had finished, he handed Willkie the sealed letter and asked him to make sure that it went directly to the Soviet premier and nobody else. Willkie gave him his word. With that, the president wished them luck and Willkie and Cowles went out into the rain and back to the city.[8]

Willkie would carry personal messages from the president to Stalin and Chiang Kai-shek, but he would travel as a private citizen rather than an official envoy, as a morale-building avatar of goodwill rather than on official diplomatic business. Willkie wanted the freedom to speak his mind, and the president presumably wanted to protect himself with a measure of deniability. This arrangement made for some confusion in the press. "He would go as a private citizen," the *Times* noted on August 8, but then on August 21 the paper observed that it was a "semi-official flying trip," only to report on August 22 that Willkie went as the "personal representative" of the president. The two leaders left the mission vague as well. The president gave him no specific charge or strategic agenda. Willkie's job, Roosevelt announced just before the *Gulliver*'s departure, would be to "tell the truth about America's war effort," symbolize the nation's unity, and "compare" for Allies and neutrals "what an Axis victory would mean as contrasted with a United Nations' triumph." Willkie would certainly fulfill that brief, but he found ample opportunity to exercise his right to free speech—much to the public's edification and the president's consternation.[9]

A frenzy of activity filled the last weeks before takeoff, as Willkie shuttled between New York and Washington, meeting with the president and government officials. He saw Cordell Hull, the secretary of state, and Maxim Litvinov, the Soviet ambassador. He sat for State Department and OWI briefings, and managed to see T. V. Soong, China's foreign minister, just before he left. Barnes and Cowles helped him get everything together. There were special wartime passports to arrange, equipment to buy, and shots to get—typhoid, cholera, smallpox, yellow fever. They'd need lighter clothes for the Middle East and overcoats for the cold night flights. The unofficial nature of the trip meant that formal dress wouldn't be necessary—or so they hoped.[10]

Edith Willkie wasn't happy about the trip. At first she had thought she might go along, but FDR had decreed that "no women were allowed." She told Wendell by telegram from Indiana that she would also go to Puerto Rico to see their son Philip. "Not every mama can go to Puerto Rico to see her son," he cabled back, "it's impossible." Edith, or "Billie" as Wendell called her, shot back: "Not every mama can go to Puerto Rico, but nei-

ther can every papa go to Russia. Love, Billie." Still, she dutifully relented and returned to New York to help him prepare for his departure.[11]

At first glance, it might seem that Wendell Willkie was singularly unprepared for a journey of this magnitude. He little resembled air-age heroes
like Lindbergh or Earhart. American political myth often casts him as a
farm boy and his hometown of Elwood, Indiana, as a bucolic hamlet, but
these stories, drummed up by his supporters to win electoral advantage,
conceal a more complicated reality. Born on February 18, 1892, as the
fourth of six children in a middle-class household, he arrived in the world
just as Elwood and Indiana were wrenched from a rural past into an industrial future. Some forty miles northeast of Indianapolis, Elwood was
a place where one could still read about the price of grain in the newspaper, but no one would have mistaken it for the country market town it
had once been. Huge natural gas deposits had been discovered under-
neath a vast swath of western Ohio and eastern Indiana in the years before Willkie's birth, and by the 1890s Elwood found itself in the middle
of the new gas belt. Wells went up in the cornfields, spouting flames into
the air, and the city swelled, its streets lit at all hours by the free-flowing
supply of cheap gas pumped straight from the ground. The population
jumped from two thousand to thirteen thousand in the space of a few
years, and by the turn of the century the small city was an industrial
boomtown.[12]

Willkie's father, Herman, was a lawyer, as was his wife, and they
found themselves in the middle of the action. In 1890 a group of eastern
bankers had arrived, proposing to finance the country's first tin-plate
plant on fourteen acres of farmland near a gas gusher locals called Vesu-
vius. The bankers hired Herman, who had come to America from Prussia
at the age of four, to investigate the terms of sale. The year Lewis Wendell Willkie was born, Ohio governor William McKinley came to town to
dedicate the new plant and launch Elwood into the industrial age. Soon
the city attracted factories turning out engines and boilers, forges and
lamp flues, glass plate and furniture.

Downtown Elwood boasted a grand hotel and an opera house, while streetcars and wagons jostled for room on newly paved streets. Glass workers from Pittsburgh and tin workers from Wales arrived in numbers, mixing on the plank sidewalks with German and Scotch-Irish farmers in for a day of marketing or a night on the town. The Amalgamated Association of Iron, Steel, and Tin Workers began to organize in the city, and they, too, hired Herman as counsel. Streets of wood-frame houses went up quickly, some sturdy and elegant for up-and-coming burghers like the Willkies, others smaller and flimsier for the working class. The gas couldn't last forever, though, and for decades the city lurched between boom and bust. The wells began to slow as early as 1900, but the city pushed on, trying to stave off the inevitable. Factories opened and closed, businesses came and went, but by the first decades of the twentieth century the trend was ever downward. In 1937 the tin works shuttered its last building, and by the time Elwood's favorite son returned to accept the Republican presidential nomination before thousands at an outdoor rally in the summer of 1940, the city had embarked on a long period of postindustrial stagnation.[13]

The Indiana of Willkie's youth was not the pastoral land of popular myth. Coming of age in a society poised between an idealized past and an unsure future, Willkie took as much inspiration from his family's cosmopolitan roots as he did from the stories cooked up to mythologize a world that was slipping away. Willkie's parents, both products of liberal German immigrant families fleeing the turmoil that followed the 1848 revolution, were more than equipped to instill in him the combination of independence and worldly ambition he would need to navigate an eventful life.

Henrietta Trisch Willkie was by all accounts remarkable. One of the first female lawyers in Indiana, she may also have been the first woman in Elwood to take up smoking. She cultivated in all her children something of her own drive and passed on the freethinking streak she had inherited from her parents. Her mother was a child of liberal Hamburg merchants who had been active in revolutionary circles, her father a blacksmith and newspaper editor. The Trisches began their married life in Fort Dodge, Kansas, in the 1850s but soon retreated to Indiana in disgust, revolted by the violence and oppression unleashed in "Bleeding

Kansas" after the state went over to slavery. Henrietta's mother found local fame as a temperance lecturer and lay preacher who rode circuit across Indiana holding forth at Presbyterian revival meetings.[14]

Henrietta was fiercely independent, even severe, with limitless energy and competitive spirit. She trained to be a teacher, taught herself the law after her fifth child was born, and practiced with her husband over the objections of some members of the Indiana bar. Avid in her pursuit of self-improvement, she read, sang, played the piano, painted china, and pursued quilting and embroidery. She hated cooking and hired someone to run the household. Some accounts suggest that she was strict and aloof, others open and engaging if imperious. The periodic impatience her children acknowledged—and there were six of them in the house, after all—was perhaps as much a product of nineteenth-century social convention as of their boisterous behavior. Henrietta resisted fealty to the middle-class doctrine of "separate spheres," which steered women toward the privacy of the home and away from any public ambitions they might harbor. At her death in the spring of 1940, her kids remembered a woman "driven by an indomitable will," so much so they had the phrase carved into her tombstone. There was some debate about adding the words "to conquer" to the epitaph, but as Joseph Barnes would later write, they were omitted for "reasons of affection rather than because they did not apply."[15]

Herman Willkie was as ambitious as his wife and almost as iconoclastic. The rangy six-foot-tall son of a farmer, he put himself through college and became superintendent of schools in Milford, Indiana, where he met Henrietta, one of his employees. Hired to run Elwood's slapdash school district in 1888, he instituted a system of orderly grades and started a high school. At night he studied law, and when he was admitted to the bar in 1890 he immediately resigned his position as superintendent to begin the practice that his wife would later join. A lifelong Democrat, Herman hosted William Jennings Bryan in the family home and traveled around the state speaking on behalf of Bryan's presidential candidacies in 1896 and 1900. Canny and principled, he wasn't quite a midwestern Farmer-Labor radical, but he sympathized with unions, workers, and the Populist Party. In the 1920s he campaigned, as the young lawyer Wendell would also, against the Ku Klux Klan. He specialized in damage suits for injured workers and even once voted for a socialist mayoral candidate when he felt the Democrats and Republicans had gone soft on vice. Herman had himself launched a moral crusade against the town's lively red-light district. Some around town called him "Hellfire Willkie" for his reforming zeal and his prowess before a jury. A few who ended up on the losing end of a decision would remember him, even decades later, as a "crooked lawyer," but most recalled him as avid about winning cases for his clients.[16]

Herman Willkie pursued business opportunities almost as aggressively as he did justice, but he wasn't as successful with his investments in real estate and industry as he was in the courtroom. The Panic of 1893 put him deeply in debt. With six children to support in an up-and-down economy, he was always behind. For a few years he kept bankruptcy papers on his desk, ready to file, just to keep his creditors at bay. Although he eventually got clear of debt and managed to buy a three-story house on the favored north side of town, he was never rich. In the end, Herman's children remembered him with boundless affection. They said he was unusually attentive for a father of the era, and kind to a degree that belied his reputation as a religious teetotaler and crusading lawyer.

Accounts of Wendell Willkie's childhood suggest that he grew up in an almost implausible atmosphere of fresh-faced bonhomie, good-natured competition, academic and athletic achievement, and free-ranging adventure. Some of this was no doubt the inevitable puffery attached to the boyhoods of famous men, but it does appear that his parents provided him with an auspicious mix of independence and direction. The Willkie kids were given mostly free rein to wander the small city and the nearby countryside. Wendell and his brothers had a motley crew of friends—the sons of a printer, a teamster, and several tin workers—with whom they seem to have had a childhood right out of the pages of a boys' adventure story.

They fished in trash heaps for cast-off machine parts and got old barrels and boxes from grocers or saloonkeepers, using the junk to build wagons and wigwams, sleds and kites and boats. Once they happened upon a huge stash of boards—the remains of the city's plank sidewalks, torn up to make way for modern pavement—and built a 125-foot approximation of the roller coaster from the local fairgrounds. In the summer, they hitched rides on wagons out into the country, jumped in a mud pit behind one of the factories, or hiked to swimming holes along a local rivulet called Duck Creek, a distant tributary of the Mississippi.

One time they got hold of a small skiff and put in, aiming to paddle down to the Gulf of Mexico. Sandbars and brush soon put an end to that dream, and they had to walk miles home. Elwood was a rough-and-tumble place, and legend held that Willkie, big for his age and not shy, got into his share of fights, sometimes with older boys not inclined to go easy on the mouthy son of a big-shot lawyer.[17]

Henrietta and Herman always worried about money. Hoping to foster a spirit of autonomy and responsibility, they required that all their children find part-time work. Summers during their college years, Herman would greet his returning boys at the train station, suggest that they spend a few days at home, and then buy them a ticket out of town and tell them to write when they found work. When Wendell was still young—not yet in his teens—he drove a neighbor's cow from town out to pasture. Later, he sorted produce, collected junk, distributed advertising hand-bills, drove a bakery wagon, and did farm work. In the summer of 1908, when he was sixteen, he went to work in the tin mill. He was tasked with "catching" hot bars of molten steel as they came out of a revolving cylinder, securing them, and returning them to the "roller" over and over again, until they were thin enough to make tin cans. This was dangerous work—"I have literally seen eggs fried on the floor," one of his brothers said—and Willkie considered it a badge of honor to have lasted the whole summer.[18]

The next summer, his last before college, he tramped around out west, hopping trains and working odd jobs in South Dakota, Wyoming, and Montana. With a western land boom on, he found work washing dishes in a restaurant, running a tent hotel for homesteaders, and baling hay. He even drove a stagecoach for tourists in Yellowstone National Park—or at least he tried to. His first time out he ran the horses off the road and flipped the whole rig. Nobody was hurt, but he was fired on the spot and returned to Elwood just in time to find all the tin workers out on strike. Herman was representing the union and he made Wendell a junior clerk, a job that involved a memorable meeting with the famed lawyer Clarence Darrow. It also brought him up close and personal with the class strife that racked American society. One evening father and son were walking near the train depot when two strikebreakers went after the union lawyer. Herman was punched in the head before Wendell could tackle the assailant. Police broke up the fight, but not before there were blood and bruises all around.[19]

The Willkies presided over a house in which discussion, argument, and reading were prized above all else. Over the years they amassed a library of nearly six thousand books, from which Wendell and his siblings were encouraged to imbibe freely. Many nights Herman would read aloud to the entire family or orchestrate ad hoc productions of Shakespeare. Herman and Henrietta formed the Hyperion Circle, a local group dedicated to strategies for self-improvement—lectures, readings, practice in oratory—recommended by the turn-of-the-century Chautauqua movement. They also organized a group of neighbors to take extension classes from the University of Chicago and raised funds for Elwood's first public library. Herman liked to rouse his kids from their beds by bellowing inspirational quotes up the stairs. At meals the boys and girls were encouraged to take and defend positions, and it was in this small debating society that Wendell learned politics, economics, and history. The Willkie dining room tackled the great issues of the day: capital against labor, the Spanish-American War and American imperialism, free silver versus the gold standard, corporations versus small business, free trade and tariffs.[20]

In his late teens and early twenties, Wendell Willkie came into his own. He was, as one of his biographers put it, "purposeful and ambitious," but with a persistent streak of the familial iconoclasm. He could be headstrong, even reckless. Always popular, he spoke his mind and attracted a following. He was proud of his principles and independence, but also drawn to the limelight. He showed an extraordinary ability to find his way to the center of the social and political action. Elected class president his senior year of high school, he founded his own independent social fraternity—called King of Beasts—when a high school sorority snubbed his Welsh girlfriend, the daughter of working-class immigrants. At Indiana University in Bloomington he dabbled in Marx and asked the head of the economics department to do a course on socialism. The chair agreed, but only if Willkie could get ten students to sign up. He had to "buttonhole almost everyone in the university," he remembered, but he succeeded, solidifying a reputation as a charismatic freethinker. Later he managed several campaigns for student offices, electing independents over the usual fraternity-backed candidates. Needing money to pay for law school, he taught history for a year at a high school in Kansas after graduation and then accepted a job as a junior chemist in Puerto Rico, joining one of his brothers who was already working for the American-owned and -run Fajardo Sugar Company.[21]

Puerto Rico made a great impression on the young Willkie. One incident in particular stayed with him. Out for a horseback ride with the manager of one of the big sugar plantations, he saw a starving peasant—likely a fugitive hiding out after a recent revolt of cane laborers—stumble out of the brush along the path. The boss, Willkie remembered, barely slowed his horse to slash at the worker with his cane knife, nearly severing his arm at the shoulder. Willkie was horrified. Already prone to sympathy for the exploited, he would always remember that moment as the birth of his social conscience. Later, as a wealthy businessman, Willkie would tell Mike Cowles that the encounter was the spur for his unorthodox social attitude. The memory "kept him from thinking like a typical American millionaire," Joe Barnes would later recall.[22]

Willkie had been an average student in college, but when he returned to Bloomington for law school he worked his way to the top of his class and was selected as class speaker. He used the opportunity of his graduation in 1916 to pay homage to his new hero, Woodrow Wilson, with a speech called "The New Freedom," which called for a reformed state constitution with more robust regulations on banks and business. The school's administrators were taken aback—"the most radical speech you ever heard," the university president later remembered—and withheld his diploma for several days. After the controversy subsided, Willkie returned home to Elwood to join his father's firm and continue his courtship of the town's new librarian, a young woman from Rushville, Indiana, with the improbably similar name of Edith Wilk, whom he had met at a friend's wedding a year earlier.[23]

Wendell and Edith married in January 1918, but their life together was soon interrupted by World War I. Willkie was commissioned as a lieutenant in the artillery, bounced around to training camps in various states, and finally disembarked for England and then France in September 1918, arriving at the front just in time for the armistice. Well known in his unit, Willkie earned the respect of his men—and sometimes the enmity of superior officers—for his democratic attitude. He mixed as freely as he could with the enlisted men and became a highly sought-after defense counsel for soldiers caught on unsanctioned larks to Paris. He told a colonel who tried to reprimand him for his breaches of military hierarchy that he was "going to associate with these men as equals after the war—and I'm also going to do it now." The conflict strengthened the young idealist's budding internationalist beliefs. He was thrilled by Wilson's advocacy for a League of Nations—and he would be dismayed when the US Senate refused to ratify American membership in the new world body. The war also gave him a new name. Early on, an army clerk misunderstood his name and reversed the "Lewis" and "Wendell" on his forms. Since everyone knew him as "Wen" anyway, Willkie decided the effort to undo the switch wasn't worth the struggle with the inevitable military bureaucracy. So from that day forward he was Wendell L. Willkie.[24]

Just before noon on August 27, Captain Kight threaded the *Gulliver* through the clouds of a passing squall, finding just enough visibility for a safe landing at Borinquen Field in Puerto Rico. The crew got a well-earned afternoon off, while Willkie and his companions took in the sights. Willkie had specifically requested a stop in Puerto Rico to visit his son, Philip, who was stationed at the Roosevelt Roads naval base. After waiting out the storm, the travelers were treated to an impromptu flight over the island in a US military plane.[25]

Almost thirty years had passed since Willkie's time as a junior chemist on the island. Memories of that time must have surfaced as he sat with his son, flying over mountains and plains and coast with the sunlight breaking through the retreating clouds. The Willkie of 1942 was far less naive than the young man who had watched in horror as the plantation boss hacked at a fugitive cane worker by the side of the road, but his hatred for injustice had only deepened over the years. He often recalled the incident as a kind of epiphany—a lesson on the savagery of power abused.

Now he too had power. But how would he use it? Back in 1915 he had worked for Fajardo, the American-owned sugar concern, and now he returned as a guest of the American military. Sugar and sailors had been the two chief instruments of American rule over Puerto Rico since its annexation in 1898. Willkie understood the injustice. He had spoken out previously in favor of Puerto Rican statehood (although not for independence).

Doubtless the memory of savagery fired his conscience. Would it challenge him to recognize how American power over Puerto Rico resembled the force of empire all over the world?[26]

Willkie grew up with the country, coming of age just as the United States entered its industrial prime, as farms and small towns gave way to cities and suburbs, companies merged into giant conglomerates, and ever-rising levels of consumption drove the economy. But he also came from a place that looked back fondly on a pioneer past. The stories told in the Indiana of his youth celebrated an idyll of progress. Children's readers and booster literature lionized the idea of an orderly march across the prairie and its culmination in the farmlands and market towns of the rural Midwest. People of Willkie's generation and class were apt to imagine their close-knit, homogenous society as exemplary and quintessentially American—a national identity defined by white people of English or northern European stock. Of course, these stories overlooked nearly as much as they revealed. They obscured the industrial realities, inequalities, and class unrest of Elwood's present as much as they omitted the history of conquest of Indian societies that had brought this settler civilization across the continent and secured its air of quiet repose and tranquil domesticity.

Willkie was not immune to the pull of these stories. They were as much his heritage as the nonconformity, curiosity, and compassion he had learned from his parents. He revered the idea that America's energy originated in the westward progress he had glimpsed in his youth, and he would struggle all his life, in ways implicit and explicit, to square a form of prideful nationalism with his belief in freedom for all. His middle-class culture offered both immense opportunity and blinkering illusions. The same corporate economy that fueled prosperity required bureaucratic complexity, which seemed to imperil cherished autonomy and independence. In a way, the family dinner-table debates never ended for him, but the anxieties of the age did not seem to trouble Willkie too much. Perhaps it was his stable sense of self that gave him the confidence to imagine a fusion of independence and interconnection, the particular rapprochement between self-reliance and fellow feeling that he would later use to encourage Americans to avoid "narrow nationalism" and greet the wider world on equal terms.[27]

Willkie grew up with the world as much as with his own country. The United States became a great power in his first decade, when victory in the Spanish-American War secured imperial possessions in the Caribbean and Pacific. What Teddy Roosevelt and other expansion-minded Americans saw as their rightful "sphere of influence" appeared to many as the logical result of pioneering progress; it was only natural that Manifest Destiny should push westward across the Pacific and extend so-called civilization to the benighted lands across the sea. As Willkie made his way from Elwood to Bloomington to Paris, the United States similarly expanded its global prospects. By 1915, when Willkie found himself in Puerto Rico, one of the chief outposts of America's imperial sway in the Western Hemisphere, the United States controlled the fifth-largest empire in the world.[28]

Americans were ambivalent about this fact. Anti-imperialists like Mark Twain and Willkie's fellow Hoosier Eugene V. Debs denounced America's overseas possessions as counter to democratic ideals, but others believed that America's rise to global influence would supplant European colonialism with a world civilization based on free trade and free ideas: Jefferson's "empire of liberty." And of course there was no shortage of out-and-out imperialism. Men of influence like Teddy Roosevelt and Senator Albert Beveridge wanted to see the United States sit astride the globe like Britain and Spain before it.[29]

The entire American imperial imagination floated on a dark and pervasive current of race thinking, which swept across the country in these years. Social Darwinism, eugenics, and other popular theories of biological determinism were fashionable and influential, masquerading as common sense and giving an imprimatur of scientific authority to the racial hierarchies endemic to American society. People at all levels of life believed that societies advanced in stages, beginning in savagery and barbarism and making their way to "civilization." These were, at their heart, theories of biological difference marked by race; the savages and barbarians were inevitably dark-skinned peoples "over there"—in the colonized lands of Africa and Asia or the less advanced regions of southern Europe—while the civilized were white people hailing from northern and western Europe and the United States.

Popular entrepreneurs of racial thought competed to supply the most compelling "scientific" accounts of where various peoples stood on the ladder of civilization. Categories we now think of as ethnic groupings held the significance, and sometimes even the legal force, of racial difference and inferiority. Eugenicists like Madison Grant, whose 1916 book *The Passing of the Great Race* found a wide audience, feared that the "Slovak, the Italian, the Syrian, and the Jew" would soon dilute the purity of America's "Anglo-Saxon" stock. There was debate also about whether natives of America's newly annexed lands—supposedly "unfit for self government," as Theodore Roosevelt and other imperialists warned— could ever advance from savagery, or whether they would need white Western oversight in perpetuity. American imperialists stood ready to direct colonized peoples, by way of the rod or the schoolbook, the bayonet or the sanitary commission, toward their rightful place at the knee of the Great White Father. Even many anti-imperialists were at heart nativists, concerned that American involvement abroad would further pollute the "purity" of the nation's bloodstream, already imperiled by immigration from southern and eastern Europe.[30]

This was the country in which Wendell Willkie reached adulthood: a nation dedicated to the ideal of the individual proprietor and open land for all, in which prosperity seemed to depend on industrial capitalism, bureaucracy, and mass urbanization. A nation founded on the principle of equality for all, but only just removed from racial slavery and the final subjugation of the Indians, roiled by debates over immigration and empire, torn apart by the contest between capital and labor, reluctant to grant women the right to vote, and riven still by the color line. The dilemmas that animated the Willkie dinner table and the headlines alike turned on the problems of American freedom at home and abroad.

Sometimes the discussions turned to wealth, power, and labor— the grand questions of political economy. Would corporate capitalism deliver an age of ease and abundance or suffocate autonomy and self-possession? Would a nation of proprietors become a captive population of wage-slave consumers? Perhaps the government could intervene to regulate business and provide economic security for all. Or was that the road to statism, a new form of the same unfreedom from which the nation had won its independence a century and a half earlier? Other questions concerned just who counted in the Constitution's "we the people." Were immigrants American? Did new arrivals jeopardize the autonomy of native-born sons and daughters? Would Negroes, as African Americans were called in polite conversation among well-meaning whites, have their fair share? Or would the rot of racism continue, corrupting American democracy as it had from the start? What did the country's conflicted embrace of empire mean for American freedom?[31]

Willkie was no stranger to these conundrums. His upbringing had nurtured in him a gut passion for both the preservation and extension of the freedom he felt to be his birthright. His father's politics had blended the prairie populism of Bryan with the Progressivism of the Wisconsin senator Robert La Follette. After early dabblings in a naive socialism, the younger Willkie sketched out a personal politics that reached for a bridge between liberal ideals. He was a liberal in the nineteenth-century sense, in that he stood for individual and economic freedom, and in the modern sense, too, in that he stood for individual rights and racial equality. However, his bridge was always a work in progress. He felt the powers of government and law should actively protect individual and group rights and opportunities, but he supported "free enterprise" in business and trade, stopping short of the regulatory and directive reach sought by those of his generation who would embrace New Deal liberalism. He hoped to discover a modern social ethic that could supply rights for all and protect the communal good without losing the free-wheeling individualism of the nineteenth-century settler republic. Willkie's struggle, his friend Joe Barnes would later say, captured "the fumbling of the American Middle West to bend its old frontier dream of the Garden of the World into the iron necessities of an industrial age."[32]

Meanwhile, family debates had convinced Willkie of the perils of empire, and World War I had taught him that government must extend to the international realm. The failure of Wilson's League of Nations suggested that internationalism must observe a careful and deliberate balance between independence and interdependence. These were the necessary virtues for individuals, communities, and nations. The chief dilemma and opportunity of his modern liberalism was to craft a politics that would hold them ever in the balance.

CHAPTER 2

Power and the Presidency

Akron, New York, Khartoum

THE COURSE OF Willkie's young adult life did not seem likely to bring him to the center of world events. He spent the decade after the war in Akron, Ohio, working as a lawyer, first for the Firestone Tire Company and then in private practice as a trial attorney for business clients. The great gusts of money the automobile boom of the 1920s sent through the "Rubber City" left a deep mark on Akron's culture and social life. If Sinclair Lewis had not invented the city of Zenith for his famous parody of midwestern "Babbitry," he might have set his tale of conformity in Akron, so welcoming was it to the spirit he satirized. Willkie prospered there, and by the middle of the decade he was widely acclaimed as one of the best trial lawyers in the city. But his personal idiosyncrasies and political convictions put him slightly outside the social life of the city's middle and upper classes.

No Babbitt himself, Willkie shunned golf and bridge for reading and conversation, and voted Democratic in an overwhelmingly Republican business culture. His public appearances during his Akron years were not boosterish speeches before the Chamber of Commerce or the Rotary Club; he was more likely to speak on the perils of war and the prospects of world peace, the legacy of Abraham Lincoln, or the problem of race hatred. His early forays into politics were similarly idealistic. In

1924, he went to the Democratic National Convention as a delegate with two purposes: to see Woodrow Wilson's League of Nations endorsed in the party platform and to force the party to go on record against a resurgent Ku Klux Klan.[1]

Willkie was no black sheep in Akron society. He may have shown little interest in the social conventions of corporate life, but he made partner quickly and was elected president of the Akron bar in 1925. He cultivated a reputation as an amiable freethinker, always up for a friendly argument, but he firmly believed in business itself. He thought that business could and should progressively respond to the great questions of the time—a faith that would later make him suspect in the eyes of New Dealers and other more radical critics. This was Willkie's way. An insider with a nose for outside opinion, his genial iconoclasm would serve him well as he rose to national and then international prominence. It would help him see that the world was changing, and that the milieu of power, privilege, and national pride in which he had so naturally ascended was facing challenges it was ill-equipped to understand or accommodate.

Much of Willkie's legal work in the 1920s was on behalf of the power industry, which was growing mightily as more and more Americans hooked up to the electrical grid. Utilities had a special allure. A modern technological drama, the expansion of the grid reached deeply into the everyday lives of Americans. Steam power, which drove nineteenth-century industrialization, depended on water or coal. It was a centralizing technology, drawing workers and capital to hubs of production. Electricity often coursed from steam turbines, but it traveled across great distances, spreading light, productive industry, and, Willkie hoped, a new kind of democracy for the industrial era. It is not a stretch to say that utilities embodied all the paradoxical possibilities of modernization he sought to reconcile: expansion and interdependence, free enterprise and systematic planning, bigness and freedom. His passion for the work must have been plain: in 1929, the head of Commonwealth and Southern, a new holding company created to represent the financial and legal interests of a host of regional utility companies, asked him to move to New York as junior partner in the law firm that handled the company's affairs.[2]

Wendell and Edith arrived in New York in October 1929, just weeks before the great stock market crash. He always said that he had been content in Akron—he once remarked that he felt "fixed for life" there—but the move to New York opened up new and thrilling prospects and brought him to the center of national life. First and foremost was his work for Commonwealth and Southern, which would thrust him into the middle of a great national controversy. Willkie's decision to work for a massive holding company seems unlikely, even an abandonment of his political and social ideals. It is hard to imagine that he overlooked how the new job might challenge those beliefs. A late nineteenth-century innovation, the holding company sprang from the era of corporate consolidation and cut against the democratic vision of dispersed power he had hoped for from the spread of electricity. Created to finance and organize the scale-up of industrial development, these private corporations existed to own the securities of other public or private corporations. They kept day-to-day company operations decentralized while radically consolidating financial, legal, and political control for the bankers, lawyers, and businessmen who sat on their boards. C&S was itself the product of a partnership between J. P. Morgan and Company and another New York bank, Bonbright and Company, cobbled together from the stock of five smaller holding companies. One 1936 study found that 70 percent of the 475 largest corporations in the country were holding companies. This sort of consolidation inspired intense public distrust, particularly in the utility industry, where more than 3,500 local public utility companies had been brought under holding company control across the 1920s.[3]

Progressives, radicals, and New Dealers would all inveigh against the "power trust." They saw it as a dangerous instrument for anti-competitive business practices, a blueprint for evasion of government regulation, and a vast opportunity for graft and corruption. Not long after Willkie went to work for C&S, a series of trials and congressional investigations of the brash power magnate Samuel Insull gripped the nation. Insull had the most extensive utility trust in history, with layers upon layers of holdings and byzantine stock structures that befuddled journalists and investigators. It was, in the end, a classic pyramid scheme. Before his empire collapsed in the early 1930s Insull bilked investors out of millions, camouflaging his deceit with an extensive public relations operation that bought consent for consolidation. By the time of the Depression Insull had become one of the chief symbols of the depredations of the Roaring Twenties. In *The Big Money,* the bitter last volume of his avant-garde *U.S.A.* trilogy, novelist John Dos Passos called Insull "Power Superpower." The utilities magnate symbolized the final demise of a free, plainspoken American republican ideal, crushed by empire, war, and big business.[4]

Willkie seemed outwardly untroubled by the dismal reputation of the holding companies. Lifted into the executive ranks at C&S not long after his move to New York, he rose quickly, becoming president and then CEO in 1934. Willkie continued to believe in business precisely because he continued to think, unlike Dos Passos, that it could be made an engine of opportunity. For him, that meant that business itself had to create the kinds of checks and balances expected of a robust democratic system through its own managerial structure. With that in mind Willkie reorganized the board of C&S. Exploiting a little-recognized divide in the industry, he removed several bankers and financiers from director positions and elevated the producers of energy—the heads of the operating companies—in their stead. He also simplified the firm's structure, stopped awarding its lawyers stock bonuses, allowed unions to organize in its holdings, and tried to keep electricity prices as low as possible. These reforms, along with his general idealism, earned him some notoriety among the more cynical power chiefs, who took to calling him "the Jesus Christ of the utility industry" behind his back. From the outside, however, Willkie appeared less a maverick than an eager cheerleader for the industry and for private enterprise in general. It was this avid spirit that brought him into conflict with Franklin Roosevelt's New Deal and, ultimately, made him famous.[5]

Of all the initiatives launched during Roosevelt's first one hundred days, the Tennessee Valley Authority (TVA) was perhaps the most daring. The legislation aimed to develop a huge area surrounding the Tennessee River watershed, one of the poorest regions of the United States. It would bring cheap electricity to rural areas by allowing the federal government to produce and sell power generated by a dam at Muscle Shoals, Alabama. This plan brought the government into direct competition with

C&S, whose subsidiaries served much of the region. The utility industry saw the TVA as unwarranted government interference in their market and a threat to their ability to compete. They launched a public attack on the plan, and for the better part of the 1930s, Willkie served as the industry's point man in a series of widely watched congressional hearings, court cases, and negotiations with the government over the fate of the TVA.[6]

Meanwhile, Roosevelt had decided that the only way to bring fairness and stability to the utility field would be to break up the holding companies. In early 1935 he had his advisers draw up legislation—the so-called death sentence act—that would outlaw the great majority of them. Willkie and the power industry fought back, using congressional hearings and the press to defend "free enterprise" and fan the flames of already intense anti–New Deal sentiment in the business community. FDR pointed out, quite rightly, that most of the New Deal was designed to save business, not usher in socialism, but this did little to placate his enemies. At the height of the Depression, public opinion did not favor industry, and Congress passed a revised version of FDR's bill in the summer of 1935. The bill gave the government the power to regulate rates and interstate transmission of power and mandated that all holding companies that held more than one utility system or did not directly supply power to customers dissolve within three years.

The industry, with Willkie still out front, kept up their attacks before Congress and in the magazines and newspapers, hoping that FDR might lose at the polls. The debate stretched to the end of the decade, ending only when the Supreme Court ruled that the TVA was indeed constitutional. Willkie actually favored some regulation of the industry and was willing to negotiate with the administration. But he tacked to the right to win advantage over his adversaries, and in the process he became a widely hailed booster for private enterprise and a fervent critic of New Deal "overreach"—ironic, given that he was a proud Democrat and had voted for Roosevelt in 1932.[7]

By the late 1930s, Willkie was a successful and visible New York executive, with an office down by Wall Street and an apartment on Fifth Avenue across from Central Park. His name appeared in the *Social Register* and, increasingly, in the newspapers and on the cover of national magazines. But despite his voluble defense of private enterprise,

Willkie remained something of a misfit among the genteel Ivy Leaguers of New York's upper crust. An oddball in business circles, he made little effort to fit in, spending vacations on a working farm near Rushville, Indiana—one of the five he bought over the years—rather than at a country home in Connecticut or Long Island. He lacked the kind of polish expected from men of his class. Restless and energetic, he didn't like to sit still unless he was reading or deep in animated conversation. When he did stop moving, he was "one of those athletic sitters," the columnist Katharine Brush reported, likely to throw a leg over the arm of his chair or prop his feet up on his desk, showing off the worn leather on the soles of his shoes to visitors. He smoked avidly, lighting one cigarette before finishing another, blowing smoke from his nose, and dropping ash all over his clothes and the floor. His suits, pressed and fresh each morning, invariably ended up mussed and wrinkled by the afternoon. His hair flopped over his brow, and there was no doubt as to why he'd gotten a D in hygiene at Indiana University.[8]

Willkie's iconoclasm showed most in his intense interest in ideas and culture. A true son of Herman and Henrietta, he preferred books, theater, and movies to country clubs or yachting, and he found most businessmen boring because they could talk about little besides business. New York provided rich soil for his interests, and he took up his reading in history, fiction, drama, poetry, and current events with renewed vigor. Edith often remarked on the disheveled state of their living room on a Monday morning, where she'd encounter scattered piles of books after Wendell had spent the weekend pursuing some literary enthusiasm. Prepared by his childhood evenings in Elwood for a life of the mind, he seemed to have a natural inclination for accumulating knowledge. The writer Janet Flanner once remarked that Willkie had a memory "something like a boy's pocket," where he stashed all manner of details and facts gleaned from his reading. He knew by heart numerous passages of prose and verse, and he delivered them with great aplomb. When he tried to read aloud from a written text, however, he lost all sense of rhythm and pacing. As a result, he tended to avoid prepared speeches or ditched them partway through, preferring to hold forth extemporaneously.[9]

The result of all his energy was an appealing mix of serious enthusiasm and unrehearsed ease that sometimes threatened to spill over into impulsiveness, arrogance, or recklessness. His appetites—for attention, conviviality, laughter, and intense political talk—powered his rough-hewn charisma. Willkie never lacked for admirers, particularly among women. The British writer Rebecca West remarked that photographs did not do him justice. "They make him look big but soft and blowsy," she said. "Actually, he has the well-organized bulkiness of a healthy bear, and singularly brilliant eyes."[10]

Willkie was not shy about returning this admiration. He apparently never considered abandoning his marriage, but he exploited the privilege that powerful men of his era enjoyed, leading something of a double life. He had a conventional marriage and a wife who dutifully provided public respectability. But he pursued a series of intimacies with other women, relationships masked in public as "friendships." These open secrets troubled some of his friends and political advisers. Raymond Buell, a foreign affairs expert who advised him during his two runs for the presidency, found Willkie's philandering distasteful and potentially compromising, a product of what he viewed as Willkie's general "vulgarity." Many people felt for Edith Willkie, too. "You couldn't help but admire her," the journalist William L. Shirer remembered. "She was probably terribly hurt. But she wasn't going to ruin his career."[11]

Rumors abounded that Roosevelt's advisers considered using Willkie's affairs to sink him in the 1940 election, but FDR could hardly take the high road on infidelity. In an age when men had the power to keep their affairs secret, it was only Willkie's shamelessness that threatened to derail him. "I had the good fortune," he wrote to a friend in 1937, "to marry a sane Indiana girl with a rare quality to bear with a restless and altogether unsatisfactory husband." In the end, most seemed willing to see his dalliances as an unfortunate by-product of the connective energy that propelled all his pursuits and made him so popular.[12]

Willkie was linked to many women over the years, but the most important was his long relationship with Irita Van Doren, the editor of the books section of the *New York Herald Tribune*, whom he met in 1937. A practiced and subtle editor and writer, she gave him the opportunity to fulfill his intellectual ambitions, introducing him to the collection of writers, editors, and foreign correspondents that gathered for an informal salon at her apartment. He wrote several book reviews for her, and she served as his personal editor and adviser, helping him to craft speeches and articles and to write *One World*. She was also close with the influential liberal Republican publishers of the *Herald Tribune,* Helen Rogers Reid and her husband, Ogden, who would, in large part thanks to her influence, become Willkie's biggest political boosters. "When you saw them together," Joe Barnes remembered many years later, "working on a speech or talking and laughing, you knew that they enriched each other and—miraculously in our day and age—hurt each other almost not at all." It wouldn't be too much of a stretch to suggest that Willkie's public career, the whole Willkie phenomenon even, depended on the uncredited good graces of two women: Irita Van Doren and Edith Willkie.[13]

Willkie enjoyed his prominence, but he backed into national politics. He had long been an active Democrat, since his early days in Akron, but seeking public office did not seem high on his list of ambitions. It is hard to know just how or when the notion of a political career occurred to him. This ambiguity stems in part from characteristics that, ironically, made him a great candidate. Willkie seems to have been most at home in public. As Ellsworth Barnard, one of his biographers, noted, "We never seem to see him *alone*." He clearly had personal convictions and "inner resources," but never slowed down much to reflect. Willkie wrote few personal letters and kept no journal, at least not one that has survived, and so he comes down to us as the sum of his public statements and actions to a greater degree than many political figures of his stature.[14]

By the late 1930s, he was gaining a national reputation as an exuberant and daring public figure—the most attractive personality among the generally dour and stuffy critics of the New Deal. His outspoken performance at the TVA hearings had brought him into the national eye, and in 1939 a group of well-connected liberal northeastern Republicans began a campaign to enlist him as a candidate for president. They suspected that his charisma would make him a consummate political actor. He had a winning combination of homespun authenticity and heartfelt idealism that drew people to him. And he had the master politician's most important assets: a sixth sense for the cadences of everyday talk and the ability to make people feel that he understood their problems. His flexible and easy temperament—one observer called it "a supreme example of elasticity of soul"—would serve him well on the campaign trail and, eventually, on his world tour. He knew his own mind, but he could also imagine how others felt.[15]

Yet he was rough around the edges. He had little feel for manners, and his tendency to run roughshod over niceties could put off those not immediately charmed by his bluster. In keeping with his overall sloppiness, he was not much for administration. He left the details of political organization and office logistics to others but was, Katharine Brush reported, "a hero to his secretaries." He had what Barnard called "personal magnetism," but his interest in the limelight could repel as much as attract. Some found him naive or glib, others unreliable, reckless, and opportunistic. And while many recalled him as kind and considerate, he could also be hasty or rude with people he saw no reason to impress or did not respect. His brash manner suggested to some that he was an intellectual lightweight. He did tend to bull his way through details or subtleties, even though he could master both when it suited him. He always preferred forthright declarations of principle when diplomacy and tact might have saved him a great deal of grief—a weakness that would get him in trouble both at home and abroad.[16]

What he lacked in subtlety or tact, he more than made up for with his obvious relish for upsetting expectations. The son of a labor lawyer who became a utilities executive, he was a midwesterner with a prairie populist bent who was at home in New York business and cultural circles. A spokesperson for free enterprise who believed in nothing as much as Woodrow Wilson's League of Nations, he could talk wheat harvests one day and address an audience at Carnegie Hall the next. No wonder his new supporters believed he could scramble the conventional left-right categories of American politics. "The greatest joy in life," he told an interviewer in 1940, "is to keep one's thoughts uncontrolled by formulas. I won't be dropped into a mold. I want to be a free spirit. If I wasn't one, I would be still sitting on a cracker box in Indiana."[17]

As the election approached, Willkie found he was born to be a politician. He'd always liked talking about issues, giving speeches, and meeting people. He'd known since the TVA struggle that he found public life exhilarating. He loved to cultivate reporters and he understood how well turned attacks or rejoinders could carry an argument in the papers. He could appeal to feeling as much as logic, boiling complex policy questions down into easily digestible aphorisms, sentiments, or wisecracks. The obvious pleasure he took in the retail side of politics was apparent. He had an unrehearsed manner and a quick tongue, a reputation for straight talk, and a jocular appeal in front of crowds and microphones—just the sort of conversational charisma crucial for political success in the age of broadcasting. "He was one of the greatest mixers I ever saw in my life," the journalist Damon Runyon would later remember, "a bar-room glad-hander, a corner cigar store back-slapper." The influential columnist Drew Pearson wrote that "for sheer force of personality and character," Willkie made "the greatest impact of any man I've ever talked to. He rings true."[18]

Not unaware of his own appeal, Willkie cultivated his natural informality, sometimes to the point of hammy folksiness. "In my business," he once cracked, "it's an advantage to look like an Indiana farmer." His hail-fellow-well-met nature and disheveled charm made this bit a cinch—but it could also backfire. He refused to let himself be photographed in overalls and reminded reporters that he was merely a "conversational farmer," but the press loved to play up his background, or their image of it, and Willkie gave them plenty of material. The *New York Times* political writer Arthur Krock thought Willkie was a long shot for 1940, but still one to watch. "He still has his haircuts country style," he wrote. Sometimes all the playing at regular Joe-ness could be, as the conservative columnist Westbrook Pegler put it, "a depressing burlesque." Not everyone bought the act. New Dealer Harold Ickes mocked the "barefoot boy from Wall Street," and Alice Roosevelt Longworth, FDR's cousin, sniped that Willkie's appeal came from "the grass roots all right, the grass roots of a thousand country clubs." This was not quite true, but it did describe the growing coterie of influential Republicans who were convinced they had their man. More and more, they thought, he was heaven sent as a challenger to a weakened Roosevelt, who was seeking an unprecedented third term amid mounting doubts about the New Deal.[19]

Willkie slowly warmed to the idea of a one-on-one debate with Roosevelt over the nation's future. In early 1940 he launched an unofficial campaign, switching parties, issuing a series of speeches and articles, and making public appearances attacking the New Deal's infringement on private enterprise. Behind the scenes, his supporters—businessmen, lawyers, admen, and influential editors like the Reids of the *Herald Tribune*,

Fortune publisher Russell Davenport, and Davenport's boss Henry Luce, the founder of *Time* and *Life*—went to work putting his name before the public. A group of young Ivy League grads organized a nationwide network of "Willkie clubs" to get the word out. By early 1940 he was still a dark horse, but one with a bit of buzz. Still, this intraparty insurgency faced long odds: most Republican voters and party leaders didn't know him. The conservative midwestern bloc that controlled the party appreciated Willkie's pro-business attack on Roosevelt's New Deal, but he had been a Democrat until that very year. Besides, it seemed unlikely that a businessman, and a spokesperson for the utilities at that, could win a national election during the Depression, even if the New Deal had lost some of its luster. Most galling for the Republican old guard, however, was Willkie's long-standing internationalism. He'd never lost his belief in the ideas behind Wilson's League of Nations, a faith that nauseated the midwestern Republican leaders whose brand of insular nationalism everyone called "isolationism."[20]

Over the spring of 1940, as Nazi armies rolled across Europe, a sense grew that both rank-and-file Republicans and independent-minded voters might welcome an unconventional candidate, one who rejected stale party orthodoxy for the active progressive Republicanism of an earlier generation. Willkie did not officially declare his candidacy until June 12, but he stepped up his efforts in April and May, giving informal speech after speech to Republican delegates and radio audiences, penning articles in newsmagazines, and even appearing to wide acclaim on the popular radio quiz show *Information Please.* He kept up his attacks on the New Deal, but he also called for sensible government supports for labor, public relief, and public health. His forthright support for civil rights, particularly an anti-lynching bill, won him wide African American support. Looking abroad, he called for aid to the beleaguered French, Belgians, Dutch, and British. He opposed war, he said, but rejected outright isolationism, damning it as a sure-fire way to bring war to American shores in the long run.

A statement of his ideas that he wrote for *Fortune,* called "We the People," got picked up by *Reader's Digest* and brought him new, influential backers. The piece attracted the attention of Gardner "Mike" Cowles Jr., the publisher of the *Des Moines Register* and the newsmagazine *Look,* one of the primary competitors to *Life*, as well as his brother John, the publisher of the *Minneapolis Star-Journal*. These prominent liberal Republicans broadened Willkie's profile and got him in front of party delegates west of the Appalachians. Meanwhile, his amateur supporters took their "Draft Willkie" petition drive national, and a host of admen, public relations experts, columnists, and editors swung their support behind the upstart candidate. Frequent articles and editorials in *Time, Life, Look, Collier's,* the *Saturday Evening Post,* and a host of newspapers across the country featured Willkie or backed him outright. He went nonstop that spring, flying around the country giving off-the-cuff speeches to delegates and jawing with newsmen. He was in rare form, showcasing his knack for candor and casual exuberance before his biggest public yet. "I'm the cockiest fellow you ever saw," he boasted to one audience in Kansas. "If you want to vote for me, fine. If you don't, go jump in the lake and I'm still for you." By the middle of June, as the Nazis raised the swastika over Paris, acclaim for Willkie was growing steadily in public opinion polls.[21]

Willkie skipped the primaries entirely, but he arrived at the Republican convention in Philadelphia in late June riding this groundswell of popular support. Still, the conventional money was on New York State attorney general Thomas E. Dewey, Senator Robert Taft of Ohio, or even Senator Arthur Vandenberg of Michigan, each of whom was more palatable to isolationist opinion. But Willkie took Philadelphia by storm, wading into the crowds and running back and forth between hotels wooing delegates. Coming into the convention, Damon Runyon had been sure that Dewey had it sewn up. But then he saw the "big and tough" Willkie bellied up to the hotel bar, holding court in the midst of a swarm of well-wishers. The candidate, Runyon enthused, "began shaking hands all around and every time he shook hands he ruined somebody's dukes. He had a handshake like a guy squeezing an orange . . . he left hundreds of guys so they couldn't pick up a fork for a week." Willkie's momentum proved irresistible, and after a dramatic floor fight and some backroom wrangling he prevailed, winning the nomination on the sixth ballot as great chants of "We want Willkie!" swept down from the public galleries.[22]

The general election proved less dramatic, even anticlimactic. Willkie ran a disorganized campaign—split between the amateur enthusiasts who had led the charge for his nomination and the professional Republicans who took over after the convention—and never managed to seriously trouble Roosevelt, despite widespread unease with the New Deal and the prospect of a third term. Willkie tried to make up for the internal divisions in his camp by sheer force of personality. He criss-crossed the country by rail and air in the last months of the campaign, hoping to keep the momentum going with impromptu whistle-stop speeches and big rallies in halls, theaters, and open fields.

The entire campaign unfolded against the backdrop of the Nazi blitzkrieg and the early setbacks for the Allies—the fall of France, Dunkirk, the Battle of Britain. The country was in something of a slow-motion panic, tearing itself apart as it struggled both to avoid war and to resist the spread of totalitarianism in Europe. Willkie's staunch internationalism proved both a blessing and a curse. As the United States inched closer to war in Europe, his refusal to embrace isolationist allies in the Republican Party seemed more and more prescient, but any points he won on that score did little to distinguish him from Roosevelt, who was already pri-vately convinced that the country would eventually have to join the fight. Willkie had promised to speak directly and simply to the voters, but events got the better of him and he found himself making small distinctions with overheated rhetoric.[23]

Two political issues dominated the campaign. The first was Roose-velt's support for a peacetime draft. Willkie was in favor of it, and said so, but he attacked a congressional amendment to the eventual Selective Service Act that would have given the government the right to take over factories and other private property as a war measure, calling it an at-tempt to "sovietize" the nation. Soon enough, however, the amendment was modified, and the challenger was left looking overeager to protect industrial interests. The second was the president's decision to swap US destroyers for British military bases—a deal that outraged the isola-tionist right and caused some consternation on the left, too, where it was seen by some as evidence of creeping American imperialism. Willkie agreed with the deal, ultimately the beginning of the massive Lend-Lease program. But in an attempt to score points he attacked the secretive means by which Roosevelt and Winston Churchill had come to terms as "dictatorial and arbitrary."[24]

This kind of rhetoric began to give the campaign the air of a free-wheeling crusade, and by September Willkie himself was calling it just that, warning that liberty itself was in danger if Roosevelt got a third term. The president said little in response until near the end of the campaign, preferring to appear above the fray, but it was easy for his supporters to paint Willkie as the candidate of Wall Street and the power trust, and thus a threat to democracy. Tension mounted all fall. In big cities Willkie sometimes found his crowds infiltrated by hostile Democrats, and he dodged his share of eggs, tomatoes, and even light bulbs and rocks on occasion. One night, on his home turf of New York, police arrested a man with a loaded gun in the Madison Square Garden crowd just as Willkie was getting ready to mount the dais.[25]

Near the end, as something like desperation set in, Willkie abruptly changed tacks and started warning that Roosevelt planned to lead the nation into the war. This reversal—a sudden attempt to please the Republican base by depicting FDR as a warmonger—was an unseemly betrayal of his internationalist principles. The switch energized the right and momentarily gave him a bump in the polls, but it undermined the morale of his most fervent supporters. In late October, President Roosevelt gave his famous and controversial speech in Boston pledging not to send American boys into "any foreign wars"—a promise he knew he could break if the country was attacked. At the same time, he charged isolationist Republicans in Congress with a failure to fully fund the defense budget—thereby painting the Republicans and Willkie as reckless gamblers with the nation's safety. These two quick strokes were enough to curb the challenger's surge. Willkie lost soundly—by 5 million votes—although he fared better than any previous Republican against Roosevelt.[26]

The failure of his "warmonger" gambit reminded Willkie that the main source of his power was his independence. Despite that momentary lapse, he had achieved his greatest acclaim by saying just what he believed, not what the polls suggested. He had drawn to his side a vast corps of support that bridged left and right, including a huge number of African Americans, who appreciated his forthright stand on civil rights issues. Old-guard Republicans resented him, isolationists had discovered a bitter new enemy, and many on the left were still suspicious of his utility industry background, but a wide swath of voters across the broad middle of American politics greeted him as a refreshing straight shooter who recognized the gravity of the times. His internationalist convictions—and willingness to agree with Roosevelt—had provided a measure of national unity in a moment of crisis. The influential columnist Walter Lippmann would write in late 1944 that Willkie had stemmed the Republican Party's "tendency to sink into know-nothingism and reactionary obstruction." If Willkie had not won the nomination in 1940, Lippmann felt, the country "should be today not on the slopes of victory, but isolated, divided, and desperately hard pressed."[27]

Willkie's lapse of principle suggested also that perhaps his greatest role in public life might lie beyond the compromising intensity of a political campaign. He would run for president again in 1944—with less success, but with an urgency spurred by a vision for the world, not simply in order to get elected. "I would gladly say to hell with the Presidency and all political offices," he once remarked to Walter White, "if I felt I could do more as an individual than as governor or president or anything else." The presidency attracted him solely, he told *Look* in 1942, because it was "the only political office through which fundamental ideas, national and international, can be made effective. I have never been enamored of mere office holding."[28]

Willkie lost in 1940, but he gained a political stardom rarely enjoyed by a private citizen. Thousands upon thousands of letters, telegrams, and calls—half a million by one estimate—poured into his New York offices in the days after his defeat, congratulating him on his upstart campaign and beseeching him to remain active in public life. Among them, he told one journalist, were forty thousand invitations to speak. The election, it was suddenly clear, was merely the beginning of his influence. Over the coming months, in the year before Pearl Harbor, Willkie, like all Americans, would be swept up in the rush toward war. Hoping to make up for his momentary compromise during the last stages of the campaign, Willkie resolved to speak out for war preparedness according to his principles.

Most accounts of Willkie's life score the 1940 campaign as the high point of his career. But by his own estimation the work that would stand as his greatest legacy had yet to begin. He had less than four years left to live, but in that brief window he would realize his most far-reaching ambition: to press upon the American people the urgent need to embrace a new form of interdependent internationalism.[29]

The world war would give him a chance to revive the old Wilsonian dream for a newly interconnected air age. Formidable obstacles remained in his way, however. Even with his newfound celebrity Willkie did not yet rival Charles Lindbergh, long the living symbol of modernity aloft. But he had a chance to fulfill some of the promise the aviator had abandoned. In the 1930s, Lindbergh's vision had curdled into bitter withdrawal from the global prospects of the air age. Turning his fame into a platform for a reactionary nativism that drifted toward sympathy for Hitler, Lindbergh would soon emerge as the most visible spokesman for the America First Committee—the organization around which those most committed to keeping the United States out of "foreign entanglements" clustered.

So-called isolationism had always been a varied undertaking—less a unified position than a marriage of strange bedfellows encompassing everything from socialists and pacifists to hard-bitten nationalists. What they held in common was the belief that the United States should pursue its own interests in its own sphere of influence and avoid European wars of empire. Preserving American democracy at home meant avoiding the alliances that had dragged the world into war a generation earlier. Those labeled "isolationists" might better be understood as "noninterventionists" for their fierce refusal to be drawn into the conflict on the continent. During the 1940 election, America First gathered all the noninterventionist tendencies—left and right, nationalist and internationalist—under one umbrella organization. But the drift toward war put the group on the defensive. Agitated by Roosevelt and Willkie's tacit rapprochement on foreign policy—the election was a choice "between a knave and a fool," one strident America Firster lamented—the group increasingly came to be identified with Lindbergh's strain of conservative xenophobia.[30]

Lindbergh and Willkie would joust in public more than once during the tense and chaotic year between Willkie's nomination and Pearl Harbor. Inflamed by the events in Europe, Lindbergh lamented the lack of a choice between Willkie and FDR, openly warned of a slide toward dictatorship, and finally let his anti-Semitic tendencies show, claiming that Britain, the Roosevelt administration, and the Jews were the "three most important groups pressing the country towards war." Outraged, Willkie labeled this "the most un-American talk made in my time by any person of national reputation." Even America First split over Lindbergh's outburst. Still, the organization made Willkie one of its chief targets—second only to Roosevelt himself—and the group's letter-writing campaigns swelled his office mail with denunciation and invective.[31]

The Japanese attack on Pearl Harbor broke the power of America First, but the appeal of what Willkie came to call "narrow nationalism" persisted in many quarters. Over the next several years he would do as much as anyone else to banish it from the public realm, but even as Willkie's fortunes surged and Lindbergh's faded—the Hoosier had more "box-office" than the pilot, one citizen wrote the president in 1941—he would continue to confront the pervasive spell that nationalist feeling cast over American encounters with the world.[32]

Willkie had little time to linger with his son in Puerto Rico. After their impromptu flight over the island, the *Gulliver* left Borinquen Field that very evening, heading for Brazil and a seven-day journey across the Atlantic to Cairo, their first official stop. The travelers were in the air for ten hours that first night, flying under a bright moon, skirting to the north and east of Venezuela, Trinidad, and Suriname to avoid stacked storm clouds massing along the coast of South America. Just as the sun was rising, they landed at Belem, at the mouth of the Amazon, alighting at the American base there to refuel and grab a meal. Then they flew on, following the coast to Natal at the easternmost tip of Brazil, the usual departure point for eastbound flights carrying Allied supplies and personnel to the front in North Africa. They slept at the airfield that night and set off early on the twenty-ninth for Africa.[33]

The *Gulliver* could cross the Atlantic in one go, but to make allowances for bad weather and save fuel for the flight over Africa—where safe airfields with secure fuel supplies were less certain—Captain Kight scheduled a stop at the secret Allied air base on Ascension Island. Out over the Atlantic, Kight and his copilot, Alexis Klotz, soon spotted a big submarine—three hundred feet in length, they judged—cruising on the surface. German U-boats were wreaking havoc on Allied shipping that year, and a TWA pilot in the same vicinity would have a confirmed sighting later on in the day. Although Kight and Klotz couldn't spot its insignia from seven thousand feet, they radioed the sub's location and bearing to the Natal base.

Captain John Wagner, the *Gulliver*'s navigator, homed in on Ascencion's radio beacon hundreds of miles out. The island's narrow landing strip, cut through the saddle of a ridge between two mountain peaks, soon came into view. The Army Air Corps called the base Wideawake Field, an apt description of the state of mind needed for a safe touchdown. As he brought the C-87 in for a landing, Kight suddenly realized that the first third of the runway was on a slight incline. It was only as the plane crested the hill that he could see the flagman waving him in. A massive colony of terns roosted near the far end of the airstrip, diving and wheeling between mountains and sea in great swoops and clouds. Only the day before, one of the birds had gone into the prop of a fighter on takeoff. The *Gulliver* managed to land safely and begin refueling. At sundown the travelers took off again, dodging errant terns, bound for Accra, the capital of the British colony known as the Gold Coast.

The *Gulliver* had smooth flying over the ocean, skimming along above the clouds, but visibility dropped to three-fourths of a mile over the Gulf of Guinea. Kight and Klotz thought it might be prudent to bypass Accra, but their options were limited. Allied planes couldn't land at Abidjan or Dakar, as both were controlled by Vichy France. They decided to reduce the plane's power and push for Kano, in British Nigeria, but just shy of Accra the weather improved, and they were cleared to land.

After a day of rest the travelers embarked on another night flight and reached Kano, where they intended to make a brief refueling stop before heading off across the continent to Khartoum in the Sudan. Perched precariously between mountains and desert, with rain-sodden farmland right at the edge of the landing strip, the British airfield at Kano was not easy to negotiate. As the *Gulliver* was taxiing out to the runway, a big Wellington bomber roared down the strip, straining for liftoff, and then crash-landed, sliding into the mud at the end of the runway. Nobody was seriously hurt, but the wreck of the "Wimpy," as the American flyers called the big-bellied British planes, cost them a day while ground crews worked to clear the runway.

The stops in Accra and Kano were hasty, informal, and largely unrecorded. The travelers scouted for war news, toured around a bit—they found the walled city of Kano with its elaborate mud dwellings particularly impressive—and took briefings on the tense standoff between the Vichy French and British forces in the region. US intelligence officers stationed there noticed something else, too: there was a "vigorous and growing nationalist feeling" among young West Africans. They were "bitterly anti-imperialist and anti-British." Whether any of this reached Willkie is unclear—the travelers were no doubt preoccupied, working to acquaint themselves with the routines of the British Empire. They neglected to bring the sunglasses, tall boots, pith helmets, vitamins, and quinine required for malaria prevention and sun protection—practical prophylactics of colonial life that the British considered essential. Not to worry, though, as the US Army had packed those items for them. They were par for the course in America's tropical colonies, too, and the army came prepared.[34]

All across Africa Willkie and his companions came and went on airfields recently built by Mason's Pan Am, now maintained by the Air Transport Command. America's military and corporate infrastructure was already there, paving the way for global expansion in the years to come. Pan Am claimed to have reduced malaria rates among its US employees in Africa from 30 percent to less than 1 percent. In its promotional materials the company even congratulated itself for cheating the "white man's grave." The evocative phrasing, with its whiff of Kipling or Conrad, partook of the imperial vernacular, suggesting a corporate faith in the United States as a more efficient and modern successor to the British. When Cowles later told his fellow alumni of Exeter prep school that he was "struck with the possibility of a great future for Central Africa when malaria can be stamped out and that area, packed with natural resources, begins to develop," he too struck a similar note, no doubt imagining Pan Am and the US military as the ultimate masterminds of that development.[35]

The flight to Khartoum on September 1 was a nine-hour straight shot across the grasslands and deserts of central Africa. Captain Kight had a bit of trouble sorting out the communication protocols with the British, but the *Gulliver* reached Khartoum's Wadi Seidna Field safely, where Willkie and his companions retired to the British governor's palace for the night. "To date," Joe Barnes wrote to his wife from Khartoum, "the great wonder and fascination is Africa—about which everything you have ever read or been told is all wrong." The continent had left Barnes "full of sights and ideas," impressions that remained indistinct, but his experience of Africa as confounding—and the notes of skepticism and exuberance jumping off the pages of his letter home—captured the searching, quizzical temperament that he and Willkie shared in the face of their journey. Barnes, a foreign correspondent by trade and a committed anti-imperialist, had spent most of the 1930s abroad, reporting from the Soviet Union. As the colonial conundrums they glimpsed in Africa made their way to the forefront of the journey, his open-ended reflections would soon find themselves ill at ease with the sorts of rote imperial assumptions Cowles took for granted.[36]

So far the travelers had skirted the edge of the war, following well-established civilian air lanes. They had traced roughly the same path as Amelia Earhart on her final adventure five years earlier. But now they were entering British military airspace, and getting their signals and codes in order was imperative. From Khartoum they would head north to the Nile, which they would then follow on up to Cairo, approaching from the south to avoid enemy aircraft patrolling the skies above the battlefields around El Alamein.

Willkie and his companions had been gone six days, but already they had seen sights to last a lifetime: sunrise over the Amazon Delta, a secret island base in the Atlantic, the walled city of Kano, and the vast expanse of the African plains. The trip, Joe Barnes wrote to his wife, was "fantastic beyond belief and beyond telling." Rest was hard to come by under the din of the engines, so reading and cards prevailed. Sleep "hangs over me like hunger," wrote Barnes, but he was "some $30 to the good at rummy." As they prepared to head north toward the war, the great stakes of the trip must have started to dawn on them all, rubbing off on their in-flight contests. Willkie, Barnes remarked, loved to play rummy. Not surprisingly, he liked to hold his cards and look for a chance to win outright.[37]

CHAPTER 3

Egypt Is Saved

London, Cairo, Alexandria

As the *Gulliver* groped north over the Nile at dawn, Willkie and his companions feared they might be too late. Would Egypt be in Nazi hands before they could reach it? "On the way to Cairo," Willkie would later remember, "bad news came to meet us." In Kano they had heard that German advance scouts were almost upon Alexandria. Surely it was only a matter of days before General Erwin Rommel would take the capital. By the time the *Gulliver* reached Khartoum, rumor had it that Rommel's Afrika Korps was eighty miles from the city and Nazi paratroopers had been seen dropping into the Nile Valley. The British Army was readying for an evacuation. Civilians were packing cars to flee. For the five hours and forty-five minutes of flight time that morning they were all on edge, unsure what to expect on arrival in Cairo. The tension deepened as they drew closer to the battle zone: the Royal Air Force had promised the *Gulliver* a fighter escort into Heliopolis, the airfield outside Cairo, but no planes appeared.[1]

Much of the rumor turned out to be exaggeration. Axis planes had been seen in the skies above Cairo earlier in the morning, but the *Gulliver* touched down unscathed to a welcome fit for a visiting statesman. Crowds raced to meet the taxiing plane, and the British and American military officers and diplomatic officials gathered on the tarmac greeted

Willkie with great relief. He emerged from the plane squinting in the hot desert sun, tired but cheerful, wearing a pith helmet and his blue suit. The "big bear-like man"—as one reporter described him—stepped down and told the gathered reporters that he wanted "sleep and more sleep." As Willkie and his friends were whisked off to the residence of Alexander Kirk, the US minister to Egypt, they said a quick farewell to the crew. Bombing raids on Heliopolis were common, and the plane was headed for an airfield near Suez and then on to Lydda in Palestine, where the crew and passengers would be reunited in just over a week.[2]

Over the next few days Willkie and his companions took a whirlwind tour—a "blitzvisit," as Frank Gervasi, a correspondent for the American newsmagazine *Collier's* called it—of Cairo, Alexandria, and the front. Willkie remembered Egypt as "full of rumors and alarms." The streets of Cairo, he wrote later, were "filled with officers and soldiers coming and going." Egypt in the summer of 1942 was in a jumpy state. Famine and malaria stalked the countryside, Nazi armies seemed to draw ever closer to the capital, and Axis spies were suspected everywhere. The British, who effectively controlled Egypt, kept a tight lock on reliable news, so Allied reporters and ordinary Egyptians filled in the gaps with hearsay and speculation. In the hotels and coffee shops and bars where journalists and diplomatic staffers congregated, people debated "a dozen different versions of what was taking place in the desert not much more than a hundred miles away." The tight leash on information heightened the already rampant bitterness with which ordinary Egyptians regarded the British.[3]

Willkie charged right in, forgoing the sleep he craved, visiting, talking, and assessing. The first two days were a succession of diplomatic receptions, interviews with British and American officials, and audiences with Egyptian leaders. "Short as it was," Gervasi reported, "correspondents worked harder and longer during Willkie's visit than at any time while away from the fighting front." Reporters in Cairo were a jaded lot, tired of covering a gloomy war that often felt like one big retreat. Gervasi was suspicious of Willkie, calling him a "breezy politician" who might have "wowed them at some multicourse dinner of superpatriots back home." His "act," the reporter wrote, "didn't quite come off" in the Middle East. The *Collier's* man was convinced that the whole trip was

PR for a presidential run in 1944, but even Gervasi had to admit that Willkie's visit had delivered a much-needed jolt to the Western press corps. "Willkie shook up their livers," he concluded.[4]

The morning after his arrival Willkie toured a US tank base. Mingling with the soldiers and mechanics, he remarked that he hoped his visit would bring more coverage to the Mediterranean theater, which didn't get the attention it deserved back home. "I just want to say I'm damned glad to see you," he told the crowd. "God bless you and give 'em hell!" Back at US military headquarters, Willkie set up on the landing of a grand staircase for a press conference for Allied and Egyptian reporters. Gervasi painted a sardonic picture of the event for the readers of *Collier's*: in his lightweight suit with his "pants belt tight around his middle," his "unremarkable tie," and his customarily "rumpled" hair, Willkie looked "very much a man of the people." Even the sun heeded the demands of central casting, throwing "a shaft of light on his face from an open door."[5]

"I've come for a definite purpose," Willkie announced. "As a member of the party in opposition to the President, I want to say that there is no division in America on the question of winning this war and the establishment of a just peace after the war." Egyptians and other Middle Easterners could take his presence as proof that "130,000,000 Americans are all behind the President to beat the Germans." Rising to the occasion, Willkie "turned prophet," as Gervasi put it. He edged beyond his original mandate—reassuring his hosts that America's industrial might was gearing up—and went for the ultimate morale booster: predicting a turning point in the war. "The days of Germany's glory are over," he proclaimed. It would still be a long war, but he was confident that "Nazism has reached the peak of its power and we now are seeing the beginning of its recession." Turning to the local situation, Willkie said that he was no military expert—he hadn't even been to the front yet—but he was sure that Rommel was "out on the end of a limb." Whether he had had a confidential briefing on the ongoing battle in the desert or was just riffing on his instincts is hard to say, but Willkie announced confidently that he believed that Rommel would be completely defeated "fairly soon."[6]

On paper Allied power appeared overwhelming, but at that moment the Nazis had the Red Army pinned at Stalingrad, the Japanese were killing thousands of American marines in the Solomon Islands and

New Guinea, and Rommel seemed to be on the cusp of breaking through and sending a stream of panzers into the streets of Cairo. Used to non-committal war reports heavily edited by British authorities, the reporters found Willkie's assurances thrilling but confusing. There was nothing to do but report them straight, which they did, including as much detail as they could get past the censors. In time Willkie would be proved more right than wrong, in terms of both the local situation and the tide of the war. But Egypt would give Willkie a great deal to think about as he began to consider more fully what the global conflict might mean for the people of the world.[7]

This was an issue that had preoccupied him since the early days of the war. In late January and early February 1941 he had visited a beleaguered Britain as Luftwaffe bombers pummeled the country. He had traveled to London as a private citizen, albeit with Roosevelt's blessing and a letter of introduction to Winston Churchill. He spent eighteen days meeting with the prime minister and a host of other British officials, as well as the royal family and a colorful cast of journalists, intellectuals, and diplomats riding out the war in London. Crowds gathered as he toured air raid shelters in the Tube, inspected coastal defenses, and visited bomb-damaged cities across England. Always keen to mix things up, he also threw darts in a pub, sat in the House of Commons as a Labor back-bencher denounced the Tory administration, and bicycled to an impromptu tea with a group of workers and their families in South London.[8]

The trip had convinced him of British resilience—"I like their nerve," he said—and reminded him of the everyday qualities of democracy that the United States ought to be willing to fight for. The visit left little doubt that the "Indiana Dynamo," as some Londoners labeled him, could use his charisma to put ideas before an international public. He returned to the States just in time to deliver testimony on behalf of Roosevelt's bid to send armaments and other aid to the Allies at a standing-room-only Senate hearing. The noninterventionists were making their last stand for neutrality, but Willkie's performance helped push the Lend-Lease bill into law and further alienated him from his fellow Republicans.[9]

By the end of 1941, with the question of neutrality suddenly moot after Pearl Harbor, Willkie found himself an immensely popular figure. Still a private citizen—and back to practicing law—he was much looked to for his take on the events of the day. He was constantly being asked to serve on committees, chair organizations, put in a word for job seekers, throw his influence behind legislation, and make speeches or write articles for the big weeklies. The mail regularly overwhelmed his office staff, and they put in a switchboard to route all the incoming calls. Stories about him appeared in gossip and romance magazines, and he would even have his life rendered as a comic book. Willkie was now a political celebrity, a public personality tailor-made for the age of broadcasting and the great mass public gathered by the magazines, radio networks, polling firms, and advertisers. Talking to a nationwide audience over the radio, he was able to bridge the gap between private life and the public sphere, to give listeners the feeling that they were hearing from a "real" person they might themselves know. That implicit trust would give him the power to make himself a medium for his audience's feelings about the world at large. By late 1941, a Gallup poll reported that voters considered him the likely successor to FDR.[10]

But as his star climbed, Willkie had more than office-seeking on his mind. He began to carve out a role for himself as a herald of worldliness, a town crier on the city walls alerting the citizenry to the great stakes of the war drawing ever closer to American shores. Like other internationalists, Willkie saw the war as a symbol of the greatest social change of his time, one playing out across the planet. "Whether we like it or not, America cannot remove itself from the world," he said in a 1941 speech. "Every development in the art of transportation, every development in the art of communication, has reduced the size of the world so that the world today actually is no larger than the thirteen original colonies were when we established our system of liberty in the United States." Planes and radios had shrunk the world and brought it closer to political and economic interdependence. The United States could not afford to ignore these epochal changes, Willkie intimated, because the nation was itself the best model for how a closer, interrelated planet could work. An international version of the thirteen colonies, a new global "system of liberty," was in the offing, and the United States had to work to bring it into being.[11]

Willkie had long tried to forge an unlikely blend of earnest mid-western patriotism and cosmopolitan worldliness. This was a delicate balancing act: he had to both celebrate Americanism and gently prod Americans toward a more international outlook. It required an ongoing calibration of his affections for both native and worldly belonging, and a real-time sense of the American public's willingness to buy his views. This tension threatened to further alienate his more parochial compatriots, but it also fueled his surging popularity. He became the chief embodiment of a new kind of international American, a worldly idealist, and rode a rising wave of global-minded thinking.

Willkie seldom acknowledged that he belonged to a larger internationalist tradition, but beyond his sympathy for Wilsonian idealism, he benefited from a long history of internationalist thinking in America and abroad. A few years earlier, internationalists in the United States had labored in the political wilderness. But as the war approached, a cosmopolitan outlook swung back into favor, helping to propel Willkie into the public eye. Like their more established allies abroad, American internationalists were a divided group, riven by disagreements over the proper use of American power. Willkie succeeded in part by transcending these divisions and in part by embracing a more expansive vision of the future.

Ideas about world fraternity date back to the ancient Stoic philosophers, but the practical internationalism of Willkie's era had more proximate roots in the nineteenth century and its imperial entanglements. Steam engines, railways, and telegraphy shrank the planet, just as planes and radio would in the next century. Finding themselves enmeshed in a new global sensibility, people in the industrial age founded internationalist social and political movements to equal the new conditions. Paradoxically, the impulse toward "internationalism"—a term coined by Jeremy Bentham—emerged alongside growing nationalism. As European thinkers and politicians sloughed off the principle of rule by divine right, they began to envision not only modern states but an international congress of nations.[12]

Some of the most adventurous of the new nationalists envisioned a sphere of political cooperation *between* nations. They hoped that the great social transformations of the time—commercial development, industrialization, trade, science and technology, professionalization, and the revolutionary rise of the working and middle classes—would create a wide-reaching civil society that could transcend the interests of any single nation and supply the driving force behind progress. A broad assortment of groups—free traders, communists, pacifists, reformers, social scientists—saw vast possibility in an international society. By the early twentieth century internationalist visions had spread all over the world. Some sought to dissolve nationalism into a world proletariat or a world government, others to amplify it into empire. But the most influential elements coalesced around a moralistic, institutionalized internationalism organized by sovereign states and run by technocratic experts. By the time the self-inflicted horrors of World War I convinced the Great Powers to embrace international cooperation, a blueprint for the League of Nations already existed. But realizing that blueprint would require the crusading fervor of Woodrow Wilson.[13]

In the pre–World War I Progressive Era, American internationalists split along lines not too dissimilar from their global counterparts. On one side were the unilateralists, a group of progressive imperialists for whom American power and idealism were indivisible. Exemplified by Teddy Roosevelt, they hoped to bring manly nationalism and patriarchal authority to a developing world. On the other side were multilateralists, feminized in the public mind by their egalitarian ideals and by the fact that many of their leaders, like Jane Addams, were women. The multilateralists sought to curb empire and encouraged the United States to engage in mutual cooperation among nations. By the Great War both sides agreed that the eventual peace must produce an international organization capable of taming the beast of nationalism.[14]

When Woodrow Wilson went to Versailles in 1919 to make peace, he carried the hopes of a great global constituency with him. Cheered throughout Europe as "the savior of Humanity," Wilson embodied both strains of American internationalism. Simultaneously aloof and evangelistic, the dour Protestant was a Progressive social reformer with ties to Addams and other peace advocates, who nonetheless had few qualms about exercising American imperial might. He had overseen military interventions into Mexico, Haiti, and the Dominican Republic, and viewed American domination of the Western Hemisphere as a model of "cooperation" between states that would ostensibly guarantee "self-determination" for citizens of those states. In Paris, Wilson walked a fine line. Wary of Bolshevism, the other great internationalist movement of the day, and of the European imperial entanglements that had dragged the world into war, Wilson wrangled support for an international body that institution-alized the concept of the equality of nations, the peaceful resolution of conflicts, and authority based on the "consent of the governed." In prac-tice, the League of Nations would fulfill few of these ideals, but the spirit of the moment resonated across the globe, inspiring thousands of inter-nationalists, from patrician statesmen and technocratic modernizers to social reformers, anticolonial activists, and young idealists like Wendell Willkie. But Wilson's own country—or at least its Senate—rejected his idea. The treaty confirming US participation in the League was never ratified, and internationalism appeared to fall from favor with Ameri-cans reluctant to bow to outside constraints.[15]

During the interwar years so-called isolationism dominated do-mestic politics, particularly in the Republican Party, but political isola-tionism in Congress and the parties masked growing involvement with the world. In the 1920s, American industry, financed by New York banks and encouraged by federal policy, widened its foreign investments and trade, particularly in Latin America and the Pacific. After a brief return to protectionism during the chaos of the Depression years, President Roosevelt and New Deal policymakers recommitted to securing Amer-ican commercial and financial interests in a world of open markets. While less bellicose than the prewar imperial internationalism, this ex-pansionary spirit nonetheless encouraged those who continued to be-lieve that the United States should exert itself on the world stage.[16]

Meanwhile, the loose assembly of multilateral internationalist organizations had kept up their work after Versailles. Some embraced the gendered discourse of "peace" and campaigned for disarmament, women's rights, anti-imperialism, and outlawing war. Others hewed to a more pragmatic line and advocated American entry into the League. But even as that hope faded, they all joined a larger network of transnational social movements that would eventually coalesce in support of the future United Nations.[17]

With the onset of World War II, internationalists of all stripes could claim a measure of prophetic wisdom. The League had been inef-

fectual, true, but only because of fatal compromises with European nationalism and empire. Without an international union strong enough to
curb fascism, militarism, and colonialism, another war was inevitable. A
reinvigorated cooperation between nations, all internationalists agreed,
must result from a second global conflagration in as many decades. Nobody could deny that now.[18]

Renewed interest in world cooperation did not ensure unanimity
of opinion, however. American internationalism remained fractious.
Time and *Life* publisher Henry Luce carried the public banner for unilateralism, announcing in his famous 1941 article "The American
Century" that the United States should lead the postwar world. He and
other expansionists refined Theodore Roosevelt's manly missionary
rhetoric and welcomed international cooperation only insofar as it did
not impinge on American power. Meanwhile, Vice President Henry
Wallace spoke for the multilateralists, calling for the inauguration of a
"Century of the Common Man" to offset Luce's nationalism. A host of
other internationalisms jostled for position as well. Pacifism was on the
wane after Pearl Harbor, but similarly idealistic ideas of a world government with broad police powers proliferated. African American thinkers
and activists, from W. E. B. Du Bois to Walter White of the NAACP,
hoped that the war would provide an opportunity to undermine racism
and colonialism. Diehard supporters of the League of Nations latched
on to the idea of a new world body to be called the United Nations. Former
president Herbert Hoover, in his popular book *The Problems of Lasting
Peace,* backed the idea of a world body controlled by the Allies. Influential journalist Walter Lippmann favored the formation of regional alliances to create stable, balanced spheres of influence.[19]

President Roosevelt, for his part, tended to shy away from overt
endorsement of any postwar plan, at least at first. In August 1941 he gave
the world the Atlantic Charter, which promised self-determination for
peoples everywhere after the war. The result of a clandestine meeting between FDR and Winston Churchill on a destroyer anchored off Newfoundland, the charter was a "joint declaration" that renounced any
British and American territorial aims, supported free trade, and advocated
peace and economic cooperation. Most important, it announced that the
two democracies respected "the right of all peoples to choose the form of

government under which they will live; and they wish to see sovereign rights and self-government restored to those who have been forcibly deprived of them." The charter initially appeared as a simple declaration of joint war aims, offering an anodyne and largely toothless commitment to liberate lands conquered by the Nazis. But its lofty rhetoric inspired colonized peoples across the globe, giving them a spotlight to highlight Allied shortcomings. Meanwhile, Roosevelt's evocative "Four Freedoms"—freedom of speech and religion, freedom from want and fear—seemed to promise an expansive American approach to the peace. Behind the scenes, however, the president's postwar planners—working in secret in the State Department—began to lay the groundwork for American leadership of the global capitalist system and a world body dominated by what FDR called his "Four Policemen": the United States, Britain, China, and the Soviet Union.[20]

Wendell Willkie floated above these competing visions, aligning himself with no organization or government official and refusing to commit himself to any particular platform or plan for world cooperation—many of which would emerge by the last years of the war. He was clearly a multilateralist, but his avid support for war preparation ruled out pacifism. He enjoyed the political backing of Henry Luce and other liberal Republicans, but his deepening belief in interdependence set him apart from the main currents of unilateralist opinion and gradually eroded his support among that faction. In many ways, he simultaneously stood apart from the two main traditions and brought them together—he tried to be the hardheaded man of politics who could popularize multilateralist cooperation. He was, he often said, interested in "creating a body of public opinion" to force policymakers and politicians of both parties to embrace the robust multilateralism he envisioned.[21]

In the tumultuous early months of American involvement in the war, from Pearl Harbor to the Nazi advance across North Africa, he had kept busy practicing law, giving speeches, and jockeying for position in the Republican Party. But he needed something more if he was really going to lead the public toward a deeper understanding of the stakes of the war. The uncomfortable truth was that his customary exhortations would not keep him in the headlines. They would soon grow stale if he could not find a new drama in which to star. Luckily, the show had found him, and now he found himself winging his way toward a whole new level of world influence.[22]

On the afternoon of his second day in Egypt, Willkie took in a speedy tour of the pyramids and Sphinx and then sat down with Egypt's prime minister, Mustafa al-Nahhas. This and the appointment with King Farouk the following morning were intended as little more than formal audiences, a chance for Willkie to express his confidence that American industrial might would soon turn the tide of war. According to the official record, the prime minister and king proved more interested in securing the delivery of specific American goods. The king, who was regarded as an ineffectual playboy and potential fascist sympathizer by most British and American officials, asked Willkie to look into a missing shipment of American cars and trucks. Al-Nahhas tried to impress upon Willkie his hopes that a host of imported items, from fertilizer to machinery to food, might come via the Lend-Lease program.[23]

Willkie's briefing materials warned him about King Farouk's friendly relations with Italians and Germans but suggested that most Egyptians were not so much pro-Axis as anti-British. Scheduling issues had pushed their meeting to Friday—traditionally the Muslim holy day, when no audiences were permitted—but the young king had honored his visitor with an exception. Willkie genially violated royal protocol, showing up in his blue suit rather than formal dress. Axis propaganda had predicted that he would ask for a declaration of war; more likely he gently urged the king to keep faith as American production swung the war in favor of the Allies.[24]

The prime minister left far more of an impression. Willkie remembered al-Nahhas fondly as full of such "gusto and good humor that I told him if he would come to the United States and run for office, he would undoubtedly make a formidable candidate." Perhaps he appreciated the way the canny al-Nahhas attempted to extract aid from the Americans while resisting full Allied control. In any event, he depicted the prime minister as a capable and savvy public figure and left his veiled political maneuvering unmentioned.[25]

By the end of the day on Friday, Willkie's visit had started to attract the attention of regular Egyptians. The previous evening, craving an escape from official British Cairo and its thickets of protocol and intrigue, he'd stolen a moment for a stroll through the streets of the city. On a whim, feeling sweaty and hot, he ducked into a department store to buy something more suited for the desert climate. "I knew him at once," the French clerk declared to some trailing reporters, and fitted Willkie for a new khaki suit and shirt.[26]

On Friday afternoon, sporting his new gear, Willkie took up an invitation from the British lieutenant general Bernard Montgomery and headed for the front in the Western Desert. A few hours of driving took him and Cowles from Cairo to Montgomery's secret field headquarters hard by the Mediterranean coast. They found the British commander in a cluster of trailers and tents hidden among the sand dunes. Montgomery, or "Monty" as his troops called him out of earshot, verged on a stock character—in Willkie's words, "wiry, scholarly, intense, almost fanatical." He treated his guests to an in-depth account of the recent action, reliable and uncensored news that was hard to come by in Cairo. Rommel's advance had been checked at the First Battle of El Alamein in July, but Allied forces hadn't been able to drive him back. In the week prior to Willkie's visit, Rommel had launched a new offensive, but thanks to overwhelming artillery and airpower, and some clever strategy on Montgomery's part, the Allied forces had repulsed the Nazi thrust.[27]

Now Montgomery felt he had the advantage for good. "Egypt has been saved," Willkie recalled him intoning again and again as they spoke. Despite his bullish remarks to the press earlier in the week, he hadn't been entirely convinced, but Montgomery brought him around. "It is now mathematically certain that I will eventually destroy Rommel," Cowles and Willkie both remembered the general saying. "This battle was the critical test." Later that night, as Willkie and Montgomery sat together listening to the breaking surf and the boom of distant artillery, the general affirmed his plans to take the war to the Germans. "I tell you, Willkie, it's the only way we will defeat the *Boches*," Montgomery said, using the old French slang for the German enemy. "Give them no rest, give them no rest."[28]

The next day, Willkie and Cowles joined their host for a look at the course of battle. They examined destroyed German tanks and greeted Allied soldiers—Englishmen, Australians, New Zealanders, Canadians, South Africans—just back from the front lines. They visited an American unit, too—a small tank corps accompanying new US Sherman tanks that had joined the battle in recent months. Willkie commiserated with the enlisted men about the food, the heat, the blowing sand that got in everything, and the flies, "the billions of flies," as Cowles put it. Indulging a penchant for hard-boiled romanticism that marked all of his accounts of regular soldiers and workers on his journey, Willkie would remark that even though the men were heading back into the fighting, there "were no heroics, no big talk." They hailed from eighteen different states, he noted, channeling the folksy propaganda narratives found in magazines and movies, which imagined American fighting units as small democracies populated by representatives from diverse backgrounds, all united in the wholesome goal of licking the enemy and getting home. "They were just a group of physically hard, alert American boys," he later wrote, "who were wondering when they'd next see Texas, Broadway, and the Iowa farm."[29]

Off to the west, Allied forces were harrying the retreating Germans. Shells whistled overhead and they could see planes swooping in to attack Nazi positions. Now and again enemy planes would appear, Willkie recalled, bent on "quick, sharp strafing raids against British artillery positions." The American visitors could watch the battle unfolding across the wide-open desert vistas, but they weren't right in amid the fighting. "Here and there above us," Willkie wrote later, "we would see in the bright sky a plane that had been hit spinning to the earth in a spiral of fire and smoke and occasionally we'd see the floating parachutes of the pilots who had been lucky enough to get out in time—all of them floating, it seemed to me, out over the Mediterranean, under the propulsion of a gentle breeze from the south."[30]

When they returned to camp, Montgomery called a press conference. He knew he could not yet claim the victory he believed he had won. If he did, he feared, Rommel might order a general retreat before the Allies could muster the full strength needed to completely destroy the German and Italian armies. But a statement by Willkie wouldn't be seen as an official declaration of victory, and it might boost morale and dispel some suspicion in Cairo and the wider Middle East. They agreed on the wording, and summoned reporters to gather under the general's tent in the hot and still afternoon.[31]

Willkie stepped up and launched into a short speech hailing the recent battle as downright historic. It was "a turning point in the war," he announced. "Egypt is saved. Rommel is stopped and a beginning has been made on the task of throwing the Nazis out of Africa." He went on to praise Montgomery's tactics and the cooperation of the Allied troops— symbolic of the "future world spirit" needed after the war—and closed with a call for more American artillery and tanks to help finish off Rommel. Used to evasive, censor-ready understatement, the reporters delighted in what Gervasi called "hot, perishable stuff." Before that day, they had known there was a battle under way, but it seemed little different from the other engagements that summer. Now, suddenly, this battle was called the most critical of the war. Egypt was saved! The reporters sprang for their typewriters, thrilled for the scoop—but many remained wary. Even Willkie could discern "a polite sort of skepticism" on their faces.[32]

The British censors severely muted Willkie's revelations. They scrubbed his comments of any suggestion that Egypt might definitively be "saved," leaving the impression that the battle was only "significant," the threat "eased," and the Germans "stopped" but not "eliminated." When Willkie got wind of the redactions he was furious. "God damn it boys," he supposedly exclaimed, "nobody has the right to censor anything I say! I'm a responsible person. Nobody's got any right to censor me—and I mean nobody." It's easy to imagine Willkie in such high dudgeon, but the self-righteous bluster betrayed genuine frustration. After all, he'd secured Montgomery's blessing. And he felt he had Allied interests at heart. News of their success would boost confidence in the Middle East. But the British authorities believed morale was best secured through control and stability.[33]

Willkie admired the discipline, spirit, and military prowess of his British hosts, but their imperial mentality troubled him. On a visit to Alexandria the next day, he was treated to dinner with a half dozen or so high-level British military and diplomatic personnel, all well informed about world events, all of them "experienced and able administrators of the British Empire." His host, Admiral Henry Harwood, was a war hero, having commanded the nervy December 1939 operation in which out-gunned British cruisers had forced the Germans to scuttle the battleship *Graf Spee*. Willkie tried to get these men to talk about the world beyond the conflict and the ultimate fate of the imperial system. He was disappointed by what he heard. For all their sophistication, they seemed little different from their predecessors at Versailles a generation earlier. They were incapable of seeing that the world was changing all around them. "Informed Englishmen" bent on reforming the empire existed—Willkie had met them during his visit to London in 1941—but these officials were blithely committed to things as they stood. The colonial system was the air they breathed. They had heard of the Atlantic Charter, but it had never occurred to them "that it might affect their careers or their thinking." So steeped were they in the folklore of the empire, in the benevolence of English rule over the benighted regions of the earth, that Willkie's talk of global self-determination fell on deaf ears. All he found, he remembered, was "Rudyard Kipling, untainted even with the liberalism of Cecil Rhodes."[34]

The dinner-table talk in Alexandria suggested that the British failed to see the most fundamental tensions unfolding right under their noses. Willkie hadn't met as many ordinary Egyptians as he would have liked, but no small measure of fresh, street-level information came to find him. His ambivalent status—part presidential envoy, part public diplomat—served him well, attracting all sorts of people with stories to tell, while his natural gregariousness enabled him to win trust quickly. In Egypt and beyond, he became a magnet for inside dope. As Joe Barnes remembered it, "Everywhere Willkie went, men in positions of great power and ordinary citizens spoke to him briefly, hurriedly, with a sense that he would be gone the next morning and that this might be their last chance to say something outside official channels." Most of these rushed confidences have been lost to time, but the impression they made survived in Willkie's expanding view of the war.[35]

The British worried that the Egyptians were too detached from the urgency of the war effort, but the Egyptians' political antennae were tuned to a different frequency. King Farouk and Prime Minister al-Nahhas were self-interested—they hoped to preserve their hold on power, but they also had to maintain their nationalist credentials in the eyes of a restive public. They looked for fissures in Britain's informal rule, openings they could exploit for a greater share of self-determination. British officials thought them shortsighted. Were the Arabs and Circassians and varied tribal peoples of Egypt likely to be treated better under a Nazi racial state? To many Egyptians any means of ending British domination counted as its own kind of long view.

Willkie was more prepared than many of the Allies to get the message, but understanding why that is so requires taking the long view, too, to see how Egypt and Willkie alike were wrapped up in the long history of race and empire. Egyptians lived in a country that was a nation in name only. An Ottoman province since the sixteenth century, Egypt had been granted partial autonomy in the late nineteenth century. British and French investors flooded the country not long after, financing the Suez Canal and the Aswan Low Dam, but also swamping the young country with debt, punishing taxes, and diminished independence. An 1882 rebellion saw a group of plotters inside the military rally behind the slogan "Egypt for Egyptians." British troops arrived to protect European interests, reinstate Ottoman power, and occupy the country. Egypt found itself lodged in a strange state of semicolonialism—ruled by Ottoman khedives with no real power and governed by a British High Commission with no popular authority. Beyond the Suez Canal zone—the strategic hinge of the British Empire—one Egyptian writer remembered the country in these years as little more than "a gigantic cotton plantation."[36]

When the Ottomans decided to side with the Central Powers during World War I, Britain made Egypt a formal protectorate. Stiffer colonial control inspired renewed resistance, and a bloody revolution broke out in 1919. The British grudgingly permitted the nationalist Saad Zaghlul to lead an Egyptian delegation to Paris with an appeal to the peace talks at Versailles. Inspired by Wilson's principles of self-determination, Zaghlul and his delegation presented themselves as a civilized people ready to join the family of nations.

They discovered, however, that Wilson was not eager to meet them. They would find, to their surprise, that Wilson and the Americans were not so different from Europeans. The internationalist tradition in which Wilson worked had an ambivalent relationship to race and imperial power. Going back to the late nineteenth century, internationalism coursed with the assumptions about civilization and race prevalent at the time. Americans who embraced stage theories of civilization and fretted about the place of the "darker" peoples shared in anxieties felt across the Western world. Shadowing the hope for international society was a crude panic about what would happen as the forces of modernity brought peoples into contact. In 1886, the British international relations theorist and government official James Bryce declared that transportation and communication technology were "making the world small." But Bryce sounded this global note not in hope but in fear. Heightened contact between "the more advanced and civilized races" and "the more backward," he would later write, amounted to a "a crisis in the history of the world, which will profoundly affect the destiny of mankind." Across the globe, from Europe to the United States to South Africa to Australia and New Zealand, several generations of popular writers, academics, government officials, and legislators worried about the fitness for "self-government" of the indigenous populations that colonization, immigration, and commerce were bringing onto the world stage.[37]

Even more surprising was overt resistance to European dominance. Japan's 1905 military victory over Russia set off a shock wave through the newly coalescing "white" world—Teddy Roosevelt had in fact first recommended his famous "big stick" as a way to keep the Japanese in line—and a surge of joy across Asia and the Middle East. Representatives of smaller countries and European colonies, emboldened by a new current of resistance to racism and empire, began to press their claims for a role in world affairs. They too wanted to claim the mantle of civilization—and they indicted the imperialist West for violating its own ideals.[38]

The early twentieth century saw a host of attempts—like the 1924 Johnson-Reed Act in the United States and other laws in Canada, New Zealand, South Africa, and Australia—to restrict immigration flows from less "civilized" regions of the earth to the so-called white men's countries. These were joined by campaigns to limit the participation of peoples of color in international trade and association and to tighten and expand imperial control over colonized regions. When W. E. B. Du Bois announced in 1900 that the great danger of the twentieth century would be "the problem of the color line," he had in mind not only Jim Crow but the growing reach of influential racists like James Bryce, Theodore Roosevelt, and Jan Smuts of South Africa, who were working to reserve democracy and freedom for whites only.[39]

Many progressive internationalists embraced white supremacy, often in the form of a widely shared, implicit common sense rather than explicit race hatred. Visions for a system of international law, for instance, came wrapped in the conventional assumptions about the stages of civilization. When the Great Powers came together to draft international laws of war they wrote them only for "civilized" nations. In European colonies in Africa, Asia, or the Americas—zones of "savagery"—or in conflicts with "barbarous" peoples like the Ottomans or the Chinese, different standards inhered. A 1914 British manual of military law declared that "the rules of international law apply only to warfare between civilized nations. . . . They do not apply in wars with uncivilized States and tribes"—and that the British commander might use his discretion in defining "justice and humanity."[40]

The universalism underpinning internationalism had a primal exception at its core. With no common humanity expected between colonizer and colonized, white and nonwhite, imperialists legitimated the brutality inevitably used to preserve order. In fact, harsh measures might even be seen as humane, strong medicine for inferiors who refused to recognize their own best interest. The brutality that marked the "race for empire"—whether carried out by the Germans in Southwest Africa, the Belgians in the Congo, the British in India or Egypt, the French in Syria or Southeast Asia, or the Americans in the Philippines—was seen as a tool of civilization, not a corruption of it. Part of the shock of World War II for some Europeans was that suddenly they were subject to the terror reserved for "savages." The wars of empire, with their race hatreds and atrocities, had come home.[41]

Some radicals, pacifists, and feminists dissented from the pervasive status quo, but these conceptions of global difference shaped both the peace and the League of Nations. Woodrow Wilson, himself a southerner and a believer in white supremacy, never doubted that Europe and the United States should run the new world body. "The East is to be

opened and transformed," Wilson wrote in 1904, "whether we will it or
no; the standards of the West are to be imposed upon it; nations and
peoples which have stood still the centuries through are to be quickened, and made part of the universal world of commerce and of ideas
which has so steadily been a-making by the advance of European power
from age to age."[42]

In Paris in 1919 anti-imperialists from across the globe gathered in
Paris to put their claims for freedom before the great champion of "self-
determination." Petitioners from Africa, Asia, the Americas, and the
Middle East (including W. E. B. Du Bois and Ho Chi Minh) joined Saad
Zaghlul at Versailles. One Cairo newspaper reasoned, in the racial logic
of the time, that Wilson and the American delegation would see "inhabitants in Egypt who are not barbarians or negroes or red-skinned, but are
rather the heirs of an ancient civilization [seeking] their due place under
the sun." But American officials, unimpressed with Egyptian claims to
whiteness, dismissed Zaghlul's group as a "native autocracy" and Egypt as
"incapable as yet of efficient government." Apparently "self-determination"
did not apply to them. Zaghlul never even got a chance to make his case:
the very day he arrived in Paris, Wilson agreed to officially recognize the
British protectorate. Like many other petitioners from smaller nations or
colonized areas, he was largely shut out of the deliberations. Wilson also
explicitly rebuffed a proposal to have the League endorse the principle
of racial equality (pushed by the Japanese, who would soon prove
themselves equally adept at racial imperialism).[43]

In the years to come Woodrow Wilson would become an unwit-
ting symbol for a whole generation of nationalists and anti-imperial insurgents, as restive peoples everywhere found a glimmer of possibility in the
disappointment of Paris. They saw a new age coming, one in which they
might take hold of Wilson's ideals and put them to work demolishing
Western empire and its global color line. They foresaw a "violent conflict
between East and West, between imperialism and self-determination,
between slavery and freedom, between darkness and light," wrote the
Egyptian nationalist Muhammad Husayn Haykal in 1924. "Fate chose
President Wilson," Haykal declared, to be the "translator and spokesman"
for an overwhelming "force built up over the ages." Two decades later
Wendell Willkie would take up the role of "translator and spokesman"

with a fervor his old hero, constrained by his own racism and Eurocentric view of the world, could never muster.[44]

By the time Willkie arrived in Egypt, he had explicitly distanced himself from the racial and civilizational rhetoric underlying so much internationalist thought. He continued to admire Wilson, but he had never embraced Teddy Roosevelt's talk of big sticks and self-government, or the strain of racial subordination it masked. His lifelong liberalism— established by his parents, deepened by his horror at Puerto Rican exploitation, solidified by his hatred for the Klan in the 1920s—predisposed him to egalitarianism. And the great tumult of the war years had pushed him toward a host of new perspectives and varied associations that he would carry with him on his world journey.

Willkie left little trace of the inspirations for his ideas, but his deepening awareness of the problems of race and empire seems to have come from three important sources. The first were his friendships with international journalists like Joe Barnes, who was part of a generation that spent the 1920s and 1930s reporting from Asia, Africa, and the Soviet Union, where new ideas and movements were reshaping the old world order. Through Irita Van Doren, Willkie met Barnes, Vincent Sheean, John Gunther, William Shirer, Dorothy Thompson, and others who questioned the complacency of white middle-class thinking on the world beyond Europe. They did not shed all the assumptions of American exceptionalism, but the plainspoken, generous style of their reporting for magazines and newspapers widened Willkie's horizons and left its mark on his thinking.[45]

Also influential were ex-missionaries trying to shed the usual paternalism of missionary work and persuade Americans to accept a vision of world fraternity beyond race. Between the 1920s and 1940s, writers like Sherwood Eddy gained a significant audience among liberal Protestants with his warnings about the dangers of the combined forces of racism, imperialism, and nationalism—what Eddy called the "white peril"—for an interconnected world. These ideas came to Willkie most directly in the form of his friendship with the novelist Pearl Buck. The child of American missionaries in China, Buck was an outspoken critic of racial discrimination and supporter of the right to global self-determination. She and Willkie met while serving on the board of United China Relief, a nonprofit organization that raised money for Chinese civilians imperiled by the Japanese invasion.[46]

Most important was the education that Willkie received in the global black freedom struggle, largely as a result of his friendship with NAACP head Walter White. They got to know each other not long after the 1940 campaign, when Willkie joined the board of Twentieth Century–Fox Studios and they collaborated on a drive to end stereotyped roles for blacks in Hollywood. They also worked for a federal anti-lynching law, for a ban on the southern poll tax, and on a radio broadcast responding to the race riots that tore apart Detroit and other American cities in 1943. White remembered his alliance with Willkie as "one of the three or four closest and richest friendships of my life."[47]

White introduced Willkie to a host of civil rights leaders and prominent African Americans, and encouraged him to see the war as an opportunity not just for American blacks but also for colonized peoples abroad. The "double V"—victory over fascism abroad and segregation at home—was a critical issue for black agitators of the era, from liberals like White to radicals like Du Bois. "The paradox of race," the philosopher Alain Locke declared in 1942, "has become our democracy's greatest dilemma." How could an "inconsistent half-way democracy" preach about self-determination abroad when it "conferred freedom for some and subordination for others" at home? A war against fascism, against an enemy that classified whole categories of people as nonhuman, was also a chance to battle American segregation and end colonialism everywhere.[48]

In the spring of 1942 White had invited Willkie to address the NAACP's national convention in Los Angeles. He did not disappoint. "We must, now and hereafter," Willkie boomed from the dais, "cast our lot as a nation with all those other peoples, whatever their race or color, who prize liberty as an innate right, both for themselves and for others. We must, now and hereafter, together with those peoples, reject the doctrine of imperialism which condemns the world to endless war." The war, Willkie said, was challenging the casual assumptions of previous generations. Americans, supposedly ill-disposed to "alien imperialism," had to recognize that the world nature of the war meant challenges to imperialism abroad and to racism at home. In the coming months he would struggle with the fact of American empire, but this was a significant step for a white politician of his prominence to take.[49]

Meanwhile, the war offered a new day for race relations and criticism of empire. For several decades, professional anthropologists like Margaret Mead and Franz Boas had worked to undermine the idea that any group of peoples could be seen as inherently inferior to another, and had begun to chip away at the idea that there was any scientific basis for "race" at all. Buoyed by the war against Nazi Germany and its racial policies, civil rights activists in the United States and anticolonial nationalists abroad found new receptivity to their ideas. Change came slowly, though, or not at all. The Jim Crow South rejected integration out of hand, and white supremacy permeated housing, policing, and employment across the nation. Racial conceptions of the progress of civilization became ideas about the lack of "maturity" of non-Western societies, and they continued to inform American assumptions about the world beyond Europe and inspire widespread faith in the spread of modernization.[50]

Still, prominent liberals and internationalists had begun to catch up with civil rights and anti-imperial opinion. Undersecretary of State Sumner Welles, for instance, held conventional views about white superiority, but he adapted to the times and announced in a widely circulated Memorial Day speech in 1942, "Our victory must bring in its train the liberation of all peoples. Discrimination between peoples because of their race, creed or color must be abolished. The age of imperialism is ended." Even as careful and influence-seeking a columnist as Walter Lippmann would declare in 1942 that "it was time to put away the 'white man's burden,'" saying that it was the moment for Americans to purge an "obsolete and obviously unworkable white man's imperialism."[51]

The Atlantic Charter, with its promise of self-government for all peoples, was the most visible articulation of Allied commitment to self-determination. The charter fired the imaginations of people far and wide, just as such promises had a generation earlier when Wilson went to Paris to make peace. But as Willkie would soon see firsthand, people across the world remembered how the promises of 1919 had gone unfulfilled. The League of Nations had merely perpetuated the rule of the European Great Powers over the rest of the globe. Still, many around the world took hope from the Atlantic Charter. Maybe this time would be different.[52]

Many Egyptians hoped so. In the years after World War I they won nominal independence from the British, who established a new constitution in 1922 and installed the cooperative King Fu'ad to oversee it. The British army remained, too, ready to safeguard foreign economic interests. For twenty years, this fragile compromise had held. The nationalist leadership tacked to the center, opting for a program of gradual reform, looking to control as much as represent the restive masses. Over time, the British came to see the nationalists as their best bet for stability. But the majority of Egyptians were still landless peasants. As the country's future leader Gamal Abd-al-Nasser would later observe: "We live in a society not yet crystallized. It is still in a state of ferment and agitation." Looking on from India in 1935, the anticolonial activist Jawaharlal Nehru spoke for many across the world who saw Egypt as typical of the halting pace of freedom: "Democracy for an Eastern country seems to mean only one thing: to carry out the behests of the imperialist ruling power and not to touch any of its interests. Subject to that proviso, democratic freedom can flourish unchecked."[53]

Political agitation had reached a perilous climax a few months before Willkie's arrival. King Farouk, a well-known Italophile, had succeeded his father, Fu'ad, in 1937, and the Allies "strongly suspected" him of sponsoring an Axis-friendly "subversive organization." In early February, with Rommel's tanks rolling eastward, the British ambassador, Miles Lampson, had given the king an ultimatum: form a new government headed by Mustafa al-Nahhas and his nationalist Wafd Party or "face the consequences." An insulted Farouk stalled, and eventually Lampson and British officers, with revolvers in hand according to some accounts, barged into the king's study to force the appointment.[54]

By this time most Egyptians bore a visceral hatred of the British that far outweighed any abstract fear of fascism. Some went so far as to cheer Rommel's advance. A number of prominent Egyptian military officers— including future leader Anwar al-Sadat—even considered joining the Axis forces. Arabic-language Nazi propaganda, broadcast daily over shortwave radio, skillfully exploited the situation. On September 3, as Willkie went to see the prime minister, Cairenes could tune in to broadcasts by the

Egyptian National Committee in Europe denouncing the British presence
as "a tumor." Elsewhere on the dial, Egyptians could hear the Voice of
Free Arabism lampoon Willkie as Winston Churchill's errand boy.[55]

Willkie began to wonder if the United States might not offer more hope
to the Egyptians. He saw tensions emerging between the Americans and
the British. For starters, Alexander Kirk and Miles Lampson couldn't
stand each other. The American ambassador and his staff saw the British
minister as autocratic and capricious. Lampson, in return, thought Kirk
too showy. In general, American troops and officials found the British
high-handed and stuffy; "hoity-toity" was the phrase one American in
Cairo used in a letter to Willkie. Some resented putting their lives on the
line to preserve the empire. Americans tended to imagine themselves as
more democratic, more honest and direct in their dealings than their allies. Willkie tended to downplay the friction in public—better, he thought,
to invoke the virtues of Allied cooperation and keep morale high.[56]

But you didn't have to look hard to find Americans themselves
adopting familiar imperial tropes. Not long after Willkie's visit, a *Time*
article about Cairo indulged in hoary Anglo-American fantasies of tropical decadence. "Despite years of English domination," the author wrote,
"Egypt was more Latin than Anglo-Saxon," as if American readers would
better grasp racial ideas imported from their own hemisphere. The
country was "old and lush, indolent and naked." It "waited—ready to be
taken." Egypt's refusal to join the war seemed to *Time* a feminized, wanton
helplessness, a failure to know its own mind. Exotic Egypt appeared
doubly degraded: an insensate slattern whose decadent passivity virtu-
ally invited rape by the Nazis and demanded protection—and control—
by her racial superiors.[57]

Yet the persistence of imperial thinking need not foreclose a peace
that would work for all people. Egyptians, Willkie hoped, still might
see Americans as committed to freedom for all. The truth was more complex. Those Nazi radio broadcasters well understood that some Egyptians remembered America's failure to support their bid for independence
in 1919. They warned listeners not to trust Americans bearing gifts: "We

cannot forget the promises Wilson gave after the Great War. He promised
to every country a fair deal which was never realized." Others held
American archaeologists just as guilty as their British counterparts for
looting the country's cultural patrimony, and resented the efforts of
American missionaries to convert Egyptian Muslims to Christianity.[58]

There were those who saw the United States as friendly, but preserving that amity, Willkie was learning, would require Americans to
see the world through Egyptian eyes. When an Egyptian student,
George Abdo Marzoog, wrote to welcome Willkie to Egypt, he greeted
the "Second Leader of the United States of America" in the name of
shared principles. "We feel the same things, and our hearts beat on the
same tune of liberty," he wrote. "Our goal is the same, namely, to fight
this total war and to gain total peace." Marzoog was a Christian who had
been educated, at least in part, in British schools. He trusted the Allies
more than most of his countrymen, but even for Egyptians with close ties
to the Allies, the meaning of "total peace" went much further than current thinking in London and Washington.[59]

Tasked by Roosevelt with ginning up enthusiasm for the war effort, Willkie was beginning to see that he would need to reframe how the
war was imagined. As impressed as he was by General Montgomery's
tactical success, winning battles wasn't going to be enough. It was that
dinner scene in Alexandria that mattered. It was there that the war
would actually be won or lost. That evening, he would later write,
"started in my mind a conviction which was to grow strong in the days
that followed it in the Middle East: that brilliant victories in the field will
not win for us this war . . . only new men and new ideas in the machinery
of our relations with the peoples of the East can win the victory without
which any peace will be only another armistice."[60]

CHAPTER 4

A Great Social Laboratory

Ankara

IF EGYPT WAS A nation still in formation, Turkey, Willkie's next destina-
tion, appeared to many Americans as a country pulled between old and
new. Built from the wreckage of the Ottoman Empire after World War I,
the Turkish republic was, as the nationalist poet Ziya Gölkap put it, "in
head European, in heart Turkish." Knowing all too well the cost of
taking sides in wars of empire, the young republic draped across the
slender hinge joining Asia to Europe was trying desperately to avoid
the fighting engulfing the planet.[1]

The Turks hewed to a strict policy of neutrality, which meant that
the *Gulliver* and its American military crew could not enter Turkish
airspace. So Willkie and his party boarded a commercial flight and
hopscotched along the eastern rim of the Mediterranean, up and over
the craggy Taurus Mountains and across Anatolia, arriving in Ankara
on September 7, a few months shy of the twentieth anniversary of
Turkish nationhood. As they taxied in, Willkie and his companions
saw evidence of Turkey's adamant neutrality: three forlorn American
B-24 bombers that had strayed into Turkish airspace after raiding Axis
oilfields in Romania. Turkish fighters had forced the planes down
and the Ankara government had impounded them for the duration of
the war.[2]

The sidelined bombers fit one of two competing narratives about Turkey, which had confounded and inspired Americans ever since its independence in 1923. According to one view, it was fiercely insular, even savage, a backward Islamic country that refused to take sides in a war for civilization. Others saw it as wholly contemporary, a model of independence and modernity for its neighbors. Willkie and his companions would find themselves leaning decidedly toward the sunnier view. For them the young republic was a fascinating social experiment—one that hinted at answers to the questions posed by colonial Africa and Egypt.

Over the previous two decades, Turkey's founder, Mustafa Kemal, had led a breakneck effort to build a forward-looking, Western-facing nation. Kemal was gone, dead four years now, but many of the leaders Willkie would meet were his followers. Their nation-building project had involved a forced, even authoritarian embrace of modernization and ethnic purity in a one-party state based on a cult of personality with no shortage of official coercion, but it claimed an enviable record of improvements in education, infrastructure, industry, and agriculture. Kemal had created a stable republic, and the generation that followed institutionalized his legacy: preserving the spirit of "Turkish" identity while promoting intensive Western-style development. In Ankara and the surrounding countryside, Willkie witnessed this potent combination of nationalism and modernization. He hoped that Turkey would eventually join the conflict on the Allied side, but he was even more taken with the promise the country showed as a model for a world beyond the war. He spied in the Turks an appetite for freedom, development, and international cooperation that proved people could throw off the bonds of empire and claim their own forward-looking path.

Willkie misjudged some of what he saw in Turkey. He soft-pedaled the authoritarianism of Kemalist nationalism. His insights often reflected either the Western assumption that progress would inevitably sweep away Eastern ignorance or blithe innocence about the impact of American influence and expansion—but the picture of a rising Turkey would stay with him. As he made his way through a Middle East aflame with dreams of freedom, the idea of Turkey as both a nationalist success story and an eager partner for international cooperation drove his understanding of the linked forces of decolonization and interdependence.

Underground Nazi broadcasts out of Istanbul had predicted that Willkie would receive the "cold shoulder" on arrival, but a retinue of officials greeted the Americans on the tarmac, and Willkie was soon putting on his usual boisterous press conference for the Turkish and Allied press in Ankara. He had come as a member of the US political opposition, he announced, to show his nation's unity. American factories were gearing up to swamp the Axis. A few days earlier, he himself had seen Rommel's tanks stopped. The war was turning in the Pacific, too, he said, hailing recent news of victories at Midway and the Coral Sea. "Anybody that bets on an Axis victory is a sucker," he cracked.[3]

But Turkish reporters had more local concerns. Did he know when the Allies would launch a "second front" to relieve the Soviets? Many Turks feared the Soviets as much as or more than the Nazis. A second front might draw Nazi armies away from Turkey's western border, but it might also give the Soviets time to consider a southern incursion. Willkie only knew what FDR had told him about war plans, much of which was confidential. So like any good politician, he hedged. Leave those details to the "technical military people," he said. The question of a second front would dog him all the way to Moscow, making pithy answers harder and harder, but in Ankara he could still duck it with a one-liner: "I think Rommel found a second front down in Egypt this time."[4]

Kemal's successor, President Ismet Inönü, was away at the time of Willkie's visit, but Prime Minister Sükrü Saracoglu and Foreign Minister Numan Menemencioglu both met with him. All three men belonged to the generation that had fought alongside Kemal—defeating the British and Greek armies that had occupied Anatolia in the aftermath of World War I, freeing the country from debt to European creditors, and securing independence with the Treaty of Lausanne in 1923—and all three had led the new country on its two-decade rush into modern life. "We want to import all traits of Western civilization to our country," wrote Yunus Nadi, the editor of the daily *Cumhuriyet* in 1928. "Not long ago . . . our social life rested on Eastern principles. We are turning them upside down." The nationalists had disestablished Islam as the state religion, replaced sharia law with a civil code sourced from Switzerland, given women the right to vote, and converted to the European clock, alphabet, and calendar. They even banned the traditional fez for men and discouraged the veil for women. Visitors could not help but notice the difference. "When Wendell Willkie dined in Cairo with the King of Egypt the monarch had his fez on," wrote the Anglo-German Turkey expert Ernest Jackh in 1944. "But in Ankara, the Turkish ministers' hats did not differ in any marked way from Mr. Willkie's Indiana model."[5]

Modernization had sharp edges, despite its sartorial veneer. The "Young Turks" envisioned an ethnically pure nation emerging from the cosmopolitan, multiethnic, and relatively tolerant Ottoman Empire. Their turn westward was matched with an emphasis on Türklük, or "Turkishness." The nationalists encouraged the spread of Türklük with both official coercion and romantic appeals to a mythical past. The Turks, they claimed, were the founders of the great civilizations of antiquity, and the Turkish language was at the root of most Middle Eastern languages. Kemal celebrated the new collective identity with a famous dictum—"How happy is the person who says, 'I am a Turk'"—while placards went up in Istanbul and other polyglot cities with the command "Citizen, speak Turkish!" He built the new capital, Ankara, in the Anatolian heartland, away from decadent Istanbul, erecting a new city of wide avenues and ceremonial edifices purpose-built as a symbol of his modern aspirations.[6]

Establishing the new nation was a delicate balancing act. "Belong to the Turkish nation, the Muslim religion, and European civilization," Ziya Gölkap declared, summing up the nationalists' carefully orchestrated appeal for a new citizen. In reality, forging this character proved an often brutal process. Despite the stated policy of equal rights before the law, Greeks, Jews, Armenians, Slavs, Kurds, and dozens of other ethnic and religious minorities found themselves suspect in the eyes of the state. Some minorities, particularly the Armenians and Kurds, had been persecuted and even massacred by the Ottomans and the rising nationalists. Some chose to leave, while others opted to "become" Turkish. Those who did not leave or assimilate found themselves persecuted. The nationalist revolution aspired to Western technocratic ideals of efficiency, but less to norms of electoral accountability. A small and precarious elite, the Kemalists ruled over a nation that was still largely rural, Muslim, and illiterate. In the end, the Turkish Republic was an

experiment in benevolent authoritarianism, a kind of top-down populism sold on the godlike persona of the benign dictator. In 1934, the government ordained that all citizens must take Western surnames. Kemal
dubbed himself "Atatürk," or "father of the Turks."[7]

The Turks wanted to be seen as members of European "civilization,"
but they remained justifiably suspicious of actual Europeans. They had
long feared Russian designs on the Bosphorus and they remembered how
the Ottoman alliance with Germany had dragged them into a disastrous
war a generation earlier. The British relinquished any designs on Turkish
territory after the Lausanne treaty, but memories of English imperious-
ness died hard. Ahmed Emin Yalman, an influential journalist and businessman, described two kinds of British: those in England, who were
"open-minded, objective, fair, courteous, one of the most perfect products of civilization," and the "Empire British—conventional, narrow, opportunistic, believing that arrogance could always uphold prestige."[8]

In the years before World War II the young republic, poised at one
end of the globe's great strategic crossroads and hemmed in by potential
adversaries, had been in a dangerous position. Playing for time seemed
the best strategy. Bent on preserving their autonomy, preoccupied with
their own development, and ill prepared for battle, the Turks saw little
reason to join another Great Power conflict. Willkie himself would find
that they spoke of both sides as "foreigners" who might jeopardize
their fragile sovereignty.[9]

In 1939 the Turks negotiated a treaty of mutual assistance with
the British and French. They had hoped to include the Soviets in the
agreement, but the Hitler-Stalin pact shattered that goal, and they settled on a plank in the treaty that exempted them from going to war against
the Russians. The fall of France in 1940 should have triggered Turkish
entry into the war, but the nationalists stalled, invoking the Soviet exception. By the middle of 1941, Hitler had taken Greece, brought Turkey's
neighbor Bulgaria into the Axis fold, and finally turned on the Soviets.
Suddenly the Turks found themselves faced with Nazi armies on their
eastern border. Fearing an invasion, they rushed to conclude a treaty of
friendship with the Germans and formalize their neutrality.

In the year before Willkie's arrival, as the Nazi threat expanded in
the Mediterranean and North Africa, Foreign Minister Menemencioglu

had declared that Turkey's policy was one of "active neutrality." Turkey would not fight, but it would not simply sit back and wait out the war. The nationalists prepared to defend the country against a Nazi invasion, maintained diplomatic and trade relations with both Allied and Axis countries, and worked hard not to be drawn too closely into either orbit. Inönü and Menemencioglu looked to play the powers off against one another, hoping the war would sputter out in a negotiated peace. "The Turkish ideal," one Italian diplomat remarked, "is that the last German soldier should fall upon the last Russian corpse."[10]

Throughout 1942, the Allies feared a Nazi attack on Turkey and the crucial oil fields of the Middle East. Whether it would come from the Balkans across the Bosphorus, down from the Caucasus through collapsed Soviet defenses, or from both sides at once, they assumed that Turkish resistance would be fierce but futile. The Turks knew they could not stop a German assault. They realized that Istanbul was defenseless, but they could at least slow a Nazi advance across Anatolia. The dreaded invasion never came—bogged down in the Soviet Union and North Africa, Nazi war planners abandoned any hopes of invading Turkey—but the possibility haunted the Allies as something of a doomsday scenario. If the Germans conquered Turkey, they would set their sights on Middle Eastern oil supplies, and perhaps even the Suez Canal, which might enable a naval "junction" with the Japanese, in turn severing supply lines to Burma, India, and China.[11]

These fears shaped Allied opinion about Turkish neutrality in the weeks and months leading up to Willkie's arrival. Turkey's refusal to take sides rankled, and in public some said that Turkey should be nudged off the fence. Behind the scenes, however, many British and American officials viewed Turkey's neutrality as all to the good: it had stalled the Nazi advance in the Balkans and left the Allies with one less battlefront to worry about. Willkie's briefing materials suggested that the Turks feared "a strong and victorious Soviet Union" and hoped for a negotiated settlement but preferred an Allied victory "because they see in such a victory a better chance for small nations to survive." Turkey was particularly well disposed toward the United States, this official policy suggested, because nonmilitary Lend-Lease aid to Turkey was increasing dramatically and "we are regarded as having no imperialistic designs in the Near East."[12]

Armed with these optimistic views, Willkie went into his meetings with Menemencioglu and Saracoglu bent on reassuring them about American intentions. The United States respected Turkish sovereignty, he said. American war production would eventually overwhelm the Axis, and his country hoped for future good relations. In return, he wanted some reassurance that Turkey did in fact lean toward the Allies. He was also looking for hints of how the Turks, so preoccupied with their national ambitions, might greet a spirit of renewed internationalism after the war.

Willkie spent more than two hours with the foreign minister. He remembered him as unwell but highly attuned to his country's geopolitical predicament. *Time* magazine reported that Menemencioglu had undergone eighteen operations for a chronic lung ailment and boasted three new platinum ribs. (The day after Willkie's visit a high fever sent him back under the knife.) His "pallor and a general frailty," Willkie later wrote, "only emphasize the courtly skill with which he seems to be watching Europe and the world. I found his mind, like his appearance, a little sad, a little cynical, very strong, and very subtle." Willkie's good opinion of the Turkish leadership grew on his final night in the capital after a late-night conference with Prime Minister Saracoglu, who had just returned to the capital. Saracoglu, Willkie cabled FDR, was a "shrewd, able, popular leader."[13]

The foreign minister told Willkie that he privately hoped for and expected an Allied victory, and both he and the prime minister said they would continue to resist Axis demands for strategic purposes, but that their ability to do so depended on increased American aid. Turkey, they said, had long acted as a bulwark against the expansion of Russia; now it served as a roadblock against Germany. The *New York Times* reported from Ankara that Turkey would not violate its "armed neutrality," but that the Turks had assured Willkie the country was "firmly anchored alongside the United Nations [the term used to denote the Allies before the UN's founding in 1945] for the duration of the war."[14]

The Turks' assurances were based on a complicated calculus. The widely respected Menemencioglu was, as Willkie remembered him, "one of the most accomplished foreign diplomats of this generation." The British thought he was pro-Nazi, while German diplomats feared that he favored the Allies. In reality, the foreign minister kept his distance from both sides. In his dealings with Willkie, he sought to keep the Lend-Lease aid coming while making no definite promises to the Allies.[15]

Willkie came away from the meeting with a sense that the Turks wanted to be friends. Nazi propaganda was widespread in Turkey, but Willkie believed it could not check "a deeper trend of the awakening of Turkey toward closer relations with the world's great democracies." The Turks may have told him what he wanted to hear, but Willkie believed they would place their trust in foreigners who dealt with them fairly and with respect. This was not true of all the Allies or even all Americans, of course. Many found it hard to accept that the Turks could just sit out the war. They saw the refusal to fight as unprincipled, and it colored how they understood the Turks as a whole. One British diplomat, irked by the affinity between Turkish neutrality and Indian nonviolence, remarked that there was "something Gandhi-esque and positively immoral" about the whole idea of "active neutrality." It was "typically Turkish and its astuteness and cleverness cannot be denied."[16]

This judgment got at the complexity of Allied opinion about Turkey, a nation that many white Westerners were at pains to categorize in their racial and civilizational hierarchies. The Turks appeared somewhere between admirably astute and immorally clever. Some Americans still saw the Turks as "the Terrible Turk," another strain of barbarous Oriental subhumanity not yet fit for self-government. This view had deep roots in popular Christian lore about righteous Crusaders bringing Muslim infidels to heel, but it had reemerged sharply during and just after World War I, when "the Turk" had joined "the Hun" in a savage attack on civilization, slaughtering Christian Armenians and refusing to submit to British and Greek control in the war's aftermath. In recent years, however, Willkie knew that this image had begun to fade as modernization-minded stories about Kemalist reforms made their way into magazines and newspapers.[17]

Writing about Turkey in *One World,* he addressed Americans as much as Turks, looking to encourage in his fellow citizens feelings of equality and respect for the modernizing nation. "The Turks are our friends," he wrote. "They both like and admire us. They do not fear us, nor do they envy us."[18]

He was particularly impressed by the afternoon trip he took with Cowles and Barnes into the Anatolian countryside, where they visited villages, farms, schools, military bases, and industrial plants. He saw shepherds grazing their flocks in the hills and veiled women gazing out from the rooftops of village houses, but also crews laying new highways, irrigation systems watering the fields, lessons under way in a teacher training academy, and modern buildings going up in village squares. In a newly built country school they watched as pupils sang the national anthem and performed folk dances before settling in for a lecture on modern agricultural science. "Opening the books to people," Willkie later declared, "was one of the decisive events of history," and it showed how the country was at a "turning in the road."[19]

Turkey was not without problems, of course. The war had interrupted trade and the country was in need of wheat and machinery. Willkie even went so far as to send a cable to Roosevelt inquiring about upping wheat shipments, but overall, he saw the archaic giving way to the modern, much as the nationalists had planned. At all levels the Turks were banishing "superstition and ignorance." Their revolution had been largely peaceful—"brought about without badges or uniforms or mass hysteria"—and it was worthy of America's respect and support.[20]

Willkie fell hard for nationalist propaganda. When he later wrote that Turkey "had set its face toward the modern world and was building, hard and fast," it was not difficult to imagine his Turkish guides eagerly approving. He could not fully appreciate the incomplete nature of the Kemalist revolution, and like many sympathetic observers, he soft-pedaled the most autocratic elements of nationalist rule. But his judgments also served his own ends. As he traveled in the countryside or talked to officials in Ankara, he sensed a need to foster American respect for their national experiment, but also to frame the country as a model for world progress measured in more than machinery, highways, and scientific schooling.

Willkie discerned the inklings of a spirit of internationalism in the elite circles he encountered in Ankara. Neutrality made Ankara a locus of intrigue, but also a site of worldly sociability. He was struck by the fact that the Turks were very much at ease hosting the "international society" made possible by the war effort. The foreign minister threw a party for the visitor at Kemal's old country house outside the city, where Willkie would remember guests from across Europe and Asia indulging in the "curious internationalism of the diplomatic world." He met Soviets, Brits, Greeks, Yugoslavs, and Afghans, along with others he could not quite place. He heard about plans for a postwar federation of Europe and about the good hunting around Ankara. They drank English whisky, ate Russian caviar, and danced to American music. This was a rarefied world, of course, but it got Willkie thinking. Internationalism had always drawn sustenance from the more robust medium of nationalism and looked to channel its narrow vision of belonging toward more expansive vistas. Perhaps the cosmopolitanism of the Turkish capital was just the right substrate in which "the necessity of international co-operation" could take hold.[21]

Menemencioglu, the ailing diplomat with the platinum ribs, struck Willkie as the great symbol of the changes Turkey was struggling to usher in. He, Willkie would write, "seemed to personify a vast leaven which is now working deep in the lives of something more than half the human race." In just two decades the nationalists had created a modern state out of a crumbling empire. It was a powerful corrective to ideas about the unfitness for "self-government" of non-Western peoples. "Like the Arabs of the Middle East," Willkie would write a few months later, "like the peoples who live around the borders of China or on the islands of the southwest Pacific, like the Indians, they had no experience with self-government until a generation ago." Yet here they were, and they had done it themselves, with no colonial supervision.[22]

Turkey had come farther faster than even the United States. Somewhere in all his comings and goings Willkie met an intelligent, English-speaking lawyer who seemed to personify the spirit of worldly self-government he favored. Of course, there was nothing particularly exceptional in a Turkish professional who spoke English. But this lawyer was a woman, in town from Istanbul to argue a case before the Turkish Supreme Court, one of a growing group of women attorneys in the country. Meeting her brought home the vast changes Turkey represented: "I could not help thinking of my boyhood days when, only forty years ago, my mother's active practice of the law and interest in public affairs were considered an unusual—almost a peculiar—thing in central Indiana." In just a single generation, Willkie observed, the Turks had founded and raised up a modern republic with the promise of gender equity. Perhaps, he would write in *One World,* Turkey "offered a possible prototype for what is happening to all the vast area that used to be the Ottoman Empire."[23]

The Turkish newspapers were full of praise for Willkie and his mission. US ambassador Lawrence Steinhardt reported that the visit had claimed more column inches than any other recent wartime event. Given the top-down nature of Turkey's democracy, the newspapers tended to reflect government opinion. In Willkie's case that suggested the Turkish government looked upon his visit cautiously but positively. Editorials in the papers appreciated his support for neutrality and his interest in postwar planning; they hailed him as a member of FDR's democratic opposition, and they offered airy and abstract endorsements of future friendship with the United States.[24]

Some writers did suggest that Willkie—and by extension the Atlantic Charter—might not amount to much more than Woodrow Wilson's empty promises. In the Istanbul-based paper *Tan,* one journalist wrote that Turkey, committed to "the doctrine that a civilized and dignified community can only consist of free and independent peoples," offered Willkie "an edifying outlook on the war, as well as on the peace of tomorrow." Peace for the Turks, he wrote, would be meaningful under only one condition: "The victims of the present war will not have fallen in vain if at the end of the present conflict the spirit of Lausanne can be extended to the entire world."[25]

Willkie left Ankara on a high note, flying from the relative calm of Turkey back into the war zones of the Middle East. He would spend just over forty-eight hours in Beirut and Jerusalem—but it was long enough to see how diplomatic intrigue and imperial diffidence might scramble his hopes for a new spirit of interdependent internationalism.

CHAPTER 5

The Imperial Dilemma

Beirut and Jerusalem

Bᴇɪʀᴜᴛ ᴡᴏᴜʟᴅ ᴍᴀʀᴋ Willkie's first encounter with the "mandate" system, a semi-imperial scheme that assigned colonies liberated from the defeated Germans and Ottomans—a host of territories spread across Africa, the Middle East, and the South Pacific—to the victors of World War I. Neither a complete extension of colonial power nor an endorsement of freedom for ruled peoples, the mandate regime was an awkward compromise forged in Paris in 1919 between Wilson's promises of self-determination and European recalcitrance in the face of global demands for an end to empire. It charged the Allies—under League of Nations supervision—with the responsibility for uplifting their new charges and bestowing upon them the "sacred trust of civilization." The rules were complicated—and loose.

For those mandates deemed to be fit for self-governance—so-called Class A mandates—"provisional independence" could be recognized. The period of paternal oversight was supposedly temporary and local elites would share governance duties with League-appointed officials and governors from the mandate power. For mandates considered further down the civilizational ladder—Class B and C areas—the timeline for freedom was longer and far more vague. Wilson had hoped the mandate system could head off a postwar European colonial land grab, but in practice it had helped to prolong imperial control. As Winston Churchill recalled it, "There were to be no annexations but Mandates were to be granted to the Principal Powers which would give them the necessary excuse for control." Wilson's hopeful internationalism had become, historian Mark Mazower concludes, not the "antithesis to empire but its civilizer."[1]

Lebanon, Syria, Palestine, and Iraq were all current or former mandates of Britain and France, and Willkie suspected he would find there the same colonial mentality that had frustrated him in Egypt. Remembering their discouraging dinner in Alexandria, the travelers resolved to do all they could to avoid appearing too connected to the European powers. They started with a simple gesture: rather than take official diplomatic lodgings in Beirut, they would stay at a hotel. Hardly a major rebellion, but it was a start if they wanted a more local—and independent—perspective.

And so upon landing at Beirut in the late morning of Thursday, September 10, Willkie came down the receiving line, shook hands all around, and announced to the American consul, William Gwynn, that he wished to be taken directly to a hotel. With this he upset several days' worth of diplomatic scrambling on Gwynn's part. The consul knew—by way of a wire from Kirk, his colleague in Cairo—that Willkie wanted to meet with the Syrians and Lebanese, but he was concerned not to offend the British and French. The colonial powers were, as he later wrote to Washington, "the masters of these two countries at present," and "to have put Lebanese and Syrians ahead of them would have caused something like a scandal and would have greatly embarrassed the local people." So he had Willkie staying at the official French residence, his official schedule well stocked with meetings with colonial officials, and only one audience with representatives of the true "local people." Willkie was angry, but he eventually relented—it was only one day, after all, and he was already late for his first meeting, a breakfast with General Charles de Gaulle, leader of the Free French forces that held sway over the region.[2]

Willkie's State Department briefing had given him a serviceable account of the recent history of Lebanon and Syria. He learned that Lebanon was divided between Muslim Arabs and various Christian sects and that Arabs dominated Syria, Lebanon's larger inland neighbor. These former Ottoman possessions had been "entrusted" to France as Class A mandates. The French had dragged their feet on bringing the two states into the "family of nations" until 1936, when the socialist government under Léon Blum finally negotiated treaties with both countries that promised independence by the end of the decade. The French parliament, not prepared to part with its empire in the Levant, rejected the agreements.

After the fall of France, the Vichy regime maintained control of the two mandates, but in the summer of 1941, the Vichy forces had been chased out by a joint British and Free French invasion. The British took over security duties and Churchill sent Sir Edward Spears—liaison to de Gaulle and the Free French—to Beirut as his minister. The Free French proclaimed Lebanon and Syria "independent," Willkie's briefing commented, and set up local governments for the Lebanese and Syrians, but "transferred practically no real power to them." De Gaulle continued "to operate the civil administration on mandate lines," ignoring his own declaration of independence and maintaining a "'preeminent and privileged' position for France." To run this precarious operation, he had installed General Georges Catroux as the high commissioner for the French mandates, headquartered in Beirut.

The United States had repeatedly endorsed the idea of independence for Lebanon and Syria, and the British officially supported freedom for the two French mandates. These stances did not please de Gaulle. The leader of the "Fighting French" had lately written to Churchill demanding that the British keep out of French affairs in the Levant. He wanted Spears recalled, and he threatened to stop working with the British if his demands were not met. The United States hoped to mediate between the squabbling colonial authorities but also wanted to stay on the good side of the local populations. It was a combustible situation, made worse by food shortages and Axis radio propaganda, which harped on the idea that Allied soldiers were hoarding food while their leaders plotted to combine Lebanon, Syria, and Palestine into one state and turn it over to the Jews.[3]

After his breakfast with de Gaulle—no record of which has survived—Willkie set off for a nonstop day of meetings. Reporters were stationed at the American consulate, where Willkie wheeled out a hurried version of his usual show, producing facts and figures on American war production and urging the Lebanese and Syrians to more firmly cast their lot with the Allies. He amused and mystified the Arab reporters with choice selections from his trademark vernacular. "Bet on the winning horse, which is the United Nations" brought smiles, while a more America-centric quip—"If you want to see the United Nations win don't just sit in the bleachers and throw pop bottles!"—earned only puzzled expressions.[4]

At noon the party took a quick drive into the mountains to meet General Spears for lunch at his house overlooking the city. Spears, a worldly diplomat and military man with an American wife and long experience in France, was amused by Willkie's manner. "I quite liked him," he recalled, "if one can be said to develop a liking for the wind that blows one's hat off." Like many diplomats, Spears underestimated Willkie, judging him to be all politician and no substance, but it was true that the abbreviated schedule had led Willkie to revert to his hurried and relentless campaign personality. The visitor "impressed" Spears with "the American technique of presidential candidates in obtaining information," particularly after lunch, when they returned to town and a rushed tour of the American University of Beirut, where Willkie greeted Bayard Dodge, the president of the college, with an abrupt demand: "Tell me what is the difficulty between the French and the British here. I can give you fifteen minutes."[5]

Bowing to Willkie's demands, Gwynn had arranged a few minutes for Willkie with Alfred Naqqash, the president of the Lebanese Republic. They met at his office downtown, in the "Petit Sérail," a two-story sandstone edifice with crenellated walls like a European castle, built in the late nineteenth century to house the local Ottoman administration. Nobody in Beirut failed to grasp the significance of the fact that the French High Commission's headquarters, a sprawling Ottoman barracks with an ornate watchtower, tellingly known as the "Grand Sérail," looked down on the Petit Sérail from a hill in the center of town."[6]

Naqqash, a member of Lebanon's prosperous Christian community, had been appointed to his seat as a wartime measure by the Vichy

French and then reappointed when the Free French took over. Catroux favored him precisely because he lacked a dedicated following. Naqqash blocked anti-French factions, be they Christian or Muslim, from holding the nation's highest office, and in that he was an apt symbol for Lebanon's short national history. Propped up as an outside power's hope for stability, he served primarily as a hedge against the swirl of factional struggle. Willkie's brush with the figurehead president offered a glimpse of the social reality beyond the simplified picture provided in his State Department briefing.[7]

Like so many nations, Lebanon was an idea before it was a place, but the place it became could never be made as pure as the original idea. Carved out by European powers as a Christian state in a Muslim region, the country was defined by its lack of a shared vision, singular people, or unified history. The only past the various peoples of the former Ottoman territory shared was their collective history of jostling for advantage and coexistence. The "imagined community" of their nation was one part European fiction, one part ethnic and religious competition and cooperation. All the internal divisions broke power among a changeable array of factions and alliances.

Lebanon's multifaceted and varied population would eternally undermine the wishful thinking behind its imperial invention, yet it provided the ground for a surprising innovation in modern nation-building. Built-in division necessitated political compromise, as each faction, unable to rule on its own, sought allies to win power and stability. Lebanon was not a nation-in-waiting, like Turkey, nurtured by fantasies of demographic purity, ready to form up around visions of blood and soil. It was instead a political experiment in which, according to one historian, "various laboriously constructed formulas for coexistence" became the shared stuff of national belonging.[8]

Before the Versailles Treaty, the lands that would become Lebanon and Syria belonged to a larger Arab-dominated region of the Ottoman Empire that many called Bilad al-Sham, an expanse that included Palestine and the future states of Jordan and Israel. Despite its predominantly Arab identity, the region was home to many religious communities, particularly in the area surrounding Beirut and Mount Lebanon, where one could find Sunni and Shi'a Muslims, and significant clusters of local sects like the Alawites and the Druze. The scattered Jewish population grew in number as Zionism gained popularity in Europe, and there was also a patchwork of influential Christian communities led by the Maronites, who dominated the commercial life of Beirut. The French, who had a host of investments in railroads, trade, and agriculture in the region, had close ties to the Maronites dating back to the Crusades. Each of these groups saw the area as a homeland, and the core of a future nation.[9]

But any national ideas brewing in the region prior to World War I ran afoul of the infamous Sykes-Picot Agreement. In May 1916 the British and French had secretly divided up postwar control of Ottoman Arab lands. The British would control Palestine and Iraq, while the French would take Beirut, Mount Lebanon, Damascus, and surrounding coastal and inland areas. A month after the secret accord, a local leader on the Arabian peninsula, the Hashemite king Sharif Husayn, launched a popular revolt against the Ottomans. With dreams of establishing an independent Arab state, Husayn joined forces with the British, who neglected to mention that they had other plans for the future of the region.[10]

When the war ended, the British held Beirut, but duly stepped aside for French troops. Meanwhile, in Damascus they grudgingly permitted Husayn's heir Faysal to set up an Arab state. Faysal, like Saad Zaghlul and so many others, traveled to Paris to make a case for an independent Greater Syria. An increasingly embattled Wilson appeared sympathetic at first, but ultimately he ignored Arab calls for autonomy. With that, the road was clear for the French in the Levant. In April 1920 they secured Class A mandates for Lebanon and Syria from the new League of Nations, while the British took Palestine and Iraq. The two powers also prepared to exploit any future oil discoveries in the region, creating a regime of ground rights, pipeline routes, and financial shares to divide up possible crude deposits. Mandate in hand, the French ordered Faysal to submit to their authority. When he resisted, French armies marched on Damascus, routed Arab forces, and expelled the Hashemites. Faysal retreated to Mesopotamia, where the British installed him as the titular king of their Iraqi mandate. The dream of a fully realized Greater Syria, or any independent Arab nation in the Levant, lay gutted on the road to Damascus.[11]

In Lebanon, what the French and Maronites had imagined as a Christian redoubt under European tutelage became instead an unruly amalgam of ethnically and religiously divided communities. A Maronite elite faced constant competition with other "confessional communities," particularly the Sunni Muslims, who believed Lebanon belonged to a unified Arab Syria. The fragmented politics suited the French, who soon discovered they could neuter all the jockeying parties by giving each enough administrative authority to simultaneously placate them and prevent unified resistance. The French saw Syria and Lebanon as key way stations on the sea-lanes to their Asian colonies and the oil-rich lands to the east. Long ago the scene of French-dominated crusading, the two countries were a fitting arena for a new crusade, the *mission civilisatrice* to the untutored peoples of the globe.

Overt resistance to French control was dealt with severely: during the Druze-Syrian Arab revolt of 1925, artillery and planes had hammered Damascus, killing more than one thousand people. The revolt—and its repression—had hastened the rise of Arab nationalism across the mandates, among Muslims and Christians of all walks of life. This fellow feeling had been mounting since Ottoman times, and now redoubled in response to the intransigence of the European powers. "Anything that inspired love of country or language, or drew us nearer to other Arab countries, had been discouraged by our colonizers," recalled Wadad Makdisi Cortas, a Lebanese woman from a prominent Protestant family. "Any movement that bred self-respect was refuted and killed in its infancy. The same desire for freedom of thought expressed by the Algerians, Egyptians, Syrians, and other North Africans applied to us."[12]

Yet despite the growing political tension, Beirut and Lebanon prospered. In the relatively stable 1930s, Beirut became the most cosmopolitan city in the Middle East, with a bustling downtown, a modern port, broad avenues, clattering streetcars, a lively intellectual life, and a Muslim and Christian commercial elite. Even France's rejection of the 1936 independence treaty did not kill national hopes. Wasn't Beirut evidence enough of a state ready for self-government? Spears, the British minister, recognized "the pride of nationhood developing in quite ordinary people; sailors in the harbor, taxi drivers, began to feel they were now citizens of a beautiful country, the loveliness of which they seemed to realize for the first time, its pale blue sky diluted from the lapis lazuli blue of the Mediterranean, visible from every corner of their privileged land."[13]

By the outbreak of World War II, the patchwork population of Lebanon had forged its own peculiar identity. Not quite subjects, not quite citizens of an independent state, the Lebanese had become what one historian has called "colonial citizens." They did not enjoy formal freedom, but the relatively open nature of the mandate meant they could make limited claims upon the state. The French had established elaborate educational and welfare operations intended to extend supervisory power to local elites and to win the allegiance of regular people. They aimed to both nurture and dominate their wards, dispensing aid and discipline as needed to entrench French culture and control. The colonial citizens of Lebanon—Maronites and Muslims alike—found ways to bend France's high-minded ideals and paternalist rule to their own ends, seeking expanded rights and their own share of the Enlightenment vision France claimed to embody.[14]

Long-standing divisions of culture, religion, and class never disappeared, but by the time Willkie arrived, many in the Sunni and Maronite elite had found a measure of common ground. In the late 1930s they had discovered a workable, French-approved governing formula—the presidency went to a Maronite and the prime minister's chair to a Sunni—even as the Maronites began to share the Sunnis' distrust of the imperial French. Gradually, each side came to understand that their fates were linked. By 1942, the Lebanese had joined their Syrian neighbors in calling for outright independence. A few months before Willkie's visit, the unified opposition had demanded a new round of elections. They hoped to unseat Naqqash in favor of a government that would push for independence—a freedom that they would finally win in 1943, even though French troops would not leave Syria or Lebanon until 1946.[15]

Willkie encountered this current of anti-imperial nationalism on his lone night in Beirut. Gwynn had satisfied his orders by inviting representatives of the current Lebanese and Syrian governments for an evening reception at the consul's residence. Willkie found himself in a heated conversation with Prime Minister Husni al-Barazi and Foreign Minister Faris al-Khoury of Syria and Naqqash and his prime minister, Sami al-Sulh.

The Syrians declared that they wanted independence and elections as soon as possible, but the Lebanese officials, knowing that elections would benefit their more unified rivals, preferred to wait until things were more stable. An argument ensued, and accounts differ as to how Willkie greeted the Syrian pleas. The correspondent for the Arab Information Agencies, a news bureau based in Cairo, wrote that Willkie said he would "recommend" to FDR "the recognition of Syrian independence." Gwynn, ever mindful of French feelings, remarked to his superiors in Washington that Willkie had told the Syrians he was only there to "obtain information." Willkie grasped one point with absolute certainty: the rivalry between Britain and France clouded the region's fate. When he asked one of the Lebanese officials if he favored the French or the British, the unequivocal reply was "A plague on both their houses." He put the same question to the Syrians, and Foreign Minister al-Khoury recalled later that he had said that Syria also favored "neither" of the European powers. Both no doubt recognized that they could play their colonial masters off each other.[16]

By this point, French-British relations had decayed into what one historian calls a "maladroit improvisation." The British, tangled in contradictory imperial motives, pushed their allies to grant greater freedoms while officially affirming the right of any colonial power to do as it pleased with its possessions. Meanwhile, the French suspected the British of designs on their territory. The contretemps climaxed with a bitter exchange of letters between Churchill and de Gaulle and the French leader's remarkable forty-page indictment of British activity in Syria and Lebanon, which de Gaulle had written just a few days before Willkie's arrival. Meanwhile, US officials tried to stay above the fray. The Roosevelt administration officially supported a policy of self-determination in Lebanon and Syria, in keeping with the principles of the Atlantic Charter, but mostly wanted the Syrians and Lebanese to join the war effort and become US trading partners after the war.[17]

Willkie's second meeting with de Gaulle, that evening just after his discussion with the local leaders, made the French position clear. Willkie probed the general for hints that he might be receptive to independence.

But the Free French leader, tall and haughty in his white officer's linens, lived up to his reputation as prickly and unyielding. Any concession on his part would mean ceding advantage to the British. He could not "sacrifice or compromise" his principles, he said. Willkie pushed a bit more—would the French end the mandate? De Gaulle stood firm. "In no place in this world can I yield a single French right," Willkie remembered him saying. As they all stood up to go in to a banquet dinner, the general laid his hand on a bust of Joan of Arc and declared, "She saved France, I will save France. Good day, gentlemen."[18]

The meeting might be seen as a minor spat between competing wartime allies, and de Gaulle would later complain that Willkie was little different from other Americans: they all indulged in "the standard malevolent banter" and seemed to think that he had a Joan of Arc or Louis XIV complex. Of course, that judgment wasn't so far-fetched, given that the diffident and proud de Gaulle had been known to directly compare his place in history to that of just such illustrious saviors of the French nation. Willkie and Cowles—Barnes did not weigh in with his own impressions—seem to have at least partially embraced the idea, common among American officials from FDR on down, that de Gaulle was little more than a self-aggrandizing troublemaker. Looking on from afar, irked by de Gaulle's demeanor, they could not appreciate the depth of his predicament, or the strength of will it took to be an exile fighting for his country with a death sentence on his head.[19]

Grandstanding aside, the exchange helped Willkie see how crucial French imperial "rights" were to the restoration of the French nation. Empire motivated everything: the Free French military effort in the region, prewar promises to the League of Nations, cynical dealings with the Lebanese and Syrians. De Gaulle would accuse Willkie of having arrived at the meeting with no experience in the Middle East and his mind made up. He wasn't wrong, but the larger truth was less comforting to his ego. The French leader simply did not like what Willkie was learning. Later he would say that Willkie had left convinced that "the friction in Beirut was merely an episode in the rivalry between two equally detestable colonial systems." Indeed, this was part of the lesson Willkie took home—that France's *mission civilisatrice* left little room for Lebanese and Syrian dreams of freedom—along with a sense that the two semicolonial peoples were moving closer together, drawn to each other by their shared interest in self-determination.[20]

The travelers' sense that Lebanon and Syria had become elaborate stage sets for Great Power wrangling took on a particularly foul air at the banquet that night. Years later Cowles would remember that he was nearly pulled into a "little bit of intrigue right out of an Eric Ambler novel." Indeed, if the sordid affair he remembered had been carried out, it could have changed French history dramatically.

Cowles recalled that he was finishing his dessert and coffee when the maître d' handed him a place card. On the front was scrawled Madame Catroux's name and the word "over." On the back, in French, was a cryptic message: "Meet me in the garden immediately after dinner."

Once the meal had broken up he wandered alone for some time in the darkened grounds of the Résidence des Pins—its gardens were like "a small Versailles," he remembered—fearing he had misunderstood. When Madame Catroux finally appeared they began a halting, difficult conversation, going back and forth between his broken French and her stumbling English. Cowles pieced it together soon enough: she wanted to get a message to Roosevelt and Churchill, and thought Cowles, as a top official in the Office of War Information, might serve as her courier. But the message itself took his breath away. She said she knew that the president and prime minister found de Gaulle an impediment to the war effort. If she could arrange for an "accident" to befall de Gaulle in Beirut, she wanted the two Allied leaders to guarantee that her husband would lead the Free French into Paris when it was liberated from the Nazis.

Cowles was astounded, but she seemed dead serious. He told Willkie about the conversation on the plane soon after, but his friend wanted no part of it. "Mike," the publisher remembered Willkie saying, "you never told me that story. If it ever gets out, I'll say I never heard it. When you get back to Washington, if you want to tell it to Roosevelt, you're on your own." Cowles decided that he had to deliver the message, and arranged a meeting with the president when they returned. According to Cowles, Roosevelt made him tell his story twice and then thought it over for a while. He then asked Cowles if he would be willing to go to London and repeat the story to Churchill if Roosevelt decided it was necessary. Cowles said of course he would, and then the president told him not to repeat the story to anyone else until the war was over. He gave the president his word and never heard a thing about it again. Needless to say, Madame Catroux failed to carry out any such scheme. Her husband went on to serve in a number of diplomatic posts under de Gaulle, who became the leading figure in postwar French politics and the great symbol of the Third Republic.

The story—which comes down to us from only one source, Cowles's memoir—seems almost too fanciful to be entirely true. Whatever the gap between his account and what actually happened that night in the garden, the whole affair no doubt served to underscore for Willkie that the Allies were more than capable of matching the Lebanese measure for measure in petty but deadly squabbling.[21]

Lebanon and Syria were colonial ideas first and national realities second. Palestine, by contrast, was the scene of two national ideas fighting over one country. The day after the turmoil in Beirut, Willkie flew to Jerusalem, where he succeeded in bypassing colonial authorities to meet directly with representatives of the two communities vying over the future of mandate-era Palestine: the Zionist Jews and the Palestinian Arabs. Fatigued by all the pomp and politics of Cairo and Beirut, he made sure that no formal dinners or receptions would distract them in the Holy City. The travelers agreed to stay at the British high commissioner's residence, but the bulk of their time in Jerusalem was spent in meetings with Zionist and Palestinian leaders. News of their journey had preceded them, and the editors of the daily *Filastin,* which since the 1920s had been one of the chief champions of Palestinian nationalism and resistance to Zionism, had heard that Willkie had promised to speak to President Roosevelt about the Syrian and Lebanese desire for independence. The Palestinians had high hopes for the Americans and the Atlantic Charter. Willkie might be the next president, and so, they wrote, "it behooves us to pay attention to his statements on the Arab East."[22]

The British high commissioner, Sir Harold MacMichael, was remarkably similar to his colleagues in Cairo and Alexandria. A veteran of colonial Africa, he was a learned scholar of Arabic who seemed to Barnes to have "stepped into real life out of the pages of Rudyard Kipling." On the eve of Ramadan and the Jewish New Year, the British official led the Americans on a tour of the old city, visiting the Wailing Wall as worshippers arrived for noon prayers.[23]

It could be dangerous to venture out in public with the high commissioner. Palestine wasn't a combat zone, and Jerusalem was relatively quiet in 1942, but all through the war, tensions between Zionists and Arabs remained pitched, and MacMichael was a controversial figure. The Arabs were suspicious of any colonial administrator, as most had come to view the mandate as a means of handing their country over to the Zionists. But MacMichael was particularly hated. He arrived in 1938 just in time to oversee British repression of the Arab Revolt—a campaign of resistance that had begun in 1936 with a general strike and climaxed in 1937 with a period of guerilla warfare and chaotic plunder, during which Arab rebel groups took control over vast swaths of the countryside. By 1939, British and Zionist forces had quelled the revolt with a brutal counterinsurgency campaign.[24]

In 1939, however, MacMichael had become the local face of Britain's dramatic postrevolt policy change. Hoping to placate the Arabs, London officials had issued a white paper that Zionists saw as nullifying their progress toward establishing a Jewish state in Palestine. The white paper curtailed Jewish immigration numbers for five years, gave the Palestinians the right to approve further arrivals after that period, granted MacMichael power to regulate land sales to Zionists, and endorsed an independent Palestine governed by Jews and Arabs together. Zionists and Arab nationalists in Palestine agreed on little beyond their shared dislike for the British high commissioner.[25]

MacMichael seemed aloof from all of this febrile unrest. Barnes later wrote that from inside Government House, the hulking British compound, "the problems of the Palestine mandate could be made to seem simple and old and eternal, and not much worth bothering about." As they toured the Wailing Wall, the Haram al-Sharif, and the Church of the Holy Sepulchre, Willkie questioned MacMichael about Britain's role in Palestine and the Middle East. The high commissioner was adamant. Palestine wasn't a British colony. His duty was to maintain order and fulfill the mandate. The details of the struggle and the lives of the population were a momentary distraction; the duties of supervision and tutelage, however, were eternal.[26]

MacMichael was a fitting symbol for Britain's role in Palestine. For a quarter century, the British had ruled a land lurching toward civil war with an incoherent policy that amounted to little more than wishful thinking. "Palestine for most of us," one early colonial official remarked, "was an emotion rather than a reality." For empire builders steeped in Protestantism, the mandate was a faith-based fantasy with no single purpose—some favored Arab rule, some a Jewish homeland in the land of the Old Testament, others Christian supervision of the Bible lands. More hard-nosed officials in Whitehall deemed Palestine just another way to protect access to Arabian oil and the Suez sea-lanes to India. A few even wondered if it was worth the trouble.[27]

From the start the British had given assurances to both Zionists and Arab nationalists. As early as 1915 some officials vaguely backed the principle of an "independent" Arab area in the region. But in 1917, even as they sponsored the Hashemite king Husayn's bid to restore the Arab homeland of Bilad-al Sham, pro-Zionist foreign secretary Arthur Balfour announced that His Majesty's Government "view[ed] with favor the establishment in Palestine of a national home for the Jewish people." The Balfour Declaration meant that the British had simultaneously pledged themselves to sponsoring Arab independence and creating a Zionist state.

In the early years of the mandate the British had deceived themselves into believing that there was no real conflict in Palestine, as Arabs and Jews were both "semitic" peoples in need of civilizational tutelage. But when Zionist immigration jumped, Arab resistance mounted and low-level unrest began to disrupt everyday cooperation between the two communities. Zionists bought land, often from absentee Arab landowners, and dispossessed poor Arabs to erect settlements. Mixed communities gave way to parallel societies. Arab resistance to the British military and Zionist settlers grew more militant. By the outbreak of war a bitter stalemate had set in. After the suppression of the 1936 revolt, the Arabs were in disarray, with many of their leaders dead, exiled, or imprisoned. The Zionists, momentarily shocked by London's seeming reversal of the Balfour Declaration, had nonetheless spent the previous decade nurturing the civic and military institutions of an embryonic Jewish state.[28]

The war turned the region into a great Allied supply depot, which kept unemployment down and tensions at a low simmer. In the weeks before Willkie's visit, however, there had been a considerable panic about the advance of Rommel's armies. If Cairo fell, there wouldn't be much between the panzers and Palestine. The Zionists were working to enlist their young men in special Jewish brigades attached to the British Army, but many Arabs welcomed the prospect of a Nazi occupation, betting that it would rid them of both the British and the Jews.[29]

The Palestinians' titular leader, the "grand mufti" of Jerusalem, Hajj Amin al-Husayni, had in fact been in Berlin since his exile in 1941. He had fled British arrest during the revolt and, after stops in Beirut and Baghdad, had made common cause with Hitler. Like other anticolonialist insurgents across the globe who turned to the Nazis—Egyptian officers, Indian and Lebanese factions, even the far-right Zionist splinter group Lehi—he had embraced the ancient principle that the enemy of my enemy is my friend. Hitler installed him as the head of an Arab Office, from which he took charge of pro-Arab Axis radio propaganda, masterminding the very programs that needled Willkie across the Middle East. But al-Husayni's deal proved to have long-lasting consequences for the Arabs. Even as Rommel's armies fought their way east in 1942, word of the grim progress of Hitler's Final Solution had begun to leak out of Europe. The mufti had let his hatred of empire curdle into anti-Semitism, and in the years ahead his decisions would do much to besmirch the cause of Palestinian nationalism.[30]

Willkie had inadvertently helped shore up calm in Palestine just days before his arrival, easing fears of a Nazi breakthrough with his announcements from Turkey and Egypt. Behind the scenes, though, some British officials despaired of ever accommodating their warring charges and solidifying their rule. General Montgomery, for instance, had been called to Palestine to put down the 1936 revolt. Despite the success of his vicious counterinsurgency—with its internment camps, torture, aerial bombings of towns and villages, and random reprisal killings of civilians—Monty had little faith in the mandate's long-term viability. "The Jew murders the Arab and the Arabs murder the Jew," he said in the wake of the white paper. "This is what is going on in Palestine now. And it will go on for the next 50 years in all probability."[31]

Tasked with enforcing the white paper and restricting Jewish immigration, MacMichael had begun to resent Zionist intransigence. In his dispatches he advised disbanding the Jewish Agency—the formal, British-sponsored Zionist administration—and disarming their militias and police. But he also admitted that such a drastic step would be well-nigh impossible. The Jewish Agency wielded the lion's share of power in Palestine, and he knew it would resist. The terms of the colonial mandate, shaped by the Balfour Declaration, gave all the leverage to the Zionists, and now they were driving events. In 1946 and 1947 they would launch attacks on British military outposts and civilians alike. Bombings, assassinations, and gun battles would kill hundreds. By the end of 1947 the British had given up and dumped Palestine into the lap of the newly founded United Nations.[32]

In late 1942, however, the *yishuv,* as the Zionists called their Palestinian settlement, had yet to take up arms. Willkie looked to grasp the situation through direct meetings with the two rival nationalist camps. With little faith that the British could be honest intermediaries, he turned to the American consul general in Jerusalem, Lowell C. Pinkerton, to arrange conferences with representatives from both sides.

Pinkerton knew he couldn't just call the Zionists and Palestinians over for coffee. The divisions between the two groups, and among factions within each camp, were too bitter. So he engineered an ingenious solution. The diplomatic residence had front and back staircases leading up from separate doors below. Pinkerton ushered one group into an upstairs sitting room from the front staircase while another was shown to the back of the house to wait. When the first group was done he led them down the way they'd come while the others came up the other staircase, unaware that their rivals were passing them on the other side of the house. Four officials alternated like this, each settling into an armchair opposite Cowles, Barnes, and Willkie, who offered them tea and cakes and tried to put them at ease. "Tell us all about it, old man," the *Christian Science Monitor* reporter Edmund Stevens remembered the traveler saying. "Tell us without pulling punches."[33]

It's difficult to know what Willkie learned from these encounters. We have only spotty accounts of what was actually said, filed by journalists who sat in on the conversations. Pinkerton had invited a "moderate" and a "radical" from each camp. From the Zionist side there was Moshe Shertok, head of the political department of the Jewish Agency, and Dr. Aryeh Altman, a representative of the right-wing Revisionist Party, the chief rivals of the Mapai Party, headed by Shertok and future Israeli leader David Ben-Gurion. Two members of an influential family from Nablus, the al-Hadis, represented the Palestinian side. Ruhi Abd al-Hadi, described by journalists as a moderate, was an Arab officer in the mandate government. The other was Awni Abd al-Hadi, who had been personal secretary to King Faysal in Damascus in 1920 and a founder of the Palestinian branch of the Arab nationalist Istiqlal Party in the 1930s. He had returned from exile after the 1936 revolt to practice law and sit on the Arab Higher Committee, the independent executive body drawn from various Palestinian political parties.[34]

Like the editors of *Filastin,* the Arab leaders were eager to see Willkie, who had direct access to Roosevelt and might himself be the next president of the nation most likely to support the Arab cause. The flash point of the moment concerned Jewish immigration quotas—a fraught issue given both the terms of the white paper and the revelations about the Nazi atrocities unfolding in Europe. Shertok, who would later change his surname to Sharett and become the second prime minister of Israel, wanted to see 2 million Jews in Palestine. Altman called for 10 million and the expulsion of the Arabs. The Palestinians wanted to hold the line at the current half million, and neither would cede Arab sovereignty over Palestine. Awni Abd al-Hadi wanted an independent Arab nation in Palestine. Ruhi Abd al-Hadi, despite his official position in the mandate government, criticized British rule. "This is our country," he said to Willkie, with no small vehemence.[35]

Each side had an intransigent commitment to its own vision of Palestine. "If I were in your place, I would be a Zionist," Awni Abd al-Hadi supposedly said to Ben-Gurion when they first met in the 1930s, "and if you were in my place you would be an Arab nationalist like me." Ben-Gurion recognized it, too, even as far back as 1919: "We, as a nation, want this country to be *ours;* the Arabs, as a nation, want this country to be *theirs.*" The contest could have only one winner—a fact Willkie was not well placed to understand. The meetings presented the conflict as a struggle between competing camps that he—or by extension Roosevelt— might treat with favor or disfavor, as if it were a contest between two more or less equal competitors. But the two sides were not playing by equal rules, and hadn't been for years.[36]

Beginning in the eighteenth century, European Jews had begun to understand themselves as a people with shared identity. Pervasive anti-Semitism fed this growing nationalism, uniting different ethnicities, classes, and sects across the diaspora as an imagined community in exile, a state of belonging in search of shared soil. Zionism arose to supply a people with a place. Palestine—which contained the lands known in the Bible as Judea and Samaria—soon emerged as a possible site. "Palestine is our ever-memorable historic home," wrote the Zionist thinker Theodor Herzl in 1896. Jews emigrated to Palestine in five waves, or *aliyot,* between 1882 and World War II, and won British sanction to form the Jewish Agency, effectively a state-in-waiting.[37]

Arab Palestinians already had "soil"—but their national movement was not as quick to form up as Zionism, nor would it prove as effective a political instrument. After 1919, Arab writers and politicians began to celebrate the idea of a place called Palestine and its sovereign people. They founded newspapers like *Filastin* and declared their loyalty to the nation: "Long live dear Palestine and its honest, sincere sons," one journalist declared in 1920, in an essay titled "Manajat Filastin," or "Communion with Palestine." This manifesto predicted an outpouring of fellow feeling in the coming years, but parochialism proved an obstacle. Local ties fostered connection to the land but elevated affiliation with clans and families and localities above the newly imagined nation. Pan-Arabism also diluted Palestinian identity with competing visions of a Greater Syria, while a vast gulf between elites and landless peasants further hindered national coherence.[38]

Over time, national feeling partially overcame social divisions. During the Arab Revolt, resistance to Zionism and the British mandate quickened the cement of a unity based on hope and defiance. Pressure from Arab militants pushed notables like Awni Abd al-Hadi to form the nationalist Istiqlal Party, while the mufti broke with his British sponsors and formed the Arab Higher Committee. But long-standing divides hampered the rebellion, and the British crackdown scattered the leadership. By the time Willkie met the two al-Hadis the Palestinians were back where they had started—fractured and on the defensive. They were unprepared for the coming "catastrophe" of 1948—the *nakbah,* as it is known to Palestinians—which scattered their population and encouraged in world opinion the idea that Palestine was not quite a nation.[39]

The Zionists were by no means monolithic, but they shared a common purpose. Perhaps their most important advantage over the Arabs was their appeal as representatives of European culture, partners in bringing uplift to a benighted land. Zionism, Herzl had argued back in the nineteenth century, could "form a portion of the rampart of Europe against Asia, an outpost of civilization as opposed to barbarism." This underlying racial logic helped legitimate Zionism in British eyes, but undergirding the high-flown rhetoric was the reality of conquest. Even Shertok, commonly thought to be a dovish alternative to Ben-Gurion, saw the Zionist project in terms of forceful seizure. "We have forgotten that we have not come to an empty land to inherit it," he wrote back in 1914, "but we have come to conquer a country from a people inhabiting it, that governs it by virtue of its language and savage culture."[40]

It would have been impossible for Willkie to have fully understood this complex history. He was left with the feeling that things were deadlocked, and he emerged from his meetings dismayed. "By the end of the day," he remembered, "I felt a great temptation to conclude that the only solution of this tangled problem must be as drastic as Solomon's." Looking for a more hopeful view of the situation, Willkie paid an evening visit to Henrietta Szold, the founder of Hadassah, the American Zionist women's organization, which ran charitable, educational, and agricultural enterprises in Palestine, where Szold had lived for two decades. Over eighty years of age and nearing the end of her life, Szold was still a Zionist, but she had become increasingly isolated from the *yishuv.* Once called the "First Lady" of Jewish Palestine, she now believed in direct cooperation between Arabs and Jews. Cross-cultural understanding would eventually result in a negotiated settlement between the two parties and a binational state. It was a hopeful vision, and increasingly (even to her) far-fetched as divisions hardened.[41]

Willkie found Szold at home, preparing for the next day's Rosh Hashanah celebration. They sat by her window, talking by candlelight as the last of the day's light fell over Jerusalem and the Judean hills. She told him, as he remembered it, that there was no "necessary antagonism between the rights of the Arabs and the hopes of the Jews." The key was to break down prejudice on an individual level, face-to-face. If Jews and Arabs got to know each other, the Arabs would see that "we are not coming as conquerors or destroyers, but as a part of the traditional life of the country, for us a sentimental and religious homeland."[42]

Szold's view appealed to Willkie. She tapped into his sense that intimate, direct connection between people could bridge any divide. They both had great faith in the power of talking things out, of working together and overcoming differences. She reminded him of his work with groups that promoted cross-national ties and raised money for war relief efforts in the Soviet Union, China, and the Middle East. Talking with Szold heartened him a bit, although she reinforced his suspicions about the British. She had to agree, sadly, when he suggested that "certain foreign powers" were "stirring up trouble" between the Arabs and Jews in order to maintain their own control. This was true, of course, but Willkie was hard pressed to appreciate that a British exit would do little to hasten Jewish-Arab conciliation. The mandate had not only warped relations between the two sides but fundamentally transformed them in favor of the Zionists.[43]

Willkie spent only one day in Palestine, but in his frustration and confusion he joined a long tradition of American hesitation. Woodrow Wilson had been a quiet supporter of American Zionists, and the Balfour Declaration won official support in both houses of Congress in 1922, but for years the default State Department policy was simple: leave it to the British and the League of Nations. Over the interwar period, however, domestic isolationism in both parties—reinforced by entrenched anti-Semitism—had undermined enthusiasm for Jewish settlement in Palestine. As a result, the influence of Zionism in the United States waned, reviving only on the eve of World War II, when Americans began to grasp what was happening to the Jews of Europe. Suddenly Zionism found influential American backing, while the Arabs had little presence in American public life and few powerful supporters. A small cadre of diplomats and intelligence officers did prefer an Arab state in Palestine. Some, from families with missionary roots in the region, genuinely sympathized with the Palestinians, while others simply wanted to preserve American access to Arab oil. A latent anti-Semitism common among the Ivy League WASPs of the Foreign Service factored in, too, while some Americans feared that a Jewish state in Palestine would drive the Arabs into the arms of the Soviet Union. But these so-called Arabists lacked influence. Sumner Welles, an avowed anti-imperialist, was strongly pro-Zionist. He reassured the Arabs that the United States fought for the self-determination of all peoples, while behind the scenes he favored Zionist ambitions in Palestine. In the end, Roosevelt and his top advisers took a practical stance. They saw a Zionist state as an expedient solution to the Jewish crisis in Europe, the best answer to a problem that anti-Semitism made them wary of solving by allowing huge numbers of Jews to emigrate to America.[44]

Led by Ben-Gurion, the Zionists were starting to see that their best hopes lay no longer in the bitter and exhausted British but with the United States, where politically influential Jewish leaders could capitalize on mounting outrage at the news from Germany. When an international assembly of Zionists gathered at the Biltmore Hotel in New York in May 1942 to formally seek American support for a Jewish state in Palestine, FDR and Welles found themselves snared between two moral commitments. On one side loomed a potential solution to the long-standing persecution of the Jews. On the other stood the claims of the Palestinian Arabs, exactly the type of people to whom the Atlantic Charter promised freedom. While Welles and other officials pushed for a greater commitment to the Zionist cause, Roosevelt delayed, vowing to consult each side and offend neither. "The more I think of it, the more I feel that we should say nothing about the Near East or Palestine or the Arabs at this time," Roosevelt wrote to Cordell Hull in July 1942. "If we pat either group on the back, we automatically stir up trouble at a critical moment."[45]

All this diplomatic wrangling unfolded against the backdrop of a larger cultural transformation under way in the United States. Jews benefited from the atmosphere of pluralism and tolerance that took wing during the fight against fascism and Nazi racial dogma. Anti-Semitism was by no means eradicated—polls recorded the highest levels of suspicion of Jews in the early 1940s—but the war ushered in a new era in which *public* anti-Semitism withered. Prejudice against Jews never disappeared altogether, but a 1955 editorial in Mike Cowles's *Look* magazine put it succinctly: "Hitler made anti-Semitism disreputable."[46]

American Zionists capitalized on this new spirit, promoting a Jewish homeland in Palestine as both a remedy for the Holocaust and a beacon of the new humanitarian ethos. More and more Americans came to agree with this program, finding in magazine articles, radio programs, and other products of the age of broadcasting depictions of Zionist Palestine that rendered it as a country just like their own, home to a kindred national spirit. If the British saw Palestine as an exotic land desperate for the light of Protestant civilization, Americans brought their own sense of frontier romance to this familiar story, discovering in Palestine a place where a special people rode on the steady wind of progress and reprised the American pioneer drama in the Holy Land. In a series of *National Geographic* articles published across the 1930s, American readers were treated to tales of modernization in the fabled "Bible lands." The magazine, a primary "window on the world" for its vast middle-class readership, depicted Jews as bringing the blessing of agricultural technology to the benighted Arabs and, in the process, "developing pastoral people to a higher plane of life."[47]

The idea that the Zionists echoed the American pioneer ethos became a common trope in American culture. Visits to the *kibbutzim* produced sentences like this one, from the *Atlantic,* in 1949: "You see the faces, lean, hard, tanned, self-reliant, intelligent, sober; yet full of faith, hope, and confidence." These faces, the article declared, explained the success of the country. Theirs was a spirit of manly endeavor, lighting out into the wild, defying religious persecution to found a new land. It was a picture in stark contrast to the older image of Jews as urbane and effete intellectuals or grasping and inscrutable moneylenders, and much like the myths held dear by Americans themselves, with their stories of Pilgrims and an open country brought to heel with the plow and rifle. "On a miniature—almost a laboratory scale," *National Geographic* declared, surveying the arrival of survivors from the liberated death camps in 1946, "a visit to Palestine today is much like a visit to America of yesterday."[48]

Arabs enjoyed rather less favor in American culture in these years. If the descendants of Jewish and Catholic immigrants were finding themselves more frequently included in the public culture of whiteness previously enjoyed only by Anglo-Saxon Protestants, the American racial imagination continued to be less welcoming to blacks, Latinos, and Asians. In a June 1942 *Saturday Evening Post* article attacking anti-Semitism and other forms of prejudice Willkie celebrated the "vast assembly of minority groups which have gone into the welding of the nation," but the truth was that if Jews were slowly joining the national story, many others remained outside, marooned by imposing racial barriers. For the small population of Arab Americans, many of them from Syria and Lebanon, many of them Christian, those barriers were not absolute. They were sometimes accepted as fellow whites by the American majority, sometimes excluded, particularly if they were Muslim. Theirs was a precarious state of belonging in a nebulous space between white, Asian, and black.[49]

Americans tended to have little explicit knowledge of Arab cultures. Beyond childhood stories of the Arabian Nights—a reservoir from which they drew images of fantasy and romance—many turned to stories told by Holy Land tourists in magazines, guide books, and Sunday school sermons that celebrated the lost glories of the Bible lands and lamented the condition of contemporary Arab society. That repertoire of stock tableaus gave those Americans who visited during the war years—mostly reporters and soldiers—shaky preparation for the conflicting experiences of the people they encountered. Some found them generous and friendly, but others complained about the supposed Arab inclination toward thievery, revenge, and cruelty. Distressed by the poverty and disease they encountered in the Middle East, many came to equate the environment with the people living there. One war correspondent called Arabs "scrofulous, unpicturesque, ophthalmic, lamentable." An army officer added a less literary litany: "useless, worthless, illiterate, dishonest, and diseased."[50]

In those *National Geographic* articles where Zionist pioneers appeared manly and authoritative, Arabs were seen most often as sheiks, peasants, or "Bedouins." They were represented as dissolute and nomadic, a weak and feudal people living lightly on thinly settled land, still mired in barbarism and in need of Western tutelage. Wild and disorganized, they supplanted the Jews in the American imagination as the quintessential wandering people.[51]

Perhaps it is no surprise that Willkie did not linger over the quandary of Palestine. He kept his personal feelings under wraps during his visit, but the truth was that he had advocated for a Jewish homeland in Palestine in the past and would do so again in the future. "The doors of Palestine will have to be opened for homeless Jews in Central and Eastern Europe who survive," he declared the month after his return, in a speech commemorating the twenty-fifth anniversary of the Balfour Declaration. He did not indulge in overtly racial rhetoric, but he was undeniably drawn to the Zionist pioneer aura. He would later remember Henrietta Szold's stories of farms and factories in Palestine as "full of youth and vitality," proof of the march of development.[52]

Like many liberals, Willkie hoped for a world where the modernizing energies he perceived in nationalist Turkey and Zionist Palestine could be reconciled. He wanted to honor *Filastin*'s freedom dreams *and* offer safe harbor for the waves of Jews escaping the smoke and fire of Europe. But in Palestine he had found those hopes at loggerheads with each other. New forces of anti-imperialism were coalescing around the globe, but they were fueled by a nationalism that might threaten his nascent internationalist vision. In Palestine, where two nationalisms were entrenched in a pitched struggle over the same ground, the idea of an interdependent society of nations seemed a distant fantasy. Caught between Zionism and the Atlantic Charter, Willkie's instincts urged him to address the immediate crisis in Europe. He knew that Palestine mattered deeply to the Arabs, but he could not foresee how consequential the dispossession of the Palestinians would prove for both the United States and the world.[53]

Besides, there was little time to reflect. Early the next morning the Americans packed into cars and drove to the British airfield in Lydda, where they reunited with Captain Kight and his crew and climbed aboard the *Gulliver* for the flight to Baghdad.

Wendell Willkie and Franklin Roosevelt were the first presidential candidates to campaign by plane. Here Willkie greets reporters on the gangway of an Eastern Air Lines flight during the 1940 election. (Courtesy Franklin D. Roosevelt Presidential Library, National Archives and Records Administration)

This drawing, which accompanied a February 23, 1948, *Life* story about the British historian Arnold Toynbee and his popular history of "civilization," revealed the lasting effects of nineteenth-century stage theories of race and progress. Development, the article argued, was still commonly seen as an ascent from primitive "subhumanity" toward maturity, in which only "Western civilization" was "making any progress." (Courtesy family of Charles E. Martin)

Edith and Wendell Willkie take in a rare vacation near Palm Beach, Florida, following his loss to Roosevelt in 1940. Most of Willkie's vacation time was spent in Rushville, Indiana, where he owned several farms. (Bettmann / Getty Images)

Willkie's stand on racial equality helped him win substantial support among African Americans. The influential *Pittsburgh Courier* broadcast its endorsement of Willkie from the façade of its headquarters during the 1940 campaign. Photograph by Charles "Teenie" Harris. (Teenie Harris Archive / Carnegie Museum of Art / Getty Images)

New York: The switchboard installed at Willkie's law office after his run for president made him into a nationally revered public figure. His charisma on the campaign trail turned him into an icon of the age of broadcasting and anticipated the global celebrity he'd find with the publication of *One World*. (Author's collection)

Cairo: Willkie greets the welcoming crowds from the hatch of the *Gulliver*, September 2, 1942. (Bob Landry / Getty Images)

Cairo: The *Gulliver* on the tarmac at Heliopolis Field, September 2, 1942. Willkie mills around among the crowd of soldiers, airmen, and officials. (Bob Landry / Getty Images)

Cairo: Willkie with Egyptian prime minister Mustafa al-Nahhas *(center)* and US envoy Alexander Kirk *(right),* September 1942. (Bettmann / Getty Images)

Egypt: British general Bernard Montgomery reviews battle plans and troop movements with Willkie in the desert west of Cairo, September 1942. (Bettman/Getty Images)

Crowds of newspaper reporters greeted Willkie at each stop on his world tour, eager to hear his fresh takes on the course of the war and Allied plans for the peace. Here he is conferring with reporters during one of his Middle East stops, likely Cairo or Ankara. (Courtesy of the Lilly Library, Indiana University)

Beirut: Alfred Naqqash, the president of Lebanon, greets Willkie, September 10, 1942. Lebanon and Syria, French mandates since the end of World War I, had recently been granted formal independence but were still struggling to free themselves from French rule. (Courtesy of the Lilly Library, Indiana University)

Jerusalem: Willkie visited with Henrietta Szold, the Zionist founder of Hadassah, a Jewish women's organization, and an early advocate for Arab-Jewish coexistence in Palestine. (Courtesy of the Lilly Library, Indiana University)

Baghdad: Whenever he could, Willkie tried to break loose from the formal itinerary of banquets, receptions, and meetings. Here he is on a walk with a guide and translator. (Courtesy of the Lilly Library, Indiana University)

Tehran: The young shah of Iran, Mohammad Reza Pahlavi, had never flown before. Willkie arranged to give him a ride in the *Gulliver* on September 16, 1942. (Hart Preston/Getty Images)

Soviet Union: In Moscow and Kuibyshev, the wartime capital, Willkie was deeply impressed by the Soviet dedication to the war effort. Here, Willkie takes in a display of Soviet propaganda with one of his traveling companions, Gardner "Mike" Cowles, the publisher and deputy director of the domestic branch of the Office of War Information. (Courtesy of the Lilly Library, Indiana University)

Moscow: Willkie with Joseph Stalin after their meeting at the Kremlin on September 23, 1942. They are accompanied by *(left to right)* Viacheslav Molotov, the Soviet foreign minister; Joseph Barnes, deputy director of the overseas branch of the Office of War Information; and Mike Cowles. (Courtesy of the Lilly Library, Indiana University)

China: In the cities of Lanzhou, Chongqing, and Xi'an, cheering crowds gathered to greet the American visitor. Willkie was stunned by the reception, although he could tell that the ruling Guomindang party, the Chinese Nationalist regime led by Chiang Kai-shek, had staged the seemingly spontaneous receptions. (From the Academy Film Archive)

Chongqing: Many Chinese were eager to hear what the most prominent American visitor to their country since Ulysses S. Grant had to say. Here Willkie, with a Chinese translator, addresses a mass gathering. (Courtesy of the Lilly Library, Indiana University)

Chongqing: Willkie with Chiang Kai-shek, the leader of the Guomindang, in October 1942 after one of their several meetings. Chiang pressed Willkie to help end the unequal treaty arrangements forced on China by Westerners in the late nineteenth century. (From the Academy Film Archive)

Chongqing: Willkie with Mayling Soong, the wife of the Chinese leader, better known in the United States as "Madame Chiang." Soong charmed Willkie, and rumors of an affair made the rounds for years afterward. (Associated Press)

London: The scene at Mansion House on November 10, 1942, where Winston
Churchill delivered his Lord Mayor's Day luncheon speech. Responding to Willkie's
provocations, the prime minister vowed that he had not "become the king's first
minister in order to preside over the liquidation of the British Empire."
(Staff/Worth/Associated Press)

Minneapolis: The *Gulliver* with Willkie and its crew on October 14, 1942, on the way back to Washington, DC, where Willkie would report to President Roosevelt on his trip. (Author's collection)

Rushville: After his return, Willkie decamped for Indiana, where he spent a week recuperating and preparing a speech about the trip. On October 22, photographers followed him through downtown, where he stopped to talk to friends and neighbors about what he had seen on his trip. (Associated Press)

New York: On October 26, 1942, Willkie delivered his "Report to the People" live to an estimated 36 million listeners over all the major radio networks. (Murray Becker/Associated Press)

Willkie with Captain Richard Kight, the Lubbock, Texas, native and pilot of the *Gulliver,* and Willkie's "ideal of a rugged, alert American." (Associated Press)

ONE WORLD

BY

Wendell L. Willkie

CLIFTON FADIMAN *says:* "I want to urge every American to read *One World*. It's not a book, it's a searchlight."

WALTER LIPPMANN *says:* "...he has a seeing eye and an understanding heart. ...He is a genuine believer in the American way of life.... Mr. Willkie's book becomes a plea that Americans should learn to understand the shrunken world in which they live...."

RAYMOND CLAPPER *says:* "No person in public life can afford not to be familiar with what Mr. Willkie has to say as a result of his flight around this *One World*."

BOOTH TARKINGTON *says:* "Written with a breathless honesty, the book tells us what we ought to know, and so a reviewer can say at once that we all need to read it."

JOHN GUNTHER *says:* "There is only one thing to say about Wendell Willkie's book—it is *must* reading for every living American."

WILLIAM L. SHIRER *says:* "It is one of the most absorbing books I have read in years, full of humor, shrewd observation, a thousand and one facts you and I never heard but should have. I read it in one gulp."

SIMON AND SCHUSTER, PUBLISHERS

—*World*

The cover of the tabloid version of *One World,* published in both hardcover and tabloid versions on April 8, 1943, to immense acclaim and unprecedented sales. (Courtesy of the Lilly Library, Indiana University)

Demand for *One World* soon outstripped supply, and the book's publisher, Simon and Schuster, was forced to run ads in major papers and magazines explaining the commotion surrounding the book that some had taken to calling the fastest-selling book in American history. (From ADVERTISEMENT for Wendell Willkie's "One World" by Simon & Schuster [New York: Simon & Schuster, 1943]. All rights reserved.)

CHAMPION OF DEMOCRACY

THE STORY OF WENDELL WILLKIE

CHIANG KAI-SHEK

WINSTON CHURCHILL

JOSEPH STALIN

HERE ARE SOME OF THE HIGHLIGHTS IN THE LIFE OF WENDELL WILLKIE, WHO WAS BORN FIFTY-TWO YEARS AGO IN THE SMALL TOWN OF ELLWOOD, INDIANA, AND WHO IS KNOWN TODAY ALL OVER THE WORLD AS A CHAMPION OF FREEDOM AND EQUALITY FOR ALL PEOPLES!

WILLKIE'S PARENTS WERE BOTH LAWYERS. HIS MOTHER WAS THE FIRST WOMAN ADMITTED TO THE BAR IN THE STATE OF INDIANA.

I'M GOING TO BE A STEAMBOAT CAPTAIN WHEN I GROW UP. HOW ABOUT YOU, WENDELL?

AW, HE WANTS TO BE A LAWYER!

THAT'S RIGHT, AND I'M GOING TO BE AS GOOD AT LAW AS MY FATHER AND MOTHER.

WILLKIE WORKED HIS WAY THROUGH INDIANA UNIVERSITY AND LAW SCHOOL AS A DISHWASHER, CORN HUSKER AND SHORT-ORDER COOK.

By 1944, when he made his last, failed run for the presidency, Wendell Willkie was a famous popular figure, a well-known idealist, and a "champion of democracy" worldwide. The April issue of *True Comics* celebrated his life, which would be cut short only six months later. (Author's collection)

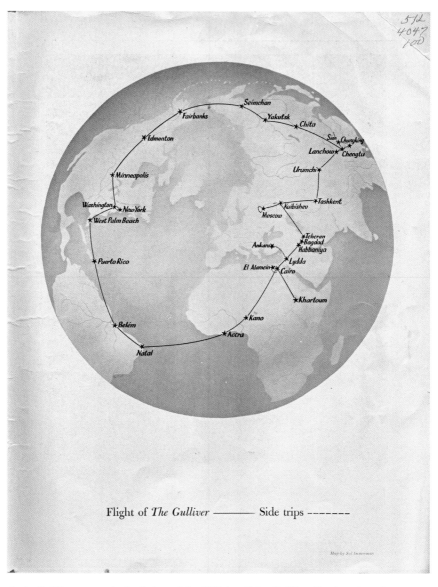

Flight of *The Gulliver* ———— Side trips --------

Artist Sol Immerman's depiction of the "Flight of the *Gulliver*," printed on the endpapers of each copy of *One World*. The map, which emphasized a stylized (and partial) representation of Willkie's voyage, depicted the air-age geography of the war years and a world of collapsing divisions free of the "splotches of color" that signified nations on a customary map. (Courtesy of the Lilly Library, Indiana University)

CHAPTER 6

How East and West Will Meet

Baghdad

Winging in from the east, the *Gulliver* dropped through the midday glare into Baghdad. The morning's journey had been easy and uneventful, as Major Kight took the travelers back over Jerusalem, across the terraced hills of the coastal ranges, above the delta where the Jordan River flows into the Dead Sea, and then north by northeast for the long haul over the pale brown expanse of the desert. It was Saturday, September 12, the first day of the month of Ramadan.[1]

Anticipation in Baghdad had been mounting all week as news of the gregarious American emissary spread across the region. His reception there would be the most elaborate yet. As he and his companions appeared at the mouth of the *Gulliver*'s hatch, the King's Guard band struck up the familiar cadences of "The Star-Spangled Banner" and the royal bodyguard, resplendent in bright white coats and blue trousers with red stripes, presented arms. Shedding his overcoat in the hundred-degree heat, Willkie came down the steps in his trusty blue suit to greet the Iraqi prime minister, Nuri al-Said, and a host of Iraqi, British, and American officials. He inspected the honor guard, and after ten minutes of shaking hands and milling about with the assembled dignitaries, he joined the prime minister in an official car and set out for the city, sweeping down freshly wetted, dust-free avenues into downtown.

Colonnaded Al-Rashid Street had been cleared of cars and wagons to hurry the group's way toward the Royal Court, where a guest suite—in a pavilion originally built for a visit from the prince of Sweden—awaited.[2]

The Iraqi royal government had arranged a busy round of visits and state dinners for the party's two nights in the ancient city between the Tigris and the Euphrates. The travelers greeted this agenda with some trepidation. Willkie had put up a brave front at the airport, smiling and shaking hands and making his customary jokes, but two weeks of nonstop travel and official hubbub had taken its toll. He was exhausted. He managed to make it through the first round of events—wreath ceremonies at the tombs of Iraq's first two kings and a luncheon—but back at the Royal Court he went straight to bed, leaving Cowles to make the arrangements for yet another state dinner that night.

So much of their time in the Middle East had been carefully stage-managed, glad-handing at buttoned-up functions with stuffy Europeans and officious diplomats. Willkie longed for more contact with ordinary people. Not since his impromptu walk through Cairo had he mixed with shopkeepers and workers, trading stories and jokes, trying to glean how their senses of the war and their nation's future aligned with those of the politicians and diplomats. Baghdad would bring no respite from highfalutin affairs—both nights were reserved for sumptuous banquets the travelers would long remember—but Willkie did manage to discover some of the city's everyday pleasures, and he encountered an undiminished strain of that same clamor for freedom he had heard ringing across the Middle East.

Baghdad buzzed with tension and rumors. Like Cairo, Beirut, and Jerusalem, the ancient city was deeply divided. From his briefing, Willkie knew that his host that night, the recently reinstalled regent, Abd al-Ilah, owed his fragile rule to the presence of British troops. The imperial battalions had arrived in the spring of 1941 from India to break the back of a military coup orchestrated by the anti-British Rashid Ali al-Gailani, an Arab nationalist ally of the grand mufti of Jerusalem who, like the grand mufti, was sympathetic to the Nazis. The regent and the prime minister stood at the head of a country that was nominally independent and officially a "nonbelligerent ally" of Great Britain, but large swaths of the public and military were not wholly committed to the Allied cause and were openly hostile to the royal government.[3]

The situation reflected the arbitrary construction of the Iraqi nation, cobbled together in 1919 from three Ottoman provinces. The British had installed Faysal, the Hashemite king expelled from Damascus by the French, as regent of the Class A mandate, but when oil was discovered in 1927, they hardened their grip. They considered themselves the rightful and benevolent tutors of an "independent Arab nation" and could never quite understand why their "support" won them so little favor. Not long after Willkie's visit, Churchill wondered at their lack of popular legitimacy. "We have certainly treated the Arabs very well," he wrote in haughty disbelief.[4]

Iraq's short history belied that claim. The nation's chaotic early years had seen a succession of military coups, ministerial reshufflings, tribal revolts, and rumors of British string-pulling. Formal independence in 1932 did little to stabilize Iraq, which was less a nation than a fractious jumble of tribal, religious, and ethnic groups. The Hashemite royals were foreigners from Arabia and Sunni Muslims, as was most of the urban middle class. Most everyone else was Shi'a and distrusted the Sunnis. Iraqis owed more allegiance to tribal sheikhs than to the national governments that came and went with such frequency. A handful of elite men traded government positions as their fortunes rose, fell, and rose again. "With a small deck of cards," one of Willkie's Iraqi informants quipped, "you must shuffle them often."[5]

Perhaps the only real social glue was suspicion of the British. Some Iraqis, particularly the vocal Arab nationalists, feared that the British might make their "emergency" occupation permanent. As in Egypt and Palestine, some sided with the Axis. The royals struggled to dispel the impression that they were glorified British stooges. Only months before Willkie's arrival the prince and the prime minister had brutally cracked down on nationalist opposition, purging the armed forces, executing plotters, and interning dissidents. Behind the scenes, the British embassy had demanded that Nuri al-Said eradicate "anti-British" sentiment from his government. Predictably, the measures he took in response only deepened resentments.

All this upheaval worried American officials. Iraq was a critical transfer point for war matériel. Lend-Lease supplies poured in from the Persian Gulf through Basra, heading north to Turkey and the Soviet Union and west to the North African battlefields, while oil went by pipeline from Kirkuk out to Haifa on the Mediterranean Sea. Little of this wartime bustle helped ordinary Iraqis, however. Prices were high and corruption endemic. The mere presence of British troops rankled, even when they were not rousting people from their homes, imprisoning suspected rebels, or hassling Iraqis in the streets. The coup had been quashed, and Iraq was in no immediate danger of going over to the Axis, but the troubled country was precisely what Roosevelt had in mind when he hoped Willkie would put some "pep" in the Allies' step.[6]

Everywhere he went, Willkie heard hints of the rancor surging just below the surface. At a formal dinner a series of whispering government officials waylaid him to confide their suspicions. There was no opposition press—the prime minister had outlawed it as an emergency war measure—but even the officially pro-British papers captured the pervasive disquiet. In *Al-Hawadith,* Salman Shaikh al-Daoud, a prominent writer and lawyer, welcomed Willkie with an editorial entitled "The Envoy of the American People and the Arab's Share of Freedom and Independence." The Arab people, he argued, had long suffered "foreign ambition and imperialistic designs," but Roosevelt's Atlantic Charter suggested that their "full hopes" might finally be realized. "The Arab countries are for the Arabs," al-Daoud continued, "and no people on earth have the right to claim our country." Willkie's arrival was proof of Allied goodwill, and made it possible to stake the kind of claims that had too long gone ignored. "The Arab people," he wrote, "will not, from today, permit their rights to be violated, or allow attempts be made to prevent their unity, or that their territories be exploited by others." Peace and "tranquility" in the "Near and Middle East" was impossible without "peace for the Arabs, recognition of their rights, and support to their unity."[7]

Other papers delivered a similar message. The editors of *Al-Shahab* used phrases like "the realization of our national unity" to placate censors, but their calls for American help were more forthright: they sought aid in the "removal of obstacles created by imperialism, and assistance toward the formation of a strong, free and independent Arab world." Meanwhile, Iraqi officials handed Willkie a memo expressing their hope that the Allies would "leave nothing undone in helping the Arab nation to achieve her aspirations for freedom and independence in conformity with the Atlantic Charter."[8]

Many American and British diplomats stationed in the Middle East had grown cynical about this kind of talk. Primed with doubts about the fitness of Arabs for self-government, they accepted at face value stereotypes about the chaotic and irrational nature of Arab societies. Willkie's well-tuned ear for public opinion helped him sort out what mattered. He sensed that clandestine murmurs signaled unspoken common feeling. He connected the dots between sanctioned pronouncements and the shadowy fears he heard in passing. He increasingly believed that Arab nationalism would soon coalesce into a political force bent on full independence, and that the Allies dismissed it at their own peril.

Willkie spent an hour with Prime Minister Nuri al-Said, talking through Iraq's role in the war and the future of the young nation. He found al-Said a savvy judge of the nation's situation. He surmised that the prime minister was a realist who listened to the British with "respectful attention" but kept his eye on his overriding goal: building "the first really modern and independent Arab state." That afternoon, Willkie learned that the prime minister hoped to use the opportunity of Willkie's visit to declare war against the Axis. Making a declaration while Roosevelt's envoy was in Baghdad would show the rest of the Arab world that standing with the Allies meant standing with the United States, not just Britain. They even discussed language al-Said might use in a speech to the press the next day. He eventually backed away from this plan. The British, fearful that it might jeopardize their already tenuous position, were against it, and the prime minister himself recognized that the people of Iraq wouldn't support it, either. Willkie kept this to himself, even leaving it out of *One World,* and only revealed the substance of the meeting in a newspaper article in July 1943, some seven months after Iraq finally declared war against the Axis.[9]

Willkie had high hopes for al-Said. If the prime minister could shape and steer the popular will, he could satisfy both the nationalists and his British patrons and guide Iraq into modern statehood. This was wishful thinking. Willkie underestimated both al-Said's debt to the British and Iraqi disillusionment with their most visible public figure. For all his insight and ability, he was only the latest representative of the country's revolving-door elite. The most powerful man in Iraq between the 1920s and the 1950s, he treated the country, one of his colleagues once remarked, as a father would a child, doling out encouragement and discipline in equal measure. He courted the nationalists with a vision of a federation of Arab states, alternately cultivated and undercut the military, reassured the British, and did not disturb the sheikhs' dominion over the rural peasantry. He wagered that oil-fed economic growth could quell the unease born of powerlessness and poverty. Eventually al-Said's time would run out. In 1958, the military coup that would lead to the rise of the Baath Party—and eventually Saddam Hussein—overthrew the monarchy. Insurgent troops occupied Baghdad. Rebels captured and shot the regent and the young King Faysal II and dragged their bodies out into the street. Nuri al-Said went into hiding, but a day later he was caught and summarily executed, his lifeless body thrown in the street like the royals he had served, to be mutilated by the revolutionary crowds surging through the city.[10]

That grisly scene lay far in the future as the two men concluded their talks. The traveler's next stop was the gardens of the Royal Court, but on the way he asked his guide and interpreter, an Iraqi major, to show him the ordinary life of Baghdad. The officer steered Willkie and his friends to a "chaikhana," one of the city's big teahouses. The crowd of two hundred men—few women were to be seen in public—was "thunderstruck" by the sudden appearance of the American they'd been reading about in the afternoon papers. The proprietor hustled out to offer Willkie a comfortable chair, but he declined so that he could mix with the patrons, finally settling on a wooden stool to watch a game of backgammon and drink

Turkish coffee. Here he was in his element, meeting and greeting as if he'd been let loose in an Indiana town meeting or a New York cocktail party. He left to cheers and applause and later joked with reporters that he wouldn't be taking up backgammon in Baghdad anytime soon. "I'm afraid I would get trimmed—they seemed to be playing it with great skill!"[11]

Prince al-Ilah received the travelers on a broad lawn under a full moon. The Americans expected a relatively reserved affair—it was, after all, the beginning of Ramadan—but the regent greeted them from a great throne at the head of a long carpet. There were other carpets scattered about the dais, each crowded with government officials and ministers. Some were in robes and turbans, while others wore tuxedos, tails, or military finery. The minister of economics, Willkie later remembered, was in traditional Arab dress, "curiously enough," and nearby was the president of the Senate, with his elegant robes and the great beard that had earned him the nickname "God" from wisecrackers in the diplomatic corps. Willkie and his friends may have been tired of ceremony, but this display was, Cowles later remembered, "a scene right out of the Arabian Nights."[12]

The brief stop in the teahouse had whetted Willkie's appetite for talk with regular Iraqis. Unfortunately, the afternoon of their second day he was scheduled to lunch with the British ambassador, Sir Kinahan Cornwallis—"another of the tall, pipe-smoking, able, quiet, and very British Colonial Office empire-builders"—followed by meetings and a reception at the American legation. So he rose early to try for another glimpse of everyday Iraq. The party visited a blanket factory, drove through one of the city's poorer quarters, stopped in at "one of the finest museums in the world filled with Ur-Chaldee finds," and topped it off with a walk through the bazaar. Everywhere he noted the rough juxtaposition of the ancient and the modern, from the "fantastic Shi'ah mosque sprouting gold minarets into the sky" to the "dusty adobe walls and houses" to the bazaar "where copper and silver craftsmen were making bowls and pitchers but the stores sold only machine-made trinkets from New York or Liverpool." He managed to squeeze in a stop at one more teahouse before his formal duties resumed.[13]

Willkie's forays into the streets of Baghdad raised quite a commotion. The *Iraq Times* commented that "the citizens of Baghdad maintain that Mr. Wendell Willkie is the ideal democrat—the finest they have ever known," and the US chargé d'affaires in Baghdad, William S. Farrell, reported back to Foggy Bottom that it was "almost impossible to describe the electrifying effect" Willkie had on the Iraqis. They loved his "democratic and American manner." It's hard to say how deep this good feeling went—the pro-Allied papers no doubt amped up the hubbub—but Willkie was surprised to find crowds gathered wherever he went. Many—even veiled women—cheered and applauded. He never needed an invitation to work a crowd, and it seems that many Iraqis responded to his jolly repartee not unlike Blitz-weary Londoners. Edmund Stevens, the *Christian Science Monitor* reporter, noticed a profound departure from the usual "hostility or apathy" with which regular Iraqis greeted Western visitors. He would later recall the impact of Willkie's visit quite clearly. "To the semicolonial nations of the Middle East, desiring emancipation above all other things," he said, "Willkie was the Four Freedoms taken out of the realm of the abstract and clothed in a rumpled blue suit."[14]

This warm reception contributed to Willkie's sense that Iraqis were genuinely hopeful about the United States. Americans, it appeared, weren't yet seen as imperialists. The British worried that Willkie's popularity exacerbated the already hot anti-imperial feeling, heightening what Farrell called an "extreme contrast" between his attitude and the "pukka sahib exclusiveness of the local British community."[15]

Americans certainly liked to fancy themselves newcomers to the region, innocent of imperial ambitions and colonial entanglements. In truth, they had been coming to the Middle East for 150 years, and despite what Willkie had seen in his week or two on the ground, the encounter had never been simple. The United States' first foreign war was in North Africa, against the "Barbary Pirates" who waylaid the young nation's shipping, but the most sustained contact came from American missionaries in the nineteenth century. Raised like their British cousins on Bible stories, dismayed by the poverty they encountered, and often disdainful of Islam, the missionaries struggled to reconcile romance with reality. They failed to convert any great number of Muslims, but many developed significant solidarity with the people of the region. Missionaries established a host of institutions in the Middle East, from universities and churches to primary schools and social service agencies. In the confusion of the Ottoman collapse, these institutions served as islands of stability. Willkie glimpsed several of these, most notably the American University of Beirut, which he visited. The university, along with Robert College, near Istanbul, became icons of modernity and progress, nurturing the small, forward-looking middle classes that had taken root across the region.

This rising generation, bent on creating new Arab nations, was cautiously optimistic about the United States. American missionaries could be high-handed in their dealings with Arabs or Islam, but they did not arrive in the region as a conquering power and sometimes even spoke out against European colonial adventurism. Woodrow Wilson may have failed to live up to his rhetoric of self-determination, ushering in the semicolonial mandate era, but this new and newly influential generation of middle-class modernizers hoped that Roosevelt's Atlantic Charter might be the dawn of a new day for the US role in the Middle East.[16]

Much of Willkie's good feeling about the stop in Baghdad, and much of his belief in the emerging affinity between the United States and the new nations of the Middle East, came from his lingering memories of the great banquet thrown by the prime minister at the town hall on his last night in Iraq. At the dinner for sixty, Nuri al-Said, speaking in English, welcomed Willkie as the representative of the "inspiring and inspired" President Roosevelt. The Iraqi leader was impressed that the president had chosen the leader of the opposition party to act as his representative overseas. Willkie's visit, he declared, was an endorsement of the Atlantic Charter's "lofty principles." It showed that the Allies meant what they said, and that if they won, "the divided Arab race" could be made whole again. Iraqis, the prime minister continued, owed the United States a great debt. American influence had promoted an "Arab intellectual renaissance without which" Iraqi independence "could never have been attained." He finished with an elaborate flourish, reassuring Willkie and the assembled officials of Iraq's support for the Allied cause, but stopping short of a full declaration of war.

Willkie replied in kind, promising a steady flow of Lend-Lease aid and affirming the American intent to establish a postwar world "in which all men—irrespective of whether they are citizens of powerful or small nations—may live free and decent lives of their own choosing." All across the Middle East, he said, he had asked leaders and Arab "common citizens" what kind of world they wanted to live in. The answer was unanimous: it was the world offered "by the United Nations, not by Hitler's New Order." Of course, Willkie being Willkie, he couldn't stop himself from drifting off script. To the amusement of the crowd, he described the prime minister as "the modern Thief of Baghdad" who had "stolen my heart," and himself as "the modern Sinbad" who had swept into Baghdad on "a modern flying carpet."[17]

The ensuing banquet was, as Willkie would later write in *One World,* an "Arabian Nights picture of the Middle East." Cowles recalled that after the speeches a troupe of scantily clad dancers suddenly appeared, and the diners, all men save for the wife of the British ambassador, erupted in applause and whistles. Willkie and Cowles were bewildered until Cowles remembered that the day before, while Willkie napped, one of the *Gulliver*'s crew had suggested that Cowles tell the prime minister that Willkie wanted to see "the famous dancing girls of Baghdad." Cowles later claimed he wasn't sure what the airman meant but figured it was a good way to show interest in Iraq's cultural heritage. The prime minister had appeared similarly confused, or perhaps pained, when Cowles made the request, but promised to arrange it. Amid the boisterous cheering, Willkie, Cowles, and Barnes realized that their crew was having one over on them: the "dancing girls" were reputed to be representatives from Baghdad's top brothels. The British ambassador's wife, seated next to Cowles, tried to distract him with a long monologue about her passion for archaeology.[18]

After the bawdy show wrapped up, the party moved outside and seven hundred men and women gathered in the gardens of the town hall under the moon. The trees were festooned with lights and a tiled dance floor had been set up on the lawn. There was a hundred-foot bar, partially concealed by an imposing carved wooden screen. Cowles watched as the Iraqi elite "lined up three or four deep putting away the booze at a rate more rapid than I'd ever seen in the United States or in Europe." The travelers were momentarily befuddled. Diplomatic protocol suggested they should refuse offers of a drink during Ramadan, but the large screen seemed to be giving everyone the cover they needed. At first Willkie abstained. He even demurred when the mayor of Baghdad asked him to join him in a drink. That seemed to annoy the mayor, though, and so when Willkie caught up to him back behind the screen with a host of other

Iraqis, "tossing back nips of American rye," he apologized for not accepting the hospitable gesture and made up for the slight a few times over.

An orchestra tuned up, and the crowd—a mixture of Iraqis, British, and Americans—took to the dance floor. Inspired, Willkie remembered "English nurses and American soldiers up from Basra on the Persian Gulf and Iraqi officers dancing under an Arabian sky." It was like a Hollywood adaptation of the Arabian Nights—a perfect romance between two worlds long held apart. "No man could have sat through that evening and preserved any notion that the East and West will never meet, or that Allah is determined to keep the Arabs a desert folk, ruled by foreigners from across the seas."[19]

These multiple turns to the Arabian Nights were telling. The travelers' offhand remarks reflected pervasive American assumptions about Arab life, preoccupations that lingered on a mythic past rather than the bright future the region's middle-class modernizers hoped the United States heralded. Like most Americans, Willkie was steeped in legends of the Middle East as a land of indulgence, ease, and magic—a place where Protestant traditions of work and self-denial could be set aside for self-transformation. Generations of American kids had grown up with the Arabian Nights in books, in comics, and in movies. Just two years earlier, the British film *The Thief of Bagdad* had captivated American audiences and won three Academy Awards. This genre of Western popular culture inspired by the imagined, exotic East was second only to the Bible in shaping American expectations of the Middle East.

These inventions relied on hoary distortions of the East as a mysterious land of sexual laxity and irrational passion. Such ideas may have inspired Willkie's crewman to request the favors of the fabled "dancing girls of Baghdad," and certainly fueled the racism endemic to Western involvement in the region. For most American diplomats, missionaries, and travelers, Orientalist tales squared with their personal experience of the decentralized—and to Western eyes disorganized—tribal structure of Arab political society. Like the British, they often believed the Arabs to be an anarchic people unfit for self-government and in need of Western oversight. No doubt some Iraqis, all too familiar with this brand of con-descension, bristled at Willkie's invocation of the "thief," often synony-mous with "Arab" in the Western mind. This was just another galling echo of the British yoke that Arabs across the Middle East were eager to shed.[20]

Indeed, sauntering through the souk in a pith helmet, Willkie looked for all the world like the typical colonialist. But the great excite-ment he generated during those walks suggests how he subtly altered the role prepared for him by the usual imperial script. In his typically ebul-lient way, Willkie invoked these familiar stories as fables of possibility about connection and freedom. They were magic tales that promised not escape but emancipation. He rode in on his "modern flying carpet" not as the latest colonial exploiter but as a herald of the freedom he knew the Iraqis desired.[21]

On Monday morning crowds clustered along the roads applauding and saluting Willkie's motorcade as the party headed out of town toward the airport. Speaking at a final press conference, Salman Shaikh al-Daoud saluted Willkie on behalf of the Iraqi press and people. "No stranger," he began, "has ever had such a welcome as you have had here." He felt sure that Willkie—and hopefully the United States—would sup-port "the hopes of the Arabs in the future." The blithe headline in the *New York Times* the next morning would read "Willkie Finds Unity in the Middle East." The truth was a good deal more complicated, of course, but Willkie knew that many Iraqis saw the war as a turning point for their national aspirations and future Arab unity.[22]

After a final round of official goodbyes, Willkie and his friends climbed aboard the *Gulliver* and Kight got the aircraft aloft. In a farewell gesture, the pilot dipped the plane's wings and made a great loop, gun-ning the four big engines over the low-slung city. This cheeky display conveyed like nothing else the promise of the future Willkie envisioned, but it also hinted at the peril the skeptical Arabs of Baghdad would find there as well. The *Gulliver* departed as a soaring herald of American freedom, but the plane must have carried with it a note of menace, too, for those used to seeing only imperial might in such bullish displays of Western power. Looking down from above, it would have been hard for Willkie to discern any jeers behind the roaring turbines and the lively acclaim still echoing in his ears. They went around one more time, looking down on the city that had given them their most thrilling prospect of world connection yet, and then Kight pulled the *Gulliver* level, straightened out, and headed east again.

CHAPTER 7

First Flight

Tehran

THE SHAH OF IRAN had never been up in a plane. That was one of the first things he told his visitor when they met for lunch at the monarch's low-slung modern weekend house in the mountains outside Tehran. Without a second thought, Willkie invited him for a ride in the *Gulliver* that very afternoon. They finished up their lunch—served at a table set on Persian rugs in a stand of trees with a view over the shah's terraced flower gardens, swimming pool, and tennis court—and Willkie made a phone call to the American legation to rouse the *Gulliver*'s crew. The two leaders agreed to meet at the airfield later that afternoon. Everyone scrambled to prepare for the royal flight—bumping a few things from Willkie's crowded schedule, securing official permissions, arranging vehicles. When Kight and his crew reached the airfield they discovered that the *Gulliver* was fully gassed up for their next leg and had to be unburdened of several thousand gallons of fuel for a safe landing on a rough field at altitude. They didn't want the shah's joyride to end in a fireball.

Willkie took his host for a half-hour spin, soaring above Tehran and the Caucasus Mountains in the evening light. The shah was delighted and didn't want to come down—until Kight suggested that a night landing on an unfamiliar airfield might not be the most prudent idea. The quick jaunt was an impromptu anniversary present of sorts. September 16, 1942, marked one year since the Russians and British, fearing Nazi influence over the shah's father, had occupied the country and forced him to abdicate, thrusting a twenty-three-year-old Mohammad Reza Pahlavi to the throne very much ahead of schedule.[1]

Ever savvy about impressions, Willkie knew the flight would help his mission—both his official one from Washington and the unofficial one that was taking shape in his mind. Giving the young shah his first flight was good informal diplomacy and a dramatic gesture of American goodwill. Far more subtle than the Baghdad flyover, this flight offered Mohammad Reza Pahlavi a new vista on his country, one he'd always remember as the gift of American friendship. It was also a deft move in the unacknowledged inter-Allied rivalry over local allegiances. Willkie's offhand invitation showed the shah an easy intimacy, a marked departure from aloof and imperious Europeans. Surely no Iranian, royal or otherwise, had ever enjoyed a sightseeing flight in a British or Russian plane. America, Willkie's gesture seemed to say, came not to occupy Iran but to help the fledgling nation take wing.

Willkie could not have guessed how apt his invitation would prove. The Swiss-educated shah appeared cautious and reserved at first glance, callow in comparison to his father, a rough-hewn former Cossack horseman. The young shah was still acclimating to his role, but he was already an inveterate thrill seeker. He had a collection of custom cars and motorcycles, which he liked to drive fast and sometimes recklessly. After his flight in the *Gulliver*, he amassed a small fleet of personal planes, and his penchant for aerial adventure nearly got him killed several times. Looking backward from the shah's eventual exile, it is tempting to read the jaunt with Willkie as a metaphor for his regime's ill-fated alliance with the United States, an omen of American power gone awry. But on that day in 1942, the flight seemed to promise new beginnings.[2]

The *Gulliver* had arrived in Tehran two days earlier, after a quick two-hour hop from Baghdad through cloudless skies. A mixture of Iranian, American, British, Soviet, and even Chinese officials and officers awaited the travelers at the Allied airfield outside the city, where the *Gulliver* pulled up near a line of Soviet fighter planes. The ground crew that hustled out to meet them was Russian and Chinese—a marker of changing political geography. Refreshed by his stay in Baghdad, Willkie jovially shook hands and found his way over to the waiting journalists. His first official duty in Tehran was an errand of the heart. A week or so earlier, Ray Brock, the *New York Times* correspondent in Ankara, had asked Willkie to find his wife, Mary, an NBC radio reporter stationed in Tehran, and give her his love. "In fact, he told me to kiss you," Willkie gleefully exclaimed when he discovered Mary Brock in the press scrum. "Mission carried out most satisfactorily on the spot," she reported.[3]

Like his impromptu flight with the shah, Willkie's kiss—the first of several smooches he would deliver in the coming days—was a clever stunt with deeper implications. His official task was to try to push Iran into the Allied camp, but these "unscheduled missions" contributed to a less defined and more important project. By stepping outside the rigid boundaries of diplomatic protocol he was making himself an emblem of interconnection between America and the rest of the world. His little escapades helped win goodwill for the Allied cause, but the greater challenge was bringing the world to America and showing his fellow citizens what the world was fighting for. Iran would reveal this mission to be indispensable. Like a cross between independent, modernizing Turkey and semi-colonial Iraq, Iran represented the stakes of the fully global war. For Iranians, the war was not a question of avenging Pearl Harbor or stopping Hitler. Winning the peace, for many of them, meant ending colonial interference. In order to sway Iran and other Middle Eastern countries to the Allied cause, Americans would have to understand that reality.

Willkie threw himself into several days packed with touring and talking. He had lunch with the shah and a meeting with the Iranian prime minister, as well as the usual briefings with the American consul and other Allied diplomats and military men. He also made two short speeches, one to the Iranian cabinet ministers and one over Tehran radio. On that first day he visited a refugee camp for evacuees displaced by the fighting on the eastern European front, where he found several thousand distraught Polish civilians occupying hastily erected tents and barracks in the desert. They were waiting for passage to South Africa, where the British hoped to resettle them. Willkie and his friends watched as new arrivals spilled out of buses, carrying their makeshift bundles to the fumigation tent. It was a forbidding glimpse of the war the Americans would witness up close in a few days.[4]

On the first night they took in the show at a Western-style cabaret, where Willkie's arrival caused a minor scene. All the newspapers were full of the news of his tour, and before he knew it Allied servicemen and Iranians alike were fishing American money out of their pockets and thrusting bills at him, asking for his autograph. Willkie was invited to stay at the guest room at the consul's residence, while Barnes and Cowles were shuttled off to a hotel. Cowles was told it was the "best" in town, but in a city that was unevenly modernized, where in many places water and sewage still flowed in troughs along the streets, he was unprepared for the communal squat toilets. The place was "extraordinarily dirty" by the publisher's standards, and he bailed out, begging a spot on the consul's living room couch, while Barnes made do at the hotel. Meanwhile, visits to the bazaar, a café, and two factories—one making concrete, the other glycerine—offered a unique perspective on a society that mixed old and new.[5]

The war had upset the usual rhythm of life, causing food shortages, soaring prices, and friction with Allied military personnel. The sudden Allied occupation of late 1941—the British had taken the south and the Soviets the north—upended centuries of sovereignty. The Iranian government still controlled Tehran, but by early 1942 the young shah had been forced to sign a tripartite treaty with the occupying powers. The terms of the treaty guaranteed Iran political and territorial integrity after the war but turned over its defense and control of transportation and communication facilities to Allied forces. Securing Iran's oil deposits, deeded to the British Anglo-Iranian Oil Company since the first decade of the century, and protecting the rail line running from the Persian Gulf up to the Caspian Sea had been the main motives for the Allied occupation. Now British and Russian troops ran the rail operation, moving tons of Lend-Lease war matériel through to the USSR at the expense of disrupting domestic commerce. The British also manipulated the food supply, withholding aid in order to win political concessions. Shortages and famine roiled the cities—bread riots broke out in

Tehran three months after Willkie visited—inflaming Iranians' suspicions about the British and Soviets.

Iran's much prized independence had long been jeopardized by its geopolitical location. Perched on the ancient trade routes between East and West, the country once known as Persia had endured invasion from neighboring powers for centuries. By the end of the nineteenth century the Ottoman Empire was no longer a threat, but Russian incursions in the north and the spread of the British Empire in the east had eaten away at Persian territory. In the years leading up to World War I, a constitutional revolution resulted in a civil war. In a preview of 1941, Russia and Britain stepped in to restore order, dividing the country into spheres of influence, making it into just another pawn in the so-called Great Game of empire in Western Asia.[6]

During World War I, Russia's new Bolshevik government denounced imperialism and withdrew its armies from Persia, leaving the British with a clear field. Like so many of their neighbors, the Persians were all but ignored at the Paris peace conference, but the British did offer a separate treaty, pledging financial assistance and a guarantee of national integrity and independence in return for control over military and civilian affairs. Outraged Persians saw this for what it was, a bid for imperial control, and rejected the terms. Since when, one proud leader demanded from the floor of the assembly, had the nation's independence even been in doubt?[7]

Foreign interference had been repulsed, but in early 1921, Reza Khan, commander of the Iranian Cossack brigade, launched what amounted to a slow-motion coup. With tacit British support, he outmaneuvered or co-opted all his rivals, and by 1925 all that was left for him to do was order the assembly to proclaim him king. The lawmakers complied, and early in 1926 Reza Khan became Reza Shah, first ruler of the Pahlavi dynasty of the new nation of Iran. Over his two decades in power, Reza Shah emulated Kemal Atatürk, pursuing a top-down nationalist modernization campaign that primarily served to consolidate state authority. He funneled money to the military, overhauled infrastructure, jump-started industrial production, confiscated land from wealthy property owners, and outlawed religious clothing in favor of Western dress. He also increased inequality and diminished the power of traditional Islamic authorities, which allowed religious dissent to drive an alternative nationalist movement that branded the Pahlavis as a surrogate of the West.[8]

The Pahlavis sought to curtail British and Soviet influence by forging relationships with other Western nations—a plan they called their "third power strategy." By the time Willkie arrived, Mohammad Reza Shah was auditioning the United States for the role of the third power. His father had courted Germany for the role, hoping to split Russia and Britain, but Iran's ties to the Nazis brought them together instead. Fearing a repeat of Rashid Ali's failed coup in Iraq, the British and Soviets demanded that the shah expel all Germans from the country. When he balked, the Allies decided to invade and subsequently forced the king to abdicate in favor of his son.[9]

By late 1942, Iran had—as Willkie's State Department briefing put it—"not yet recovered from the shock of these events." Its much-vaunted military had crumbled at the first sign of the Allied advance and the once-fearsome Shah had ended his defiance in a matter of days. He left the country on a British ship, headed for exile in South Africa, never to return. His heir was young and inexperienced, and the ensuing power vacuum encouraged tribal and religious leaders to reassert their lost authority and empowered the usually quiescent and divided constitutional legislature—tendencies the Allied occupiers encouraged. Social and economic dislocation drove political insurgency, as new parties and factions formed and dissolved with alarming frequency. The result was a momentary fissure in the otherwise solid edifice of Pahlavi rule, as a host of competing voices clamored to represent the people's nationalist aspirations.[10]

Willkie's meetings with the shah and the prime minister reflected this parlous state of affairs. The prime minister, Ahmad Qavam, had been in office for only a month, but he had long experience in Iranian politics, most of it in opposition to the Pahlavis. A wealthy landowner from the north, he had previously served as prime minister in 1922, but he had run afoul of the shah and been packed off into exile for two decades. Qavam tended to treat Mohamed Reza Pahlavi less as a supreme ruler than as the little boy he had known during his first stint in government. He would hold the office three more times in the coming decade, much to the young shah's chagrin. Allied diplomats could never quite get a fix on Qavam. Some saw him as pro-Nazi, others pro-Soviet; most felt he was anti-British, but he had British support in late 1942 as a counterweight to the new shah.[11]

Willkie was privy to little of this internal drama. Many years later, one former Iranian official would claim Qavam had actually tried to prevent the American from seeing the shah. Apparently the prime minister was among those who found Willkie's informality less than charming. According to the story, Willkie was in some discomfort during his meeting with the prime minister. At one point he removed his shoes to scratch his itching toes, offending the prime minister, who was unaccustomed to such informality. Even worse, Qavam believed that Willkie had, as the shah's biographer Abbas Milani puts it with elaborate delicacy, "allowed himself the luxury and liberty of freeing himself, noisily, of superfluous bodily gasses." The prime minister considered this sock-footed farting American unfit for a royal audience, and he tried to warn the shah off hosting Willkie for lunch the next day. The shah, suspecting Qavam's motives, ignored the advice and ended up enjoying his first flight thanks to his unruly guest.[12]

Whatever their political differences, Qavam and the shah both took the same line with the American. When the envoy fulfilled his official mission, pressing each leader for a public declaration of Iranian commitment to the Allied cause, both demurred. They professed friendship for the United States but refused to compromise Iranian neutrality. Both wanted increased American aid and advisers—particularly for the military—as a condition of any move toward the Allies. They were careful, however, to keep relations cordial and open. Currying favor with the United States would check British and Russian power and increase Iranian autonomy.[13]

Willkie was only the most visible of a stream of American visitors that year. A number of official advisers—including a general sent to support the nation's military—joined thousands of American troops tasked with improving the Lend-Lease supply line to Russia. But the nature of that involvement, and of US influence in the Middle East as a whole, was up for grabs. American diplomats tended to read Iranian requests for aid and assistance as an invitation to greater involvement in their society and a chance to prove their good intentions, when Iranians simply sought a countermeasure to Russia and Britain. American consul Louis Dreyfus called Iran the perfect "proving ground for the Atlantic Charter." After the 1943 Tehran conference, where Roosevelt, Stalin, and Churchill pledged to respect their host's sovereignty, the president remarked to Cordell Hull that he was "rather thrilled with the idea of using Iran as an example of what we could do by an unselfish American policy."[14]

Just how "unselfish" that policy could be was Willkie's unspoken dilemma. Throughout the Middle East he had urged wary governments and people toward the Allied cause. Now, in a much-reported short address to government officials in Tehran he appealed to the ideal of "sacrifice for the common cause." He assured the Iranians that the Allies were fighting to allow the citizens of "small countries as well as large" to "live decent and free lives under governments of their own choosing." The United States, he said, "seeks no advantage—it wants no territory, no additional power, no control over others." But American assistance, Willkie told his audience, required Iranian skin in the game: "As has always been true and always will be true in time of basic struggles, those peoples make the most advancement who share, and share fully, in the sacrifice and the cost necessary to win." It was time, he concluded, "for men and nations to stand up and be counted."[15]

But trying to put "pep" in the step of unsure neutrals—as FDR had asked Willkie to do—often ignored what neutral nations really wanted. A truly "unselfish" American policy, one that sought "no advantage," would recognize the desires and demands of those it sought to court for the war effort. So far, most of the conversation surrounding Willkie's tour in the Allied media fixated on the idea that the peoples of the region had to "stand up and be counted." "Those Who Give Most Will Get Most," read the banner headline on the front page of the British-controlled *Palestine Post* the day after the "genial, bluff, hearty" Willkie stopped in Jerusalem. Mr. Willkie, the Jerusalem paper declared, "seems to have intuitively grasped the fact that the Middle Eastern countries must hang together if they do not want to hang separately." For the British, Willkie's arc through this corner of their empire had to be framed as a lesson in the fealty owed by colonial subjects.[16]

American accounts echoed this narrative of shared sacrifice but also saw Willkie selling Middle Easterners on the benevolence of American aims. The *Los Angeles Times,* reporting on Willkie's stop in Beirut, noted that Willkie told the "nationalists of Syria and Lebanon" to see that "what they got out of the war would depend largely on what they put in." Willkie urged them to pull their weight. "The powers are committed to give them independence," the reporter observed Willkie saying, "but meanwhile, 'don't sit back and crab. Get in and push.'" Meanwhile, the *Christian Science Monitor* opined that the Middle East simply needed to know about the Allies' "absolute determination to win." Willkie was spreading the news, and soon "the gentlemen of the fez, tarboosh, kaffiyeh and caftan" would join the "team."[17]

A photo essay in *Life* magazine, Henry Luce's great icon of the age of broadcasting, encapsulated the overall tenor of the stateside press. "Willkie Sells U.S. Victory to Middle East" arrived on newsstands just as Willkie made his way from Moscow to China two weeks later. The story, accompanied by a two-page spread of pictures of Willkie inspecting troops and meeting officials, farmers, and workers, highlighted his exhortation to the Iranians to "stand up and be counted." Willkie, it said, "set out three weeks ago to win the shaky Moslems of the Middle East for the cause of the United Nations. This 220 lb. American from the Midwest was like nothing the Mideast had ever seen before." He was a traveling salesman for the American war effort, a public relations man for Allied unity, whose job it was to get "shaky Moslems" off the fence and into the proper camp. They had to, *Life* suggested, "pick their winning colors right now."

Life, however, was willing to say what few other news outlets would. The people of the Middle East were not simply unreliable, the story hinted. They were aggrieved. "The Egyptians were not very happy about the war," *Life* remarked. "The Palestinians, Iraqi[s], Syrians, Iranians positively hoped the British would lose. For them it was only another British war." This complexity quickly gave way under the bright rush of can-do Americanism: "But when a Willkie appeared, the war suddenly became something else. Willkie stood for the confident idealism, the careless generosity of America." Willkie, *Life* maintained, was imbued with the "simple magic of being an American." He "swept up his welcomers in a cheerful, raucous blast of confidence that blew right out of the heart of America."[18]

The assumption that Willkie's transparent idealism could not fail to win hearts and minds revealed a central conceit of American foreign policy. Willkie stood in for the innate "simple magic" America could bring to the Middle East. Americans need not trouble themselves too much with Middle Eastern desires; they only cared that Middle Easterners "stand up and be counted" in the war effort in exchange for American benevolence. This conceit ran deep in official US policy toward winning the war and positioning the United States for the postwar world.

In practice this meant, as *Life* hinted, displacing European rivals. Willkie had already noticed how Americans in the Middle East were often uneasy with the depredations of the British Empire. The situation in Iran was no different. The State Department had observed the 1941 Soviet-British invasion with some disgust but refused to intervene for fear of offending their allies. During 1942, as the occupation plunged Iran into chaos and the British manipulated the food supply, the American consul, Louis Dreyfus, had grown more and more alarmed, writing that the British had "robbed the country of its internal security, its communications, its morale, and finally its food." More than any other country in the Middle East save Saudi Arabia, Iran seemed ripe for the "unselfish" American role Roosevelt imagined. Dreyfus and his State Department colleagues in Washington hoped a growing American presence in Iran would simultaneously win support for short-term war goals and increase long-term influence. State Department officials like Wallace Murray thought Britain's days were numbered. It's "obvious," he wrote just prior to Willkie's arrival, "that we shall soon be in a position of actually 'running' Iran through an impressive body of advisers."[19]

In Iran, as in the rest of the Middle East, key policymakers looked to balance the Atlantic Charter's promise of self-determination with the demands of American national interest. If they saw a *chance* to protect the independence of emerging nations, the *need* to assert an American role in a crucial region was never far from their minds. Enlisting Iran as a junior advisee and trading partner would protect access to Iranian oil and offset British and Soviet influence. American officials like Dreyfus and Murray were "pro-Iran," insofar as that denoted suspicion of British imperialism and Soviet communism. They nurtured their own assumptions about the "simple magic" of American involvement, just as *Life* magazine did in hailing Willkie's arrival: the United States would become the indispensable and inevitable guardian of Iranian well-being. Iranians, for their part, would surely welcome the American vision of their future as congruent with their own desires for autonomy. But what if they didn't?[20]

Few Americans stopped to consider that. Most considered themselves natural democrats, straight-shooters who could relate to subject peoples whom the stuffy British treated as inferiors. After all, they had once been colonial subjects, too, and thrown off the British yoke. But here, as elsewhere, Americans often shared the racial assumptions of their British allies. Typical generalizations about the Iranian "character" abounded. An Office of Strategic Services report—the OSS was the precursor to the CIA—labeled Iranians "obdurate, supersensitive, hypercritical, completely lacking in social consciousness, corrupt, selfish, and given to exploitation of their helpless masses . . . a corrupt and backward race not worthy of help." Even when Americans did deign to "help," it was in the spirit of civilizational uplift. "The Iranians are children," another OSS report declared, "and like children they must be obliged to go to school and to learn and practice discipline if they are to occupy a responsible place among democratic nations."[21]

This current of thought saw Americans displacing the British in more ways than one. They would supplant British influence in the region and take over their civilizing mission. Even an "unselfish" American policy would involve a certain degree of training in the ways of Western modernity. Roosevelt himself once hazarded an offhand guess: it would be forty years before the "backward" Iranian house could be cleansed of "graft and the feudal system." An independent Iran would benefit from what FDR and his advisers considered benevolent American influence, all under a new global order in which US interests and the Atlantic Charter were neatly reconciled. They did not trouble themselves over what it might mean if Iran were to determine that it wanted control over its own destiny.[22]

Iran, Saudi Arabia, and other emerging nations in the region would be the beneficiaries, in other words, of a new Good Neighbor Policy, modeled after the strategy Roosevelt and his advisers had pursued with Latin American nations in the 1930s. The United States honored the independence of these nations, backed off the more aggressive financial and military interventions of "dollar diplomacy," and offered advice and aid in exchange for recognition of America's economic and military predominance in the region. In a sense, Iran offered a chance to extend the American hegemony of the Monroe Doctrine outside of the Western Hemisphere. It could reject formal European colonialism in favor of American patronage.[23]

Unsurprisingly, Iranian nationalists like Qavam and Mohammed Mossadeq eventually saw this as empire by another name. By 1953, when Mossadeq, as prime minister, tried to pull free of American, British, and Soviet influence, radically modifying Iran's third power strategy by nationalizing oil production, a British- and CIA-backed coup brought him down, embittering many Iranians toward the United States for good.[24]

But in 1942, Willkie offered a sunnier prospect for US involvement in Iran. The magical thinking of American exceptionalism had yet to harden into policy. Wartime uncertainty left much that would later be decided still in flux. As he prepared to leave Iran, Willkie hoped he could move American policy in a truly "unselfish" direction. Many of his hosts believed he might, judging by the fulsome praise he received in Iranian newspapers. Hailing him as "the Great Man" or "the second man of America, rival and colleague of President Roosevelt," editorials welcomed him as a symbol of international friendship.[25]

On the surface, Willkie's trip through the Middle East seemed to be a triumph. Reporting on the conclusion of the Iran tour, the Palestinian nationalist paper *Filastin* enthused that "no better envoy could have been sent to stir our emotions than Mr. Willkie." The editors confirmed the impressions of all who watched Willkie's journey unfold in the American press: "In Egypt he was very popular; in Palestine he won the admiration of the Arabs; in Iraq he was warmly welcomed everywhere." Even his off-the-cuff remark about the "thieves of Baghdad" having "stolen his heart" won approval from *Filastin*. He had, the paper said, a "deep understanding of the Iraqi position and that of other Arab countries."[26]

This hearty approval surely gratified Willkie, but he sensed that the public ardor masked deeper, less comforting sentiments, too. Few of the major Tehran papers made more than passing reference to Willkie's official mission, choosing instead to focus on what the Allies could do for Iran. This was in part a matter of timing. Willkie had arrived in Tehran at a moment of opportunity for the press. Amid the disorder of the Allied quasi coup and the resulting weakness of the shah, new voices were popping up everywhere, staking a claim on Iran's future.

Many of these new outlets thought Willkie's visit might herald a shift in Allied policy toward the struggling nation. "The Iranian government," the cautious editors of *Iran* wrote, "has announced its policy to be one of cooperation with the Allies . . . Iran has therefore reason to expect every assistance from the Allies." The nation needed goods and supplies—wheat, sugar, trucks—but it also needed less material forms of assistance, too, ones that couldn't be announced so overtly. Surveying the impact of Willkie's visit, the paper asked "whether the promises of assistance given by our two great Allies will be fully met. This is what we hear from the people of this country in an undertone."[27]

The left-leaning *Mardom* brought that "undertone" to the surface. "Democracy must be established in the world," its editors declared, "or else world peace will not last long." They welcomed Willkie's declarations of fealty to the Atlantic Charter, but their loyalty to the Allied cause included an unmistakable warning. "After this war the Iranian people will no longer submit to anything but a democratic government. . . . We know that in this fight for liberty the liberty-loving Great Powers will support the people of Iran."[28]

Willkie himself recalled the "sober undercurrents" coursing beneath the gaiety, surfacing now and again in insinuation and rumor as much as direct challenges. "Again and again I was asked: does America intend to support a system by which our politics are controlled by foreigners, however politely, our lives dominated by foreigners, however indirectly, because we happen to be strategic points on the military roads and trade routes of the world?"[29]

Across the Middle East Willkie's journey had brought to light the tangle of fear and expectation with which so many around the world looked toward the postwar peace. In stepping out of the usual diplomatic routine he had become a medium for those hopes and fears—all of which, he had begun to see, turned on how America would greet the political groundswell building across the region. Nationalists from Egypt to Iran looked to the United States as a wedge they might use to pry themselves free from their imperial past and semicolonial present. They knew about the Four Freedoms, but they had heard similar Western promises before. As one Arab diplomat put it, they had "Four Fears": French imperialism, British insincerity, Zionist expansionism, and American isolationism. They might embrace global American power, but only if it fulfilled the lofty promises of the Atlantic Charter and the openness embodied by Willkie's cheery jaunt across their lands.[30]

"That vast and ancient portion of the globe," Willkie later wrote, "which stretches from North Africa around the eastern end of the world's oldest sea and up to Baghdad on the road to China may well be the area in which our war will be won or lost." But it would take more than tanks and planes to win. In this "great social laboratory where ideas and loyalties are being tested," the war was "being fought, and won or lost, in the minds of men." The two weeks he had spent traversing this vast and restive zone had shown Willkie the necessity of heeding what its people wanted from the world waiting beyond the war. He was no stranger to the comforts of American exceptionalism. He believed in his own "simple magic" of connection and democratic appeal. But he understood the need to reassure Iranians and other Middle Easterners that demands for freedom would be heard, not discounted as insufficient ardor for the Allied cause.[31]

On his last night in Tehran, just after he took the shah up in the *Gulliver*, Willkie delivered a radio address to the Iranian people. The first part of the broadcast simply repeated the previous day's talk with its themes of common sacrifice. But then he launched into a broader discussion of the stakes of the war for his hosts. "Some pessimists," he said, believed that after an Allied victory "the smaller nations must remain under the guidance and protection of one of the great powers. I believe this view wholly fallacious." He had faith in the potential of Iran— "which has given civilization more than fifty centuries of art of the highest quality"—to develop a "free and stable political system." The reference to Iran's "illustrious past" subtly rebuked the still-powerful logic of race and civilization, and underscored his faith that Iran had "the character and the determination to go forward when victory is won as a completely free nation unhampered by any great power." From there, Willkie went out on a limb, with nothing but the Atlantic Charter to support him: "That is what the American people wish for Iran. That is what the chief United Nations have pledged to Iran." In closing he linked the fight against Nazi racial ideology to the push for universal self-determination. Once the Nazis and their "horrible thesis of the super-race dominating the smaller nations as slaves" lay defeated, Iran could join with the Allies to "build a new world composed of free people having governments of their own choosing, enjoying complete independence to work out their own destiny."[32]

The address confirmed Willkie's talent for cheerleading, but his real work lay ahead of him. He could reassure the Arabs and Iranians all he wanted. What he couldn't yet do was guarantee the direction of American opinion or policy. He could not permanently win hearts and minds in the Middle East without convincing Americans that their vision of the postwar world needed to validate the freedom dreams of colonized peoples. America was poised to make those dreams a reality, if it could be stirred from its isolationism and encouraged to abandon imperialism. Willkie was beginning to understand that in order to change how the world saw America, he would have to change the way America saw the world. That would be his next campaign. Could his "simple magic" reconcile American ideals, Middle Eastern demands, and political realities?

For now, that challenge would have to wait. The morning after his speech, the travelers departed Tehran with two new crewmembers. The Soviets required that any flights coming north into their airspace stick to strictly defined air corridors. Word was that there was no such thing as an unidentified aircraft to the Soviets. Planes that couldn't be hailed would be shot down and then identified. So Kight and Klotz deemed it wise to bring aboard a Russian navigator and radio operator. Joe Barnes spoke Russian, so it would be easy enough to communicate with the new comrades, but the addition indicated the stiff and wary nature of American-Soviet relations. They were bound for the Soviet Union proper, and into the uncertain future the two incipient superpowers, simultaneously allies and rivals, were in the process of shaping.[33]

CHAPTER 8

Working with Russia

Kuibyshev, Moscow, Rzhev

In a sense, Willkie's journey started in the Soviet Union. The unexpected invitation from three American newsmen in Moscow had given him an opening to see the world at war, but it also put the visit to Russia at the center of the trip, just as the imperiled nation was at the center of the war. Careening across the Middle East, Willkie had learned all he could about the region's insurgent nationalisms. In Russia, he arrived with a far clearer sense of what was at stake. The whole trip hinged on what Willkie could accomplish there. The chance to build a collaborative world order, he believed, would stand or fall on the prospect of the Soviet Union and the United States, two nations accustomed to looking askance at one another, learning to see eye to eye. Both his official errand of rallying unsure nations to the Allied cause and his unofficial mission of planning a truly international peace rested on delivering a message of goodwill and cooperation to the Soviet Union.

Willkie would find Russian morale at its lowest ebb since December 1941, when the initial Nazi advance had stalled just west of Moscow. The Soviets had regrouped and thrown the invaders back from the capital, but in the early fall of 1942 they faced even graver threats. To the north, Leningrad, under siege for a year, was still encircled, while in the south the Germans had pushed toward the Caucasus and the great heartland beyond the Volga River. By the time the *Gulliver* made its way north from Tehran, Nazi divisions had reached the outskirts of Stalingrad. Win there and they might sweep across the Volga and cut Russia in two, severing the supply lines coming up from Iran. The Germans could then turn north to hit Moscow from behind, or break south to take the oil fields at Baku and challenge the Allies' weaker Middle Eastern flank.[1]

The Soviets needed all the help they could get. Since the Nazi invasion they had pressed for big boosts in American Lend-Lease shipments—more guns and tanks and trucks and food, and especially more planes to give close air cover to troops fighting house-to-house in the streets of Stalingrad. Most of all they wanted the British and Americans to open the much-discussed second front and launch an invasion of western Europe. In the midst of the most devastating land war in history, as Russians buried soldiers and civilians by the millions in their scorched fields and bombed cities, Stalin and his people had little patience for stingy aid shipments and stalled invasion plans.[2]

Gloomy war news and tension among the Allies were nothing new for Willkie. The tide of war may have turned in North Africa, but the Soviets were still fighting for survival. Bent on forcing their visitor to feel the great cost of the war, the Soviets wanted him to confront the fact that the Red Army stood alone against Hitler in Europe. Anger over Lend-Lease delays and impatient questions about a second front dogged Willkie everywhere he went. The fearsome spectacle of Russia at war would convince him to convey those worries back to President Roosevelt and the American people. This meant less of a chance to probe Stalin and other Russians on the prospects for postwar cooperation. But prompt, full hearings for Soviet concerns, he hoped, would lay the groundwork for future partnership. His eagerness to please the Soviets irked the diplomatic corps and landed him in hot water back home, but he stuck to his conviction that the future depended on nurturing friendly relations with Russia.

Shepherded between stage-managed glimpses of Soviet life—his days were spent in factories and on collective farms, his nights at the opera and ballet—Willkie displayed his customary brio, meeting Soviet propaganda with a public relations campaign of his own. Indeed, the entire Soviet visit amounted to a carefully choreographed performance in his larger quest for international fellow feeling. He didn't shy away from friction with his hosts, and he actually enjoyed impromptu debates over the merits of capitalism and communism with workers, farmers, and officials, but this elaborate effort did require him to downplay his feelings about the true horrors of Stalinist communism. Still, like many American observers, he was genuinely inspired by the Russian people's resistance to the Nazis, and saw the country's rush into industrial modernity as a blueprint for political and cultural rapport with the United States.

Willkie aimed to use his voice to swing the clamorous stateside debate over the Soviet Union toward collaboration and away from stringent anticommunism. He saw the Russian and American peoples as more alike than different, and seized on the idea—popular among many American liberals and leftists, and even some in the Soviet Union—that the wary Allies were like two great ships headed into harbor on a returning tide. Believing that the two countries were subject to underlying forces of development and modernization that would ultimately bring them alongside each other, he wanted the role of harbormaster, nudging here and there with his tugboat, directing the arrangement of bumpers and belaying lines as the two vessels swung together. Orchestrate the rapprochement correctly, he thought, and the old ideological mistrusts would give way to a partnership between peoples strong enough to foster international cooperation around the world.

By these lights, the US-Soviet alliance provided a chance to coax the Soviets away from their defensive isolation and establish connections that went deeper than politics or ideology. Nourish goodwill at the personal level and Willkie might help push the two rising powers toward partnership, or at least understanding. Pair that personal touch with an expansive vision of reciprocal trade between the two powers, and the Soviets might temper their authoritarianism, tame revolutionary socialist internationalism, and invest in a shared vision of worldwide cooperation and global prosperity. Critics would call this naive, but he believed that easing mutual suspicion would bring the ultimate goal of a postwar world free of imperial exploitation that much closer.

The *Gulliver* sped north from Tehran on Wednesday, September 17, vaulting the Alborz Mountains and soaring across the gray-green expanse of the Caspian Sea and the reddish salt flats of the Ural River delta, gliding over the endless expanse of the Russian interior, speeding above mile after mile of fields turning from green to tan. With his two new Russian crew-members as guides, Kight followed the official Soviet air corridor, making his way along the intangible seam between continents, Europe on his left and Asia on his right. Three hundred miles west lay Stalingrad, where the Red Army was digging in for a desperate stand against the Nazis. Several hours later, the *Gulliver* crossed the Volga hundreds of miles upstream from the embattled city and banked a few degrees to the right to follow the great river to Kuibyshev, the inland industrial city the Soviets used as an emergency wartime capital.[3]

Willkie had wanted to skip Kuibyshev and fly straight to Moscow, but most of the foreign embassies remained in Kuibyshev, awaiting the all-clear from Stalin and the Politburo, who had never left the Kremlin. Admiral William Standley, the American ambassador, insisted that Willkie begin his tour in Kuibyshev, where he could be received by the diplomatic community and make his first official Soviet contacts. The long-distance wrangling over this point, conducted through State Department channels as Willkie made his way east, aggravated both ambassador and envoy. At the only modern airfield near Kuibyshev, a strip attached to an aircraft plant where the Soviets built the famed and feared Stormovik dive bomber, Standley and a host of Chinese, British, and American officials went out to meet the *Gulliver* and its crew. They found Willkie tired and cold, shivering a bit in his lightweight suit against the fall wind.[4]

Occupied by the war effort, the Soviets sent only a Foreign Office deputy and his staff to receive Willkie at the airfield. Standley thought it something of a slight—"the representation for a Very VIP was on the short side," he quipped in his memoirs—but Willkie shrugged it off. Despite the chill that greeted him on the tarmac, the weather was strangely sunny most of that month, as if to mock the grim course of the war. Outside of scheduled events, Willkie had free time to wander around, often during the bright, cool mornings. Bodyguards and the Soviet secret police, the NKVD, were never far off, but in the wooded outskirts of Kuibyshev he sat alone by the Volga watching barges carrying lumber to heat shops and homes bereft of the coal supplies captured by the Nazis. In Moscow he breakfasted daily with American journalists and took walks with Cowles or Barnes. He went to Lenin's tomb—closed for the duration of the war, the guard said—and then walked on past the Kremlin to a nearby book-store where shoppers seemed more interested in propaganda pamphlets than their fellow patron. Later he took a ride on the famous Moscow subway, with its mosaic friezes and cavernous domed archways, and joined the crowds headed for workshops, offices, and guard posts.[5]

Despite the lackluster tarmac reception, the Soviets had planned a slate of activities calculated to impress their visitor. In Kuibyshev and Moscow, the itinerary included the usual press conferences and meetings with Soviet officials and a host of teas, luncheons, and dinners with menus bor-dering on the obscene given the severe wartime shortages. Caviar, lamb, pigs' feet, sturgeon, and countless vodka toasts had Standley in "gustatory agony," but Willkie attacked both his schedule and the menu with gusto. Later, one Soviet minder laughed that if he were writing the story of Willkie's visit his title would be obvious: "Vodka, Vodka, Vodka."[6]

Willkie took a riverboat up the Volga to a state-run farm and toured industrial plants around Kuibyshev and Moscow, seeing everything from a foundry and a power station to factories churning out airplanes, candy, artillery shells, and canned goods. He visited an antiaircraft battery, schools, hospitals, the Lenin Library, and the Red Army Museum, saw the opera *Eugen Onegin* and the Bolshoi Ballet's *Swan Lake* and heard a Soviet jazz band. He took in Shostakovich's Seventh Symphony, newly composed to honor the defense of Leningrad, where Soviet citizens and the Red Army were famously holding the Germans at bay. The city had been besieged since September 1941, cut off from almost all aid, the pop-ulation living under relentless bombardment. Hitler had vowed to starve the city, kill or imprison its people, and scour it "from the face of the earth." By the time the Red Army finally drove the Wehrmacht back in early 1944 and lifted the "900 day siege," close to 1 million people had died of starvation and many thousands more from bullets, bombs, shells, and disease. More people would die in Leningrad than all British and American war casualties combined.[7]

Government-run newspapers carried only short notices of Willkie's arrival, and it wasn't until he finally got a meeting with Stalin, almost a week into his visit, that they printed his picture. Radio was strictly controlled, too—until earlier in the year the government had even suppressed news from Leningrad, fearful that stories of starvation and cannibalism might destroy morale—and the censors kept a tight rein on Willkie's most avid followers, the Western press. But that didn't stop him from getting noticed. The first highlight of his charm offensive was his appearance at *Swan Lake*. Rushing from a dinner at the Chinese embassy, he delayed the Bolshoi curtain by fifteen minutes, a rarity for the invariably prompt company. As he was getting settled in his box an official parted the curtains and announced the presence of the special representative of President Roosevelt, touching off a standing ovation from the audience of diplomats and Soviet military brass and high officials. During intermissions, people crowded around to shake his hand. "What a charming American!" cried one Russian from among the throng of well-wishers.[8]

At one point, Willkie wondered if he could get some flowers for the Bolshoi's prima ballerina, Irina Tikhomirova. There were no bouquets to be had in wartime Kuibyshev, but an employee of the American embassy scrounged some blooms from a nearby garden. At the end of the show Willkie clambered out of his box and leapt over the orchestra pit to the stage ("just clearing a bass drum," one correspondent remembered) and delivered a makeshift bouquet and a firm kiss to the dancer. This bit of bravado brought the house down, sending cries of "Weeel-kie!" and "Tikho-mi-ro-va!" echoing through the hall.[9]

Willkie would later say that his glimpse of the Soviet Union was "chosen entirely by chance." This was not true. Since the 1920s, the Bolsheviks had welcomed visitors from capitalist countries with elaborate stagecraft. These carefully organized campaigns highlighted tidy examples of working factories, farms, schools, hospitals, and other institutions that they hoped would, as one historian of these efforts writes, "prompt foreigners to generalize from unrepresentative samples." Willkie the Hoosier was right at home on the state farm, looking over the cattle and admiring the breeds of pigs. And Willkie the utility executive had ample experience with industrial plants. He knew how to ask probing questions about working conditions, productivity, and technology. But the "cultural show" that worked for fellow travelers like André Gide, Paul Robeson, George Bernard Shaw, and Theodore Dreiser also swayed Willkie—and became the scene of a mutual courtship between him and his Soviet hosts. Both sides were engaged in elaborate public relations campaigns.[10]

The factory and farm visits aimed to reveal an industrial war machine running full tilt and a people giving everything to defeat the Nazis. Willkie found bustling shop floors running three shifts, reviewed operations staffed by professional engineers and specialists in scientific agriculture, and met dedicated workers, many of them women or young boys. Some of the production seemed to him to "rely too much on hand labor," but he saw factories full of modern machinery—some of it built in Russia, some in Cincinnati or Sheffield and delivered via Allied aid. Soviet officials refused to give definite answers about production figures, but, "as an American used to high standards of efficiency," Willkie was duly impressed by what he saw. "If I had not known I was in Russia," he told American journalists, "I should have thought that I was in Detroit or Hartford."[11]

These offhand analogies—Willkie indulged in them frequently—suggested how he hoped to bridge the gap between the two nations. "The greatest desire of my life," Standley recalled Willkie saying to a Russian official, "is to improve Soviet-American relations." Standley even remembered the visitor going so far as to suggest that he would downplay anything that might create "an unfavorable impression" of the Soviet Union. The ambassador was a particularly unfriendly witness to Willkie's visit, and no doubt cast the traveler in an unflattering light, but that particular memory squared with Willkie's own strategy.[12]

One of Willkie's Soviet minders, Georgiy Zarubin, reported that he never missed a chance to perform for the cameras that followed him from factory to farm. He sidled up to workers and milkmaids and repeatedly urged Zarubin to make sure the photos and films were sent to the States. He knew how these tours worked, he told his minders. He was willing to follow the route they laid out for him, but they would need to make sure he met ordinary people. Americans would see right through a tour that only had him encountering "official" Russians, he told his guide.

They would say, "Oh, rubbish! Nonsense! Horsefeathers! Willkie didn't speak with the people and didn't get to know the real life of the country."[13]

Zarubin reported that throughout their travels together Willkie talked openly about the mutual benefits of a good relationship between the two countries "now and after the war," and how he was the man to nurture that relationship. "I am the 23 million Americans who voted for me during the presidential elections," he supposedly declared. "These people will believe me and follow me." Zarubin remembered the American saying his trip would "draw the countries together a great deal, and that he intended to work hard to draw the USSR and the US together even more." With support from the Russians, he could better achieve that rapprochement. The Soviets, recognizing a willing audience for their pageant of socialist progress, were happy to oblige.[14]

The most memorable stop on the tour was a visit to the Stormovik dive bomber plant. Ambassador Standley, along for the ride, realized he had been in this factory before—only it had been near Moscow, eight hundred miles to the west. The plant that the Soviets called "Factory no. 1" was part of an astonishing wartime improvisation. In the months after the German invasion in June of 1941, more than two thousand industrial plants in the western Soviet Union were moved hundreds or even thousands of miles east to put them out of reach of the advancing Nazis. In October the Stormovik plant had been dismantled and moved to Kuibyshev by rail. By December it was up and running again, and hitting production targets not much later.[15]

During his three-hour factory inspection Willkie interviewed the manager, Comrade Tretyakov, about the plant's capacity, talked with workers about their jobs, watched a recently completed Stormovik put through its paces above the tree line beyond the grounds, and sat in one of the planes himself, test-firing its machine guns and cannons. His most memorable experience was not firing weapons of war but rather a lengthy debate with the chief engineer, the "bright young man" of the plant, over the nature of freedom under capitalism and communism.

In *One World*, Willkie recalled doggedly pressing the "short, wiry young fellow" to admit to the failures of state socialism. After "ten minutes of hot colloquy," he thought he had forced him to admit that it was impossible for Soviet citizens to "hold different ideas" from official

Soviet ideology. "Then actually you've got no freedom," Willkie declared. But this elicited a stern rebuke: the chief engineer had far greater freedoms than his peasant parents or grandparents, who had never learned to read or write and spent their lives as "slaves to the soil." "Remember," Willkie recalled him saying, "we are in the developing stage of our system. Someday we'll have political freedom, too." Willkie countered with his trump card: "How can you ever have political freedom and economic freedom where the state owns everything?" This, he said, brought forth a "seemingly endless rush" of political theory justifying state-mandated equality as a form of freedom.[16]

Willkie cut off the debate there—he figured he had asked a question "to which Marxism gives no answer." But his "hot colloquy" had not been intended to win the contest. He aimed instead to both assure his American readers that he had talked frankly to the Soviets and to present his integrity to Russian officials, who he knew reserved a measure of hardheaded respect for foreign "class enemies" who were frank about their adherence to capitalism. The staged tête-à-tête sought to make a larger point, too. Willkie the capitalist doubted that state-run systems could foster real freedom. Even if he had been tacking left in recent years, his attacks on the TVA and the New Deal and his advocacy of free trade and free enterprise rested on deep convictions. But this scene with the chief engineer hinted to US readers that Soviet evolution was possible, or at least imaginable.[17]

Despite their conflicting political ideologies and modes of economic organization, Soviet communism and American capitalism shared an underlying faith in modernization and economic growth. Each system was based on harnessing mass industrial development, technological precision, and efficient methods of planning to fuel the steady advance of progress. They differed over the proper degree of state control, but Soviet communism and the technocratic liberalism of midcentury America both embraced a commitment to state-backed progress—a shared trait that some believed, or at least hoped, would lead to postwar cooperation rather than competition.

Soviet life, the American diplomat George Kennan observed in the 1930s, was fueled by a "romance of economic development." The push for progress was everything. While development was ordered from above, a great many Russians were proud of what they had accomplished under socialism and eager to tell the world about their "alternative path to modernity." For the Soviet people, modernization offered a ready-made analogue to Willkie's favored American pioneer myths, a tale of coming glory that would ennoble the sacrifices of the recent past. All the turmoil they had endured since the revolution of 1917—collectivization, forced industrialization, famine, the brutal purges that cemented an authoritarian state—would be worth it if agricultural Russia could be re-made as the industrial utopia of socialist theory and Bolshevik dreams.[18]

This narrative of modernization brought the Soviets in line with the Western world, committing them to the same stage theory of civilization that Americans and Europeans had embraced for generations. The Soviets, relative beginners on the path up from barbarism, pursued progress with the zeal of true converts. Stalin said so explicitly in 1929: "We are advancing full steam ahead along the path of industrialization— to socialism, leaving behind the age-old 'Russian' backwardness. We are becoming a country of metal, a country of automobiles, a country of tractors. And when we have put the USSR on an automobile, and the *muzhik* on a tractor, let the worthy capitalists, who boast so much of their 'civilization,' try to overtake us!"[19]

As Stalin well knew, Americans often saw Russians as not quite civilized. Russia had a decided "national character," journalists, diplomats, and scholars argued, shaped by its land and geography. It was not only largely rural but "Asiatic" to boot. Some saw it as static, a "halfway station between the advanced West and the backward east," as one political scientist put it, while others believed that it was capable of change and that its ordeal under communism was a dynamic stage in a painful and precarious development upward and westward. They hoped the Soviets could follow the trajectory the United States had traced not so long before. The country, Kennan and other more prominent Russia-watchers argued before World War II, was precariously balanced on the ladder of racial civilization only a few rungs above barbarism. It could move up or fall back.[20]

Following this logic, even some dedicated anticommunists could see Stalin's brutal economic programs as necessary evils, the only way to wrench a backward feudal society into modernity. The Russian people, the journalist Louis Fischer once remarked, were immobilized by their "bovine equanimity." Stalin's cruel and unseemly tactics, while unfit for America, gave this inert mass a necessary jolt into the future. For the correspondent Walter Duranty, the Soviet passage "from oxcart to airplane" inspired an oft-uttered refrain: "You can't make an omelet without breaking eggs." Duranty attributed the original omelet quip to Stalin, but regardless of its provenance, the saying entered English as a way of dismissing suffering (usually that of others) in service of a greater goal.[21]

Willkie did not indulge in cynical talk about Asiatic masses or egg breaking, but he appreciated a heroic narrative of economic growth. He was particularly entranced by plans for a massive hydroelectric project on the Volga. The war had put the dam on hold, but Willkie saw the future undertaking as an icon of modern mastery over nature. He figured it "would produce twice as much power as all the TVA, Grand Coulee, and the Bonneville developments combined." Willkie may have opposed the TVA on political grounds, just as he disapproved of the state socialism behind the Volga dam, but he had faith in their shared drama of rough progress. The drive to block the river's waters, flood the lands, and move people from the path of the rising lake was all worth it to send electricity coursing out to homes and factories and schools, knitting them together and pushing the story of civilization forward.[22]

Willkie's infatuation with the planned Soviet dam reflects a little-remembered warm spell in US-Soviet relations. The year leading up to the appearance of *One World* in April 1943 was the highwater mark of friendship between the two wary allies—due in large part to the news from Stalingrad and, to some degree, Willkie's exertions on behalf of the Soviets. Russians remained skeptical about American commitment to the war and suspicious of capitalism and imperialism, while many Americans, wary of communism, feared that the Soviets would make a separate peace with their "totalitarian" cousins the Nazis. But despite these doubts, between early 1942 and the end of 1943 the percentage of Americans who trusted Russia, according to one summary of opinion polling, rose from 39 to 51 percent, while those who felt distrust slipped from 39 to 27 percent.

The level of trust wavered according to current events and how pollsters phrased their questions. Opinion also differed by region, age, education, political bent, and interest in global affairs, but the general trend was toward increased trust.[23]

Two larger ideas drove this era of relative good feelings. The first, largely the domain of intellectuals and academics, held that the two societies were inevitably headed toward political and economic rapport—a view often called "convergence theory." The second was less an idea than a feeling: that shared wartime sacrifice would reveal a fundamental affinity between two energetic peoples on a common path to a bright future. Willkie would draw on both in different ways.

Convergence theory updated the standard romance of economic development, in which growth conquered all. The Soviets, its adherents suggested, were not lagging a generation or two behind the United States. They were on the verge of equaling their rivals as both countries moved away from their traditional economic systems and "converged" on a similar status as industrial giants with state-driven economies. As the Russian émigré sociologist Pitirim Sorokin put it, the United States under the New Deal was not "purely capitalistic," while the Soviet Union, propelled by "irresistible sociocultural forces," was tacking away from its "purely communistic" ideals. The war years had certainly seen increased Soviet tolerance for religion, as well as a celebration of Russian national culture over communist internationalism. Sorokin argued that these were not emergency measures to hearten a battered people but an inevitable drift toward increasing civil liberties.[24]

Convergence theory enjoyed a wartime vogue among some American Soviet observers and other thinkers hopeful of future cooperation with the Russians. Even President Roosevelt, never one for political theory, adopted an offhand version of this view. As Sumner Welles remembered it, the president hoped that "if one took the figure 100 as representing the difference between American democracy and Soviet Communism in 1917, with the United States at 100 and the Soviet Union at 0, American democracy might eventually reach the figure 60 and the Soviet system might reach the figure of 40."[25]

Willkie, too, dabbled in convergence theory. The nations shared a similar "outlook," Ambassador Standley recalled Willkie saying to his

Soviet hosts in Kuibyshev. "He was convinced that the United States and the Soviet Union from a social point of view were approaching each other and believed that within a few years the social systems of the two countries would be very similar." The Soviets, Standley said, received the idea "coldly." Willkie's dalliance with convergence theory appears to have been both casual and unquestioned, less a considered belief than an assumption spurred by his larger faith in modernization. That faith led him to believe that even if the two nations were not necessarily converging on a shared economic or political model, they might be *brought* together if their leaders downplayed ideology.[26]

Approval for the Soviet Union in the United States was driven not by intellectual abstractions so much as sympathy for the Soviet people and their struggles. Some Americans began to see Russians not as members of a fundamentally different civilization but as akin to themselves. Russians were not bovine and passive but stoic and steadfast, resolute before the Nazi threat and imbued with a spirit of independence that Americans cherished in their own national imagination. The idea that Americans and Russians were somehow similar—they wanted the same things; they shared parallel histories; they suffered wartime sacrifices for aligned ideals—entered popular consciousness through government propaganda, journalism, and Hollywood movies. Approving portraits of the Russian worker, peasant, and soldier leapt from the typewriters of the journalists Willkie met in Moscow, and from Standley's predecessor Joseph Davies, whose Soviet-friendly 1942 book *Mission to Moscow* was made into a popular film. Even the suspicious Standley got into the mood, telling an audience in New York that it was "the united effort and self-sacrificing devotion of the people of Russia that has touched my heart as much as it has won my everlasting respect and devotion."[27]

This idea was neatly crystallized in the November 1942 issue of *Fortune* magazine. In an ad for *Life,* another of Henry Luce's magazines, a picture by the famous news photographer Margaret Bourke-White showed a group of Russians clustered wide-eyed around a radio on June 22, 1941, the day the Nazi invasion began. These, the title said, were "The People with the Halos and the Horns." Public opinion about Russia was divided, argued the ad. Were true Russians the brave soldiers who stood against the Nazis, "helmeted and haloed like some knight of the grail"? Or were they the hard-bitten revolutionaries of American fears? Would they be inevitable foes in the postwar world? Was the alliance simply concealing "the Bolshevik horns that sprout on the Russian forehead, the cloven hoof of Communism hiding in the Russian boot?"

Reading *Life*, the ad said, could help Americans see the truth "somewhere between these two melodramatic extremes." The real Russia, "unhaloed, unhorned Russia," could be found in Bourke-White's expressive photo, and in the faces of the Russian people Americans could get to know in the pages of *Life*. "You know the look on these faces," the caption reminded readers; "you have seen it before your own radio on a day of crisis." Americans and Russians, linked together in the age of broadcasting, could offer each other long-distance sympathy for their shared sacrifice and hope for a potential shared future. The impression was underlined at the bottom of the page by a series of smaller images showing Russians—in church, defending their land, and debating mathematics— as simultaneously steadfast and opening to the West.[28]

Throughout his visit Willkie worked this same vein, collecting encounters with anonymous people Americans might admire. Whether it was the "bright young man" of the Stormovik plant, milkmaids on a state farm near Kuibyshev, or women workers at a munitions factory in Moscow, he tried to see Soviets as people and not stand-ins for communist ideology. His Soviet minders noticed that he went out of his way to engage people one-on-one, asking about their lives and their outlook on the war. As he toured the munitions plant he hurried through the technical material he usually relished—briefings from the director about equipment and output—and made a point of stopping to speak with the women toiling at the machines. He inquired about their families—whether they had brothers or fathers or sons at the front—and then probed them about the appeal of a separate peace with Hitler. They were all, as one teenager declared, working to "finish off the Germans." Reflecting on his visits, Willkie told American reporters that he could find no evidence of ebbing spirit: "I found universal devotion to the homeland. It was inspiring."[29]

This confused the journalists at first. Anybody familiar with the course of the war would find doubts about Russian determination preposterous. But they soon understood the purpose of Willkie's pointed affirmations of Soviet commitment. The comments were, the reporter Henry Cassidy remarked, "designed to convince any waverers at home that Russia was a sturdy ally." This was "ammunition for a political battle," Cassidy wrote, part of a larger campaign to sway public opinion. Willkie wanted to reveal actual Russians as beleaguered but steadfast, committed to the defense of their homes and families, and thus natural partners for like-minded Americans in both war and peace.[30]

Willkie mined similar stories from his grueling trip to the front— the highlight of the visit. The journey began near midnight in Moscow on September 23, several days into his visit, when he piled into a limousine with Cowles, Barnes, and several American military advisers and drove northwest from the city. The lines were only about a hundred miles away, but the trip through the war-torn woods and swamps took fourteen hours each way. They enjoyed hard-packed roads for the first few hours, but at daybreak they reached Staritsa and switched to American Lend-Lease jeeps. From there to the front near Rzhev the roads were barely passable, swept by unrelenting rain and fog. Mile upon mile of the route was over "corduroy" roads made from tree trunks lashed down tightly over swampy ground. Dozens of cargo trucks stood abandoned on the roadside in the mud.

The jeeps stopped and started, bucked and plunged. Mike Cowles remembered that it was ten days before he could sit comfortably again. Willkie suffered, too, but the trip took on an air of romance for him, and he would later think of it as a scene of Russian sacrifice that Americans would naturally appreciate. The pain brought back tales of frontier sacrifice from his boyhood: as they "bumped and bounced on roads so rough and muddy and rutted and corduroyed," he "finally understood the stories my father used to tell me of conditions in pioneer Indiana." The effect was heightened by the sight of evacuated Russian peasants returning to their homesteads, their belongings piled high on wagons, "surging back with a kind of elemental strength to the land which the Red Army had won back from the enemy."[31]

Willkie could see little from the command post eight miles behind the lines, but he could hear artillery firing and shells landing somewhere in the smoky gloom over the city of Rzhev. A few miles further on the party reached a small village on a gentle rise where the Red Army had overrun a Nazi fortification not long before. In the muddy trenches and blasted bunkers and ruined houses Willkie saw tired Soviet soldiers, some of them women, eating and talking not far from the splayed bodies of German dead.[32]

Willkie's Soviet minders were surprised that he seemed little interested in troop movements or strategy. The former World War I artillery officer had the necessary military expertise, but he was bent on treating the visit like one of his factory tours: a chance to gather tales about Red Army morale and sacrifice to take home to America. He also spent quite some time with wretched German prisoners languishing on a muddy roadside near the wrecked village. He asked the POWs how old they were, where they were from, and how their families were doing at home. These "miserable, homesick boys and men," he would later write—some close to forty, some as young as seventeen—did not resemble the "terrifying Huns, the unbeatable soldiers about whom I have read so many tales."[33]

A young general named Dmitri Lelyushenko, only thirty-eight years old, commanded all sixteen Red Army divisions along the Rzhev front. Willkie pressed him about the German prisoners—was this what they were up against? The general replied that Willkie shouldn't be deceived. The Nazis were well organized and led. But the Red Army was fighting for its homeland, and if they got all the help they needed from the Allies, they would throw back the invaders. Lelyushenko stood out in Willkie's mind as the ultimate representative of Russian resolve and character. Willkie wanted Americans to savor the difference between the German prisoners, "thinly dressed, emaciated, consumptive," and the Soviet general, whom Willkie would describe as "powerfully built, a born horseman with bowed legs betraying his Cossack origin, ruddy, vital, alert, full of animal spirits." Back at the command post, over a supper of cold bacon, black bread, potatoes, and cabbage, Willkie idly asked how much ground the general was defending. "Sir," Lelyushenko shot back, "I am not defending. I am attacking."[34]

The young general cemented Willkie's general impression of the Soviet Union at war. Visits to the factories, the farms, and the front had convinced him that everybody was united in sacrifice and determination. It was "the Russian people in the fullest sense who are resolved to destroy Hitlerism," he later wrote. This great spectacle of the Soviet war may have been partly staged, but in this case what Willkie was shown and what he hoped to show his fellow Americans was, as it happened, more or less true. The Russian people, galvanized by the threat to their land and families, fought with great determination for the same government that had repressed and divided them for so many years before the war.[35]

Willkie would do his part to sell Americans on Russian resilience, but the Soviets, he learned as his visit progressed, were losing faith in their allies. Everyone from General Lelyushenko to the workers at the Moscow munitions plant gave him not-so-subtle reminders of the lagging pace of American aid. And everywhere he went, soldiers, workers, peasants, writers, and even fellow attendees of the ballet expressed their doubts in the form of a persistent question: when would the United States and United Kingdom open the second front?

The question, Captain Kight would say, "just bugabooed everyone of us. How the heck did we know?" Willkie had little knowledge about Allied war plans. Roosevelt had kept him in the dark, not even mentioning Operation Torch, the North African invasion planned for November, which the Soviets would refer to as "front one and a half." Stalin already knew about the plans for Torch, but he also knew there would be no invasion of Europe in 1942. He had learned as much in August, when Winston Churchill flew into Moscow to smooth ruffled feathers. The prime minister's arrival climaxed a summer full of controversy over the question of a second front. Churchill's visit had tamped down the fire in London and Washington, but disappointment had transformed Soviet hopes into resentment. Willkie's visit would revive the ardor of their complaints.[36]

He had arrived in the Soviet Union at a perilous moment. In late September the defense of Stalingrad looked to be a lost cause. The desperate Red Army offensive that would turn the tables and trap the Germans in the city was still two months off. All along the Eastern Front, from Leningrad to Rzhev to Stalingrad, the fate of the war hung in the balance. The Nazis had been repulsed from the outskirts of Moscow, and history tells us that the German advance had run its course, but that was far from clear at the time. Nobody knew whether Stalingrad would hold. Everyone lived daily with the fear that it might not.

Willkie had lent his name to calls for an early second front at rallies in New York, but he was not eager to get caught between Stalin and the other Allied leaders. These were military and diplomatic matters over which he had little influence. Behind the scenes, he told Soviet officials that the Allies weren't ready yet and a failed landing would be worse than a delayed one. In public, to the press, he tried to cast the issue as one of shared sacrifice, a kind of preparation for the cooperation he hoped to see after the war. Stalingrad is "as much a British and American front as Russian," he said, "because this war is global in nature. All fronts belong to all allies and no nation can afford to become individually self-protective."[37]

The line about global reciprocity was in keeping with the larger view of the war Willkie was working toward—but it did little to assuage the immediate crisis. Faced with the relentless questioning, he changed tacks, going from "bugabooed" to true believer in just a few days. A second front was, he realized, "a symbol" to the Russian people of their expectations for Allied aid. And he started to come around to the idea that his raising the issue in public could improve relations between the two countries. Soon it would become the linchpin of the visit.[38]

He must have known that speaking out on the topic would further strain an already tense relationship with the American embassy. Standley, bemused by the bizarre frequency with which Russians buttonholed Willkie about the second front, felt sure the questioning was the result of a Kremlin propaganda campaign. This was no doubt true to some extent. The workers in the plants and random farmers and citizens on the street all seemed to be following the same script. But as any American journalist or lower-level diplomat knew, the hard-pressed Soviets were genuinely obsessed with the prospect of relief from the Nazi onslaught. The second front was a constant subject of rumor, gossip, and inquiry when Russians and Americans met that summer and fall. The Kremlin's top-down agitation was real, but Standley misread the situation. The Russians in this instance were willing participants in an effort to influence the course of the war and end their own suffering.[39]

Willkie could sense that the idea of a second front offered the essential commodity of hope to a war-weary but determined people. Several hours spent talking with a group of Russian writers won him over.

They included the reporter and novelist Ilya Ehrenburg and the writer and propagandist Konstantin Simonov. The writers had indeed been given a mission, Simonov recalled—to "lay out to him everything we thought about the fact that the Americans and English had not opened, and did not intend to open in the immediate future, a second front." This assignment was hardly unwelcome: "In fact, we did not want to talk about anything else."[40]

Willkie, with Barnes translating, tried to ask the writers about a range of issues: the state of German morale, the impact of Allied aid, even the possibility that Shostakovich might tour the United States to improve mutual understanding. The writers parried all his queries. Russian reporters did not speak to the soldiers who butchered their country. The gift of any American tank was well and good, "but so far it isn't an American who sits in it, fires from it, and burns in it, but a Russian." And the idea that the Soviets needed to send a musician to appeal to Americans was an insult. Willkie, taken aback by their intransigence, realized that they were "embroiled in a fight to the death." Ehrenburg had been advocating for a second front for months, and Simonov was just back from Stalingrad, where Red Army troops defended the bombed shell of a city, their backs to the Volga, fighting the Nazis street by street, house by house, even room by room in the burned husks of factories and apartment buildings. The great horror of the war was with them at every moment. The only thing that mattered was the second front.[41]

Willkie found the mounting clamor for a second front merging with his deepening appreciation for the sacrifice of the Soviet people. As he pondered how to bring this welter of facts and feelings alive for Americans, he inevitably landed on the person of Joseph Stalin. The meeting between the two leaders almost never happened. When Willkie arrived in Moscow he went with Standley to meet with Stalin's right-hand man, Viacheslav Molotov, the head of the Foreign Ministry. Willkie told Molotov that he had a personal letter for Stalin from President Roosevelt, but Molotov could offer no guarantees about a meeting. The Soviet chief worked long hours, mostly late at night, and saw few outsiders. Foreign visitors frequently endured days or weeks of waiting for an audience that never came. Sometimes the silence suddenly ended with an impromptu middle-of-the-night summons to the Kremlin. Willkie got off comparatively easy. On September 23, three days after he saw Molotov, word arrived that Stalin would see Willkie at seven-thirty that evening.[42]

The circumstances of the invitation—and its pointed circumvention of the American embassy—brought the simmering tensions with Ambassador Standley to a head. Willkie had repeatedly provoked Standley, at one point insinuating that he was a "little man" for holding to protocol and at another embarrassing him by proposing a drinking contest between some Soviet officers and the stiff and proper former admiral. He even upstaged the ambassador right before the meeting with Stalin, offering to take up a particular matter of military supply coordination with the Soviet leader. He was the president's envoy, Willkie said, and Standley had "been so long out of touch." That was the final straw. Banging his fist on the table, Standley angrily reminded Willkie that "that there is only one United States representative in the Soviet Union, and I, the American Ambassador, am that representative."[43]

It's not clear who cut Standley out. The ambassador was certain that Willkie had instructed the former Kremlin correspondent Joe Barnes to set up a back channel with Stalin's office, but Molotov and Stalin could have engineered it, too. They may have wanted to woo the president's envoy without the suspicious Standley present. Regardless, the kerfuffle served Willkie well. Whatever the extent of his cavalier behavior with Standley—and neither self-importance nor mischievous provocation would have been out of character—he no doubt preferred to see Stalin one-on-one, so that he could position himself as Stalin's near equal, a leader who did not have to abide by the artificial conventions of diplomatic protocol. His missions—official and unofficial—depended on being "in touch" with both Roosevelt and Stalin, and making the most of his status as a personal go-between for the president.

It is hard to imagine how Willkie thought he might charm the Soviet dictator. It was a meeting, the *New York Times* commented, of obvious opposites: the brash capitalist and the taciturn communist, the "breezy, casual, open-faced American and the short, compact, strong-armed and wary-eyed chief of the Soviet government." Willkie's freewheeling rise to

influence in American political life could not have been less like Stalin's
ascent in Soviet society. Where Willkie had made his name promoting
"free enterprise," Stalin's fame came from his exertions as a state-builder,
his character forged in the fire of a bloody revolution and tempered by his
dogged struggle to ascend the brutal Bolshevik hierarchy. The Soviet experiment was fragile, he warned throughout the 1920s and 1930s, its modernization imperiled by "capitalist encirclement" and the inevitability of
war with its imperialist enemies. To fortify the state he had relentlessly
pushed for industrialization from above, championed the destruction of
private property, and overseen the exile or murder of "class enemies"
and fellow Bolsheviks alike—and then, when the war he had predicted
arrived, he rallied the Soviet people to the defense of their homeland.[44]

Where Willkie was loose and ribald, cheerfully intent on mas-
saging the public opinion of a capitalist democracy, Stalin was rigid and
controlled, fixated on mastery of a calcified social and political order. In
his drive to wrench the nation out of its "backwardness," Stalin had
championed state power that, more and more, accrued to him alone. He
and his fellow Politburo bosses reflected a tragic irony: they had intended to create a classless modern industrial society, but they were fast
becoming an isolated aristocracy ruling over an empire of exploited peasants. Stalin was the executor of a brutal "agrarian despotism" that
pitted favored urban workers and cowed party bureaucrats against the
backward peasantry. In little more than a generation he had spurred the
transformation of an agrarian empire into a rough industrial behemoth,
one that offered a measure of security and social mobility to those who
could work harder and faster than their comrades, elbowed their way
into a favored post, or showed fealty to the party, which was increasingly
a cult of personality devoted to Stalin himself. Yet Stalin could be a
shrewd and pragmatic improviser when he needed to be. Suspicious of
foreigners and outsiders, he was nonetheless open to wary cooperation
with his allies, particularly Roosevelt, whom he trusted more than
Churchill. The question of future cooperation would turn on eastern
Europe, the region he considered the Soviet Union's rightful sphere of
influence and a buffer zone against another attack from the west.[45]

Willkie reached Stalin at an opportune moment. The war had
helped him solidify power, but it had also forced him to relax his

persecution of the Orthodox Church, back off on pushing for a worldwide communist revolution, and encourage nationalist sentiment in Russia and other Soviet republics. He even seemed willing to collaborate with the Allies in a future world organization, provided that the British and Americans would do their part to help defeat the Nazis and make the necessary concessions in eastern Europe to secure the Soviet Union's western borders. Much of this flexibility, it turned out, was wartime expedience. The rest would soon dissipate in a cloud of mutual suspicion between former Allies. But as Willkie made his way to the Kremlin, the prospect of a fruitful collaboration seemed to be on the table.

The encounter got off to a shaky start. As Willkie rushed from the embassy reception to his residence and then to the Kremlin, he realized he had lost track of his most tangible responsibility: delivering FDR's letter to Stalin. Cowles would later say that the perpetually disorganized Willkie had forgotten about the letter and couldn't find it as they prepared to leave the residence. He joined Barnes in a frantic search. They turned out all of Willkie's bags and pockets and finally discovered the letter, a bit crumpled, at the bottom of a laundry bag.[46]

With that minor catastrophe averted, Willkie joined Stalin and Molotov around a conference table in a wood-paneled reception room on the second floor of the Kremlin. There was a desk piled high with papers in one corner and a huge globe visible in an anteroom. Noticing this, Willkie began with some pleasantries about his trip. As he told *Life* correspondent Walter Graebner a few days later, "I said I had enjoyed my air journey immensely, adding that one had to ride in airplanes really to understand how small are man and his works. 'Aha, so there's something of the philosopher in you,' Mr. Stalin said, with a twinkle in his brown eyes." He observed that the Soviet leader was stocky and shorter than he expected—"he would have to stand on tiptoes to look over my shoulder." Even more surprising was Stalin's taste in clothes. The dictator's famous military tunic was a soft gray and his pants a light pink.[47]

Willkie's account of these talks—Stalin in his pastels, eager for a "frank heart-to-heart discussion"—hit some deliberately iconoclastic notes. His portrayal jibed with a tendency among Soviet-sympathetic Americans to sentimentalize Stalin. Liberals and fellow travelers often imagined "Uncle Joe" as the gruff but kindly patriarch of an unruly nation in need of his firm hand. The Stalin Willkie discovered was no less a projection than these fantasies, but it drew on his more specific hopes. He cast Stalin as a clever, hard-boiled antihero rather than a stern but loving paterfamilias. The war had "turned some of his jet-black hairs gray," Willkie told *Life*, but also "steeled his heart more than ever against the fascist tyranny."[48]

"Stalin is a hard man, perhaps even a cruel man," he would write in *One World*, "but a very able one. He has few illusions." His mind was "tenacious" and "driving." And he "asked searching questions, each of them loaded like a revolver, each of them designed to cut through to what he believed to be the heart of the matter that interested him." In another passage he described him as a "simple man, with no affectations or poses." He laughed "readily at unsubtle jokes or repartee." Willkie, always ready with cocksure banter, obliged. Midway through a story about his visits to Soviet schools and libraries, he let slip with a coy warning: "But if you continue to educate the Russian people, Mr. Stalin, the first thing you know you'll educate yourself out of a job." Stalin, Willkie claimed, laughed long and heartily at the gibe.

Simple and hard, but sophisticated enough to laugh at the lightly subversive jokes of his capitalist guest, Willkie's Stalin was not unlike an American businessman or lawyer. He had a "logical and practical mind," one that might suggest the capacity for compromise and cooperation. Frank and informal, Stalin appeared open to Willkie's out-of-bounds diplomacy. He felt they connected on a personal level. When he thanked the Soviet leader for speaking so candidly, he remembered, Stalin replied with real warmth: "Mr. Willkie, you know I grew up a Georgian peasant. I am unschooled in pretty talk. All I can say is that I like you very much."[49]

With all this joshing, the meeting became an odd hybrid: part international summit, part cultural exchange, and part negotiation over the nitty-gritty details of Lend-Lease. Each side treated the talks both as a private back channel to President Roosevelt and a public relations opportunity intended to reassure the other side of their good intentions. Still, they ventured into a number of sticky areas. Willkie told Stalin that he would "exert every effort" to strengthen the collaboration between their two nations during and after the war. In that spirit, he said, the president wanted to know how they could further aid the Soviet resistance.[50]

Stalin was unequivocal: the United States and Britain were not living up to the promises of their Lend-Lease agreement. The only way the Allies would win the war, Stalin said, was if the Soviets held out until the British and Americans were ready to invade Europe. It was Soviet sacrifice that allowed them to prepare. But recent reverses in southern Russia stemmed in part from shortages of cargo trucks and crucial planes. Just under half of the pledged material was making it up the Persian Gulf supply lines, and only 15–20 percent of the tonnage promised by the northern sea route was arriving. Some of this was due to intensifying Nazi attacks on Allied shipping—one recent convoy had been hit so hard it had turned tail and returned to the British Isles—but Stalin was furious about reports that a shipment of American P-39 Airacobras, vital for providing infantry cover against the Luftwaffe, had gone missing on the docks in Scotland.

He ticked off a list of needed supplies, which Willkie promised to take directly back to Roosevelt. The Red Army would need 500 planes, 10,000 cargo trucks, and 5,000 tons of aluminum, as well as food: 2 million tons of wheat from US reserves, plus corn and other grains, lard, and canned meats. In hindsight this shopping list may sound a bit prosaic, but Willkie knew how consequential these basics were for Stalin and the Soviets in their time of crisis. This end run around the Lend-Lease bureaucracy was his chance to deliver "something concrete" and would go a long way toward winning a greater share of Stalin's trust.[51]

The tense tone surrounding the aid question extended to the rest of the conversation. Willkie wondered if the German will to fight was flagging. Stalin contended that enemy morale was still strong. They were fighting, he believed, to avoid another generation of privation and chaos like that caused by the unequal terms of the Treaty of Versailles. Willkie leapt at this, venturing the idea that public statements about a more equitable peace might nudge the German people away from Hitler. Stalin responded that German resolve would only be broken by force. He said the Allies needed to step up their bombing of German cities. This set off a small debate about the effects of bombardment on civilian morale, with Willkie arguing that air attacks on Britain and the Soviet Union had actually served to stiffen resolve. Stalin admitted as much, but then grimly suggested that the Allies, including the United States, needed "to be bombed a bit," because they "suffer from complacency and overconfidence."[52]

As they prepared to close things out, Willkie sought Stalin's approval for a statement to the American public pushing for "maximum assistance" to Russia. In the United States, he said, "public opinion controls everything," so he needed to make the story of Soviet sacrifice come alive for Americans. When they truly understood what was happening at Stalingrad and Leningrad they could not fail to support increased aid. There was a saying in the United States, he continued, that "the squeaky wheel gets the most oil." Stalin, not quite catching the subtlety of American slang, bristled a bit at this imputation of Soviet weakness. He would not "let our wheel squeak," he retorted, but he would admit that the situation was serious and approved of Willkie's idea, with one caveat. Don't stress the hardships of the Soviet people, he said. Don't praise them too much. They were fighting for their motherland and did not wish to be patronized or treated like children.[53]

Willkie gladly acquiesced to Stalin's terms. As Barnes and Cowles joined him for a picture with Stalin and Molotov, he felt the meeting had been a success. He had his list of critical war matériel to take back to President Roosevelt. He had established a one-to-one rapport with the Soviet leader and positioned himself as an eager medium between the two nations. All of his exertions, he hoped, had laid the groundwork for future collaboration. There was only one catch: disorganized and cavalier as ever, he walked out of the Kremlin with Roosevelt's letter to Stalin still in his pocket. The note, it turned out, contained no vital diplomatic overtures, merely a formal introduction to the Soviet premier. But the minor gaffe, only made public much later, suggests how much Willkie intended to make the trip his own.[54]

The meeting with Stalin left Willkie feeling emboldened to launch a fresh salvo in his campaign to win American support for the Soviets. Soviet "coolness" toward the Allies required action. In a short speech he gave in Moscow near the end of his visit he hailed the sacrifices of the Russian people and their "people's war" and urged Americans to "build a bridge of supplies" to the embattled country. Buried in the middle of his remarks was a stick of political dynamite. "Personally," he announced, "I am now convinced we can best help by establishing a real second front in Europe with Britain at the earliest possible moment our military leaders will approve. And perhaps some of them will need some public prodding. Next summer might be too late."[55]

This statement was an inspired bit of strategic bravado. It simultaneously recognized the scheduling authority of Allied "military leaders," delivered a careful poke at the British, and legitimized "public prodding" in war planning. Willkie knew the Allies weren't ready for a European landing that year, but the potential gains in Soviet confidence outweighed hedging. Staking his personal support against Allied conventional wisdom might have appeared naive, but it could pay dividends later, when Willkie hoped to be involved in negotiating a more expansive peace with the Soviets.

Willkie's statement immediately became the noisiest controversy of the entire trip. For a week or two afterward, as he continued east, the newspapers and airwaves in America and England rang with charge and countercharge over his second-front stance, renewing the rumpus briefly quieted by Churchill's visit to the Kremlin. Willkie's calculated provocation earned him a few cheers from friendly columnists—he was the "outstanding goodwill ambassador of these times," wrote the syndicated columnist Ernest Lindley. Right-wing reaction was predictable: in courting the Soviets Willkie made an "everlasting nincompoop of himself," spat the *New York Daily Mirror*. Meanwhile, officials in Washington and London considered his statement "ill-considered" or "irresponsible." Members of Congress and Parliament lined up to denounce him. Clement Attlee, the deputy prime minister, rejected both the "need for public prodding" and "demands made by irresponsible people." Still, the British ambassador to Washington reported that Willkie's comments had likely increased his "popularity with the man in the street and middle-of-the-road opinion generally."[56]

Roosevelt and Churchill tried to stay above the fray. For a week or so, the president deflected or ignored questions about Willkie, even though he worried that the envoy was thinking less about the nation and more about his own political ambitions. Churchill, who considered

Willkie a friend, rose in the House of Commons to denounce the "undesirability of public statements or speculations as to the time or place of future Allied offensive operations." Not long after Willkie's departure from Russia, however, Stalin fanned the debate by giving the American journalist Henry Cassidy a surprise statement affirming that the second front had a "very important, one might say a prime place" in Soviet strategic considerations.[57]

Journalists began to badger the president. Did Willkie speak for him? This exposed the nebulous nature of Willkie's trip, a topic the cagey Roosevelt did not want broached. He remarked that he had seen the headlines about Willkie's statements but had not read the stories, because they were "purely speculative." He left it unclear whether he meant the stories or Willkie's opinions. Back on the other side of the globe, Willkie, by then in China, suddenly found reporters asking him to respond to the president's statement that his comments were not worth his time. Wasn't he the president's envoy? Always touchy about his former opponent and possessed of no shortage of vanity when his own seriousness of purpose was called into question, Willkie said the president had asked him to perform certain specific tasks and he had carried them out as best he could. "But when I speak for myself," he declared, "I'm Wendell Willkie and I say what I damn please."[58]

Roosevelt finally offered a vague affirmation: everything was all right with the Willkie tour as far as he was concerned. With that, the controversy began to fade. It would be put to bed entirely a few weeks later when Operation Torch went ahead as planned and the Allies fulfilled Willkie's predictions of Rommel's defeat. While "front one and a half" may not have been quite what the Soviets wanted, it eased the wait for a full invasion of Europe.[59]

The culmination of Willkie's visit—and his own campaign to woo the Soviets—came at the state dinner Stalin hosted for his new friend the night before his departure. Stalin and Molotov invited the entire party, along with a select group of Soviet officials, Standley and his embassy aides, and the British ambassador. As Kremlin banquets went, it was an intimate affair, just twenty-five guests all told. Fueled by the usual "over-powering dinner" and liberal offerings of wine and vodka, the evening took on a raucous and freewheeling air. Willkie later boasted, improbably, that he downed fifty-three vodka toasts, all of them "bottoms up, glass over the head."[60]

Not surprisingly, loose talk abounded. Much to the disgust of Standley and his staff, some of Willkie's companions loudly hailed him as "the next President of the United States" to their Russian hosts. Meanwhile, off in a corner, Barnes got into an ill-advised argument with Lavrentiy Beria, Stalin's infamous security chief, about the purges of the late 1930s. Fortified with drink and recalling his days as a Moscow correspondent, he accused the Soviets of executing some of his friends. Bystanders watched aghast as Beria stormed out, but the drunken antics soon resumed a more jovial tone as his colleagues Mikoyan and Voroshilov amused Stalin by handing out joint bear hugs to Archibald Clark Kerr, the British ambassador. Steeled with liquid courage, Clark Kerr wrote later, the threesome resolved to go to Stalingrad and "try our luck with the Germans."[61]

All of a sudden Marshal Voroshilov offered to demonstrate the use of a new Soviet machine gun. He began waving it around, all the while reassuring everyone that it was unloaded. A boisterous argument about how to properly aim and fire the weapon ensued, and the gun began to go around the room, with each guest demonstrating his prowess in mock battle. "Shooting from the hip," Clark Kerr remembered, he "raked the bellies of Stalin, Molotov, and Willkie." Voroshilov snatched the gun back, exclaiming that it should be fired from the shoulder like a rifle, and mimed a fusillade back at Clark Kerr. "Then Stalin seized it and fairly decimated his guests. This he seemed to enjoy immensely." Sometime around midnight, Stalin capped off the boyish rites with a screening of a short propaganda film about the defense of Moscow. Cowles would long recall the gruesome film, including footage of Nazi soldiers beheading a baby. Already staggered by the food and drink, he struggled to keep his dinner down.

The mix of macho bonhomie, recrimination, and gore lent the whole affair a potent atmosphere that peaked during the obligatory rounds of toasts. They started innocently enough, with the expected exchange between Willkie and Stalin, and toasts to Churchill and Roosevelt and the ambassadors. But before long, Stalin was upbraiding the interpreters for their lack of enthusiasm—apparently he felt their translations were not mirroring his guests' vigor. Willkie jumped up to propose a toast to the interpreters, "the only ones who are working here tonight." Stalin drank the toast and remarked that this was the first time they sounded like they meant what they said. Then Barnes rose and, speaking in Russian, drank to journalists. It was a minor landmark moment. No American had ever offered a toast in Russian at a Kremlin dinner before, and Molotov replied by saluting Barnes as a correspondent who had been "fair and just" in his time in Moscow. Not to be outdone, Cowles brought cheers with a round for the "unknown Russian soldier—who is winning this war!"

Getting into the spirit, Major Grant Mason, Willkie's Air Corps attaché, rose to toast the Allied pilots. Just as everyone was sitting down they realized that Stalin was still on his feet, launching into what Barnes recalled as a "rude and truculent" diatribe about the missing Airacobras diverted on the docks in Scotland. (Rumor had it that it was Churchill himself who had ordered that the planes be held back, although later reports suggested that the Americans diverted them for use in Operation Torch.) Clark Kerr tried to assure Stalin that the planes were being put to their best use for the Allied cause. Before the premier could reply, Willkie broke the tension with a one-liner: Stalin certainly "kept his eye on the ball." The Soviet leader was baffled by the American slang until Willkie got the interpreters to explain.[62]

Having seized the floor, Willkie went for broke, paying tribute to Soviet sacrifice and imploring Stalin to look past the inevitable tensions of the alliance and remember their common goals. The British and Russians had each stood alone against Hitler, he said. Now the Allies had to stick together to win the war. If "we could learn to stick together after the war," Barnes remembered him adding, "we would have a period of peace and prosperity such as the world had never seen." Willkie reached over and grasped Stalin's arm, turned the Soviet premier to face him, and raised his glass to the Allies, "united now and who, for the peace and economic security of the world, must remain united after the war." Stalin took the mild rebuke in stride and drank the toast. Then he leaned over and spoke directly to his visitor. "I like plain-spokenness," Barnes heard him say, "but you wouldn't have stolen 152 planes from me."

Over the years, many have discounted Willkie's visit to the Soviet Union as little more than a naive and high-spirited romp. By these lights, he was either a self-serving buffoon looking to advance his own political career or just another dupe of the wily Soviets, used as cover for cynical authoritarian maneuvers. Willkie exploited the war for future electoral advantage or crashed dumbly about, failing to see how the Russians were using him. He was craven or, even worse, credulous.

The first judgment was based on the idea—common among journalists and politicos at the time—that Willkie was just trying to stay "in the public eye." This is in part true, but it ignores *why* he hoped to maintain his profile, slighting his oft-stated interest in, as the Moscow correspondent James Brown put it, "guiding public thought" at home. There is no doubt that Willkie was eager to please Stalin and the Soviets, and that they sought to game his visit to their advantage, but his head-to-head with Stalin was never likely to go down in the annals of Great Power diplomacy. Willkie was not there to win concessions at the negotiating table. He had a subtler agenda.[63]

A better way to understand Willkie's meeting with Stalin, and his trip as a whole, comes via *Time* magazine's report on the Russia visit. Willkie was, in a classic of *Time*-speak, "naive-shrewd." Putting his open and gregarious nature to work as a strategic asset, he was imagining a role for himself in a game played with a currency greater than the diplomatic coin of wartime tactics or national interest. The little melodrama of the banquet toasts exemplified this vision in action. A complex display of informal diplomacy, Willkie had used his final toast not only to openly announce the global stakes of US-Soviet cooperation but also to show how the two rising superpowers could wrestle their fragile alliance into a working partnership. Mixing defiance and supplication, he hoped to earn the respect and affection of the Soviet leader. The rough intimacy called up by their banter—what later thinkers would have labeled the bonds of "homosocial" manhood—might prove the basis for international cooperation between their nations, each an industrial behemoth on the same modernizing trajectory, but only if the two leaders had a personal stake in supporting each other.[64]

There's no doubt that Willkie left with an overly hopeful view of Stalin and a rosy take on the Soviet Union as a whole, but he was not ignorant about the Soviet communists. He knew that Stalin's revolutions had killed millions, destroying an entire generation. He knew the secret police had been watching him during his visit, just as they watched over the Soviet people. His idealism about future cooperation stemmed from a faith in mutual pragmatism. Surely each side could be wooed into cooperation so long as the political and economic benefits were great enough.[65]

He was not blind to the possible pitfalls of his approach. He told the British that he distrusted Molotov, who he thought would try to sway Stalin against the United States in the long run. Like Roosevelt, he felt that Stalin was more amenable to cooperation with the Allies. His visit had led him to believe—against the doubts of Standley, Kennan, and other Foreign Service officers—that the Allies had to handle Stalin gingerly, coaxing him away from ideological opposition to capitalist imperialism and an even deeper Russian suspicion of the West. Stalin, Willkie would say later, had to be made to "feel like a life member of the club and not like a temporary one." If he was treated well, Willkie believed, "he would play the game."[66]

For his part, Stalin did feel some measure of rapport with Roosevelt—and, it seems, with Willkie—despite his belief that capitalist Americans could not be trusted. A wary optimism also emerged among ordinary Russians. Ilya Ehrenburg, one of the writers who schooled Willkie on Soviet sacrifice, remembered believing that "after victory everything would suddenly change." Many in his generation, he recalled, "believed that victory would bring justice, that human dignity would triumph." Time, needless to say, would not prove kind to this fragile prospect. And unlike Willkie or Roosevelt, Ehrenburg lived to see his hopes dashed. He watched as US-Soviet relations went into slow collapse, caving beneath the pressure of deepening mutual mistrust and conflict over the boundaries of postwar Europe. In a few years Stalin would again order Beria to "open fire on his own people" and the United States would be "threatening us with the atom bomb."[67]

Later, the Soviet writer would ruefully admit that he had mistaken his "desires for reality." Perhaps the same can be said of Willkie, but that judgment was far from clear in the fall of 1942. Most journalists and officials on the ground in Moscow believed that his visit had given US-Soviet relations a necessary jolt of good feeling. Watching the *Gulliver* depart, *Life*'s Walter Graebner felt as if he was seeing off an old friend. Ambassador Clark Kerr, standing next to him on the tarmac, remarked that it had been an unusually stimulating week.[68]

CHAPTER 9

The China Mystique

Lanzhou, Chongqing, Xi'an

As Willkie winged east from Moscow, the United States was buzzing with talk of his travels. Even as he headed for China, his final stop, commentators were checking the scorecard on Willkie's trip. The second-front scandal had kicked up the most dust, outraging those on the right *and* left. Old-guard Republicans and New Deal Democrats alike could agree: Willkie was reckless and self-serving. To these critics, Willkie had told tales out of school in a craven bid to keep his name in the headlines.

Others found his enthusiasm refreshing. Even if his reports seemed "over-optimistic," a *Washington Post* editorial argued, the mission as a whole appeared a "wise move." In Egypt, Turkey, and Russia, the *Post* editors felt, Willkie had boosted support for the Allied cause. "We doubt," the paper continued, whether foreign leaders had "ever before dealt with anybody quite like him." Willkie represented "the robust, sincere, American spirit" of the US war effort. For many back home, his journey was welcome proof that the nation could greet the world on its own terms. "Here we have John Doe in the person of Mr. Willkie," wrote one fan in a letter to the editors of the *New York Herald Tribune*, "speaking with dramatic conviction on the international stage, and the world listened." In his blue business suit, Willkie was "an average American in the uniform of Mr. America, representing the inquisitive, probing, want-to-know-why attitude typical of American thinking."[1]

Even before Willkie left Moscow he could sense the surge of state-side attention. Telegrams from supporters suggested the trip was going over well but urged him to keep his priorities straight. "Go a little easy on tone of superoptimism," his former campaign manager Russell Daven-port advised. "Suggest attitude mature deliberation taking account doubtful factors as well as good so as to represent your own judgment," he continued in telegraphese. Reports on the trip were good, Irita Van Doren cabled, but so far they "emphasized presidential mission." Willkie should try to stress the "independent knowledge-seeking aspect of trip." Tamping down his natural "superoptimism" didn't mean playing it straight. He would have to be himself, rather than Roosevelt's messenger. His pronouncements in Cairo and Moscow had announced his free agency; now he needed to make that independence count.[2]

A *Post* editorial suggested that despite Willkie's charms, "deeds and not merely assurances of great things to come are what will count with the Turks, the Russians, and with the Chinese, whom he will now visit." In the air above central Asia, making his way from one nation under siege to another, Willkie no doubt pondered what sort of deeds would truly count. Success, he had already discovered, would turn not on boosting morale or coaxing unsure peoples more firmly into the Allied fold. Winning required more than planes and tanks and aid, and he would need to convince his fellow citizens to do more than don the uniform of "Mr. America" and flex their self-congratulatory national muscles. The true challenge was not defeating fascism but sowing the seeds of an interdependent postwar world order.[3]

On the long journey east Willkie considered everything he had seen and heard in Russia. He worried about the Soviet leadership. "When he was talking with Stalin, Molotov, Vishinsky, and other members of the Politburo," Cowles wrote, "he detected in them a rebirth of the brutality and imperialism of the old Czarist governments." Willkie believed the Russian and American people could get along, but their leaders were another question. How, Cowles remembered him musing, might he get them to join together in "a real league of nations strong enough to preserve peace, promote more equality between have and have-not nations, and break down trade barriers so all people might have a chance at a rising standard of living."[4]

The Soviet problem was the linchpin of an even greater challenge. The war, Barnes recalled Willkie saying as they flew, "was much more than a military episode in an old balance of power struggle." Millions saw it as a chance to end empire once and for all. The second-front bombshell, with its naked appeal to "public prodding," had been designed to keep the Soviets engaged in an alliance that might blossom into cooperation for a reworked world. Now he would need to deliver a similar prodding to Americans who could not yet see what his journey was really about. China would give him the perfect opportunity to bring home, for himself and his fellow citizens, the true stakes of the war.[5]

From Moscow, the *Gulliver* and its passengers began a 4,000-mile, six-day passage to western China, heading for Chongqing, the dusty, hilly city where Chiang Kai-shek's Nationalist forces, reeling from the Japanese invasion, had sought refuge in 1937. They were back in Kuibyshev the first night, and took off early the next morning for Tashkent, where they spent the night in a primitive hotel run by a hospitable old couple. "Bedbugs," the crew reported drily. September 29 found the plane skirting the western flank of the soaring Tian Shan Mountains. By afternoon Captain Kight had banked east and discovered a pass through the range. As the *Gulliver* roared 13,000 feet above ancient caravan routes, the party could look up at 18,000-foot snow-capped peaks looming out of the mist and glare. Just beyond the Chinese border, Kight brought the plane down in Urumqi, in China's westernmost province, Xinjiang, on a rock-strewn dirt runway running up the side of a mountain.[6]

Only a handful of Americans had ever set foot in Xinjiang before. Hollington K. Tong, the American-educated minister of information in Chiang Kai-shek's Nationalist government, had come west from Chongqing to meet Willkie, but the Soviets (who were funneling aid to both the Nationalists and their chief adversaries, Mao's communists) seemed to be in charge of Urumqi. The cars, the travelers noticed, were Soviet-built. The goods in the stores had Russian labels. Even the street signs were in Russian. Sheng Shicai, the warlord-turned-governor of Xinjiang, treated the travelers to a review of Soviet-built mechanized military and old-fashioned cavalry. The "lithe, wiry Mongols and Kazaks," Willkie recalled, "sat their saddles as if they were part of their horses" and wowed the visitors with their deft exploits on the mounted saber course.[7]

The next morning Kight coaxed the *Gulliver* down the inclined runway and up into another breathtaking mountain pass. Their maps listed some peaks at close to 19,000 feet, but many were labeled with question marks. From the lofty prospect of the *Gulliver*'s cockpit, these seemed to tower over 20,000 feet. At last they broke through into China's vast interior. The rest of the flight to Lanzhou, Cowles remembered, covered "miles of desert, red loam hills, [and] cultivated green fields." The radiant spectacle "unfolded beneath us like a slowly opening fan."[8]

The *Gulliver*'s route had been kept secret as a precaution against Japanese attack, and for several days the outside world lost track of its progress. Misinformation abounded. A BBC radio report had the travelers arriving in Chongqing three days after their departure from Moscow, when they were still thousands of miles to the west. American papers carried notices about the elaborate welcome the Chinese were laying out for Willkie, and some reassurances, too. He wasn't overdue, Nationalist officials told the press. "They don't want me to become a clay pigeon for the Japanese," Willkie later quipped.[9]

For the journey east to Chongqing, Kight had taken on board a Chinese radio operator to work the Nationalist codes. The system was imperfect, however, and some messages came through in the clear. Between Urumqi and Lanzhou an uncoded message arrived asking if Willkie might make it to Chengdu, just west of Chongqing, by 1:00 p.m. the next day. The lapse almost led to disaster. As the *Gulliver* prepared to leave Lanzhou the next morning, reports arrived that Japanese planes, tipped off by the errant communication, were scouting the route ahead and the skies near Chongqing. Luckily, cloud cover along the flight path and unsettled weather over Japanese-held territory to the east reduced the risk, and they soon had the all-clear. That 400-mile leg still proved to be the hairiest yet. Midway through the flight one of the plane's big props sputtered, began to smoke, and stalled out. Kight and Klotz had to nurse the *Gulliver* into Chengdu on three engines. The *Gulliver* stopped there—the field at Chongqing was deemed inadequate for the big transport anyway—and the next day, October 2, Willkie and his companions took a Chinese DC-3 into Chiang's wartime capital.[10]

The further east they went, the more lavish the reception. In Urumqi, Lanzhou, and Chengdu they met high officials, toured industrial sites, and attended banquets—the usual. But in Lanzhou, the capital of Kansu province, thousands of people lined the road into town, cheering and waving American and Chinese flags. Similar scenes, and even larger crowds, awaited them in Chongqing and Xi'an. "Men, women, young boys and girls, bearded old gentlemen, Chinese with fedora hats, others with skullcaps, coolies, porters, students, mothers nursing their children, well dressed and poorly dressed," Willkie recalled, lined the streets and hillsides for miles, "packed from curb to store front" in the sun in Chongqing and the rain in Xi'an. It felt, Barnes remembered, like "a kind of national ovation," a heartfelt outpouring of faith in the alliance between the United States and China.[11]

However heartfelt they seemed, the demonstrations were not spontaneous, and the visitors could sense it. They could see the pre-hung banners. They noticed that the little fluttering flags were all identical and brand-new, no doubt handed out just beforehand. Willkie found the smiles genuine, but the full truth might have discouraged him. Days before, Nationalist authorities had assembled official committees in each city to festoon the streets with banners. Youth groups, neighborhood organizations, and police were mobilized to gin up crowds. Newspaper editors were ordered to run Willkie-themed editorials. On the morning of his arrival, police forced shopkeepers along his route to stock flags and then required people to buy them. When authorities determined that there weren't enough flags waving, they distributed thousands more, much to the annoyance of those who had bought them. Hours before the Americans were due, police lined up the crowds and drilled them in slogan shouting and flag waving. Boy Scouts and Girl Scouts bustled about filling gaps in the crowds. Just before the cars arrived, police fanned out into the surrounding streets to round up stragglers. As Willkie rolled slowly past, many people, not entirely sure what was happening, just stood and stared. The most willing groups shouted and waved at every car that went by, long after he and his party passed.

Not since President Ulysses S. Grant had toured China in 1879, Nationalist propaganda proclaimed, had such a reception greeted a visiting dignitary. Willkie had been given the proper respect—or "face," as the Chinese called it. The production hit all the right notes. Willkie had seen adoring crowds before, but not quite like this. He felt wooed, his ego stroked. Whatever his doubts about the manufactured nature of the spectacle, he soaked up the adoration.[12]

But the contrived reception didn't please everyone. John Stewart Service, a State Department official, was on the ground in both Lanzhou and Xi'an as the police and Guomindang officials prepped the crowds. Later famous as one of the "China hands" unjustly blamed for "losing" the country to the communists, Service was also one of a handful of Americans in the diplomatic corps who spoke Chinese. He found the elaborate preparations dismaying, further evidence for his sense that Nationalist rule was both authoritarian and hollow. The Chinese dissenters he knew called them a sign of the party's fundamental "psychology." The Nationalists were unable "to understand the people and to permit them to show in their own way any spontaneous feeling." Mingling with the crowds, Service saw a missed opportunity. The general goodwill of the Chinese toward Americans "would have resulted in some manifestations which, though not as obvious as organized cheering sections, would at least have been obvious enough to impress Mr. Willkie or persons around him familiar with China."[13]

As it turned out, the staged crowds were only the beginning. "He's to be smothered," wrote General Joseph "Vinegar Joe" Stilwell, the top US adviser to Allied forces in the China-Burma-India theater and a caustic critic of Chiang's leadership. As the general predicted, the Nationalists laid it on thick. Willkie and his companions were soon enjoying—and eventually enduring—the most intense round of banquets, receptions, luncheons, visits, and conferences of the entire trip. Over ten days in China Willkie met hundreds of officials and ordinary people. He toured arsenals, training camps, military academies, factories, orphanages, universities, and the front. He was given frequent access to the press and made a series of speeches at banquets, luncheons, and over the radio. At one point he drew a crowd of thousands to a university amphitheater. City officials in humid, dusty, and ramshackle Chongqing—then undergoing a forced modernization campaign to make it fit for its new role as a national capital—went so far as to clear out a shantytown (and its residents) near Willkie's lodgings—"so that it might not offend his eye." The man the Nationalists thought might be the next president of the United States was being "thoroughly immersed in soft soap, adulation, and flattery," Stilwell sneered in a letter to his wife. "The idea is to get him so exhausted and keep him so torpid with food and drink that his faculties will be dulled and he'll be stuffed with the right doctrines."[14]

Willkie, however, was in his natural element. The constant round of visits and events gave him ample opportunity to work his charms. Newsreel cameras captured him wading into throngs of people to shake hands, reviewing lines of troops, smiling and waving as he led processions of dignitaries through historic sites, talking intently with workers in a paper factory. Reporters found him good-naturedly puzzling over the offer of a hot towel as he stepped off the plane—an "old Chinese custom"—and fiddling with chopsticks at a banquet. (Accounts of his dexterity varied.) He even deployed his patented "kissing technique"—as the *Washington Post* called it—for "spreading American goodwill," planting a kiss on the cheek of a little girl at a reception for war orphans hosted by Mayling Soong, the formidable, American-educated wife of Chiang Kai-shek.[15]

Willkie's backslapping bonhomie did not always come off well in China. His natural informality could violate traditional ideals of order and propriety, and his indifference to hierarchy startled people accustomed to deference toward elders, educators, or others whose high station merited proper respect. At a banquet given by a Chinese general known for his many children, Willkie let loose with several jokes about his host's potency. Another time, as he signed autographs in a swarm of college students, he asked his interpreter to tell the crowd that China had the best looking "co-eds" he'd seen in his travels. Elsewhere he interrupted a reception with the demand that he meet some regular people. Officials scrambled to bring in several confused rickshaw drivers for a photo op.

The most bizarre of these minor dust-ups happened when a Chinese official detailed to Willkie's residence came into his room and was startled and embarrassed to find the big, bearish traveler sitting naked at his desk, trying to beat the unseasonable fall heat by working on a speech in the buff.[16]

These incidents embarrassed American diplomats and military men, too. Willkie's antics seemed foolish and possibly harmful to the war effort. He was just a grasping office-seeker, a "fat peanut politician" in Stilwell's acrid description. Another China hand, John Paton Davies, remembered Willkie as all ego, someone who assumed "that his unbuttoned personality exuded persuasive allure." For his part, Willkie willfully alienated the American ambassador, Clarence Gauss, a businesslike career diplomat only recently installed in Chongqing. Described by one American observer as "a rather acid but agreeably shrewd man who greatly disliked his present position," Gauss bore typical disdain— "treaty port superciliousness"—for the Chinese. Willkie never gave him much of a chance. Before leaving Russia, he had told American officials that he wanted no interference from the ambassador.[17]

Whether or not the message had reached him, Gauss was unprepared for what was to come. Minutes after Willkie landed in China they quarreled over the ambassador's advice on whom to see, what to say, and how to behave. Willkie spurned Gauss's offer of lodgings in his own residence in favor of a richly appointed guesthouse courtesy of Chiang Kaishek. Ever wary of mental and physical embassy walls, he made sure that the ambassador would, as Gauss himself later remembered, see "as little of possible" of him. In return, the humiliated Gauss did as little as he could to help Willkie. "What was all that excitement?" the irked Gauss griped after Willkie was gone. "What was that fellow so eager about? Didn't he know that none of these Chinese, not even Madame Chiang, can vote in American presidential elections?"[18]

In the end, most of the Americans posted to China looked askance at the courtship between Willkie and the Nationalists. They had started to believe that Nationalist rule was bad for the war effort and bad for China, and they saw all the orchestrated excitement as a ploy to fool an influential but gullible traveler. In a way, they were right. Willkie admitted that he was falling hard for China. Upon his arrival in Chongqing, he laughed about the foiled Japanese attempts to waylay the *Gulliver*. They were a special kind of "flattery," he said, but there was "more danger of my being killed by the kindness of the Chinese than by enemy bullets." What he *was* worried about was the integrity of his mission, he joked. "During the three days I have been in China I have fallen so much in love with the Chinese people that it is going to be difficult to carry out my fact-finding mission with the correct critical approach." Willkie's discernment was often lacking in China, and as a result, he found himself drawn into Sino-American political intrigue over the Nationalist war effort.[19]

The primary dispute—much chronicled in memoirs, histories, and Cold War–era recriminations over the "loss" of China to the communists—raged between Stilwell and Chiang. By 1942, the American general had become convinced that a dishonest and cowardly Chiang was refusing to take the fight to the Japanese. Chiang, not surprisingly, saw things differently. Knowing how hard it had been for the Nationalists to unify China—they had been trying since the 1920s—and how tenuous his rule was in a country divided into fiefdoms ruled by warlords, the communists, and now the Japanese, he preferred a defensive strategy. The Nationalists had suffered massive losses in the first few years after the 1937 invasion—retreating from the coastal cities of Beijing, Shanghai, and Nanjing—but the Japanese advance had eventually bogged down into a wary stalemate. With his armies disorganized and ill-equipped, Chiang decided to "trade space for time." By late 1938 the Guomindang had moved its industry and capital city far to the west, beyond the great gorges of the Yangtze River. There they hunkered down—enduring withering Japanese bombing of Chongqing and other Nationalist cities—to await help from the Allies. There had been thrusts and counterthrusts in the succeeding years, but Chiang's main goal was to outlast this latest round of invaders—just as the Chinese had for millennia.[20]

In the months after Pearl Harbor, Chiang continually pressed the Americans for greater aid, particularly more airplanes, but Stilwell was convinced that he mostly wanted the armaments for a coming war with Mao. President Roosevelt, for his part, valued China's contribution to the war effort, but Allied strategy privileged the European and Pacific theaters over the China-Burma-India front. The Nationalists were useful—they kept several million Japanese troops tied down—but never a priority.

American aid increased over the course of the war, but China remained an afterthought in Washington. The British likewise saw China as secondary, important only to distract the Japanese from India.[21]

By the fall of 1942, the bitterness between Chiang and Stilwell was nearing fever pitch. Chiang found Stilwell rash and arrogant. Stilwell believed the Chinese leader was a foolish weakling and a corrupt dictator. Each blamed the other for humiliating Allied losses in Burma earlier that year, when the Japanese had defeated a British and Chinese campaign to secure the Burma Road—the main supply route into "free China" from India. Chiang complained that in Stilwell the United States had sent not an adviser but a "king of the China theater." Vinegar Joe took to calling the Nationalist leader "Peanut," mocking the round dome of the generalissimo's shaven head.[22]

Stilwell halfheartedly tried to get Willkie to see the situation his way. At one of their conferences Willkie seemed to him uninterested or too tired to fully engage. "Poured it on him, to prime him before he saw the G-mo," Stilwell recorded in his diary. "Don't know whether he heard me or not. Afraid he may be just a politician. Christ, haven't we *any* big men?" A day later, after Willkie's first conferences with Chiang and his wife, who acted as his translator, the general reported that the envoy was "completely sold on CKS and Mme." Willkie, he noted, did advise him to "put it on with a trowel" if he wanted to convince the Chinese, but Stilwell had nothing but disdain for his visitor's showy retail diplomacy. "To hell with that stuff," he barked to his diary. By the end of the visit, Stillwell found Willkie "utterly indifferent" to him. "I'm very small fry in his great plan, of course."[23]

The only American Willkie showed much interest in was Stilwell's subordinate and rival, General Claire L. Chennault, whose "Flying Tigers," a roguish unit of Army Air Force fighter pilots, were celebrities in their own right. By the summer of 1942 they had inflicted such heavy losses on the bomber squadrons plaguing Chongqing that the Japanese all but ceased the campaign. Chennault's exploits had been celebrated in the stateside press and in China itself, where he was revered by the Guomindang. But he was not universally beloved among US military personnel. In fact, as Captain Kight noted upon their arrival in Chongqing,

Americans in China were divided into the "Stilwell faction" and the "Chennault faction," army grunts against air force flyboys.[24]

Chennault's camp argued that with the proper supplies his pilots could drive the Japanese out of China, all via airpower. In fact, with enough planes, Chennault thought he could win the entire war. From the skies, he would destroy Japanese supply lines, free up the US Navy's drive across the Pacific, support a renewed Chinese ground offensive, and pound the home islands into surrender. Stilwell and his backers found this scenario ridiculous—a "jackass proposition," the general wrote in his diary. Stepped-up air attacks would just lead to a massive Japanese assault on Chennault's vulnerable bases. Stilwell thought China needed to train its patchwork, semi-independent armies into a modern force and take back the overland supply route. With matériel flowing via the reopened Burma Road, Chinese armies could mount a series of offensives—supported by airpower—and push the Japanese back to the sea in both Burma and China.[25]

Not surprisingly, Willkie preferred Chennault's bravado to Stilwell's more measured calculus. Chennault was "tall, swarthy, lean, and rangy," Willkie would later write. He had "something hard about his jaw and his eyes which contrasts curiously with his Louisiana drawl." Plus, Willkie felt that Chiang favored Chennault's strategy. In truth, Chiang's main goal was to pit the Americans against each other in a play for time, but Willkie thought that supporting Chennault might show support for the Chinese and give him a vital role as a medium between Chiang and Roosevelt. During their two-hour meeting, Chennault told Willkie he had never had a chance to put his plans before the lead war planners in Washington. Seizing the opportunity, Willkie asked the general if he would draft a detailed letter laying out his plans, which Willkie, as the president's personal representative, would carry back to FDR. Chennault agreed, and several days later the letter arrived by special courier. Willkie took it to the president, who liked what he read. This set off a major row in the War Department, where the army chiefs backed Stilwell over the renegade Chennault. Willkie would give a glowing account of Chennault in *One World*—"what he asks for is amazingly little; and what we have sent him falls far short of even that little"—and in the spring of 1943, after a showdown over China strategy, Washington okayed some of Chennault's ideas.[26]

Ultimately, however, Stilwell's recalcitrance, Chiang's evasiveness, and the War Department's aversion to an air-first strategy thwarted Willkie's efforts. His dive into the Stilwell-Chennault tiff never made headlines, largely because he kept his efforts out of the papers. Whether his support for the controversial air-first strategy was wisdom or folly—postwar appraisals have largely favored Stilwell's strategy—the entire imbroglio was something of a sideshow for Willkie, who mostly hoped it might foster closer relations with the Chinese.

Putting aside warnings from his stateside advisers and his own misgivings, Willkie plunged headlong into mutual courtship with the Nationalists. His China speeches overflowed with rhetoric praising Guomindang democracy, sacrifice, and martial spirit, and his account of China in *One World* is the least reflective or critical in the book. Filled with glowing mini-portraits of the many Nationalist officials he met, each one a representative of China's "best men," it often reads like propaganda. One depiction of a general—"a thoughtful, patient, untiring fighter for China's victory and a better world"—could stand in for all the rest. They seem to reflect Willkie's own sense of himself: by turns resolute, wise, and serious, but nonetheless good-humored and eager for hearty fellowship with their Allied counterparts.[27]

Willkie had three long talks with Chiang Kai-shek, accompanied by either Madame Chiang or Hollington Tong as translator. Chiang won Willkie's approval early on with his fondness for one of the American's favorite subjects: industrial development. Having visited a number of primitive factories relocated from the coast, Willkie tried to convince Chiang to embrace mass production rather than "the widely distributed small plants" the Chinese leader favored for a country emerging from agricultural feudalism. Most pressing were discussions about the postwar world. Hoping to reassure Chiang of American benevolence, Willkie told him that Roosevelt did not see the US-British alliance as unilateral. He hoped for strong US-Chinese cooperation after the war. Pleased, Chiang expressed his hope for a postwar settlement that would keep peace in the Pacific region and work to dismantle the force of racism. The primary thing he wanted from Britain and the United States, however, was an immediate end to the system of unequal trade agreements forced upon China in the nineteenth century by the Western powers. Abandoning those "unfair treaties" would be true proof of American ideals.[28]

"I have come to China to pay homage not only to the Chinese people," Willkie announced on his first day in Chongqing, "but also to one of the truly great men of his time, your Generalissimo." The Nationalist leader was "one of the best known men in my country, and one of the best-liked." Willkie found Chiang a man of contrasts: he had a soft-spoken "reflective manner" and "quiet poise" set against a severe and dignified military bearing. American audiences, already well primed by the Guomindang's influential US backers to appreciate Chiang's "aggressive spirit," heard from Willkie that he "came to power the hard way" and displayed an almost "unreasonable" loyalty to his comrades and their cause. In Willkie's speeches and *One World,* Chiang came across much as he did to the most fervid pro-China boosters: the determined leader of an emerging democracy and a staunch ally of the United States committed to unifying his country and defeating the Japanese.[29]

This image struck many Americans in China as absurd. To people like Stilwell, Gauss, or Service, Chiang stood at the head of a corrupt and sclerotic authoritarian state. He refused to fight the Japanese, while his secret police terrorized the people in the name of suppressing dissent. His government instituted capricious controls on commodities in the cities and blockaded the communists in the north, while allowing smugglers from occupied China to set up a burgeoning black market for profiteering Nationalist elites. His officials taxed landless peasants in grain and rice to feed their stagnant and rebellious armies. Lavish banquets greeted Willkie even as famine stalked the countryside. Inflation crippled the economy while government officials, rural landlords, and other backers of the regime enjoyed Western-style luxury, sweeping through the bombed cities and starved countryside in their limousines.

For the Vietnamese socialist revolutionary Ho Chi Minh, Willkie's celebrated visit was the height of irony. Earlier in 1942 he too had set off for Chongqing, in order to try to negotiate terms of an alliance between

Chiang and the Viet Minh against the Japanese. Seized by the Guomin-dang police before he could reach the capital, he spent fourteen months in Chinese jails, biding his time and writing poetry. Reading about Willkie's visit in the paper, he noted it with a rueful sense of fatalism:

> We both came in amity,
> Wartime allies of the KMT.
> While you were feted at the seat of honor
> I was fettered in this penal horror.
> Diplomatic affections may run hot and cold,
> Such is the way of the world,
> Or as the French say, *C'est la vie,*
> All waters flow down to the sea.[30]

Chiang may have been a righteous anticommunist, the American OWI official and journalist Graham Peck observed, but his party "had been founded through opportunism, treachery, and murder." The bloody coup that brought them to power in 1927 determined the character of their rule—and ensured they could only masquerade as a democracy. The Guomindang was a vast and terrible façade, foreign observers and Chinese dissidents alike concluded, a cynical exercise in propping up the traditional "face" necessary to reassure gullible Americans to keep the aid coming.[31]

Two episodes of such "face"-making—one minor, one major—suggest how Willkie's eagerness to see the Chinese as postwar partners blunted his critical faculties. At one of the innumerable banquets in Chongqing, the Princeton-educated mayor of the city announced that a rare treat was in store. For months, the mayor said, dairy products had been banned due to a cholera outbreak traced to the milk supply. But Willkie's visit was so special that he had repealed the ordinance for one day. The guests enjoyed "good old-fashioned vanilla ice cream" with wary pleasure. "For the next few days," Willkie joked later, "we waited anxiously to see if our anticholera inoculations were really any good."[32]

But on the streets of Chongqing, the great ice cream ban of 1942 told a different story. Over the course of a scorching summer and fall, Graham Peck reported, ice cream parlors, cafés, and tea gardens—which popped up everywhere after the Japanese bombing eased—had been sub-ject to capricious closures by the authorities. From elegant pleasure gar-dens to holes-in-the-wall, the city's snack spots closed, opened, and closed again. Chongqingers either sweltered or paid high prices for bootleg ice cream. By the fall, more well-to-do cafés and bars had re-opened, but ice cream remained a black-market commodity. Impromptu speakeasies served cold treats for exorbitant prices, while soda and tea prices skyrocketed in the sanctioned cafés.

Various explanations for this strange policy traveled the Chongqing gossip circuit, or what Americans called the "bamboo-telegraph." Peck remembered that the whole thing started when the generalissimo, "hur-rying through the town in his cavalcade of bounding black limousines," became upset at the spectacle of people enjoying themselves during war-time and ordered all the cafés shut down. The police complied, but be-fore long they took bribes to let some well-connected places reopen. When owners of more modest shops complained, the authorities allowed them to reopen—for a price, of course. When one group of proprietors com-plained about others reopening and threatened to report the police to higher-ups, the police hastened to shut down the newly opened offenders, and so on in a confusing round of openings and closings and reopenings. Whatever the truth—and Peck, the narrator of these events, was predis-posed to believe the generalissimo's role in the affair—the gap between these tales of bribery and corruption and the mayor's benevolent story of cholera precautions was telling. For critics like Peck, the ice cream saga perfectly captured how Willkie was screened from the chaos and corrup-tion of Nationalist China.[33]

A more consequential glimpse behind the façade came on Willkie's journey to the front. The trip was long and eventful, though not nearly as arduous as the trek to the Soviet front two weeks earlier. On the evening of October 7, Willkie and his companions flew northward to Xi'an for another flag-waving parade. After climbing a long lantern-lit path to a hilltop military academy and another rich banquet, they boarded a special sleeping car headed east toward the Yellow River. Early in the morning they switched from train to handcar, facing forward on benches in front of soldiers who pumped the cars down the line. Finally, their escorts had them walk the final few miles along a great cut in the earth, shielding them from the river and the front. All night, they learned later, Japanese planes and artillery had been lobbing explosives here and there to try to score a kill. One report said four shells landed near the train station not long before Willkie's car pulled in. Another claimed that the Japanese had bombed nearby Luoyang, destroying a decoy sleeping car and killing 150 refugees camped in the rail yards there.[34]

In a village surrounded by trenches at a bend in the river near the town of Tungguan they found the front. From an observation post, Willkie and his companions could peer 1,200 yards across the water at the Japanese positions. It was strangely calm, Cowles remembered. Every so often firing popped off as they came or went, almost as if the battle was coming to life just for them. Their guide was Chiang Wei-kao, one of the generalissimo's sons, who was a captain in the artillery. After a review of the troops and a brief speech the party returned to the railcar, where lunch was served. Captain Chiang, Willkie remembered, appeared with gifts for the travelers. The Peking beer, French wine, and Japanese cavalry swords, the captain claimed, had been captured from the enemy on raids across the river.

Willkie pointedly wrote in *One World* that he was convinced the front was "more than a showplace." Behind the scenes, however, he may have been less sanguine. He knew it was set up for visitors—Henry and Clare Boothe Luce had stopped there during their worshipful tour of Nationalist China in 1941—and Cowles later said he suspected that the shooting might have been staged for their benefit. They both remembered Stilwell joking that the front was the greatest market in China, where the opposing forces traded openly across the lines. They concluded that the front was "relatively dormant." But they kept their doubts private, and Willkie's public show of belief would earn him ridicule and scorn. An American journalist recounted how he had often been shown stacks of captured guns, swords, and helmets on trips to the front. Suspicious, he had once surreptitiously scratched his initials on a helmet only to encounter it again a few months later, on a tour of a different front. Graham Peck scoffed at Willkie's credulity, saying he could have found French wine in any store in Chongqing, alongside other luxuries smuggled across the Japanese lines.[35]

Willkie was not blind to the troubles facing China, some of which he realized stemmed from the Guomindang. Stilwell's grievances had been plain enough. And one letter from an anonymous Chinese student put it bluntly: there was no democracy in China. The "masses" had "no voice whatever in the government. No freedom of speech, of press, or of association." No doubt he took these criticisms seriously, but he also downplayed the problems they revealed. He heard from semi-independent editors and economists that corruption—particularly by officials—was swelling the rampant inflation set off by the government's policy of printing money to finance the war. The inflation problem was so serious that he dedicated an entire chapter of *One World* to it. He concluded that the government needed to democratize land ownership and loosen currency controls, but he stopped short of directly blaming Chiang or the Guomindang and lapsed into hopeful bromides about their good intentions.[36]

There was one person he met who was sure to give him a jarring take on the Guomindang: Zhou Enlai. The future premier of the People's Republic of China was living in Chongqing in 1942, serving as the Communist Party representative in a short-lived governing coalition set up as a show of unity between the country's many factions. Educated in France, Zhou—"this excellent, sober, and sincere man," as Willkie would later describe him—was well practiced in charming Westerners. He spoke harshly to Willkie about the Guomindang's corrupt officials and misguided domestic policies. Their grain tax contrasted sharply with the peasant-friendly land and tax policies the communists had implemented in the northern regions they controlled. Zhou did praise his old comrade Chiang's devotion to the national ideals of Sun Yat-sen, who had led the revolution that founded the Republic of China in the 1920s. He hoped the unified front would last the war, but he could make no promises as to what might happen once the Japanese had been dispatched.

Willkie came away from the meeting with guarded optimism. He reassured himself that the communist movement was "more a national and agrarian awakening than an international or proletarian conspiracy." This view was accurate in some respects, but it downplayed the Soviet role in the rise of the Chinese communists and soft-pedaled Mao's inclination for ideological purification, which had already inspired a cruel "rectification" campaign in the north and would bring so much disaster in the years to come. Willkie indulged in delicately arranged wishful thinking about both sides, viewing the Guomindang and communists as fellow devotees of Sun squabbling over a shared nationalist and anti-imperialist heritage. A rapprochement seemed unlikely, but it was not to his mind impossible.[37]

Barnes would later write that Willkie well understood the "central weaknesses of Chiang's regime," but he chose to touch on them only lightly in his later account of his journey. Willkie noted the "centralized control of Chinese life" imposed by the Guomindang in *One World,* but he explained it in terms that Chiang himself would have favored: the Nationalists were taking China through a "tutelary stage" of political and social development on the upward path of modernization. They had to educate the masses in "new habits of living and thinking designed to make them good citizens of a complete democracy, with electoral rights, at a later time."[38]

This was an accurate reflection of the Nationalist leader's intentions—Chiang hoped to lead his country to democracy and tried from time to time to intervene in the rampant corruption in his party, but he did so with less and less success as the war ground on. Chiang was proud, diffident, and driven, and his greatest virtues were also his faults. The persistent will that sustained him in a two-decade-long quest for unification read as complacency or foolishness to outsiders, rather than wisdom drawn from a long view of history. His confidence that he alone could finally end colonial dependency and make China modern was seen as stubborn arrogance. By 1942 the country was nearly ungovernable, fractured by years of war, occupation, famine, and inflation. Several years later, as the communists surged, Chiang fretted over his fate to one of Stilwell's successors: "When I die if I am still a dictator, I will certainly go down in the oblivion of all dictators." Willkie politely described the Guomindang elite as wearers of an "old-school tie," refusing to recognize that they were less an establishment than a narrow caste of loyalists who told the generalissimo what he wanted to hear. He excused or concealed the paternalism, elitism, and exploitation that would eventually undermine the regime.[39]

Stilwell and Willkie's other American detractors had no doubt that he had fallen prey to the Nationalist propaganda machine. The endless parade of "schools and factories and girl scouts and sewing circles and arsenals," the general griped, was a regular snow job, ensuring Willkie would be "stuffed with the right doctrines." But Willkie had come to China already well stuffed with his own doctrines. Hard-pressed to shed many of the romantic assumptions Americans often carried on their actual or imagined journeys to the "Far East," he was ill prepared to receive the kind of un-official wisdom he had searched for in the Middle East and Russia, and eager to believe the best of Chiang.[40]

Willkie's complex investment in the idea of China had deep roots. The Americas were, after all, "discovered" by Europeans seeking a western route to China, and many Americans saw the two countries as inextricably linked. "We people of America," one missionary said in the late nineteenth century, "may be said, in some sense, to owe to China the discovery of our continent." The search for a northwest passage, the wagon trains and pioneers, the conquest of Native Americans, the estab-lishment of an empire in the Pacific, all the stories of progress, expan-sion, and "manifest destiny" that Wendell Willkie and others of his gen-eration had told themselves—all could be traced back to China.[41]

By the late nineteenth century, American missionaries and traders had joined Europeans in "opening" China to the global market and Western cultural influence. Some saw China as fated for partnership with the United States, believing that the American "open-door" trade policy (a pledge to keep the China market available to all the Western powers, favoring no one imperial trade network) would separate Ameri-cans from imperialist Europeans in the eyes of modernizing Chinese. Others, however, recoiled at closer relations with "Orientals," whom they saw as not far removed from Africans and other racial subordinates. The result was a complex current of fantasy and fear. Eastern exoticism and inscrutability could be a seductive threat to self-government or a re-storative source of spirituality. Either way it appeared as the extreme op-posite of the modernity, progress, and reason Westerners assumed was their gift to the world. In novels, plays, travelers' tales, and sermons of the time, venturesome, masculine Westerners carried out their civiliza-tional duties by penetrating the impassive, feminine East, taking Chris-tianity and capitalism to China while bringing silks, spices, or Buddhism home for consumption in a burgeoning mass market hungry for novelty and revitalization. Declarations of friendship, offered by well-to-do Americans with religious or financial interests in China, vied with the darker currents of racially inflected xenophobia that inspired the exclusion acts and other anti-Chinese laws. In the end, both competing tendencies dovetailed to perpetuate the stage theory of civilization underlying racist exclusion and benevolent paternalism.[42]

Racial nativism never disappeared—in fact, it prospered with the popularity of "scientific" racism and the 1924 Immigration Act—but middle- and upper-class Protestant whites, many connected to the missionary movement and with access to the press, sustained the idea that China and the United States were fatefully linked. They saw the open-door policy as evidence of American good intentions and deplored the exclusion acts. They greeted the rise of nationalism in China, and of Chiang's regime, with his American-educated wife and his conversion to Christianity under her tutelage, as evidence that the country was entering the modern age. They imagined Christian, democratic, capitalist America as a model for China, and China as the ultimate fulfillment of American ideals.[43]

By World War II this romantic narrative offered a new take on American Orientalism: the so-called China mystique, which held that China's evolution toward modernity and civilization had transformed it into a proto-America. If much American China talk was, as one critic put it, an "opportunity for striking self-adoring poses," influential figures like Pearl Buck and Henry Luce updated China's image, casting the ancient land as both needy and worthy. Raised in China as the children of Protestant missionaries, they differed in their politics, but they worked together, along with Willkie and other prominent internationalists, on the board of United China Relief (UCR), which raised money for humanitarian aid and conducted its own propaganda campaign on behalf of the Nationalists.[44]

Luce, who nursed a nostalgia for the China of his youth, took a messianic view of America's benevolent role on the world stage. Across the 1930s and 1940s, in the pages of *Time, Life,* and *Fortune,* Luce operated a de facto public relations wing of the Guomindang. He and his editors puffed up the "great Chiang" (and the "Missimo," as his magazines liked to call Madame Chiang) while treating as a fait accompli his efforts to bring Christianity, democracy, and capitalism to China. Chiang "sits like a mountain, moves like a dragon, and walks with the sure step of a tiger," one typical account in *Time* exulted, hailing the Guomindang's determination to defeat Japan and install democracy in China.[45]

In his zeal for an "American century," Luce tended to ignore his country's imperialist adventures in the Pacific and the closed door to Asian immigration. He could not conceive of the idea that many Chinese understood the open door trade policy not as a guarantee of fair play but as a free hand for American exploitation. This blindness only amplified the prevailing sentiments of his version of the mystique: China, via the Guomindang, was the beneficiary of the world-historical progress unleashed when American power strode freely across the globe.[46]

Pearl Buck was far less triumphalist than Luce—she was, by 1942, a cautious critic of the Guomindang—but no less committed to the China cause. Winner of the Nobel Prize in 1938 for her bestselling novels of Chinese life, particularly *The Good Earth* from 1931, she shaped many Americans' conceptions of China. She joined Willkie in encouraging Americans to abandon empire and racial discrimination if they hoped to win the world's favor, and she placed her faith in one-to-one connections between peoples. The goal of her work, she once said, was "to help ordinary people on one side of the world to know and understand ordinary people on the other side." She offered herself as an expert on China for Americans, and in particular on the life of rural peasants, whom she depicted not as exotic or inscrutable but as long-suffering, striving individuals comparable to beleaguered Depression-era Americans.[47]

Her sentimental portrayal of Chinese peasants as *Grapes of Wrath*–style salt-of-the-earth types had great appeal for Americans. At first the husband-and-wife heroes of *The Good Earth*, Wang Lung and O-Lan—famously played by Paul Muni and Luise Rainer in the hit 1937 Hollywood adaptation—seem to exemplify a foreign, premodern patriarchal peasant family. But in rendering a family triumphing over famine, war, and corruption, Buck sketches the couple's virtues in terms that would have been very familiar to most Americans. Their imperiled domesticity jibed with American expectations of "traditional" gender roles rooted in the ideal nuclear family. In the end it read as a fable about the fundamental qualities Americans and Chinese shared. It encouraged Americans to greet the Chinese as partners in a hoped-for new world beyond the war.[48]

One part Luce, one part Buck: that was the China mystique at work. Heroic Guomindang Christian democrats on the one hand and the steadfast, long-suffering masses on the other, persevering just as plucky Americans would do in hard times. Stilwell, Service, and Peck thought this risible, of course, but their objections would not be heard until after the war. Many more Americans imbibed the saccharine offerings of United China Relief, whose posters trumpeted "China: First to Fight!" or "China Shall Have Our Help!" over images of battered and bruised nuclear families—father, mother, and child, styled to look at once "peasant Oriental" and 1940s glamorous—suffused with the inward determination and far-seeing gazes found in propaganda posters and golden-era Hollywood movies. The images echoed *The Good Earth* and rhymed with story after story in *Time* and *Life:* China was made up of relatable families, resolute but in need of American help.[49]

"Ever since I was a little boy," Willkie said at a UCR event in 1941, "I have had a sentimental feeling about China." The millions who followed his journey and later read *One World* heard an account of China that dipped deeply from this well. "China Has Been Fighting Five Years," blared one chapter title. "What Free China Fights With," another proclaimed. Willkie's praise for the generalissimo as an "aggressive spirit" and his roll call of China's "best men"—with their Luce-ian tones of devotion—was paired with Buck-esque celebrations of "the inexhaustible human resources" of the country. "People who know China," he wrote, had alerted him to "the vitality, the resourcefulness, the courage and devotion," of the Chinese people "to their cause of freedom."[50]

Willkie found this spirit everywhere, but particularly in the nation's far west. The vast landscape unrolling beneath the *Gulliver* inspired a characteristic rhapsody, one that he shared with Chiang at a Chongqing banquet. "I came to China," he said, "not through what used to be called a 'treaty port,' but through the great and wealthy provinces to the west of here." As in Russia, Turkey, and Palestine, Willkie found modernizers wresting civilization from a recalcitrant land. "I have lived and worked in the West of America," he continued, "and I know from first-hand experience the kind of aggressive self-confidence which is developed in pioneer regions by men who are not afraid to take chances, sometimes very grave chances, in pursuit of what they believe in." The people of China's west, he wrote later, seemed "tall and resourceful, a more rugged type" than urban Chinese. They did not complain about wartime losses. "Instead, they talk big and a little boastfully and very much like the men of my father's generation in the United States." This was Willkie's version of the mystique. "The opening up of this new China," he wrote, "compares only, in modern history, with the opening up of our own West. We know the struggle of those people. We know the hope. . . . The economic aim of the leaders of modern China is to develop their country much as we developed ours." It all left him feeling that China was "not an alien country, full of strange customs, but a warm-hearted, hospitable land filled with friends of America."[51]

The most telling evidence of Willkie's immersion in the China mystique can be found in his encounter with Mayling Soong, the inimitable Madame Chiang. The generalissimo's wife was the youngest daughter of China's most famous family, one of six siblings who all held positions of great influence. Her eldest sister was married to the Nationalist finance minister, H. H. Kung. The middle sister was the widow of Sun Yat-sen, who had never forgiven Chiang for massacring rival nationalists back in 1927. Two brothers held high positions in Chinese banks; the third, T. V. Soong, was the foreign minister and Willkie's first Guomindang contact in the United States.

Mayling was the most famous of the Soongs and stood at the center of all the currents swirling around China. A Methodist Wellesley graduate and a consummate master of her own image, she was canny and manipulative, a fount of calculated charm. In the years leading up to Pearl Harbor she had shrewdly positioned herself in the American media, one of her biographers observed, as "the frail yet valiant symbol of distressed China." Behind the scenes, critics said, her haughty manner, love of power, and taste for luxury exemplified the Guomindang's corruption. In the public eye, however, she shined as a charity matron for "warphans" and a selfless crusader for a modernizing nation. The "Missimo"—part wife, part national leader—seemed to be the perfect bridge between China and America.[52]

In Western diplomatic circles she had a reputation as a seductress who knew how to disarm men with her charm. Even the acerbic Stilwell, it was said, found her beguiling. These accounts, most often crafted by men, little appreciate how perilous it was for a woman to operate at her level of influence in China. If she exploited Orientalist expectations, she also cultivated an image as a practicing Christian and proper wife. "No woman can be said to have dedicated herself to her man with the devotion of Mrs. Chiang Kai-Shek," one *Washington Post* editorial declared. And yet, the editors continued, she combined "feminine charm and understanding with the vitality and directness which are supposed to be masculine traits."[53]

She relished confounding expectations. As symbolic mother to China's orphans, she became a kind of social worker to the whole nation. As an adviser and translator for her husband, appearing at his side when he met with Allied leaders, she staked out a role in official life. In 1943 she would make a much-ballyhooed trip to the United States—encouraged by Willkie—to rally support for China. Her image neatly reconciled two Western impressions of China: the older trope of the passive East waiting for "opening" or aid, and the newer idea of China as resolute and modern, ready to meet the world. She confirmed the reigning view that China could become just like America—with the proper tutelage, of course. She was, in short, the perfect spokesperson for the US-China alliance and the embodiment of the China mystique.[54]

Willkie got a full dose of Madame Chiang the charmer. Mike Cowles remembered that they "met all three sisters during our visit, but it was Madame Chiang who most fascinated me—and Wendell." Clare Boothe Luce had given Willkie a letter of introduction to Mayling, whom she had visited in Chongqing the year before. "You are bound to hit it off magnificently," the soon-to-be Republican member of Congress from Connecticut assured her friend. She was more right than she knew.[55]

Americans following the visit in the papers sensed only a hint of the sparks that flew between the two restless and charismatic figures. Soong hailed Willkie as "a distinguished personality so wholeheartedly and essentially human that he is the very embodiment of the warmth and spontaneity which we so admire in Americans. He is a living vibrant symbol of the free nations." Chinese reporters recorded something noticeably more charged. "I think Mr. Willkie is a very disturbing personality," they heard her say. She had a pro forma speech all prepared for the occasion, but meeting him had "knocked it into a cocked hat." She would speak from the heart because her visitor was "so spontaneous, so warm-hearted, so essentially human that anything written down would not express the welcome felt in our hearts for him." Willkie responded in kind: "I accept as the quintessence of all the compliments I have ever received that I have been complimented by"—Chinese news sources rendered this last bit as "have proved disturbing to"—"such a delightful lady."[56]

Behind the scenes, gossips said, their mutual admiration went much further. Stories abounded of their disappearing from receptions or lingering privately behind closed doors. Years later Cowles would claim that Willkie had asked him to cover for him during an assignation with Madame Chiang. The two had absented themselves from a banquet, Cowles said, leaving him to confront an angry generalissimo and three of his gun-wielding bodyguards—later inflated to "sixty" in Washington gossip circles—who searched the guesthouse and found nothing. The next morning a giddy Willkie announced that he had invited Madame Chiang to fly to America with them on the *Gulliver*. Cowles, astounded at this lack of discretion, had to convince him that it would be unwise for the president's envoy to arrive home with the famous wife of Chiang Kai-shek in tow. After Willkie thought better of it, he dispatched Cowles to tell Mayling. He found her and delivered the brush-off. "Before I knew what was happening," Cowles claimed sensationally, "she reached up and scratched her long fingernails down both my cheeks so deeply that I had marks for about a week."[57]

The professional political gossip Drew Pearson would later write that Willkie had supposedly let slip to Cowles and Barnes that it was "the only time" he "had ever been in love." Mayling Soong was said to have told an American friend in the late 1950s that she had been ready to give up anything, even Chiang and China, for Willkie. But many observers concluded that Willkie was little more than a tool in her quest for influence. Frances Perkins, FDR's secretary of labor, remembered a conversation between her boss and Madame Chiang during her 1943 American visit in which Roosevelt, presumably up on his gossip, asked what she had thought of Willkie. She replied that he was "really an adolescent, after all." As the China diplomat John Paton Davies later put it,

"Little Sister" had "accomplished one of her easiest conquests." Whatever the truth behind the stories, there's no doubt that Willkie lost control of himself in Chongqing. Madame Chiang, one of his biographers remarked, "completely anesthetized his critical judgment."[58]

Still, the energy thrown off by their encounter proved useful for his unofficial mission. In the midst of their initial flirtations Madame Chiang hailed him not just as "disturbing" but as "a living and dynamic symbol of a new world society of free nations." He reciprocated, in typically exuberant fashion, by launching into a soliloquy—again reported with slight and telling variations—about how he intended to "howl and howl throughout this world" for a world in which "all nations and all peoples will be free." Carried away, no doubt, but perhaps also recognizing "howling" as the role he was most fit for, he built to a climax: "And I want to show to you that when I howl, I howl. And Madame and I are going to howl in chorus when this war is over."[59]

Later, Willkie would explain one of their disappearances from a party as a visit to Mayling's eldest sister, who was sick and could not attend. They got so lost in conversation, he said, that they forgot the time. "We talked about the revolution of ideas that is sweeping the East—a subject that came up wherever I went—of India and Nehru, of China and Chiang, of the overpowering surge toward freedom of Asia's hundreds of millions, and . . . for the right to their own governments, independent of the West." Willkie may have been in thrall to Madame Chiang and to China; he may have, as the historian Barbara Tuchman would later put it, "treated any imperfections of Chiang Kai-shek's rule with the loyal reticence required by the Allied cause and the customary idealization of China," but he was also working to inspire faith in the ideals he believed he and Mayling shared. When Stilwell remarked that he was "small fry" in Willkie's "great plan," he likely meant the 1944 presidential election. But Willkie's objective was altogether grander and more tenuous: an interdependent world free of racism and empire.[60]

Madame Chiang aside, no small degree of Willkie's exuberance stemmed from his sense that he had found his most likely partners in remaking the world. The Chinese, he was discovering, had a long history of fighting for anticolonial internationalism. Ever since the nineteenth century, Chinese nationalists had bristled at Western domination. Even Chiang had mentioned to him the most visible of the "concessions" forced on Chinese rulers by Western governments: the "treaty ports," foreign enclaves in Chinese cities where Europeans, Americans, and even Japanese doing business could live, trade, and enjoy what was called "extraterritoriality"— immunity from Chinese law. By the height of Western power in China, just before World War I, there were at least forty-eight of these hated enclaves.[61]

The treaty ports were sites of exchange and conflict, where new ideas gathered and cultures met. Many Chinese, however, resented the concessions as a source of dependency and degradation. They were well aware—from the cruel ways Europeans and Americans treated ordinary Chinese in the treaty ports, and from reports about the gathering tides of nativism and legal exclusion in America—that they were viewed as racially subordinate, unfit for full participation in the game of civilization and modernity. Repurposing ideals of democracy and equality venerated by hypocritical treaty port Westerners, they pioneered new forms of nationalism and anticolonial ferment. Years of humiliation at the hands of strangers many Chinese considered inferior fueled intense anger. The essayist Yang Yibo, writing about life in the most famous of the trade zones, voiced these frustrations in florid and vivid terms: "I hope to utterly destroy this old Shanghai, to smash asunder this oriental bastion of imperialist domination, to inter forever those golden dreams of bloodsucking vampires."[62]

In Paris in 1919, Chinese attempts to abrogate the treaties and end extraterritoriality had proved futile. Like other anticolonial nationalists, petitioners from Beijing found that Woodrow Wilson honored their demands only in the breach. A few years later, when Sun and Chiang set out to unify the nation, they remembered the slights of 1919 and made full sovereignty their goal. "Wilson's proposals," Sun declared, "once set forth, could not be recalled." Like others around the globe, the Chinese "saw how completely they had been deceived by the Great Powers' advocacy of self-determination and began independently and separately to carry out the principle of 'self-determination of peoples.'"[63]

Brutal, corrupt, hypocritical: Chiang, the Soongs, and the Guomindang were certainly that. But they also sought a sovereignty rooted in the end of racial imperialism and a new international system of cooperation between nations large and small. This sovereignty had been partially achieved in the late 1920s, with initial agreements to end extraterritoriality. These promises were left in limbo by the Japanese invasion, but the Guomindang hoped to emerge from the war with full independence. Not long before Willkie arrived, the generalissimo and Madame Chiang had returned from a trip to restive, freedom-minded India. Much to the chagrin of the British, they had met with Gandhi and Jawaharlal Nehru to discuss the war, their nationalist movements, and a future internationalist society.[64]

Willkie knew something about this history. He had been following the rise of anticolonial nationalism all along his route. Unlike most Allied officials—who treated the Chinese as second-class allies and tended to ignore or downplay their demands for freedom—Willkie recognized the Chinese as partners whose anti-imperialist credentials could give the war effort true worldwide appeal. The pointed reference to the treaty ports in his first speech in Chongqing suggested that he hoped to be a new kind of American—one who would greet the Chinese not as peons or exotics but as fellow climbers on the ladder of progress. Further travel in China convinced him the country was the most fruitful prospect yet for the new international society he'd first glimpsed back in Turkey. And everywhere he went, Chinese nationalists—whether officially affiliated with the Guomindang or not—expressed their hope that his visit could help break the strictures of race and empire.

Chiang pressed Willkie on extraterritoriality, hoping he might help them shed the unequal treaties. The major independent Chinese daily, *Ta Kung Pao,* welcomed him as a champion of racial equality, hailing the NAACP talk he had given earlier that year. "He said in that speech: 'The day is gone when men and women of whatever color or creed can consider themselves as superior to those of other creeds and colors. The day of vast empire is past. The day of equal peoples is at hand.'" Now, the paper argued, America needed to follow Willkie's lead. The nation had to renew the commitment to internationalism squandered by Wilson, update it with a commitment to racial equality, and make good on the promises of the Atlantic Charter.[65]

Throughout the visit, Chinese editors and other commentators picked up on these themes, following Willkie's comings and goings with a steady stream of public conversation. A Catholic newspaper, *Yi Shih Pao,* declared Willkie had suggested that in a true democracy the "color line" could not be the fundamental political dividing line. This principle was the "most fundamental basis for reconstructing international peace." A group of Chinese professors, writing directly to Willkie, echoed this view and presented a picture of the world situation that questioned the usual racialized story of "civilization." "The different races and nations of the present-day world," they wrote, "have become interdependent politically, economically as well as culturally, and have constituted a great society with their manifold interests closely interwoven. This is the natural consequence of the development of civilization." The way forward, they said, required doing away with "racial superiority" and instituting "cooperation and liberty" for "world peace on a permanent basis" in accordance with the "Atlantic Charter proclaimed by President Roosevelt."[66]

In *One World* Willkie would say that the gesture that had touched him the most in China was an earnest letter he received from a Kunming student named Wong Pong Hai. The letter laid out a homegrown plan for world fellowship: "every country may freely adopt her own political system"; "all small nations ought to be independent"; a new league of nations open to all peoples. But Wong also issued a polite challenge. He remembered the last Western promises of a remade world. "I hope this time," he wrote, "the Atlantic Carta [*sic*] will not be Wilson's fourteen points." The point was politely made but clear. A repeat of the old, flawed peace would not suffice.[67]

A consortium of "people's organizations" in Xi'an put it more emphatically. They too recalled Wilson's failure. Now their hopes turned on the Atlantic Charter, which, they argued, had "become a world charter, or the charter of humanity." But would it suffer the same fate as Wilson's Fourteen Points? "The question at present," they declared, "lies not in the validity of the Charter but in the fulfillment of the terms of the signers." The raw materials of a just peace were there. But if the charter was not "thoroughly enforced, the reconstruction of a new world order will never be realized and the possibility of third world war is unavoidable."[68]

Remaking the world would require squaring the pull of national feeling with the hope for international organization. This quandary had long dogged internationalists, and it would bedevil Willkie, too. Both the Guomindang and their rivals reassured him, as the left-leaning *New Szechwan Daily* put it in an editorial welcoming Willkie, that "Chinese nationalism is, in short, international nationalism." The war had given the old dreams new legs. Even if the Chinese were treated as a second-class member of the Allies—in fact, *because* they were treated as a second-class member of the Allies—they understood what Willkie had long believed: the war had to be more than just a victory of arms. In a speech for United China Relief, T. V. Soong claimed the Guomindang fought not for nationalist glory but "to uphold the new world of justice and freedom." Back in 1919 the Allies had failed to plan for the peace during the war. But now, with Allied cooperation a fact—Soong sugar-coated the divisions behind the scenes—there was an opportunity to "form our international society while we are still fighting the war."[69]

Even institutions steeped in the China mystique saw Chinese-American wartime cooperation in the spirit of anticolonial internationalism. The Chinese-American Institute of Cultural Relations, an organization set up to promote China's interests in the United States, whose top officers were Madame Chiang and the notoriously corrupt finance minister H. H. Kung, sent Willkie a letter during his visit. Along with typical calls for upping American airpower in China and making the China front equal to the European front, their memo concluded with the widest possible conception of the war: America and China would cooperate in "rebuilding a new and better world order in which every people, irrespective of color, race, or religion, shall enjoy equal freedom to develop its national life according to its cultural pattern and in which no war for predatory conquest shall ever be allowed to happen again to the civilized world."[70]

American skeptics discounted much of this talk as Guomindang window dressing and little more than empty and cynical idealism calculated to boost support among influential Americans. For these critics, Nationalist propaganda about world cooperation reflected only the elite cosmopolitan internationalism of Chinese elites. This was true: almost all of this conversation happened within a small sliver of Chinese society. Whatever their true interest in equality and democracy, they could not claim to truly represent their fellow citizens, most of whom were impoverished and disenfranchised.

And yet, as Willkie traveled around listening to Chinese concerns, he could see how issues most Westerners found parochial or tendentious were quite immediate for many Chinese. He became convinced that they had a firm handle on the vision he had been chasing most of his life, echoes of which he had heard from Cairo and Ankara to Baghdad and Tehran. In fact, he found their belief in a real peace so persuasive, and their fears that the Atlantic Charter would prove hollow so galvanizing, that he revised some of his own long-held assumptions. As early as his stop in Chengdu, he pondered the legacy of his old internationalist hero. America's failure to support the League of Nations was a great tragedy, but perhaps a blessing in disguise. "Even if the ideals of Woodrow Wilson and the world that he visualized had been realized," he said in a rare critique of his childhood idol, "that would not have been enough." They would have failed anyway, he said, because they "included too many old shibboleths of imperialism, colonies, mandates and such by which one nation tries to rule another."[71]

Wilson had failed to establish peace, Willkie decided, because he overlooked two key problems: "economic collaboration and the Far Eastern racial question." From here on out he intended to make the "high ideals" of "economic collaboration and racial equality"—at home and abroad—a "religious faith." The whole point of his trip, he told a crowd of 1,200 gathered in Chongqing, was to help "build a new world order where every people will have the right to determine their own social and political systems and live in a world of freedom and justice regardless of their race, creed, or color." The Chinese, witnesses said, erupted in "thundering applause."[72]

Willkie decided to cap off his visit to China with a major speech on the war and the world to come—the sort of "howl" he had promised Madame Chiang. Delivered to the press on October 7 in Chongqing, just before his trip to the front and subsequent departure, it was broadcast live and reproduced in full in papers around the world. In this improvised attempt to make his two missions one, he heeded Roosevelt's call to rally the reticent, but also pushed for an expansive view of the war. Drawing on all he'd seen across "thirteen countries," in "kingdoms, soviets, republics, mandated areas, colonies, and dependencies," he said that the conflict was "not simply a technical problem for task forces" but "also a war for men's minds." True worldwide commitment to the Allied cause would only come when the hopes of the millions in those thirteen countries were heard.[73]

Willkie announced that he had found four truths everywhere he went. The first two were simple. People everywhere wanted the Allies to win the war and to "get on the offensive now." There had been a lot of big talk, from Allied leaders and from Willkie himself, about the power of American industrial production, but comparatively little material contribution. China and Russia were bleeding heavily—suffering by some estimates 5 million casualties so far—but seeing little in the way of US aid. They wondered, as Willkie put it, "how much longer they will have to eat, like children, at the second table." Willkie himself believed that the time was ripe for "an all-out armed offensive everywhere by all United Nations." But he admitted that even his extravagant assurances— including the second-front bravado—would prove cheap without a basic understanding of what the war meant in all the countries he had visited.

If the Allies wanted to win the "active, aggressive, offensive spirit of nearly three-fourths of the people of the world who live in South America, Africa, Eastern Europe and Asia," Willkie asserted, they needed to recognize two other truths. First, people wanted to "live in liberty and independence." Second, they doubted "the readiness of the leading democracies of the world to stand up and be counted upon for the freedom of others after the war is over." Such doubts, magnified by the relative trickle of US aid, prevented "their enthusiastic participation on our side." In Asia, for instance, where "freedom and opportunity are the words which have modern magic," even the name of the Atlantic Charter troubled "thoughtful men and women." Did "all those who signed it, these people ask, agree that it applies to the Pacific?"

Allied leaders needed to "make a clear and simple statement" of support for global freedom. The "war must mean an end to the empire of nations over other nations," he continued. "No foot of Chinese soil, for example, should be or can be ruled from now on except by the people who live in it." But the Allies had to back it up with concrete plans, too. There had to be "firm timetables" and "ironclad agreements" among all the Allies to help colonial peoples who joined their cause to "work out and train governments of their own choosing" so they could "become free and independent nations." Not all peoples wanted "democracy handed to them next Tuesday on a silver platter," he conceded. "But they are all determined to work out their own destiny under governments selected by themselves."

This effort had to begin now, during the war. Those who said such "subjects should be hushed until victory is won" would repeat the Wilsonian failures his Chinese friends had never forgotten. Only "sincere efforts to find progressive solutions now" could win the confidence of unsure nations and boost the Allied cause. Roosevelt and other American officials seemed to think that if Willkie simply reassured nervous small nations that American power would win the war, they would rally to the flag. Willkie's retort—carefully couched as a discovery, not a rebuke of the president—was that it was the other way around: the small nations would only join up if they saw it as their war, too. Americans had to accept that for many around the world the war was only worth fighting if it actually secured the freedoms Americans claimed to champion. Willkie's two missions had merged: rallying global support meant redefining the war as a fight for global freedom. True victory meant freedom not only from fascism but also from empire.

Besides, Willkie argued in closing, Americans would prosper in a more free and open world. With "trade routes strong enough to give all people the same vested interest in peace which we in America have had," the "individual freedom and economic liberty" of his own country would be guaranteed by guarding the freedoms of others. This argument may have rung false to some Filipinos or Hawaiians, or the Puerto Rican cane laborer whose maiming Willkie had witnessed all those years before. But Willkie hoped a just postwar settlement would make Americans more interdependent with the fates of others around the world and help truly realize American ideals. "The way to make certain that we do recover our traditional American way of life with a rising standard of living for all," he concluded, "is to create a world in which all men everywhere can be free."

The Chongqing speech was suggestive rather than definitive, thrown together on the fly to answer the gathering urgency he felt. It touched only lightly on knotty topics like global trade, and left others—the problem of race in particular—unmentioned. But the speech was his boldest declaration yet of an anti-imperialist internationalism. As he flew for home he felt he was leaving China transformed. He was not only infatuated by the country and its leaders but thrilled by how China provided him fresh understanding of the war's meaning and new inspiration for the work of urging Americans to see and feel all he had learned across the arc of his journey.

CHAPTER 10

A Report to the People

Yakutsk, Washington, New York

O N NOVEMBER 10, 1942, Winston Churchill made his way east from 10 Downing Street to the City of London, winding through streets lined with cheering crowds. He was heading to Mansion House, the residence of the mayor, for the annual Lord Mayor's Day luncheon, where the prime minister by tradition delivered a speech on foreign affairs. Taking the dais, Churchill exulted in the recent war news from North Africa. In late October, the British had launched a successful offensive at El Alamein, and just two days earlier the Operation Torch landings had gotten under way. With Rommel all but defeated in Egypt, and American and British troops preparing to sweep east from the beaches of Morocco and Algeria, the prime minister could hail an Allied victory in Africa to match the tide-turning battles at Midway and Guadalcanal in the Pacific. "Now, this is not the end," he warned. "It is not even the beginning of the end. But it is, perhaps, the end of the beginning."

Those are the remarks most often remembered from the Mansion House address. With their hopeful, rolling tenor, they stand in the pantheon of steely Churchillian phrasemaking somewhere just beneath "we shall fight on the beaches" after Dunkirk or the grim image of an "Iron Curtain" descending across Europe from "Stettin in the Baltic to Trieste in the Adriatic." Less remembered today is a passage that touched off an immediate uproar in the fall of 1942. After surveying the state of the battle and pledging himself to Roosevelt as an "ardent lieutenant" in the Torch invasion, the PM turned to general war aims. The British, he said, fought with "no acquisitive appetite or ambitions" for territory. "We have not entered this war for profit or expansion, but only for honor and to do our duty in defending the right." All of a sudden, however, Churchill swerved from noblesse oblige into defiance. "Let me, however, make this clear, in case there should be any mistake about it in any quarter. We mean to hold our own," he declared to spirited cheers from the floor. "I have not become the King's First Minister in order to preside over the liquidation of the British Empire."[1]

Churchill's frustration arose, in part, from the insistent gibes of his erstwhile friend Wendell Willkie. In the month since the *Gulliver* had made its way back to Washington, carrying its chief cargo to a summit with President Roosevelt, Willkie had been showered with both acclaim and condemnation. His calls for a second front and his speech at Chongqing had unleashed a tumultuous debate that would engulf both Roosevelt and Churchill, leaving him as their rival rather than the ally he had been in the dark days of the Blitz and Lend-Lease. Churchill's defense of imperial privilege capped several weeks in which Willkie had filled the airwaves and newspapers, reporting on his trip and jousting with his critics. He opened up a new front all by himself—a battle of ideas over the postwar world. He was solidifying his role as a spokesman for a new vision of the war and the world, but he was also delivering a message, he would say, from "the peoples of the East," whose war was too often ignored. The Allies needed to think about winning the peace now, and for much of the planet that meant bringing an end to imperialism.

The PM's Mansion House speech aimed to quell the criticism of Britain's war aims ginned up by Willkie's voyage. Instead Churchill only amplified the American's message. At a moment when people all over the world were looking to the Allies in hope, he reasserted the right of one people to rule over others for their own good. Britain, he announced, fought for the glory and sustenance of the empire. It had no desire to give up its overseas possessions to satisfy the dreams of freedom of peoples unfit for self-rule, or the wooly ideas of an irresponsible American. The PM's intransigence fueled Willkie's cause. The coming months would witness his greatest turn on the world stage, as he tried to push the United States away from "narrow nationalism" and exclusive imperialism toward a more unified and interrelated world.

The last days of the trip had unfolded in a rush. The *Gulliver* had left China on October 9, swinging northwest to avoid Japanese fighters. Then it had banked northeast again, passing over Mongolia and on into Siberia, landing at Chita, Yakutsk, and then Seymchan, following air routes that were never taken by civilian aircraft over miles of snow and pines. They stopped only to refuel, sleep, and greet Soviet officials deep in the Russian hinterland. Willkie marveled again at the likeness between the Soviet Union and the American frontier of his youth. Yakutsk, near the Arctic Circle, reminded him of "a western town in [America] a generation ago," he later wrote. The pavements were boardwalks, like those of Elwood when he was a boy. The houses could have been in Minnesota or Wisconsin, with a "neat, buttoned-up look . . . with light from the windows and soft smoke coming from the chimneys." It was all, he thought, like "our own early and expanding days—especially the hearty, simple tastes, the not too subtle attitudes of mind, the tremendous vitality."[2]

He was particularly impressed by the head communist official in Yakutsk, a short, stout, energetic man called Muratov who showed him the town library and museum and squired him to a performance of a "gypsy opera." Muratov oversaw the type of bold modernization Willkie favored, building roads and railways that would open the Soviet interior to the world. Yakutsk was still dependent on river barges—and even reindeer-driven sleigh—but Muratov was eager for the commercial boom that surely awaited after the war. He assured Willkie that he would barter Siberian wood pulp for American machinery. "We're not so far away from you," Willkie recalled him saying. "Come and get it; we'll be glad to swap." Much like the bright young man of the Stormovik plant, Muratov struck Willkie as a Soviet version of the self-made man, a capable conduit for the energy he felt in the cold Siberian air. Muratov was "a man who would do well in America." He talked economic development "like a California real-estate salesman."[3]

At the same time, Willkie and his crew realized that many people they met were unwilling Siberians, exiles from the Soviet experiment, sentenced to the frigid east for crimes against the state, real or invented. Still, Captain Kight reported, it seemed like some spoke more freely than people back in Moscow. Willkie met a rueful Polish waitress who "poured into my ear an account of the Soviet system which hardly accorded with official propaganda."[4]

At Seymchan the travelers rose well before dawn for the long pull over the last of Siberia, across the Bering Sea, and into Alaska. In the early morning gloom great bonfires illuminated the dim runway and the surrounding forest. A red lantern hanging from a tower beyond the edge of the field gave Kight a marker to clear. Once aloft, they found storms glowering to the north beyond the Arctic Circle and south over the Aleutian Islands. Kight cut between them and then angled south to avoid the chop, skipping Nome and landing at Fairbanks instead. From there they went on to Edmonton in Canada, and then Minneapolis, where they said goodbye to Mike Cowles.

Forty-nine days and more than 28,000 miles of near-constant smooth skies and clear visibility: Kight and Klotz couldn't believe their luck. Even when the forecast had called for trouble, the clouds had seemed to part before them. They had taken to calling it "*Gulliver* weather." The spell wasn't broken until the very last day, en route to Washington. The initial plan was to head from Minneapolis home to New York, but an invite from the White House changed the plan. Somewhere near Cleveland they found themselves in dense clouds and rain, flying on instruments toward the capital. The control tower at National Airport told Kight he would come out of the cloud curtain at 800 feet, but on approach he was in the murk for much longer, leading to a tense few minutes until they broke into the clear 400 feet above the airport and landed safely. Willkie—shaggy-maned and ten pounds lighter than when he had set off—hopped down, declared himself "damn glad to get back," and hurried off to meet the president.[5]

Over the previous week Willkie had been out of contact with the world. As he flew, papers across the country carried accounts of his Chongqing address and his supporters and enemies squared off in the editorial pages and on the airwaves. The speech was kicking up the kind of turbulence Willkie had come to relish, pushing long-suppressed issues to the front of public conversation. Forgotten now, it was in its time heralded as a landmark event.

A number of journalists and editors with internationalist leanings greeted the address as a refreshing disruption of the status quo. Willkie's allies at *Life* welcomed it as "one of the most important statements on the war that anybody has made." The *Christian Science Monitor* called Willkie's take on empire the "most advanced position yet taken by a responsible spokesman for American public opinion." Public figures like Sumner Welles had announced the coming end of imperialism, the paper noted, but none had urged upon Americans the duty to see it destroyed. "Millions of Americans" would embrace that cause, the paper argued. The Cowles-owned *Minneapolis Morning Tribune* predicted that the speech would be discussed from New Delhi to Ankara to Lisbon, and hailed Willkie's "militant idealism." The editors hoped that Americans would soon "convince the peoples of Asia that the Atlantic Charter is in fact of worldwide scope, and in no sense limited to a single ocean."[6]

Critics weighed in, too, attacking him for sowing discord. Congressman John Rankin of Mississippi took to the House floor to denounce the traveler. "Mr. Marco Polo Willkie has already caused more embarrassment to the Allies than any man abroad," he lamented. The *Chicago Tribune* argued that Willkie had made a fool of himself by unnecessarily provoking Churchill. "They Can Keep Him," the paper's editorial sneered in its headline, and went on to joke that "the ebullient Willkie has put political baby kissing on an export basis." The New York *Daily News* wondered if he was aiming for the 1944 Republican nomination "on a platform of anti-Britishism, free trade, and Communism." He would make the United States the "world patsy," the tabloid charged, ending tariffs and immigration restrictions in a bid to "buy happiness for the world even if we pauperize ourselves."[7]

Surprisingly, the speech won kudos from progressives traditionally inclined to distrust the former corporation lawyer. The left-leaning *Dallas Morning News* hailed Willkie's "unvarnished wisdom" and his plea for a "Pacific Charter," arguing that "Asiatics" would fight, but not if it meant "a shift from one master to another." Next to the editorial the paper ran a cartoon of Willkie accepting congratulations from thankful Russians, Indians, and Chinese. The performer and progressive activist Paul Robeson, writing in the *New Masses,* argued that "no more patriotic speech has been made in this war."[8]

It had been some time since simply going around the world warranted much notice. But Willkie's journey supplied the public with some breakthroughs to catalogue. The *Gulliver* had made the first passenger circumnavigation of the world via the North Pacific; it was the first plane to go from China to the United States via Alaska, the first American plane to fly over the Gobi Desert and Mongolia, the first American plane to go through Siberia during the war, and the first American plane ever to enter China from Russia over the western backcountry. But the mounting excitement had little to do with the mere facts of the flight. The press was sure something of momentous geopolitical significance was afoot. Clearly Willkie had done more than put some "pep" in the step of the Allies, even if the trip's wider significance was not yet clear. "In seven and one-half weeks Wendell Willkie had seen the war as no other private citizen had ever seen it," *Time* magazine ventured, "perhaps more of it than even Winston Churchill has seen so far." *New York Times* publisher Arthur Hays Sulzberger, trying to sum up the impact, mused, "There have been statesmen who have met as many interesting people before, and there have been explorers who have traveled that far before, and there have been aviators who have flown that fast before, but I don't know whenever before in history so much has been packed over such a large space into such a short period of time."[9]

Initial assessments drew parallels to famous journeys, literary and actual. "If it has the proper effect," the *Monitor* argued, "Mr. Willkie's trip may turn out to be more important than Phileas Fogg's and Marco Polo's put together." Estimations of that "proper effect" were necessarily tentative but sweeping, in keeping with the references to Jules Verne's hero and the fabled spice route traveler. In his weekly radio address, the reporter Raymond Clapper allowed that Willkie's trip was "not exactly a second front." But the "sympathy and encouragement" the traveler gave to unsure allies in Moscow and China had more than symbolic value. Having seen the war close up, his "free-hand needling" brought the ideals of the Atlantic Charter and the Four Freedoms closer to realization. The *New York Times* argued that the world tour marked a subtle but critical shift in outlook that doomed the isolationist tradition. "The world is our business now," the paper declared, and it was Willkie's vision of an interrelated globe, where "Indiana's soil will remain free if Africa's, Turkey's, Russia's, China's does," that counted now. "The earth moves altogether, toward freedom, or away from it."[10]

In the *New York Post* Samuel Grafton hailed the trip as "a turning point in the war" and claimed that Willkie had "made himself a world figure in three weeks." Out there "on the road" he had "met the democratic upsurge" and recognized it. That made him powerful, but in a curious way. "History may call him the first United Nations statesman; a man without power in any country, who has suddenly developed enormous power in all free countries."[11]

The attention returned Willkie to the spotlight he'd enjoyed during the 1940 campaign. He was the central character in his own drama again, his outsize personality once more blurring the lines between politics and celebrity. As the reports and letters marveling at his winning style multiplied, a minor "Hoosier abroad" genre emerged. "There is something about a Hoosier," the *New Yorker* joked, commenting on the kisses Willkie delivered around the world, "even a Hoosier with a Fifth Avenue address, that makes him go what they call hawg-wild when he gets abroad. All the rough poetry and romance of the man come to the surface." Willkie had left on his journey "rather quietly," one columnist joked. But "with each stop of his magic carpet . . . he got noisier and noisier. Finally you could hear him on quiet nights from as far off as Moscow and Chungking."[12]

Clearly, Willkie's foreign affairs adviser Raymond Buell wrote to him, the tour had "caught the imagination" of the American people. But here, too, people were divided—and they weighed in directly to say so. Mrs. J. D. Gardner of Waco, Texas, told the Dallas paper that she thought Willkie had displayed too little tact. She wondered if he'd be welcomed home "with a band or a switch for talking out of turn." Lars Halstad wrote to the *Chicago Tribune* to protest that Willkie "would be the chief comic of his age were the moment not so tragic."[13]

Some of the clamor stemmed from continuing confusion about his role. There seemed to be two Willkies, the *New York Times* said, "the President's Mr. Willkie" and "Mr. Willkie's Mr. Willkie." The trip's success seemed to turn on the success of the second persona. Despite the occasional "heedless" word, Willkie still managed to reflect "the best of American character in his friendliness, his instinct for justice, and the unfeigned warmth of his emotions."[14]

A host of letters confirmed this impression. Mabel Wyeth of Hanover, New Hampshire, wrote to the *New York Herald Tribune* to compare Willkie to Benjamin Franklin. Both spoke to peoples abroad with "the authentic voice of unofficial America." Willkie had replaced Franklin's "coat and high fur cap" with an "old blue suit worn for occasions both formal and informal," but she saw this garb as the proper package for "Mr. Willkie's Hoosier heartiness." And Frank Fowler, of Columbus, Ohio, writing to Willkie himself, judged the trip "the greatest thing that has happened . . . since the war began." The country needed "another Lincoln," he went on, "and I believe you are the man of destiny."[15]

His "simple, impulsive Middle Western ways and speech," *Times* political correspondent Arthur Krock reported, "were ideal equipment for the journey." He should be seen as a "bearer of good-will," the paper suggested, not a professional diplomat. Everywhere Willkie went, the *Times* commented in an editorial called "When Indiana Goes Visiting," his "ease of manner, his un-feigned friendliness" testified to his uncanny ability to connect with the ordinary and the exalted alike. "He swaps data about raising hogs with the managers of a Russian state farm. He kisses a Russian ballerina. He yanks a smile from the serious Joseph Stalin. He hops out of his plane at Chungking, takes a long flight of steps two at a time and beams on the 'man on the street'—as he himself calls him." With a "heart half as big as the State of Indiana," Willkie seemed to embody midwestern openness. His plain, avuncular spirit invited reciprocity: he "likes people and likes having them like him—as they do."[16]

Taken as a whole, these accounts conveyed the sense that Willkie was becoming more than a politician. The "enormous power" Samuel Grafton had watched him suddenly accumulate "in all free countries" suggested a new kind of role. Already a quasi-celebrity, he was on his way to becoming the lodestar around which hopes and fears about internationalism would gather and a model for Americans looking to seek equal relations with the world at large in the coming years. Beyond well-known advocates like Henry Luce, Sumner Welles, Pearl Buck, Eleanor Roosevelt, and Henry Wallace stood a jumble of mainstream organizations dedicated to organizing a new postwar world order. With names like the Commission to Study the Organization of Peace, the Commission on a Just and Durable Peace, Citizens Council for the United Nations, the Non-Partisan Council to Win the Peace, the Women's Committee for Victory and Lasting Peace, and the Christian Mission on World Order, the movement was fervent but inchoate.

This blizzard of commissions and committees folded together Wilsonians and feminist peace advocates with world government planners, balance-of-power realists, and backers of Anglo-American unity. Organizations started and closed, merged, quarreled and reconciled, changed names, and swapped staff. Urgency made for strange bedfellows, bridging divides of right and left that would loom much larger in the future. The members of the Commission to Study the Organization of Peace, for instance, included Wilsonian liberals like James Shotwell and Clark Eichelberger as well as the left-leaning Asia scholar Owen Lattimore, the Popular Front writer Max Lerner, and the arch Protestant and future cold warrior John Foster Dulles. Wartime possibility lent the movement an air of heady collegiality, but the good feelings would be short lived.[17]

These peace-planning advocates shared a sensibility born of a common class background. Largely white and Protestant, the mainstream movement was made up of professionals from the coasts and big cities working in the fields of social work, academia, the law, and the elite banking and business communities. They sometimes shared the anti-imperial and antiracist convictions of their African American allies, but held little appeal for workers. Churchy and prim, ready with high-toned lectures on proper parliamentary procedure, they were influential but not broadly popular.[18]

Yet they appeared to be having an effect. The proliferation of local and national chapters, speaking tours and letter campaigns to Congress, and innumerable meetings and publications had laid down a substrate of favorable feeling for the cause. According to polls, Americans appeared ready to embrace their views. Since Pearl Harbor, support for internationalist ideas had spiked. In May 1941, a Gallup poll asked whether Americans should join a renewed League of Nations after the war; at that time, 38 percent approved and 39 percent objected. By the middle of 1942, however, "a profound change in viewpoint on international affairs" was under way, George Gallup reported. Now 59 percent chose yes and only 22 percent no. Another poll, conducted by a national opinion research organization, asked if the United States should join "a union of nations" after the war, and found 72 percent in favor and 15 percent opposed.[19]

Closer examination left this profound shift looking tenuous—or at least unformed. Only 34 percent of respondents to a June 1942 *Fortune* poll preferred participation in a "league or association" of nations after the war. A majority wanted to postpone any peace planning until the fighting was done. There was a buzz around internationalism and world cooperation, but as an expected formality to follow the conflict, not a practical endeavor to embark on now. "Everybody" one met in America, the Turkish writer Ahmed Emin Yalman said of the journalists and officials he had come across on a journey through the States that fall, while Willkie visited his country, "agreed that the future would require a new structure of world relationships, but actual steps towards it seemed to be clear to almost no one."[20]

People seemed unsure whether they favored unilateralist nationalism or multilateralist interdependence. Pollsters at Princeton University discovered that 59 percent of respondents said they had "given thought" to the role the United States should take in the postwar world (26 percent had not, 14 percent skipped the question, and 1 percent weren't sure). When asked what part the nation should play, 25 percent of those who had "given thought" selected the Luce-ian "American Century; United States take leading part; run the world our way." Another 4 percent selected "Prepare for and guard against next war; police world; strong army and navy." However, 19 percent chose "Active participation; vague phrases; partnership; United Nations," and another 5 percent went with "Advisory; promulgate democratic ideals; four freedoms," while 2 percent selected "Propose an international conference for peace." Only 2 percent chose "Stay out of world affairs, mind our own business." Old-school isolationism had lost its appeal, but a split re-mained: 29 percent leaned toward unilateralism and 26 percent favored a more interdependent direction.[21]

The survey's own use of the term "vague phrases" suggested the un-settled, up-for-grabs nature of internationalist opinion. There was a great deal of activity and wide support for expansive internationalism among politically active women, African Americans, and those on the left. But on the whole, for most Americans in 1942, it was still, as the historian Robert Divine has argued, "an incoherent movement, split into too many com-peting units" that had not taken full advantage of a receptive climate.[22]

Before his trip Willkie had been among the elite internationalists, but not of them. Many of them no doubt voted for him, forming a solid element of his electoral base, and he could speak their technical language to push the Republican Party his way. "When the war is over," went a pledge he asked party members to sign in August 1942, just before he left on his trip, "we must set up institutions of international political and eco-nomic cooperation and adjustment among the nations of the earth" and "devise some system of joint international force." His activity had little effect on the old guard of prewar nationalists, but it contributed to a big jump in internationalist support among rank-and-file Republicans—only 23 percent had favored the League of Nations in 1937, while 70 percent backed US membership in a postwar organization in the summer of 1942. Meanwhile, he had his eye on driving public opinion at large.[23]

Less a joiner than a one-man show, he felt the internationalist cause did not need another committee or petition drive. There would be cause for parliamentary models in time, but at the moment a flesh-and-blood symbol of connective energy was wanted, someone to embody the spirit of the undertaking and bring the abstract debates home for all Ameri-cans. Willkie did not hesitate to volunteer for this role—and stake out his own position. More expansive and idealistic than the nationalistic Luce, less enamored of state planning than Wallace, and more democratic than the aristocratic Welles or the elite committees, Willkie was second only to the two Roosevelts, Franklin and Eleanor, as a popular *and* influen-tial advocate for internationalism. Yet his internationalism was not just a promise but also a challenge to Americans. Looking to make his quasi-celebrity status work on behalf of the world-altering energies he had witnessed abroad, he hoped to jump-start the home front leg of his unofficial mission.

In fact, that mission already seemed to be bearing fruit. Two days after the Chongqing speech, American and British diplomats issued a joint communiqué. The two nations would end all claims to extraterritorial rights in China. This was huge news in Asia. The Nationalists celebrated it as the final achievement of Sun Yat-sen's revolution and as China's full arrival as an independent nation on the world stage. "The satisfaction," Chiang Kai-shek exclaimed, "is indescribable." Though many Westerners never even heard about the announcement or, if they did, underappreciated its significance, observers around the world did not fail to notice that the announcement came on the heels of Willkie's speech. In truth, preparations for this decision had been under way for some time in London and Washington, with debates about terms and timing going back months. Still, in the eyes of many, Willkie shared some small degree of the credit with those who had been agitating for years.[24]

Wherever one looked, the Chongqing speech was unleashing a flood of anti-imperial sentiment. On October 12, as the *Gulliver* made for Fairbanks, the editors of *Life* magazine published an "open letter" to "the people of England." Playing off themes Willkie had been developing for months, the magazine invited its allies to join in a fight for something bigger than simply survival. Americans, the editors announced, were dedicated to principles—particularly the principle of freedom. The United States had yet to dedicate its own war effort to any such high principles, but *Life* declared itself "not convinced" that Britain "would fight for them, even if they were defined." Of course, "one thing we are sure we are *not* fighting for is to hold the British Empire together. . . . If your strategists are planning a war to hold the British Empire together they will sooner or later find themselves strategizing all alone." *Life* congratulated the United States for principles it had not yet fully committed to, revealing that the magazine's anti-imperialism was rooted in the very narrow nationalist outlook that Willkie hoped to challenge. Still, the demand that the British quit fighting for colonial privilege revealed that the problem of empire had made its way to the center of wartime debates.[25]

Willkie heard little of this commotion as he flew home. In part, he was distracted by tensions with President Roosevelt. He had been stewing for more than a week, ever since the president had called his second-front statements "purely speculative." The slight still rankled. In Edmonton, when asked about the president's remarks, he said it would be in bad taste to reply "to flippant statements made by certain public officials" while he was still out of the country. Roosevelt, wanting to prevent renewed misunderstanding and dissuade Willkie from further inflammatory public statements, got a message to him in Minneapolis with the offer of an immediate meeting. Willkie was worn out and looking forward to getting home to New York, but he felt he couldn't refuse what amounted to an order from the president.[26]

There is no official record of their meeting on October 14. All that remains is a draft of Willkie's notes for the conversation. Later accounts had Willkie raising his voice with the president—dressing him down and challenging Roosevelt to "throw him out" if he wouldn't listen to what he had to say. Another story, relayed by the diplomat Dean Acheson, suggested that FDR had been planning to offer Willkie the post of secretary of state, to replace the ailing Cordell Hull, but reconsidered after a quarrelsome meeting. Both were likely embellished. Willkie's notes never mention the second-front contretemps explicitly, but he did consider a strongly worded rebuke—labeled "possible, but questionable" in his notes—in which he would remind the president that he had kept his promise to uphold a united front while abroad: "I think I should tell you, frankly and bluntly, that during the entire period of my trip, I uttered no single sentence of criticism of you or your policies."[27]

The majority of their talk would have covered practical matters. Willkie had a laundry list of items to go over, including accounts of his meetings in the Middle East; the need for food and other aid in Turkey, Iraq, and Iran; Stalin's specific requests for stepped-up flows of Lend-Lease matériel; an endorsement, despite "difference of opinion among competent experts," of Chennault's expanded airpower plan; and—although this was labeled "questionable"—a condemnation of the "wholly deplorable" work of his nemeses in China and the Soviet Union, Ambassadors Gauss and Standley, as well as Minister Dreyfus in Iran.[28]

Turning to geopolitical questions, Willkie hoped to give the president a taste of the dilemmas facing Americans. In Chongqing, he planned to say, he had been "speaking for very large numbers of Americans and in complete consistency with my special mission for you" in China. He wanted to ask the president to "cooperate in an effort to make the trip a symbol of national unity on the war." He worried, however, that FDR did not fully appreciate the political situation in China and the Middle East. British resistance to freedom for India loomed large for the Chinese, while sympathy for the Nazis was brewing in some parts of the Middle East. In both regions "the traditions of British rule" rankled. The United States had to protect its alliance with the British, of course, but in the Middle East Willkie thought "we must work no less hard to give these peoples a feeling they do not have: that we are not committed to an indefinite perpetuation of British imperialism in this area, but rather to the establishment of political freedom and economic liberty." America's reputation was on the line. There was "deeply-rooted suspicion" in China that "America has given at least acquiescence to British plans for restoration of its earlier imperial position in Asia." Such tacit tolerance for imperialism, or even the suspicion of it, he said, using for the first time a metaphor he'd deploy to great effect in the months to come, threatened "to deplete the reservoir of good will" the nation enjoyed abroad.[29]

Whether Willkie raised these topics with the president remains unknown. At the very least, he left the meeting somewhat pacified. Perhaps Barnes or Cowles—or Roosevelt himself—convinced him that the "purely speculative" comment was directed at the media or the second-front chatter as a whole. When Willkie emerged from the ninety-minute meeting he told journalists waiting in the lobby that the president had "specifically" said that "any report that he had criticized me while I was abroad was entirely wrong." He was less forthcoming about the meeting itself, promising a full report on the trip in due time. When pressed, he reiterated his support for a second front, but stressed that it was the overall course of the war that really mattered. The Allies would win—the advantages in resources were too great—but "a lot of us, including public officials, are going to have to stretch our muscles and our minds before we win." Besides, winning was not the crucial issue. There was "another question involved. That is, how soon are we going to win, at what cost in human values, and what kind of world are we going to have afterwards?"[30]

Much remained unsettled. The welter of issues the trip had stirred up awaited a strategic mind to distill a coherent program from the noise. But for now Willkie caught a cab for Union Station and boarded a train to New York. From there, he would head west to reunite with his wife and son in Rushville. In Indiana, he would enjoy some much-needed rest and prepare to tell the nation what he'd seen and heard.[31]

Just shy of two weeks later, on the evening of October 26, Willkie took to the airwaves of all four major radio networks to deliver his "Report to the People." The highly anticipated speech came at a precarious moment. Success in North Africa was shadowed by grim news from the Pacific: that very day, the navy announced that the aircraft carrier USS *Wasp* had been sunk off Guadalcanal a month before.[32]

Willkie would have sensed the fragile state of public morale and understood his rare chance to bolster it. Despite the pressure he must have felt as he approached the microphones, he delivered one of the most gripping speeches of his career. Usually his prepared speeches suffered in comparison to his off-the-cuff style, but he was seized by the moment and delivered a near-sermon. He spoke steadily and deliberately, forgoing his usual frenzied pace, for close to forty minutes, running over the half-hour slot the networks had provided. Less an account of what he had seen on his trip than an essay on American responsibility in the world, the speech was animated by Willkie's conversational charisma. It reverberated with "something of the evangelist's fervor," the writer Frank Kingdon reported. Willkie's "personal experience" became a "public ferment when he projected not only his words but his feeling over the radio." Almost as forgotten now as his Chongqing address, the "Report to the People" was hailed as one of the great addresses of the war years. It was "a milestone," Kingdon said, "in the reorientation of American thinking toward the realities of our world society."[33]

Willkie began by setting the record straight about his role abroad. The trip had been his idea, he declared. He had traveled with the president's blessing and "certain specific tasks" to carry out, but beyond that he was a "free agent." He had paid his own way, and he pledged that any proceeds from writings about the trip would go to various war relief agencies. That clarification out of the way, he plainly stated his big idea: Although he had just circled the planet, the overwhelming impression he carried home was of a shrinking world. There were, he announced, "no distant points in the world any longer." The result of the new closeness was, in his estimation, a central role for his own country.[34]

"There exists in the world today a gigantic reservoir of good will toward you, the American people," he said, pronouncing it "reservahr" in a broad, elongated midwestern timbre that would amuse many of his listeners. But there was a problem with this supply of goodwill, he warned. It was leaking from a "thousand points" through "steadily spreading cracks and holes." These leaks were the work not of the Axis enemy but rather of America itself. Goodwill was ebbing, he had discovered, because of censorship, failures to deliver on promised war matériel, and the high-handed way American diplomats treated the leaders and peoples of the Middle East and Asia.[35]

Yet the most significant problem was the American failure to clearly define war aims. The people of the world, he said, were waiting for the United States to say exactly what the nation was fighting for. The enemy's cause was clear. The fascists fought for fantasies of racial superiority, for a militarist empire fed by dreams of blood and soil. The Allies seemed only to be fighting *back*. They fought for "freedom," perhaps, but freedom for whom? Even as the war appeared to be at a turning point, short-term pragmatism and grim expedience prevailed.

All across the globe, Willkie said, doubts about Allied commitment collected under one overarching concern. Would the Allies honor the terms of the Atlantic Charter? Like many Americans, he had initially taken the charter more or less at face value. It promised "self-determination" for all peoples. That meant everyone. But outside America and Europe, he had learned, many remembered the betrayals of Wilson's war to "make the world safe for democracy" and viewed the Atlantic Charter with both hope and suspicion.

All along his route from Egypt to China, people asked him about it. Everyone from prime ministers to journalists to students wanted to be sure that "all peoples" truly applied to them. The ordinary and the exalted, Willkie said, "know what they are fighting for. They are not so sure of us." "What about a Pacific Charter; what about a World Charter?" they asked. Willkie summarized the fears he'd heard around the world in stark terms: "Is freedom supposed to be priceless for the white man, or for the western world, but of no account to us in the East?"[36]

Such questions were justified. The limits of the charter had been an undercurrent in American political discussion throughout 1942. The idea, as the journalist William Allen White put it, that Roosevelt and Churchill had "spoken of freedom but with their fingers crossed for Asia and Africa" did not seem far-fetched to many. At the very least, the columnist William Shirer wrote, the charter was "too vague" and "left out Asia." Willkie himself claimed to remember hearing Cordell Hull, during a pre-trip briefing, say that it did not apply to the Pacific. African American activists had seized on the document, joining with African anticolonialists to demand that the charter be applied to British West Africa and South Africa. American officials, including Roosevelt, Hull, and Welles, had tried to clear the air. The charter, each had reiterated several times that year, covered the whole globe. In fact, a secret committee assembled inside the State Department was working to draft an actual "world charter" to amplify the document released from Placentia Bay in 1941.[37]

Much of the continued suspicion and confusion came from the United Kingdom, where from the beginning the charter had sowed discord. Many liberals in the Labour Party welcomed it, but more committed colonialists, particularly in the prime minister's own Conservative Party, viewed it as an American scheme to undermine the British Empire and open the door to US expansion. Some derided the declaration as nothing more than a "press release," without the force of actual policy, while others, particularly inside the Colonial Office, argued that it only applied to Europe. Some allowed that certain colonies ought to be prepared for "self-government" at some indefinite point in the future, but wanted all such decisions left to Britain. In September 1941 Churchill argued that he and Roosevelt "had in mind, primarily, the restoration of

the sovereignty, self-government, and national life of the states and nations of Europe now under the Nazi yoke."[38]

Churchill's clarification had carved out significant wiggle room to
his left and right. What he meant differed according to who was listening. British audiences heard a refusal to give up the empire, and many
Americans heard either a simple reaffirmation of Allied war goals or
British high-handedness, depending on their taste. But many others
around the globe, antennae tuned for the slightest signal bearing news of
shifts in colonial policy, heard it as a defense of imperial privilege.[39]

Willkie's "Report to the People" would push the charter back into
the headlines. If there was to be a "redefinition of the meaning of the Atlantic Charter for the benefit of the poor and the mistreated of the earth,"
the *Daily Oregonian* would comment, surveying the speech's impact,
Willkie had supplied the necessary provocation. Roosevelt would be
forced to reiterate his belief that the charter applied to "all humanity."
The pact, Willkie drily retorted, was "signed by two men." And the "bewildered despair" he had encountered across the globe reflected the fear
that a repeat of 1919 was under way. War and peace were being imagined
on purely "Anglo-American" terms. In fact, Willkie had anticipated this
impasse, designing the report to provoke discussion of the most sensitive
"Anglo-American" imperial conundrums, particularly those involving a
place he hadn't even visited.[40]

India was not on the front lines of the war, but in 1942 imperial
tensions there were boiling over. Earlier in the year, with the British
colony in Singapore occupied and the Japanese pushing into Burma,
Indian nationalists had seized the opportunity to press for an end to
British rule. Churchill had sent Labour politician Stafford Cripps to
India to offer increased self-governance in exchange for full cooperation against the Japanese. Nationalist leaders Mohandas Gandhi and
Jawaharlal Nehru refused the deal and called for immediate independence instead. Their "Quit India" resolution, delivered on August 8,
promised a united front against the Japanese—in the form of both
armed and nonviolent noncooperation (a hard-won compromise between Nehru and the pacifist Gandhi)—if independence was granted at
once. The British did not simply reject these demands: they cracked
down and arrested hundreds of nationalist leaders. As Willkie made his

way across Africa and Asia, India was swept by unrest, with strikes, protests, and armed resistance breaking out across the country. The British responded by opening fire on crowds, sometimes from aircraft, and jailing tens of thousands.[41]

Up until World War II, most Americans had little connection to India. A few reformers and civil rights pioneers had tried to draw attention to the colony's plight—making analogies sometimes to racism in the United States—but many considered India a British affair, even if they did not particularly approve of imperialism. Small committees of solidarity established by Indians and Americans—particularly black organizers—emerged in the early years of the war and did garner modest support for independence. Willkie's civil rights allies, led by Walter White, Pearl Buck, and Paul Robeson, saw India as a key element in winning "global double victory": defeating the Axis and ending segregation at home and empire abroad. They had urged Roosevelt to take more definitive steps to support Gandhi and Nehru, but with little success.[42]

Even when Americans frowned on the idea of British colonialism, approval for actual Indian nationalists was rare, and confined mostly to the anti-imperial left. Any chance of broad-based American backing for Gandhi and Nehru evaporated when the Cripps mission failed. Newspaper editors in the United States, with little understanding of the particulars and limited sympathy for any vision of "double victory," reacted angrily to Indian intransigence, with many editorials castigating the nationalist leaders for rejecting a supposedly generous deal and refusing to fall in line for the war effort.[43]

Like many of his fellow citizens, Willkie came late to sympathy for India. Walter White had schooled him on its resonance for African Americans, but he remained wary of provoking Roosevelt and the British, and rarely mentioned the colony explicitly before his trip. The president had steered him away from visiting the subcontinent, but the problem of India refused to go away. Many people Willkie met—particularly the Nationalists in China—pressed him on India. The Indian nationalists tried to court Willkie as well, hoping he might serve as an effective mouthpiece for their cause. When they heard about the trip, representatives of the leading Hindu nationalist organization, the Mahasabha (at least those who were not yet in jail), asked the American consul in New Delhi to arrange a visit. Their interest redoubled by the Chongqing speech, they cabled Willkie directly care of Chiang Kai-shek to try to lure him south. Their Muslim rivals, who proclaimed Willkie "the obvious man" to negotiate a settlement between the British and the Indians, also tried to contact him, but by that time he was already headed for home.[44]

Two weeks later, in his report, Willkie was still not ready to talk about India in depth—or so he said. He had not been there and so he would not discuss "that tangled question." But, he observed, India had become "a symbol all through Asia." This made it an American problem, too. In fact, it was not the British who suffered from the oppression of India—defense of empire could be expected from that quarter. No, it was the United States. Silence about India taxed the reservoir of goodwill. The "wishy-washy attitude" of the United States government, its "vague and vacillating talk," he proclaimed, left in doubt "whether or not we really do stand for freedom, or what we mean by freedom."

Conventional wisdom in the United States held that the Indians needed to commit to the cause, and that freedom would have to wait until after the war. Now Willkie would argue for the reverse. Granting India freedom would not be a liability for the war effort. (The same went for the Philippines, he suggested, to which the United States had promised independence as soon as the Japanese occupiers were dispatched.) Action was necessary to win the confidence and cooperation of the world at large. The war had created "a world forced to choose between victory and slavery, between freedom and Fascism," he said, and the way to create an alliance in which all had "confidence in each other" was not to demand shared sacrifice but to reward that sacrifice with either immediate benefits or concrete promises.

Willkie made some concessions to the conventional wisdom in order to win over skeptical listeners in both Britain and America. "Not all peoples of the world are ready for freedom, or can defend it, the day after tomorrow," he said, echoing the usual civilizational story Westerners employed to justify the persistence of empire. But, he continued, "today they all want some date to work toward, some guarantee that the date will be kept." By giving comfort to imperial gradualism, Willkie pulled his punches, but he had to walk a fine line between encouraging anti-imperial opinion and alienating America's foremost ally. So he allowed that some saw the Raj as "benevolent imperialism." And he reassured listeners that he admired the British Commonwealth of Free Nations and backed any effort to extend "the Commonwealth in place of the colonial system." This seemed to put Willkie on the same footing as the Cripps mission or other internationalist liberals who hoped to gradually dilute the imperial system by adding India and other colonies to the ranks of Canada, Australia, South Africa, and New Zealand in the British Commonwealth.[45]

Willkie might have regretted floating a Commonwealth compromise had he dug a little deeper. Its chief advocate was Jan Smuts, the South African internationalist and racial theorist. The former Boer guerilla commander's ideas for the legal framework of the League of Nations had influenced Woodrow Wilson, and he had advocated preserving the sovereignty of the "white men's countries" through the mandate system. For Smuts, the Commonwealth served a similar civilizing mission as a "trustee" of advancement. As an institution in which "advanced" peoples oversaw the development of "backward" peoples, it forged what historian Mark Mazower describes as "an organic melding of the (white) nations of the British Empire." By World War II Smuts was a general in the British Army. He had recently spoken before Parliament, Willkie noted in the report, and proposed the evolution of the empire toward a Commonwealth model.[46]

In December 1942, Smuts would publish a long defense of the empire in *Life*, writing in explicit reply to the magazine's recent open letter and to Willkie's anti-imperialism. The old British Empire, he maintained, was long dead, replaced by the dominions model of the Commonwealth, which had grown into the "widest system of organized human freedom . . . in history." Eventual membership in the Commonwealth would guarantee self-determination for the colonies and provide a model for a new postwar world. Smuts argued that in any future international order "mother countries should remain exclusively responsible for the administration of their colonies and interference by others should be avoided." Lofty rhetoric aside, it was clear that in this "moderate" vision little about the detested mandate system would change. The African American historian and mandate expert Rayford Logan saw it plainly: Smuts meant to preserve "white supremacy, segregation and the continued effective disfranchisement of the native peoples."

The Commonwealth-style solution to empire, particularly for the non-white world, simply meant more empire.[47]

If Willkie's invocation of the Commonwealth plan was intended to reassure the British, it did not succeed. The nods to gradualism were immediately drowned out by his bolder, headline-grabbing phrases. "In Africa, in the Middle East, throughout the Arab world, as well as in China and the whole Far East," he proclaimed, "freedom means the orderly but scheduled abolition of the colonial system. . . . I can assure you that the rule of people by other peoples is not freedom, and not what we must fight to preserve."[48]

Willkie closed his report with a rousing appeal for a "new world idea." American and British listeners, he argued, had to see the coming world as shaped not by Western progress and "civilization" but by Eastern urgency. A war rooted in European power politics had become a true world war, and the peace would have to be global as well. He was only a messenger, he said, "passing on an invitation which these peoples of the East have given us." Americans had to see that in much of the world, the status quo had been put in the dock and found wanting. The "western world and our presumed supremacy are now on trial. Our boasting and our big talk leave Asia cold." There were essentially two wars now, Willkie argued, one to defeat fascism and one to end the empire practiced by the Allies. Could Americans commit to both conflicts?

The global surge of anti-imperial feeling would have effects far beyond the war, Willkie predicted, for America and Britain alike. All over the world people were "on the march, physically, intellectually and spiritually," he proclaimed. "They are no longer willing to be Eastern slaves for Western profits." The war was only a prelude, and soon "the peoples of the East" would challenge Americans to embrace an upended global order, one that would not only redress exploitation but reimagine international relations on cooperative and equitable terms. "They are beginning to know that men's welfare throughout the world is interdependent," he concluded. "They are resolved, as we must be, that there is no more place for imperialism within their own society than in the society of nations. The big house on the hill surrounded by mud huts has lost its awesome charm."[49]

More than 36 million people tuned in to hear Willkie's "Report to the People," according to one estimate—double the audience of a top-flight commercial radio program. Mail flooded his New York headquarters and his Rushville house—more than for any other speech he'd ever given—and the editorial and letters pages once again filled up with charge and counter-charge. Comments ran at flood stage in New York, Washington, and Chicago, but also arrived from cities and towns all over the country. Approval far outweighed attack, but the divisions within the public response hinted at the shape of coming debates over the postwar world.[50]

Willkie's supporters greeted the speech as a major political event—a fulfillment of the promise shown by his Chongqing statement and the trip as a whole. The *Minneapolis Tribune* (owned by the Cowles family) predicted that the report would be remembered as "one of the war's real turning points." The speech, Mrs. O. L. Ewing of San Mateo, California, wrote to President Roosevelt, was "the first time I have ever had a crystal clear picture of what we are supposed to be fighting for." The *Christian Century* exulted over "a battle cry for freedom—the freedom of all men everywhere. It was a victory—for humanity!"[51]

For some, Willkie had announced the emergence of a new political force. His attack on empire and his advocacy for an expanded Atlantic Charter made him the chief herald of a movement that transcended national boundaries. Columnist Roscoe Drummond, surveying liberal opinion for the *Christian Science Monitor,* wrote that Willkie was "emerging as a United Nations statesman." It was "widely agreed that he is giving expression to a world-wide democratic movement which when welded into a cohesive entity by Allied leadership will become a powerful weapon against the Axis."[52]

"Everybody has been talking to the common man since the war began," the *New York Post* commented. "Last night, in the person of Wendell Willkie, the common man talked back." The speech embodied "the common earthy talk of men around the world, which has at last found its way into the council-chamber, rapped for order, and has said its say." He had made "himself one with the aspirations of the plain people of the world." Willkie's speech, one letter writer from Decatur, Alabama, informed FDR, "said the things we've said at our work benches, on the street cars, at the dinner table." Virgil MacMickle of Portland, Oregon, wrote to Willkie directly, hailing him as "the symbol and the personalization of the best aspirations of the common people of America and of the world."[53]

To supporters, Willkie's personal magnetism gave him the jump on typical politicians. He sensed what was only "dimly perceived in London and Washington," the *Christian Century* declared. The veteran foreign correspondent Anne O'Hare McCormick argued in her *New York Times* column that Willkie revealed the people of the world to Americans not as masses but as "people like you and me." He had sensed a shift in the political center of gravity, from West to East: "The New World we are accustomed to locating in the Western Hemisphere is no longer here but there, in ancient nations being reborn in the profound convulsions of war and change." This was no mere "local phenomenon" but a "universal movement."[54]

For the coalition of middle-class liberals, Republican and Democratic, who formed the core of Willkie's support, he looked like a new world leader. In his letter, Virgil MacMickle admitted that he backed Roosevelt, but he volunteered Willkie for a role as a delegate "in the formulation of the peace that shall follow. The international reorganization of this world, during and after this war, will need you." Clare Boothe Luce sent a one-line telegram: "Last night the world heard the message of a global Abraham Lincoln."[55]

Willkie's intensified commitment to civil rights and anti-imperialism had begun to attract more support from the left, particularly among African Americans, but some remained skeptical. In the *New York Amsterdam News*, A. M. Wendell Malliet celebrated Willkie's "great and courageous speech" but lamented that his "knowledge of world affairs is still inadequate." Willkie had given the impression that before the war the peoples of the East were "a docile and servile lot." But the Atlantic Charter did not mark some "awakening" of colonized peoples. "Asia and Africa," he wrote, had long campaigned against "white interference" and the "world rule of Westerners." Willkie was just now catching up to that fact.[56]

More vociferous dissent arrived, too, and began to coalesce around common themes. Some argued that his harping on the Atlantic

Charter and India was disrupting the war effort. Columnist Dorothy Thompson, a former ally, scored the speech as both hot air—"we know nothing more, on any matters of fact, than we knew before"—and pure politics, an attempt to appeal to FDR's "chief following—the progressive workers and middle classes." She worried that if the British Empire became the main issue of the next presidential campaign, it would deeply undermine the coalition to defeat fascism. Conservative columnist Mark Sullivan regretted Willkie's focus on the postwar situation and his neglect of the simple elements of wartime leadership: providing people with the "tonic to fight, incitement to the simple, primitive emotion of hunting down our enemies, destroying them."[57]

Doubt began to surface in the tribunes of establishment opinion, where Willkie had found his staunchest allies. The *New York Times* published a skeptical account of his India comments, rehearsing the conventional narrative of gradual progress toward self-determination often used by defenders of the British Empire. In his syndicated column, Walter Lippmann wrote that he hoped Willkie had not only listened to Eastern grievances but also stuck up for the Allies. If "Britain were remotely the cynical imperialist power that ungrateful men make her out to be," he argued, Churchill would long ago have struck a bargain with the Axis to save its empire. In private, Roosevelt lamented that Willkie had been too hard on the British. He could only see "the little things," the president reflected, and was not concerned enough about national and Allied unity.[58]

Sullivan complained that the speech was "almost wholly about our duty to other nations," while Senator Millard Tydings of Maryland, a conservative Democrat and fellow internationalist, thought Willkie would benefit from being a little more "pro-American than pro-this and pro-that." The old isolationists at the *Chicago Tribune* gloated over Tydings's attack; it was a sign, the paper's editorial crowed, that the public would soon become fed up with "world savers." The *Tribune* was perennially eager to see Willkie go down—but the comments from Tydings, Lippmann, and Roosevelt suggested that Willkie was steering into a gathering current of nationalism, one that would buoy the fortunes of a liberal internationalism that prioritized American interests over international interdependence.[59]

The report had its most immediate effects in London. Some British opinion writers greeted Willkie's remarks with cautious optimism, reading them as encouragement for what the *Times* of London called the "settled British policy to transform dependencies into free partnerships" on the Commonwealth model. Others were less appreciative, defending the civilizing virtues of imperial oversight against the wayward jabs of an irresponsible American. In the *Daily Mail,* Negley Farson complained that the "virtues of British rule" had gotten short shrift. An American émigré, he discounted Willkie's speech as an unwarranted attack on "the mission of the British Empire."[60]

Willkie's report arrived just as British colonialists were formulating a coherent response to the Atlantic Charter. It provided them with a chance to give their vision of the postwar future a public airing. Even "moderate" officials, like Sir Edward Grigg, a former colonial administrator and current member of Parliament, still saw the empire as indispensable for "the peace and progress of the weaker races and of the world in general." Perhaps Willkie could not appreciate how it remained a "sacred trust of civilization," but Grigg and other officials hoped that after the war the Americans could be convinced to join Britain in taking over the mandate system, overseeing the gradual progress of colonial peoples toward the Atlantic Charter's promise of "self-determination," and preserving the essential form of the empire.[61]

At the highest levels of British government, Willkie's speech prompted significant disturbance. Stung by Willkie's speech in Chongqing, Churchill and his ministers had been worried what might happen if Willkie—whom they much preferred to the old ultranationalist Republicans—were to make a complete break with Britain. Viscount Halifax, the ambassador in Washington, contacted Willkie in the days before his "big speech." The British knew he insisted on "untrammelled outspokenness," Halifax said, but the PM wanted to ensure that "he should say nothing that will embarrass us." Halifax found Willkie personally friendly but bitter about Churchill and Attlee's response to his second-front comments and angry about the British censors in Egypt. Willkie felt he had risked his reputation with his party by visiting England during the Blitz; surely he was owed better treatment. Halifax passed on his views to Eden and Churchill, saying that he was "behaving like a badly spoilt child." He nonetheless assumed that with the right petting and coaxing Willkie could be brought into line.[62]

The report deepened Churchill's agitation, but he hoped "not to lose him entirely." He thought he could bring him to Britain again to soothe any personal animus, though he eventually abandoned that idea. Over the coming months the British would try to bring Willkie back into the fold, sending a series of interlocutors—the historian Arnold Toynbee, Walter Lippmann, the philosopher Isaiah Berlin—to assuage him. At one point Willkie suggested that a commission with one American member be created to study the "colonial question" and fix a date by which the British would leave India. The British ignored this overture, no doubt viewing it as illegitimate interference in their affairs. Many British statesmen, like their American counterparts, saw Willkie as unruly and erratic, an "emotional creature" who failed to observe the gentlemanly norms of respectable diplomacy.[63]

In the weeks after Willkie's report, Churchill considered how to respond. He would later write to Willkie personally to try to mollify him, but in the short term he decided something more overt was warranted. As support for Willkie's view of the charter arrived from the White House, further unrest in the colonies seemed imminent. The Indian overtures to Willkie had been irritating enough, but in early November it was reported that Jamaican nationalists had issued a public invitation to Willkie to visit the island colony. The irascible Churchill finally gave vent to his irritation with Willkie, telling one visitor that the American was like "a Newfoundland dog in a small parlour, which had wiped its paws on a young lady's blouse and swept off the tea cups with its tail." Emboldened by the improving war news, the "King's First Minister" decided to use the upcoming Mansion House address as a response, and prepared the proud and intransigent speech in which he would refuse to "preside over the liquidation of the British Empire."[64]

Willkie greeted Churchill's defiance in kind. He answered the Mansion House address with a widely broadcast speech a few days later at an annual world issues forum hosted by the *New York Herald Tribune*. It had become clear to him, he said, that declarations like the Atlantic Charter were not enough. The meaning of the war—the "idea" of the war—had to be, in its rough essentials, agreed upon by everyone, so that it couldn't be betrayed by opportunistic leaders when it came time to make peace. That could only happen if the United States would "discuss and learn and exchange" with all its Allies, as people. Americans had to exchange ideas not only with the British but with the Russians and the Chinese, too, and also with the "hundreds of millions" of other potential allies around the world.

Previewing ideas he would explore in *One World,* Willkie argued that making the war count for all those potential allies required not just talk but action. He called for the reduction of barriers to trade across the globe, so that all peoples could have "access to the materials indispensable to economic self-government." And he offered the basic outlines of a collective "United Nations" effort to oversee the political and economic process of granting independence to those peoples that some seemed to think should be "ruled perpetually by some nation's colonial imperialism."[65]

"A war won without purpose," Willkie declared, "is a war won without victory." This credo marked the distance between him and Churchill—and Roosevelt. While the British were fighting for their lives and for the empire, and official American intentions for the postwar peace were still evolving behind closed doors, Willkie stood as the foremost voice calling for a public, democratic, and worldwide plan of action for an equitable peace.[66]

Willkie's challenge to the old world moved him back into the center of public life. But many who saw him in these months found him agitated and touchy, thin-skinned and anxious about his relations with Churchill, Roosevelt, the State Department, and the press, and on fire with the vision of global freedom he had glimpsed abroad. The public confusion about his role and the uproar over his strident anti-imperialist declarations seemed to have uncovered a vein of insecurity he struggled to keep buried. In November and December, he waded into ill-advised private and public scraps on a number of fronts. He jousted with the British envoys, argued with editors at *Collier's* and the *Saturday Evening Post* over their depictions of his trip, and bridled at the slightest hint of disrespect from the president.

Like many Americans, Willkie was dismayed by the news that Roosevelt and General Eisenhower had made a deal with the defeated Vichy admiral Jean François Darlan to remain the political leader of French North Africa after the American invasion. Willkie had prepared to denounce the deal in his *Herald Tribune* speech, but a last-minute phone call from Secretary of War Henry Stimson—who warned that, with Operation Torch still under way, criticism of the deal might endanger sixty thousand American lives—convinced him to hold off until Roosevelt had had a chance to address it in public. Willkie would become the most vocal critic of the deal with Darlan in the coming weeks and months, earning kudos from critics of the president and renewed condemnation from those in both parties who saw him as too much the headstrong armchair general.[67]

Willkie was eager to keep his name in the press as a freethinking Republican, a critic of the administration, and a leader with a global anti-imperial vision, but he also hoped to avoid coming off as a loose cannon. He wanted to be free to speak his mind, but he also sought to protect the off-the-record access accorded a political insider. It was as if he expected to join a private club *and* claim carte blanche to criticize its members at will. To some he came off as both heedless and easily affronted. "This is a dangerous man and unaccountable," Forrest Davis of the *Saturday Evening Post* wrote to his State Department sources after Willkie had called him to complain about an upcoming article on the second-front controversy.[68]

If Willkie posed a danger to anyone, it was to himself. Acting like an outsider while being an insider was rarely simple. As the new year approached, his quarrels with Churchill and the British receded—it had become clear that they had profound differences of principle but shared short-term goals—while confrontations with the president, old-guard Republicans, and liberal internationalists emerged on the horizon. Willkie had become the best-known advocate for a vision of global freedom, setting himself apart from those more careful not to offend imperial conventional wisdom. He had also done much to hamstring the old isolationism,

only to find that hard-line nationalism now lingered in its place. A bellicose liberal internationalism was gathering, too, and it was no less nationalist in its determination to see the United States at the top of the Great
Power pile. For the remaining twenty-two months of his life, Willkie would
mount a quixotic undertaking, one that was only partially successful, to
disarm these rival outlooks and win over the American people to his vision of a war fought for worldwide liberation.

Friends and supporters had long suggested he write a book or publish a volume of his speeches. He had always put them off, but with the
enormous excitement that had greeted his "Report to the People," Irita
Van Doren and others renewed their pleas. Van Doren's son-in-law, Tom
Torre Bevans, a Simon and Schuster executive, suggested he consider a
book-length version of the report, accompanied by his other post-trip
speeches. Willkie's next act was coming into view.

CHAPTER 11

One World Barnstorming

America and the World

O *NE WORLD* BURST INTO the American consciousness in the spring of 1943, jumping off store shelves and to the top of the bestseller lists. On a train trip to Dallas and Houston in May, Mrs. H. W. Kight of Lubbock, Texas, spotted at least five fellow passengers reading or discussing the book. In downtown Houston, she wrote to Willkie, riders on city buses clutched copies, and "the show windows were full of it." In fact, *One World* was the reason for Mrs. Kight's trip in the first place. She was the mother of Richard Kight, the *Gulliver*'s pilot, and the whole family had been invited to a theater in Dallas where they watched a local writer give a live review of the book for the crowd. Later, back in Lubbock, they listened to an adaptation of the book on the NBC radio network and exchanged letters full of Willkie talk with excited family members across the country. The Kights saw more of the hoopla surrounding *One World* than most, given that their son was a supporting character in the tale and that the book was dedicated to him and his crew, but the depth of their immersion hints at the book's huge reach.[1]

One World appeared in stores on Thursday, April 8, and by the weekend another Willkie boom was on, this one longer and more consequential than the commotion that followed the Report. Simon and Schuster, Willkie's publisher, expected they had a hot ticket, but they still underestimated the burst of interest. The firm had brought the book out in two versions, a $2 hardcover and a $1 tabloid format resembling a magazine. The cheaper edition, racked front and center at newsstands and cigar stores, ran ahead of the traditional hardcover four to one, driving sales far beyond expectations.

Booksellers sold out so quickly that back orders began to pile up. Sensing a phenomenon brewing Simon and Schuster quadrupled its promotional budget, running a series of ads in fifty newspapers and magazines that simultaneously apologized for the shortage and trumpeted the book's success. With two sets of plates running in two printing plants on a 24-hour schedule, they soon caught up with demand. One week in and "the Willkie," as it came to be called around the publisher's offices, was already in its fourth printing; 370,000 copies were in circulation, but orders kept coming in. Two weeks later, readers had bought 650,000 copies, averaging 50,000 a day at one point. One news chain stocked the book in 75,000 cigar stores and stands across the country. By early May sales reached the 1 million mark, and by July they topped 1.6 million.[2]

One World was the iconic title of the great reading boom of 1943, a moment in which Americans, hungry for news and knowledge about the world and the war, defied paper rationing and bought books like mad. The editor of *Publishers Weekly* hailed *One World* as a "record breaking non-fiction best seller," a phenomenon "unequaled since the days of the old blue-backed 'speller'"—Noah Webster's Revolutionary-era guide to the new American English. Most books that sold over a million, he observed, like *Gone With the Wind* or *Ben Hur*, were fiction, and typically took years and several cheaper reprints to get there. Sales figures also undercounted true readership. Each book sold "gets at least three readings," the editor estimated, as people lent copies to friends and relatives. Pollsters at Gallup figured three and a half readers per copy, and estimated that by the middle of 1943 "something over four million people" had read Willkie's book. Some even deemed it the fastest-selling book in American history.[3]

One World stayed on the bestseller lists throughout the summer and appeared in a Book-of-the-Month Club edition, a twenty-five cent reprint, an edition for soldiers overseas, and a raft of foreign editions in English and in translation, including samizdat printings on underground presses in occupied Denmark and Czechoslovakia. Millions more would read the book over the next year as it made its way into libraries. We don't know how many people eventually bought or read the book, but any sales tally doesn't fully capture the popular passion for *One World* and for Willkie himself. For those who didn't pay attention to books—which, despite the record sales, was most people—Willkie authorized a condensed version for magazines and newspapers. Beginning in late June of 1943, over 100 papers in the United States, Australia, Britain, and Canada, with a combined circulation of more than seven million readers, ran the abridged *One World* in their pages. In July, NBC broadcast its live adaptation of the book, and soon afterward, Darryl Zanuck of Twentieth Century–Fox announced that he would personally produce a feature film version.[4]

In just a few months the book became a talisman of wartime life, its title a new shorthand for a whole worldview and a slogan around which internationalists everywhere rallied. By the fall of 1944, Simon and Schuster would hail *One World* as "the most widely read and discussed non-fiction book of the twentieth century." The book became almost ubiquitous, joining the songs from *Oklahoma!*—which debuted on Broadway in the spring of 1943—in the shared backdrop to wartime life. One reviewer judged it the most influential book of the war years: "Like *Uncle Tom's Cabin* it was part of the country."[5]

The extent of the furor caught Willkie by surprise—and boosted his spirits. The unexpected proceeds, he decided, would go to the war relief agencies aiding Britain, Russia, and China. "I'd be kidding you if I said I hadn't expected it to sell, but I didn't expect it to go over a hundred and fifty thousand," he told the *New Yorker* a month into the fever. "This has been one of the most richly satisfying experiences in my life."[6]

The immediate fervor burned bright, but *One World* ended up in second place on the nonfiction bestseller list for the year, runner-up to *Under Cover*, John Roy Carlson's expose of America's Nazi underground. While *One World* surely had a greater impact than *Under Cover*, its second-place finish does speak to its shooting-star nature. The craze would bring Willkie to the height of his popularity and influence, but it also would reveal the limits of his influence in the debate over internationalism, at least in the United States.[7]

For it was in the United States, and with Americans, that Willkie would face his steepest challenge. Remembering Woodrow Wilson's failures, Willkie understood that for Americans to appreciate the news of global anticolonial insurgency they would have to be brought face-to-face with the fact that they were already connected to people in faraway countries. In a world shaken by war, divided by empire, and shrunken by flight, ignoring global *interdependence* would jeopardize American *independence*. To land that argument, the account of his travels would have to both entertain and evangelize. It needed to grab attention in terms Americans could understand, in a language they recognized, to win approval for ideals and policies they had long held at arm's length. He needed to get these ideas to stick in a country distracted by mobilization, divided among itself, and anxious about the course of the war.

Willkie offered a new geopolitical vision of a world remade, a world in need of new maps and a new kind of global imagination. His was an idealistic vision, of a planet united in cooperation through a new world body designed to succeed where the League of Nations had failed. But it was strategic as well, envisioning the United States cooperating with the Soviet Union, championing decolonization, and managing a reinvigorated network of global trade. In his version of the future, America remained indispensable, not as the proprietor of a new empire but as the guarantor of the freedom and equality imagined as the country's birthright. This was a treacherous path. He was trying to tiptoe between two nationalisms: the lingering parochial hawkishness on the right and an emerging expansionary liberal nationalism that he both disputed and sometimes epitomized. In the end, Willkie revealed Americans' contorted and conflicted feelings about the world at large.[8]

The *One World* sensation was sudden but not entirely unexpected. In the months between his return from the trip and the book's publication, Willkie hardly dropped from public view, even as he delved into the work of drafting the book. In fact, the pace of his speeches, writings, and political and legal work barely let up during the run-up to the book's release. "He must write, speak, argue, convince," one journalist who encountered him in late 1942 commented. "He must keep going that tremendous upsurge of good-will that greeted him upon his return from his world tour."[9]

Much of his activity was political and legal. In a bid to placate party bosses irked by his leaving the country at the beginning of the midterm election season, he campaigned for liberal Republican candidates, including his former primary rival Thomas Dewey, who was now running for governor of New York. But he then infuriated party officials and rank-and-file Republicans when he went before the Supreme Court in November 1942 to defend the civil liberties of William Schneiderman, a Communist Party leader and Russian immigrant facing deportation.[10]

Republican irritation with Willkie would only grow over the coming months, but he was increasingly at odds with Roosevelt, too. They saw more or less eye to eye on foreign policy, and Willkie's recent swing to the left should have brought them even closer together, but he was loath to trust the president. Fallout from Willkie's outspoken criticism of the Darlan deal, his second-front statements, the back-and-forth over the Atlantic Charter, and even a presidential wisecrack over Willkie's pronunciation of "reservoir" contributed to a growing wariness. By the beginning of 1943 Willkie was telling the journalist Marquis Childs that he thought FDR and the other official peace planners would like to see him silenced or embarrassed. The president, Childs wrote in *Look*, had one eye on the 1944 election, and might be trying to damage his chief internationalist rival, "who has actually been ahead of FDR in advocating that the peoples of the earth cooperate in a new and realistic congress of nations." Roosevelt wrote privately to Willkie to try to reassure him, but the damage had been done.[11]

Despite frictions with party and president, Willkie continued to speak out for civil liberties, liberal causes, and internationalism. In the *New York Times Magazine* and *This Week* he backed future cooperation with the Soviet Union and China. But he also continued to reach beyond New York and the political classes of Washington to a general audience. From pithy accounts of war scenes in mass-market titles like *Look, Reader's Digest,* and *Coronet* to compact briefs for internationalism in *Parents' Magazine* and *The Woman,* Willkie sought to reach as many American households as he could, implicitly insisting they resemble the household he'd grown up in, where the public business of the world was also the business of family life and of "woman's work," too.[12]

Much of his writing time went into his book. That winter he set up shop most mornings in Irita Van Doren's living room. The early idea for a volume of speeches went quickly by the wayside, and he turned instead to the story of the new world he had glimpsed during his travels. *One World* was not, as Willkie's political detractors sometimes claimed, ghostwritten. Neither Van Doren, Joseph Barnes, nor Mike Cowles did the work for him. Willkie wrote longhand, in pencil, or dictated to Van Doren, and she helped him edit and rewrite. He worked from memory, from notes and memos supplied by Barnes and Cowles about their trip, and from the texts of his speeches and writings, which he adapted for use in the book. From late November into February, he labored on the manuscript, talking through his thoughts with Van Doren as he wrote, then poring over typed drafts with a thick black pencil like a newspaper rewrite man. Even in mid-February, after the pages went into galleys and he was out in Indiana, he would call in small changes, altering phrasing or deleting words to better bring the world home to his fellow citizens.[13]

Meanwhile, the country Willkie had come home to was unsettled and divided. We tend to remember the "good war" fought by a "greatest generation," but these slogans obscure the actual paradoxes of wartime life on the home front. A society riven by long-standing divisions had been called to unity and was obsessed with the war, but it was also disconnected from faraway fighting and suspicious about an alliance with the communist Soviets and imperial British. Americans chafed under restrictions and rationing but exulted in prosperity not seen in a generation. They found themselves uprooted by mobilization but thrilled to be able to get out and about, go to the movies or a show, even take a little vacation if they could get around gas rationing. Yet they also felt cajoled, and even forced, to sacrifice and produce for the common cause. They fought for political freedom abroad, but they granted immense new powers to the government that directed the war effort, and they heard big business claim that the fight was for "individual initiative" and "free enterprise," not democracy or a "New Deal for the world," even as it profited from massive federal war contracts.[14]

More than 400,000 Americans would die in the war, so it touched the whole country intimately, but America proper was spared the carnage that turned European and Asian cities to rubble. US war deaths were grievous but small compared to the estimated 3 million Japanese, 6 million Germans, 14 to 20 million Chinese, and more than 26 million lost in the Soviet Union, the last a country ravaged like no other in human history. Only in the United States, among the major belligerent nations, was it necessary for the government to churn out propaganda posters asking the obvious: "Don't you know there's a war on?" Americans, one commentator observed, were "fighting the war on imagination alone."[15]

Many Americans experienced the war primarily as a disruption of everyday life. The fighting was overseas, but mobilization uprooted millions from their homes. More than 15 million people, men and women, went into the military. Another 15 million more moved for work. Six million new women workers took jobs, about 2 million of them on the assembly lines of defense plants. A great current of people, black and white, flowed from south to north. Another, even larger, went east to west. They left families and farms for towns and cities, traveling to places they had never expected to see, following war news from places they had never heard of before. Trains and busses ran extra routes, packed with soldiers traveling to and from training camps, airfields, and seaports. NO VACANCY signs popped up across cities swollen with war workers. Streetcars overflowed with workers commuting from plants running around the clock to rooming houses where people bunked in shifts.[16]

Salaries and wages jumped, but so did prices and taxes. People dutifully planted victory gardens while griping about supposedly disloyal unions and profiteering. They bought war bonds but might admit that it was mostly in the hope of converting them into a new refrigerator or washing machine when the fighting ended. New tires were hard to come by in many places, but the well-connected seemed to have all the gas, meat, and new clothes they wanted. For the first time in a long time, people had money to spend, and spend they did, on whatever they could find that wasn't rationed. "People are crazy with money," a jeweler in

Philadelphia reported. "They don't care what they buy. They purchase things . . . just for the fun of spending."[17]

Movies, advertising, and government propaganda spun stories of a democratic war effort to an uneasy nation. Every platoon appeared as a diverse microcosm of the country eager to fight for a united and free world; every shop floor had to seem like a well-oiled machine supporting the boys overseas. But outside the movie palaces and glossy magazines, African Americans had to threaten a march on Washington to force open segregated factory gates, while white workers staged "hate strikes" to prevent working with them. Black men wearing the uniform of a segregated military doubly resented it when whites refused to serve them at restaurants, while race riots shook Detroit, Los Angeles, Harlem, and a host of other places. Men grumbled about women enjoying life outside the home, rumors of Jewish subversion swept the country, and many thousands of Japanese Americans were corralled in detention camps for the duration of the war. In Detroit, homegrown fascist Gerald L. K. Smith, still furious at the New Deal, outraged by the supposed influence of "Jewish bankers," and determined to thwart internationalists like Willkie, rebooted the America First movement with hate-filled pamphlets that found plenty of eager readers across the country. Shorn of its original noninterventionist cause, America First veered hard to the right, shedding pacifists and other antiwar skeptics to embrace the bellicose, quasi-fascist nationalism that would fuel the conspiracy-minded right wing of the Cold War years.[18]

Late 1942 and 1943 were particularly unsettled times. The turning point Willkie had announced at El Alamein and the news of victories at Midway, Guadalcanal, and Stalingrad suggested that the Allies would eventually prevail. But American casualties in the Pacific were mounting, and the late 1943 invasion of Sicily ramped up the human cost of war, while the full second front in France seemed forever forestalled. The wartime economy did not reach full gear until the spring of 1943, close to a year after shortages and rationing took hold in much of the country. With prolonged uncertainty came impatience. People began to talk openly about hoarding, price gouging, and the black market in rationed goods.[19]

Home front strife had made itself felt in the 1942 midterm elections. Republicans gained fifty-four seats in Congress, mainly in the rural and small-town districts of the Midwest, boosting the fortunes of both old-guard GOP nationalists and southern Democrats. In 1943 they united to chip away at the New Deal, dismantling or shuttering many of the agencies Roosevelt had established to fight the Depression. The president acknowledged the shift, telling the nation at the end of the year that "Dr. New Deal" was out and "Dr. Win-the-War" would see them now. Willkie looked on with some foreboding. The conservative upsurge may have damaged his rival, but a setback for liberalism hurt his own chances at the 1944 Republican nomination—and threatened his internationalist hopes for the future.[20]

In the depths of the war, seemingly the only thing almost all Americans could agree on was support for the troops. The "GI," and later the veteran, was an "idealized figure of masculine virtue and patriotic sacrifice," as historian James Sparrow puts it. Through the symbol of the GI, lofty official "war aims"—the fight against fascism, the Four Freedoms, the promises of the Atlantic Charter—rode alongside everyday nationalism to motivate a distracted and divided populace for the war effort. Willkie was as susceptible as any American to the idea that "the boys" possessed virtues of both hardy independence and resolute commitment to duty. But for Willkie those idealized virtues had to inspire more than an image of gritted-teeth resolve or sentimental heroics for the Stars and Stripes. They had to become a symbol of what Americans might be capable of in concert with others around the world. Luckily, he discovered just the right prototype for this cosmopolitan version of the GI.[21]

Over the course of his trip Willkie had come to admire the intelligence, resolve, and steady hands of the *Gulliver*'s pilot. But it wasn't Captain Kight's skills at the controls that most stuck with Willkie. "It made no difference whether we were with Stalin, Madame Chiang Kai-Shek, a laborer in a Baghdad factory, or a coolie in China," he wrote to Kight's mother not long after *One World* appeared. "Dick always conducted himself with such sympathy and understanding that he became to all of us an ideal of a rugged, alert American." For Willkie, Kight had all the ingredients of a representative type, the American flier: reliable and "rugged," a salt-of-the-earth son of Lubbock, he was nonetheless adaptable and "sympathetic" everywhere he went, connecting with people of all nations and classes.[22]

Richard Kight embodied a significant trend, one that ran counter to the narrow nationalism surrounding the GI. The war had broadened the experiences of a whole generation of women and men, promoting the rapprochement between Americanness and cosmopolitanism Willkie discerned in Kight. An influential fraction of young Americans found themselves uprooted from farms and working-class neighborhoods, only to discover that they hungered for a wider outlook on their country and the world. This broadening was not absolute—Willkie's offhand use of "coolie" in his letter to Mrs. Kight revealed the persistence of older ideas—but it proved a powerful force for a decisive cohort, many of whom would support Willkie and later use the GI Bill to ascend to the professional and business classes. As one soldier put it, the war did not change his outlook toward the rest of the world; it *created* it. "I suddenly became from a very provincial person to a person that was very much internationally oriented. I think that happened to many of us."[23]

Richard Kight helped Willkie rough out a model for his ideal everyday internationalist. This plainspoken cosmopolitan ideal could appeal to the rising worldly generation. It could breach the divides between America and the world. It could bridge the gap between the elite internationalists and ordinary patriotic Americans. For the star turn in this role, however, he cast himself. After his return from abroad, Willkie worked even harder to position himself as a medium between the world's ordinary people. Already widely hailed for his connective abilities, he looked to personify the disposition Americans would need to adopt to meet the world on equal terms.

The moment seemed opportune. Despite the uneasy wartime climate, a real surge in internationalist opinion was under way. One polling outfit recorded a jump in approval for US membership in "some sort of organization of nations after the war" from 62 percent in November 1942 to 72 percent in January 1943. And now it also seemed that Americans—or at least 72 percent of them, according to a December 1942 Gallup poll—were, like Willkie, ready for policymakers to "take steps now, before the end of the war," to start a new world organization.[24]

President Roosevelt and the State Department remained mum about any such plan, unwilling to divulge details of the postwar planning going on behind closed doors. In March 1943 a group of internationalist

US senators put forth a resolution calling for the United States and its allies to form a new world organization. The new world body, it said, courting controversy, should have police powers "to suppress by immediate use of . . . force any future attempt at military aggression by any nation." The resolution initially went nowhere, but Willkie duly wired his support, offering to do anything he could to help. Meanwhile, his greatest contribution was already on the way. *One World* would bring his customary exuberance to bear on otherwise airy and abstract debates about rights, government, police powers, and parliamentary structure.[25]

Most of *One World* is a travelogue, a pacey recounting of Willkie's journey from Cairo to Chongqing. It followed his encounters with colonialists and newly confident nationalists, his attempts to woo the Soviets and Chinese, and his hopes for modernization and development in lands thus far subject only to Western rule. Combining two of Willkie's characteristic modes, folksy raconteur and earnest cheerleader, the book became the culmination of his campaign to arouse public opinion. He mobilized the sentiments that collected around him during his trip, and made the book his greatest act of personal diplomacy. Throughout its pages Willkie himself shone through: curious, jaunty, garrulous, a template for what it would *feel* like for Americans to assume equal and interdependent relations beyond their borders.

One World moved quickly on the page, drawing on popular genres familiar to its broad audience. At first glance it resembled pure travel writing, and it exploited some tropes of revelation common to tales of discovery, but it ended up reading more like the reporting in *Life* or *Look*. Willkie's breezy, authoritative voice conveyed a touch of fascination at the new and wondrous, particularly when he slipped into Arabian Nights–style rhapsody or wishful thinking about the Chinese Nationalists. But he usually stopped short of breathless exoticism. And though *One World* was the story of a personal quest for some ineffable goal, Willkie's holy grail was not some lost mystery, hidden treasure, or spiritual gift. The news he brought back to Americans was not of dark continents, strange peoples, or backward customs. He promised more subtle and unsettling revelations. The book issued a challenge to American thinking about race and empire, yet discovered a globe unified by qualities of interconnection he believed were already shared by all.[26]

Willkie's world was one in which people were united by their similar, even conventional motivations. From Nuri al-Said to Joseph Stalin to Chiang Kai-shek, he rendered the leaders he met as resolute and capable, sensitive and forward-looking. The perfect partners for Willkie's forthright persona and his message of coming world unity, they came off like the heroes of boys' literature or glossy magazine profiles. All of this made for an odd combination. Fundamental challenges to political orthodoxy arrived along with stock characters straight out of middlebrow Hollywood. That blend of provocation and reassurance proved appealing, but the cheery and headstrong execution left it feeling a bit slight, too. *One World* "wasn't a very good book," the essayist E. B. White would later remark, "but it was an important book and will take its place on the permanent shelf of this groping, hopeful planet."[27]

Less than convincing as literature, *One World* succeeded as popular exhortation. What began as travelogue ended as manifesto, as Willkie went into campaign mode for an idea in the final third of the book. As he wrote, mining his speeches and articles for a central theme, Willkie had searched for some striking phrase that might galvanize hearts and minds, that might convey for his audience the grand stakes of everything he'd seen as he circled the globe. Simon and Schuster had been calling the manuscript *One War, One Peace, One World,* but his friend Tom Bevans suggested the whole gestalt could be conveyed in two words: *One World.*[28]

Willkie was not the first internationalist to use this phrase. The famous science fiction writer H. G. Wells—who declared himself a "confirmed Willkie-ite" in 1943—had employed it for a 1940 speaking tour called "Two Hemispheres or One World," and it popped up in the writings and thought of other internationalists, too. But it was Willkie who made it shorthand for an entire zeitgeist. "One world" joined old and new, updating the internationalist convictions of his youth for the new age of flight. Think back to the end of the last war, he urged his readers, and the failure of Congress to ratify membership in the League of Nations. The politicians had turned away from a robust and equitable internationalism, but not Americans themselves, he felt sure. The coming years would challenge the truth of that faith, but he doubled down nonetheless: at this point retreating from the world would be absurd, "sheer disaster" even.[29]

"At the end of the last war," Willkie wrote, "not a single plane had flown across the Atlantic." But now, he continued, "that ocean is a mere ribbon, with airplanes making regular scheduled flights. The Pacific is only a slightly wider ribbon in the ocean of the air, and Europe and Asia are at our very doorstep." Steamships and telegraph wires had brought the planet together during the last half of the nineteenth century, but the last thirty years had upped the ante, with radio and flight compressing both time and space in unprecedented ways. "There are no distant points in the world any longer," he announced in the book's opening, preparing the reader to take in his quick transit across the embattled globe. The "myriad millions of human beings of the Far East are as close to us as Los Angeles is to New York by the fastest trains." In the years to come, "what concerns them must concern us." The conclusion was inescapable: "our thinking in the future must be world-wide."[30]

Worldwide thinking, Willkie argued, would reveal not just closeness but wholeness, the very oneness of the new world. "We can stop thinking of the world today as a geographical map—splotches of color that stand *only* for nations and national possessions," he said in a speech a few months after his book was published. "We can begin to think of the human beings who live within those splotches of color as living also within a larger map that marks a single world." On this new map, conventions of "natural and man-made geography" would give way, to reveal the fundamental shape of the air age. Old divisions of political and national geography were collapsing, he announced in the explanatory text he contributed that summer to a major Museum of Modern Art show called *Airways to Peace,* and now "the world is small and the world is one."[31]

In fact, *One World* included a map of this "small and completely interdependent" planet. The inside cover carried a pictorial map of the "Flight of the *Gulliver*" that traced Willkie's flight path in a great circle around the globe but did away with national borders and the traditional "splotches of color." It showed instead a great blue-green spread of ocean and continents connected only by the vector of his voyage. For Willkie, this image had clear political implications. "When I say that peace must be planned on a world basis," he wrote at the close of *One World,* "I mean quite literally that it must embrace the earth." All the demarcations on the old maps—the "continents and oceans"—were "plainly only parts of a whole." From up in the air, "England and America are parts. Russia and China, Egypt, Syria and Turkey, Iraq and Iran are also parts. And it is inescapable that there can be no peace for any part of the world unless the foundations of peace are made secure throughout all parts of the world."[32]

To capitalize on this situation and "win the principles" of the peace would require political action. The Four Freedoms and the Atlantic Charter had done some of this work, and he had seen firsthand how people around the world looked to them with hope, believing that the global conflict was, as Stalin had proclaimed, "a war of liberation." But Willkie feared that Roosevelt and Stalin's idealistic slogans—to say nothing of Churchill, who had publicly reverted to a defense of imperial privilege—left room for a return to "old divisions of small nations, each with its own individual political, economic, and military sovereignty." The people, Willkie claimed—even the people of Britain—wanted more than that. The key to getting there was forcing their leaders to work toward a real United Nations—and to do it now, before the war's end.[33]

It's often forgotten now, but during the war the phrase "United Nations" referred to the economic and military alliance of more than two dozen nations fighting the Axis. As the war progressed, some internationalists adopted the term to describe a potential successor organization to the League of Nations tasked with overseeing a multilateral peace. This kind of United Nations, Willkie urged, had to be actively made, not assumed or cobbled together at the end of the war like Wilson's League. It had to be a coequal gathering of all the Allies, he wrote, a "common council, not only for the winning the war but for the future welfare of mankind."[34]

Willkie did not have a blueprint for a postwar organization, like those being prepared behind closed doors in the State Department and Whitehall or floated almost weekly in the pages of magazines, academic journals, and books. Plans were good, but they did not matter without a popular constituency behind them. When the time came, he would advocate for specifics, but in the middle of 1943 he was focused on getting public support behind a wide-ranging world organization. Remembering Wilson's failures, he believed that the viability of any such organization would depend on the United States and on the American people.

One World turned on this point. It was a book about the newly small world, but above all it was about the place of the United States in that world. Americans, whether they liked it or not, would have to nurture and sustain international connection. In the past, Willkie wrote in the book's culminating exhortation, many Americans had been sure that they could go it alone. But now a fundamental change was under way, one that directly implicated him and all his fellow citizens. Airplanes and war had shrunk the world in a practical sense, but newly shared ideas made it small "not only on the map, but also in the minds of men." Chief among these ideas, Willkie argued, was the "mixture of respect and hope" people everywhere felt for the United States. All along his route—from "a prime minister or king in Egypt" through to "a fur-capped hunter on the edge of the trackless forests of Siberia"—people everywhere had "one common bond, and that is their deep friendship for the United States."[35]

Here he reprised a theme from his radio "Report to the People": the gigantic "reservoir of good will" for America. Regular Americans, he believed, had filled the reservoir, avoiding the bad reputation of so many Europeans abroad with earthy fellowship and everyday sentiment. American teachers and missionaries had established schools and colleges in Turkey, Lebanon, Egypt, and China, where they had educated many in the middle and upper classes of the rising generation. Then there were his favored modernizers—the builders and planners. They opened "new roads, new airways, new shipping lines" and gave Americans a reputation as people who "move goods, and ideas, and move them fast." And of course there were the movies. People "from Natal to Chungking" could see Americans on the silver screen, and everywhere he went, everyone from "shop girls" and waiters to royalty plied him with questions about Hollywood stars.[36]

People wanted to trust the United States. But the reservoir had leaks, he warned, and could drain entirely if the country failed to live up to its own ideals. People across the world were uneasy for all the reasons he had often cited before—they could not discern the true nature of American war aims, they were unsure how far the Atlantic Charter would really go, and they were not sure that Americans could be trusted to help see

European empire off the world stage. But there was one other danger—one he had long excoriated and now made a central antagonist in his story of the imperiled world.

Americans, Willkie cautioned, needed to remember how "calamity" had been baked into their otherwise fruitful democratic experiment. During the Revolutionary era, Americans "won in the peace exactly what they won in the war—no more and no less," including a failure to "agree concerning the freedom or slavery of the Negro." Racial division had thus been fatally enshrined in American life, ensuring that a slave economy prospered in the South and making inevitable nine decades later another, far more devastating war between Americans themselves.[37]

In 1943, seventy-five years on, during another great war, the insidious curse of race still haunted not just America but the world. But the war had also altered the political calculus around race. "The moral atmosphere in which the white race lives is changing," Willkie wrote, drawing on his NAACP speech a year earlier. "It is changing not only in our attitude toward the people of the Far East. It is changing here at home." The United States, he charged, had long "practiced inside our own boundaries something that amounts to race imperialism. The attitude of the white citizens of this country toward the Negroes has undeniably had some of the unlovely characteristics of an alien imperialism—a smug racial superiority, a willingness to exploit an unprotected people." But now, "thoughtful Americans" were recognizing "that we cannot fight the forces and ideas of imperialism abroad and maintain any form of imperialism at home. The war has done this to our thinking."[38]

Inspired by Walter White and his other civil rights allies, Willkie pushed himself to go further than most other American whites, "thoughtful" or otherwise. Many understood the Atlantic Charter as a challenge to European empire, but few public figures saw it applying to Alabama and Mississippi, or even Detroit and New York. "Our very proclamations of what we are fighting for," he declared, "have rendered our own inequities self-evident. When we talk of freedom and opportunity for all nations, the mocking paradoxes in our own society become so clear they can no longer be ignored. If we want to talk about freedom, we must mean freedom for others as well as ourselves, and we must mean freedom for everyone inside our frontiers as well as outside." The biggest leak in the reservoir, Willkie argued, was the persistence of "our imperialisms at home."[39]

Willkie would have no shortage of chances to renew his arguments about the dangers of racism. The wartime culture of pluralism, steeled by a newly militant black civil rights movement, put pressure on white supremacy. And the horrifying news from behind enemy lines, stories of death camps and the mass killing of Jews and the other outsiders of Europe, which began to reach the United States in 1942 and 1943, redoubled commitment to racial liberalism. But progressive ideals had little purchase in many parts of the country, and even in northern cities segregation and discrimination would become extended facts of American life. War mobilization and the mass migration of black and white southerners had in some respects expanded and inflamed racist reaction. Skirmishes between black and white soldiers broke out in southern training camps. Protestors at segregated lunch counters in several cities in the South were pelted with food. In June, white mobs, with soldiers and sailors in the lead, attacked Chicano teenagers in the streets of downtown Los Angeles, stripping them of the flamboyant "zoot suits" many whites saw as disrespectful violations of rationing and insults to the common war effort.[40]

That same month, fighting between black and white kids at a Detroit city park set off almost two days and nights of racial violence. With Detroit police overwhelmed, and sometimes sympathetic to white mobs, federal troops arrived to quell the uprisings. Twenty-five African Americans and nine whites died. Willkie joined with Walter White to produce a CBS radio show about the Detroit riots. On the airwaves he condemned the "mob-madness" as detrimental to the war effort, particularly when "two-thirds of the people who are allied with us do not have white skins." News of race riots gave global audiences pause. Would Americans cooperate as equals after the war? The only solution, Willkie argued, was immediate and full legal, political, and economic rights for African Americans—a campaign to eradicate the white racial fascism that menaced the United States from inside its own borders.[41]

"Our imperialisms at home" threatened the reservoir of goodwill. But what about America's imperialisms abroad? Several reviewers of *One World* raised this question. Writers on the left, still skeptical of Willkie's progressive streak, took him to task for missing what Max Lerner, writing

in the left-liberal magazine *P.M.*, called "the imperialism of our corporations and cartels." On his trip, Lerner charged, Willkie retained a residual
Americanism. He "judged most things as he went by an American yardstick." Willkie's global vision was all well and good, critics like Lerner
suggested, but he remained naive about the reach of American power and
its shift in emphasis from territorial control to a more informal but no less
potent economic empire. Like so many of his fellow citizens, they reasoned, Willkie mistook the nation's retreat from foreign conquest for an
abandonment of empire altogether. By these lights, the "one world" he
envisioned would simply be an American world.[42]

This critique ignored Willkie's stated opposition to American
empire in both its territorial and informal guises. In China he had decried the "treaty ports" through which Americans and Europeans had
controlled trade, exploiting the so-called open door. In recent years, he
had also explicitly condemned "dollar diplomacy," the practice by
which US government advisers offered "assistance" to smaller nations
with troubled economies. Too often, this assistance left those nations in
debt, dependent on American capital and political advice. Sometimes,
as in the case of the Dominican Republic or Nicaragua, the loans were
followed by a US military occupation tasked with restoring the "order"
undermined by the original financial intervention. Willkie believed in
"free trade," but he opposed "one country entering another with its superior economic power in order to dominate it politically." He also criticized Roosevelt's Good Neighbor Policy with Latin America. Based
merely on "pretty adjectives," it preserved the unequal relations established by the Monroe Doctrine and prevented mutually beneficial trade
policies.[43]

But Lerner's accusations of naiveté hit home. Comments scattered
throughout *One World* waved off any concerns about American power.
"It has been a long while," Willkie wrote, "since the United States had
any imperialistic designs toward the outside world." Many Mexicans,
Hawaiians, Puerto Ricans, Cubans, and Filipinos would have found
this ludicrous, but he argued that in this war the United States was not
fighting "for profit, or loot, or territory, or mandatory power over the
lives or the governments of other people," and so did not incite the widespread "dread of imperialism" he found everywhere along his route.
The impression that America had no "sinister designs" on the world

guaranteed its stores of goodwill. It was, he said, "the biggest political fact of our time."[44]

Willkie's untrammeled confidence on this question may have had something to do with the route of his trip. Most of his destinations were relatively untouched by American empire, and his route only skirted Latin America and the Pacific, where public opinion about the United States was deeply divided. Brief stops in Puerto Rico, Brazil, and West Africa gave him little chance to gauge the impact of naval base expansion in Puerto Rico or Air Transport Command activity in Brazil and Africa—the most visible instruments of US expansion during the war. Overall, the air of wartime expediency and the sense of a global crusade against the Axis served to keep less savory impressions at bay. From what he could see, American soldiers, sailors, and airmen were great ambassadors of goodwill. If Willkie made any connection in his mind between the gruesome scenes he had witnessed in Puerto Rico almost three decades earlier, when US power had a direct role in propping up an oppressive labor regime, and today, when the military had joined sugar companies as the chief symbol of American sway over the island, he did not record it. If he understood how American missionaries and American business abroad could prompt as much resentment as inspiration, he did not mention it.[45]

Like many of his fellow Americans at midcentury, Willkie believed that American empire was disappearing. "America's hands are clean, thank God!" declared one of his correspondents, R. J. Malley of Cleveland. The United States had "freed Cuba" from Spain, Malley argued, while the 1934 US guarantee of self-determination for the Philippines convinced Willkie and Malley alike that the United States was moving toward the end of its ill-fitting turn as an imperial power. Willkie admitted that the United States had "not yet promised complete freedom to all the peoples in the West Indies for whom we have assumed responsibility," but surely those promises and their fulfillment were inevitable.[46]

One World treated American empire as an afterthought, assuring readers that the tide of American expansion was receding, while distracting them from transformations in that imperial power at a crucial moment in its development. American empire, one newspaper columnist remarked in 1928, had created something new. It was "intangible, invulnerable, an influence over the minds and customs of mankind which is confirmed every time the world installs an adding-machine, dances to jazz, buys a bale of cotton, sells a pound of rubber, or borrows an American dollar." Willkie could see the looming end of the European imperial system, but he was less able to recognize how a US empire of cultural, economic, and military influence was gathering power—call it the "goodwill empire," perhaps—and the ways it might endanger the democratic internationalism he favored.[47]

Willkie's anticolonial barnstorming excited more forthright critics of American empire, some of whom saw him as a potential champion of their cause. William Prescott Allen, publisher of the *Laredo Times,* in Texas, released an open letter urging Willkie to tour the border region and Latin America in the name of promoting "equitable solidarity" with our "allies to the South." He cabled Willkie as well and offered to host a summit with Mexican officials. Willkie was open to the idea, and while the trip never happened, Allen's invitation—"Wendell, Go South young man! Go South!"—spooked the State Department, where Allen was considered a "pernicious element" in US–Latin American affairs. A visit to the "Good Neighborhood" by two loose cannons would stir up too much trouble. Let Willkie loose south of the border, officials worried, and he might actually begin to put Puerto Rico on the same footing as Egypt or India. He might begin to argue, as *Chicago Defender* world affairs columnist John Robert Badger did in critiquing *One World,* that "until Puerto Rico obtains self-rule, all our talk about the Good Neighbor policy and our efforts to promote good will south of the border will be taken with a grain of salt." Willkie might realize that the "reservoir" was leaking, Badger argued, because of American as much as European empire.[48]

Willkie never went as far as allies like Allen or Badger hoped he might. He largely met Americans where they were, embracing fundamental assumptions about the central role the United States should play in the world to come. When Max Lerner accused him of measuring with "an American yardstick," he captured how Willkie's "one world" would ultimately be joined together by American goodwill. Willkie may have been "passing on an invitation" from "the peoples of the East," but he was also convinced that the future of the world depended on the power of the United States.

Much of Willkie's appeal still rested on a picture of him as rough around the edges, a hale and hearty midwesterner. "Mr. Willkie's Hoosier heartiness," one letter writer commented, ensured his fundamental Americanness. Another correspondent enthused that he was "an average American in the uniform of Mr. America, representing the inquisitive, probing, want-to-know-why attitude typical of American thinking." The *New York Times* discerned in Willkie "a kind of good nature and good fellowship" that was "quite general in this country" and that prepared "millions of Americans to see the Russians and the Chinese not as problems but as neighbors." He no doubt enjoyed glowing accounts of his famed ability to connect with everyday people anywhere, and the praise likely reaffirmed his own belief in American generosity and boundlessness. But this confidence had its perils. Americans had long been invested in the idea of themselves as neighborly and openhearted, intent on making personal, one-to-one connections that could overcome differences. These were too often stories of American niceness as innocence, tales in which friendly Americans blithely greeted the world with goodwill and ignored their own histories of conquest and inequality. This conceit threatened to lodge a persistent note of American triumphalism at the heart of his call for one world and suggested how powerful a motivating force that kind of national pride would be for his audience.[49]

For all his newfound worldliness, Willkie framed much of what he saw in particularly American terms. He favored a specific take on the story of American capaciousness, one in which his Indiana roots tied him to a frontier past. Letters like one he received from William C. Rourk, a Florida minister who thought Willkie's journey showed "the 'Pioneer' spirit of our forefathers," no doubt encouraged Willkie to double down on the frontier trope throughout *One World*. In Russia and China in particular, landscapes and people put him in mind of the American West or the Indiana of his boyhood. He was, the journalist Marquis Childs noted, "constantly being reminded of American attitudes, American vigor, American enthusiasm." Rutted roads on the way to the Eastern Front brought back childhood stories of "conditions in pioneer Indiana." Yakutsk recalled a "western town" and China "our own American West in the days when it was being opened up." The many references had a pointed purpose: folding his experiences abroad into a national narrative familiar to

American audiences. The stories of Russians and Chinese were our stories, or perhaps our stories could become theirs.[50]

Willkie's discovery of proto-Americas abroad turned on a particular and popular understanding of history. The familiar westering, settler narrative was fundamental to American self-understanding. Of course, this sentimental story of frontier vigor and perilously won domestic order was as much ideology as history, a myth that occluded the cruel conquest—of nature and Native Americans—that propelled "Manifest Destiny." That Willkie—or the Soviets or Chinese, for that matter—would omit the darker side of their national stories is not surprising, but it suggested how Willkie's recourse to the "American yardstick" obscured the imperial drive that took Manifest Destiny beyond the limits of the nation and continent.

Willkie's frontier romances served other purposes as well. He hoped to convince readers that the Russians and Chinese were not only *like* Americans but poised to join the United States as potential partners in an interdependent world order. By creating modern societies, the Russians and Chinese would show that they were on the familiar path up from barbarism toward civilization. Frontier stories were inevitably modernization stories, too, and Willkie had made his faith in industrial development clear everywhere he went. All his praise for Soviet dams and factories and his excitement over the Chinese north and far west—"irrigation projects, power plants, fertile fields and pastures, whole cities could be built in this region"—stemmed from a fealty to the stage theories of economic growth and social development Willkie shared with so many of his contemporaries, at home and abroad.

Of course, he knew that highlighting "technological backwardness, along with poverty and squalor" in places like Egypt and the Middle East could make him appear squeamish and condescending. Americans tended, he said, to be "overconscious of bathtubs." What he hoped to emphasize was how growth and freedom were linked. His worries about public health conditions—open gutters in the streets of Tehran; the malaria, bilharziasis, and trachoma he found in Cairo, Jerusalem, and Baghdad—were closely tied to his support for greater self-government throughout the region. Across the Middle East the lack of self-government meant poverty and deficits in public health, education, and industry. Empire created underdevelopment. He also steered clear of the race thinking that shadowed fables of progress. "They call them 'natives,'" he told a reporter as he was preparing to write *One World,* "as if they're a fixed mass, fixed in time, immutable, incapable of change. But 'natives' aren't a mass, a native is an individual. Give him a crack at health, sanitation, education—and the marvel is how much he can develop, not how little."[51]

At the same time, when he reassured Americans that the Soviets or the Chinese planned "to develop their country much as we developed ours," the "American yardstick" was at work again. Being "overconscious of bathtubs" meant not only a prickly and superior colonial attitude but also the assumption that "natives" must learn to adopt Western ways. All countries, he suggested, needed to ascend the same ladder of development lately mounted by the United States as it leapt from frontier adolescence to industrial powerhouse.[52]

Modernization ideals spread across the world at midcentury. Nationalist dreams of mastering nature and unifying peoples brewed in all the countries Willkie visited, just as they did back home. But Willkie's account tended to bend these desires toward an established American pattern. Ironically, Willkie had jump-started his political career with a campaign against the greatest world symbol of American-led modernization: the Tennessee Valley Authority. Roosevelt's plan to nationalize and mobilize the energy industry for rural electrification, the very plan Willkie had denounced as a radical imposition on "free enterprise," had by the war years become a symbol for a liberal brand of large-scale industrial development with populist appeal. The TVA and like-minded projects, the writer Lewis Mumford said, were great monuments to American civilization, the "democratic pyramids."[53]

A "grand synecdoche," as one historian calls it, the TVA stood for top-down efforts with grassroots cooperation. Keen to ward off further Willkie-style attacks, the TVA's New Deal backers advertised its suite of improvements—dams, power plants, electric grids, household appliance distribution programs—as a plan to nurture rather than smother individual freedom. Willkie's fellow Hoosier and chief rival in the power hearings, David Lilienthal, marketed the TVA as sweeping yet decentralized. Willkie's friends at the Office of War Information would distribute thousands of copies of Lilienthal's 1944 book, *TVA: Democracy on the March,* promoting the TVA as a global icon of American technological modernity. Before long, cold warriors would deploy this idea in direct opposition to similar Soviet visions of progress—the TVA, they thought, could offset efforts by "totalitarians" toward the same ends. But during the hopeful wartime moment in US-Soviet relations, Willkie could paint American modernization efforts as complementary, not competitive. He stressed the anti-imperial power of development, but he was certainly not immune to the assumption that the American genius for development was a universal model for the world.[54]

This backdoor nationalism slipped into Willkie's economic thinking as well. A chief pillar of his vision was his belief in "free trade." This ideal—first articulated in the mid-nineteenth century by British internationalists like Richard Cobden and revived periodically since then—aimed to reduce tariff barriers and spur unchecked exchange of goods and ideas. With commerce went understanding and civilization, free trade idealists believed. Republicans like William McKinley and Democrats like Woodrow Wilson had looked to ease tariffs. Even Karl Marx judged the notion to be on the right side of history. Its most avid contemporary proponent was Secretary of State Cordell Hull, whose argument that freer trade would serve the ends of peace helped earn him a Nobel Prize in 1945.

In *One World,* Willkie painted open trade as a chief instrument of robust interdependence. Barriers to trade "imposed by the high walls of a multitude of individual nationalisms," Willkie argued, led to war and poverty. International cooperation should reduce those barriers. It should open up a global field for exchange and reciprocity—an area for trade "large enough so that the economics of the modern world could successfully function." The Allies fought, Willkie said in a speech early in 1943, for the "freedom to trade. Not through cartel systems, subsidized by governments, not with international doles, but commerce in the best sense of the word—self-respecting commerce, conducted as far as we are concerned by free citizens."[55]

Willkie hoped for equitable trade relations between independent nations. Free trade in practice, however, tended to benefit those nations with the largest economies and trading networks and thus the capacity to dominate the market. No surprise, then, that its most eager champions were

British in the nineteenth century and Americans by the middle of the twentieth century. For its most eager advocates, like Hull, free trade was the true path to global modernization, a "one world" of hegemony for American business in the global capitalist economy. "Leadership towards a new system of international relationships in trade and other economic affairs," Hull said in 1942, "will devolve largely upon the United States because of our great strength. We should assume this leadership, and the responsibility that goes with it, primarily for reasons of pure national self-interest." His critics—including, ironically, many British statesmen—tended to see advocacy of free trade as a way to crack open preferential imperial trading networks. For them, free trade appeared more acquisitive than idealistic, a building block for a future US global empire.[56]

Whether Willkie recognized it or not, his "free trade" was likely to benefit American interests far more than those of the smaller nations he hoped to champion. Free trade was like another favorite Willkie slogan, "free enterprise." Both promised a level playing field, but their advocates often ignored or concealed how advantage inevitably accrued to the big players in the market. With "free enterprise" at least, Willkie had begun to suspect that the term aligned him with Lerner's "corporations and cartels." It did not appear in *One World*, and when asked about it he looked for alternatives. "That's another term such as 'isolationism' that has been used pretty hard," he told one interviewer in 1943. "Make it 'individual opportunity.'" Later he suggested to the prominent writer and libertarian John Chamberlain that he preferred the term "responsible enterprise." Right up until the end of his life he was searching for the right way to cast his economic ideas. "Free trade" and "free enterprise" wanted balancing with something properly democratic, something that suggested freedom within mutually agreed-upon limits and a careful balance between Americanism and internationalism.[57]

It was John Chamberlain, in fact, who was most attuned to the great conflict between internationalism and nationalism in Willkie's thought. Reviewing *One World*, he argued that Willkie's political success would depend on his ability to "somehow convey to the American people that he is interested in freedom for China because it has a close connection with the well-being of Rush County or Poker Flat." His ideas would fail if "the people get the idea that he is more interested in the problem of Yakutsk and Chungking than he is in the problem of Indiana." He had to be seen as "an internationalist because he is an American."[58]

Chamberlain's critique captured Wendell Willkie's quandary. Winning Americans over to internationalism would require catering to their nationalist impulses. If he hoped to expand his political appeal and shore up support among Republican voters, he'd have to court favor beyond the cities, the coasts, and the educated middle class already inclined to support him. Doing so, however, might backfire and alienate his liberal constituency. But with his journey, his book, and the very idea of "one world," Willkie had unsettled conventional nationalist thinking. He had shown the people of the world as not other, inferior, or in need of American stewardship. He asked Americans to confront their demands for self-determination and insisted on the extension of self-determination to minorities at home. He imagined a new form of reciprocity with the world, one that millions of Americans responded to with unprecedented urgency. And yet that reciprocity was undermined by the subtle undercurrent of national exclusivity he revealed in his fondness for frontier stories, for modernization, for free trade and free enterprise. His reliance on Americanism as a standard of global measure—Lerner's "yardstick"—was intended to render the foreign familiar, but his effort to convince his readers that there was an interdependent "one world" might falter if they only had to imagine that world as fundamentally like America.

Of course, all nations subsist on a measure of exceptionalism. By its very nature nationalism encourages the "imagined community" to cherish their stories of belonging above all others. Willkie both distrusted and embodied this fact—it was a dilemma of his times. At every point on the *Gulliver*'s itinerary, nationalism and internationalism jostled for primacy. Internationalism was at its highest tide since 1919, but Willkie still feared that a "growing spirit of nationalism"—necessary fuel for the anticolonialism he favored—would eventually win out. That was "a disturbing thing to one who believes that the only hope of the world lies in the opposite trend." Of course, nationalism was not simply internationalism's opposite but also its source and precondition. Willkie's embryonic movement had no chance of dispelling nationalism completely. But he had come away hopeful, from Turkey, China, and elsewhere, that nationalists had struck a robust compromise with their less fervent commitments to internationalism. Could the same be said for the United States?[59]

Most American reviewers of *One World* were less skeptical than John Chamberlain. "It's not a book," exclaimed the *New Yorker*'s Clifton Fadiman, "it's a searchlight." John Temple Graves, writing in the *Birmingham Age-Herald,* found "a bookful of magnificent worldliness." Willkie had made himself "to internationalism what Walt Whitman was to democracy, its singer and the breather of its spirit." Like the poet, he mixed airy abstraction and earthy enthusiasm, helping many reviewers to attach stories of actual people to internationalist idealism. The book "took us behind the battle lines," a Philadelphia rabbi remarked in a sermon devoted to *One World,* to "see the millions of common folk who make up the United Nations . . . listen to their words, learn of their accomplishments, their dreams, their hopes, their thoughts for a better world, so that the phrase 'United Nations' might take on flesh and blood." Magellan may have been a great explorer, a *Chicago Sun* writer remarked, but Willkie "was the first man to bring the world back with him."[60]

What was most refreshing for reviewers was how Willkie unsettled the dogmatic tenor of wartime opinion. Even his blunders and hasty declarations were evidence of a mind at work trying to sort out his own take on events. "He does not live by a daily reassembling of old and unworthy prejudices," remarked Ralph McGill in the *Atlanta Constitution*. Willkie had "a seeing eye and an understanding heart," Walter Lippmann wrote in his syndicated column. Lippmann would soon begin to distance himself from Willkie, but on his first reading of *One World* the influential commentator ranked the Hoosier "among the few best American observers who have gone abroad." The theologian Reinhold Niebuhr, another barometer of respectable opinion who would shortly sour on Willkie-esque idealism, hailed him as a "keen observer, and some of his most casual reflections on men and events betray a remarkable grasp of essential realities."[61]

The overall gist of the press response suggested that Willkie had carved out a position that, while still short on particulars, was both idealistic and acceptable to respectable opinion on the left or right. In the *New Republic*, Malcolm Cowley congratulated him for getting up to speed so quickly. He was now "exactly 128 years ahead of the State Department," which Cowley feared still thought in terms of the Congress of Vienna and its world of warring states. Speaking for the rightward-leaning, Guy L. Smith, editor of the *Knoxville Journal*, commented that Willkie offered no "mush-and-milk utopia." He "returned to his native heath as neither a Communist, nor a British imperialist, nor as a Henry Wallace."[62]

Any contrast with Roosevelt's vice president must have pleased Willkie, who was always at pains to distance himself from his fellow internationalist. He had considerable sympathy for Wallace's general ideas—they were remarkably similar, right down to the rhapsodizing about air-age global shrinkage—but Willkie knew that the political center distrusted Wallace's fondness for government planning. He sensed that a link to Wallace—who would, within the space of five years, lose his vice presidency, launch an ill-fated presidential run under the banner of the communist-backed Progressive Party, and find himself Red-baited out of public life—was politically risky. Though a borderline radical on questions of race and empire, Willkie remained a classic liberal on economic questions. "Frankly, I am unable to follow some of Vice President Wallace's pronouncements," Willkie told a journalist when the inevitable comparison came up. His political instincts suggested a more realistic brand of internationalism: best to keep those "who think they can blueprint tomorrow" at arm's length.[63]

Doubters remained, of course. Willkie was never going to win over conservatives keen to lump him in with the world blueprinters. The right-wing syndicated columnist Paul Mallon argued that Willkie had turned the "mechanical fact" of a newly small world into a "political argument" that was little more than a "a plausible fable." Irresolvable difference between peoples would persist. Commentators like Mallon were the respectable face of America First–style hypernationalism. And while America First itself would gradually fade away, suspicion of Willkie-style racial liberalism and progressive internationalism lodged itself firmly on the American right. The attacks were sometimes personal. George R. Baldwin of Van Nuys, California, wrote directly to Willkie, assailing him as "an attenuated American, an Anglophile, a Russophile, a Globophile."[64]

British imperialists joined American nationalists, whom they usually abhorred, in their distrust of Willkie's agenda. Churchill quipped that his book should really have been called the "Gullible's travels." Other Whitehall officials deemed it a clever move in the great game of empire. Its attack on British colonialism, they said, was really advocacy for a new, informal American empire. "Political tutelage of backward peoples is wicked," one British official commented, "but commercial exploitation without responsibility is apparently to be encouraged."[65]

Less expected was dissent from places where Willkie had been rapturously received the previous autumn. Some Egyptians objected to his descriptions of Cairo's poverty and political dependency on Britain, and some Iranians did not appreciate his dwelling on the sewage in Tehran's streets. Perhaps Willkie himself appeared "overconscious of bathtubs." Far more favorable notice came from Baghdad, where the Iraqi government released a statement, carried in all the major newspapers, hailing Willkie for his judgment that Iraq's capacity for self-government revealed the East's readiness for freedom.[66]

Overall, domestic and foreign rebukes were lost under a swelling chorus of praise. "The truth is that the American people are awakened, fully and wholly, to the fact that there is a big world of which we are a part," wrote the editor of the *Lexington* (Kentucky) *Herald*. "It will do more to win the war and to win a real peace," the paper's reviewer commented, "than any one book I have read."[67] By the summer of 1943, Willkie did seem to be having a concrete impact on public opinion. "Several million" had read him by then, the historian Henry Steele Commager observed, and Congress "appears awake to new responsibilities." The staunch nationalist bloc, which "demands the acquisition of stray parts of the British Empire" or "warns us against Russia," was now "tolerated rather than applauded."[68]

This surge of interest swelled Willkie's office mail, which had tripled since the book, forcing him to hire two new secretaries. He had "letters from men and women of all conditions throughout the United States," he said that summer, and their approval goaded him to press his case. In a July 4 national radio address he proposed that the United States add a "declaration of *inter*dependence among the nations of this one world" to its own Declaration of Independence. Americans, he felt sure, would recognize that many of the peoples of the world stood at a similar turning point in 1943 as the thirteen colonies had in 1776. Wars of liberation, then and now, made clear that the desire for freedom transcended regions, peoples, races, and cultural traditions. Americans would choose equality with the world rather than "narrow nationalism" or "international imperialism," both of which would produce "the certainty of recurring wars."[69]

Confident that Americans were already making that choice, in July Willkie published and broadcast an "epilogue" to *One World*. Nine months after his trip, he declared, "the climate in which men and women on our side think and live and hope has changed more sharply than the change from autumn to summer." The tide of war was turning, and several neutral countries he had visited, like Turkey and Iraq, had swung into formation with the Allies. Iraq had even declared war against Germany. The lesson was clear: when the Allies fought for their true ideals, the undecided would rally to the cause. The "citizens of the United Nations have learned that we do, in fact, live in one world." Americans, Willkie had no doubt, were "not likely to be laggards in an enterprise as great as this."[70]

Late 1943 brought mounting evidence that Willkie's faith might be rewarded. All summer the Senate internationalists toured the country, supported by funds and staff from the major internationalist organizations, holding meetings and speaking on behalf of their resolution to create a postwar organization. The tours were a major success. The movement remained largely middle-class, but the message seemed to be reaching a broader range of people. Polling on internationalist questions trended further upward. In September, one poll found, 81 percent of Americans—up from 70 percent in June and 63 percent in February—thought it was "a good idea" for the United States to become a partner in a "union of nations" after the war.[71]

Even the Republicans, meeting on Mackinac Island in Michigan in September to outline a postwar policy, seemed to be coming around. Old-guard party leaders, angry with Willkie for his independence and his tack to the left, did not invite him to the conclave. He was still planning another run for the White House, so he had his allies in the party push to get a plank supporting a postwar peace organization included in the conference declaration. The vague statement they won sought a middle ground between the hidebound nationalist wing of the party and Willkie's idealism. Obviously drafted by committee, it pledged Republicans to support "responsible participation by the United States in a postwar cooperative organization among sovereign nations to prevent military aggression and to attain permanent peace with organized justice in a free world." The pledge reserved the right to inspect any potential obligation for "its effect upon the vital interests of the nation." But the statement put the mainstream right on the road to supporting some form of international organization. "The issue," Anne O'Hare McCormick declared as the conference concluded, "is no longer whether this nation will cooperate in maintaining peace; it is how, to what extent and in what ways we will cooperate."[72]

That fall, Roosevelt finally gave permission for the State Department to unveil its postwar planning efforts—or at least the fact of them. Meeting in Moscow in late October, Cordell Hull and his Russian and British counterparts, Viacheslav Molotov and Anthony Eden, released an agreement that would guide the war's endgame. The fourth article of the declaration pledged to jointly negotiate the peace and create "at the earliest practical date a general international organization, based on the principle of the sovereign equality of all peace-loving states . . . for the maintenance of international peace and security." The Moscow agreements gave a great jolt of adrenaline to the Senate resolution, which had been mired in committee since the spring, held up by a shrinking band of prewar isolationists in both parties who decried the effects of "supergovernment" on American independence. A vague compromise resolution, with the fourth article of the Moscow declaration added and all reference to an international police force or compromises to US national sovereignty struck, passed by an 85-to-5 vote.[73]

Willkie was pleased but not satisfied. He called for the "democratization of the relationship between the four great powers and their smaller allies—some of them not so small—and a liberalizing of the relationship of colonial powers to their colonies." The Moscow agreements needed to be "enlarged," he said, pitching his flag well outside the careful Senate compromise. There needed to be a true "United Nations declaration," prepared and signed by a council of *all* the Allies. Otherwise, the drive for international cooperation launched in Moscow might degenerate "into a mere alliance of four powerful countries for the ruling of the world."[74]

Still, as 1943 drew to a close, Willkie's work seemed to be paying off. The general bump in support for internationalism had been accompanied by a positive view of Willkie himself. Overall, his approval ratings in 1942 and 1943 hovered around 50 percent—good numbers for a losing candidate. But he had become a polarizing figure, too. In late 1943, Darryl Zanuck of Twentieth Century–Fox surveyed audience reaction to newsreels carrying excerpts of Willkie speeches. He heard from seven theater managers in Southern California who found that feelings about Willkie ran high. In four out of seven theaters his appearance drew both immediate applause and equally vociferous booing. Willkie could split a crowd down the middle.[75]

In polling from late October 1942, just before his "Report to the People," 48 percent chose "good man, very capable and sincere" as their primary opinion of him, but only 2 percent of those polled thought to select "approve his trip, did a good job as good-will messenger." Eight months later, just as the *One World* mania was getting going, when asked for their opinion about "Willkie's ideas on the part this country should play in the postwar world," 31 percent approved, 14 percent disapproved, and 55 percent had no opinion. By September 1943, with millions of copies of the book in circulation, 66 percent of those polled thought he had "a good understanding of world opinion," 17 percent thought not, and only 16 percent professed not to know. In just those few months, a sizable portion of the public had swung toward his position. Willkie had become an icon of internationalism, a status that increased his political celebrity but would also expose him to the dangers of close association with such a fraught issue in the year ahead.[76]

For now, his work seemed to be having some practical effect. The banker Thomas Lamont wrote that Willkie's "ceaseless public exhortations" had helped bring the Republican Party around to the need for international cooperation. His position in the party was compromised, but no doubt some measure of the credit for the "overwhelming" win of the resolution in the Senate, Lamont argued, could go to him. By the last months of the year, Allied meetings in Cairo and the summit in Tehran had built upon the promising beginnings of Moscow. "The democratic ferment which I saw rising among the peoples whom I visited on my trip around the world last year now has found tangible expression," Willkie said in a speech in December. "At Moscow, Cairo, Teheran," he exulted, "the hum of the people's voice crescendos."[77]

But "one world" was still more idea than reality. Roosevelt might yet fall back on a Great Power solution for the peace. The lure of empire and its seductive fables of white racial purity might yet prove too powerful for Europeans, or Willkie's fellow Americans, to resist. While Willkie made headlines and formal approval for international cooperation seemed likely, a powerful undercurrent of nationalism also gathered strength among both liberals and conservatives. It worked deeply in Willkie himself, whether he recognized it or not. The next year, 1944, promised to be a fateful one.

CHAPTER 12

The Narrows of 1944

Kansas City, Wisconsin, Rushville

Wendell Willkie spent the closing act of his life trying to sustain the momentum unleashed by his trip and book. He ran for president again in 1944, but that would not be his greatest legacy. For most of a year, between the Moscow declarations and the first conference on international organization, which opened in late August 1944 at Dumbarton Oaks in Washington, DC, he urged his fellow citizens to see that any distinction between foreign and domestic was meaningless. American freedom, he argued, depended on true global freedom. But he found himself working against a gathering current that eventually settled the peace on terms far less expansive than his own. The forces of nationalism, empire, and racism remained resilient, and they would do much to constrain the possibilities of the new United Nations, even as the dream of one world would live on—faintly in the United States but more robustly around the world Willkie had toured in 1942.

By early 1944, as he prepared to mount another presidential campaign, Willkie had established himself as the foremost independent tribune of internationalism, admired all over the world for his brash idealism. But his popularity in his own political party had plummeted. His campaigns against colonialism and racism—not to mention his work for civil liberties—were too much for many Republicans. The midwestern old guard and the party leadership had never much trusted the converted Democrat anyway. But it was his book that was most likely to cost him a second presidential bid in 1944.[1]

Throughout 1943 and into 1944, even as *One World* broke publishing records, conservative Republican insiders bankrolled a nasty smear campaign against its author. Pamphlets, books, and articles appeared, trading in lies, rumors, and small doses of the truth, floating innuendo about Willkie's ties to Roosevelt and his plans to "broker away" American sovereignty. Meanwhile, many liberals who appreciated his internationalism shied away from supporting him as a candidate, recycling the old stories about his ties to Wall Street and the country club set. The attacks riled Willkie, despite his insistence that he cared more about promoting his ideas than jockeying for the Oval Office.[2]

In late 1943, when a group of Republican officials from Missouri led by Edgar M. Queeny, the head of Monsanto Chemical Company, challenged him to come to St. Louis to defend his views in public, Willkie reluctantly accepted. Queeny had supported Willkie in 1940, but now he baited him, sending nine leading questions about his internationalist views to conservative columnists. "Do you believe," one question sneered, "that it is desirable for America to permit flooding our country with alien individuals and alien ideas?" Another asked if he thought the United States "should become a member of a world supranational state." When Willkie learned that Queeny was selling box seats to the event for $50, he rented out the St. Louis hall and opened it to the public for free.[3]

On the day of his speech, he ignored the gotcha questions and unleashed a lively attack on the Democrats for evading open debate on world cooperation. Much to Queeny's chagrin, the stemwinder brought a standing ovation and a raft of favorable editorials. The next day, at a private lunch with sixty St. Louis businessmen, Queeny reportedly introduced Willkie as "America's leading ingrate." Whatever was said, Willkie lost his temper and his patience. "I don't know whether you're going to support me or not," he retorted, "and I don't give a damn. You're a bunch of political liabilities who don't know what's going on, anyway."[4]

His showing in St. Louis gave him a quick bump in the polls but did not bode well for his chances in the upcoming Republican primaries. In the months after the trip, Joe Barnes later wrote, Willkie had become "a man without a party, but by no means a man without a country." So he pushed ahead, crisscrossing the country in late 1943 and early 1944 as he had in 1940, meeting local party officials, making speeches, and wooing delegates. Polls showed Tom Dewey, with his more careful, patriotic brand of internationalism, as the favorite among likely Republican voters. Willkie was a close second, ahead of other challengers like Minnesota governor Harold Stassen and the arch-nationalist General Douglas MacArthur. But tallies of professional Republicans had him much further behind. Mike Cowles told Willkie that too many in his own party saw him "as a carbon copy of Roosevelt." No longer a dark horse, he was in a strange position: a leading candidate among the public at large, he enjoyed little support inside his own party. His only hope was to go after the same broad middle of American politics he had courted four years before, starting with undecided Republicans voters. Win enough momentum and he could sweep up independents and wavering Democrats in November.[5]

This strategy had narrowly failed in 1940. It would fail rather more dramatically in 1944. With the backing of few party leaders outside the Northeast and West Coast and most of his young and eager Willkie Club supporters off at war, his shaky handle on electoral strategy and organization eroded even further. He knew he could not repeat his 1940 game plan, when he skipped all the primaries. His strength was still with independents, but he had to prove that he could win over solid Republican voters, too. So he decided to enter the primaries in New Hampshire, Wisconsin, Nebraska, Maryland, and Oregon. He did well in New Hampshire but failed to sweep the delegates, winning six out of eleven from a region where his support ran deep. The Wisconsin primary in March would be a crucial test of his appeal in the Midwest. He would make a big push there, and if he failed, he told his supporters, he would withdraw from the race.

This was a rash decision. A stronghold of prewar noninterventionism, Wisconsin had large pockets of German Americans who resented the war and hated Willkie's internationalism. Many newspapers were in his camp, but most local Republicans were cool or downright hostile toward him. None of the other leading candidates bothered to campaign in Wisconsin, relying on their state-level surrogates to drum up anti-Willkie fervor. He went all in regardless, spending thirteen days in Wisconsin in the two weeks before the primary, going back and forth across the snowbound state by car, rail, and even horse-drawn sleigh. "Willkie has conducted throughout the state," wrote a reporter for *The Nation,* "one of the most fantastic presidential campaigns in American history. He has hit the towns and countryside with the personal zeal of the old-time circuit rider on the glory trail."[6]

For a moment it seemed his exertions might pay off. The crowds at his rallies skewed older, particularly in the small towns and the countryside, where most young people had gone off to work or war, but the throngs swelled as he traveled. By the end Willkie was drawing big crowds and warm praise in most newspapers. He gave himself a fifty-fifty chance of winning the majority of delegates. Come election day, however, the votes never materialized. Willkie was in a hotel room in a small town in Nebraska, gearing up for the primary there, when the returns came in: Dewey won seventeen delegates, Stassen took four, and MacArthur claimed three more. Willkie had won none at all.

He was disappointed but far from deflated. Frustrated at his inability to win over his fellow midwesterners, he took comfort in knowing that he had not repeated the compromises of the 1940 campaign. He withdrew from the race, returned to New York, and considered how to use his influence to sway the nominees from each party toward support for civil rights and a more robust internationalism. The pollster Elmo Roper estimated that somewhere between 2 million and 5 million Americans still wanted Willkie. His endorsement of Dewey, the eventual Republican nominee, or President Roosevelt was worth quite a lot. The GOP political professionals, Joe Barnes was to write, finally "had their revenge for 1940," but Willkie could extract a price for his continuing support.[7]

While Willkie bided his time, weighing how to best use his influence, a sea change in the mood of his fellow citizens was under way. By the middle of 1944 the uncertainty of the early war years had given way to something like grim determination. Few had ever doubted that the war must be fought—the nation had been attacked, after all—but the question of what, exactly, Americans were fighting for had always been less clear. As American involvement pushed toward three years, soldiers and civilians began to see the war in stark utilitarian terms: a job to get done in order to bring everyone home.

At its darkest, getting home meant killing "Krauts" and "Japs" until they gave up. For all the celebrations of wartime pluralism, Americans (and Japanese) in the Pacific theater waged what amounted to a race war, embracing brutal means for expedient ends. Official and unofficial depictions of the Japanese drew on familiar images of slant-eyed, devious, and warlike demons—or even monkeys or rodents—and those images contributed to exterminatory rhetoric. "We kill yellow rats," one Marine captain exclaimed to a reporter. "If we don't kill 'em, we won't be around for any peace. So we hate and kill—and live."[8]

Even in its less virulent forms the expedient mood began to eclipse idealistic wartime pronouncements. The Four Freedoms and the Atlantic Charter had always struggled to find a broad public embrace. Back in 1942, polls had revealed that seven out of ten people approved of the two statements when they actually knew or read them, but not that many people had even heard of them—35 percent for the Four Freedoms, 21 percent for the Atlantic Charter. By 1944 they were better known, but two Americans out of every five still said they had no clear idea what the war was really about.[9]

A portion of the shift in attitudes toward the war resulted from changes in American propaganda—some of which were the work of Mike Cowles, Willkie's friend and traveling companion. In 1943, the Office of War Information, bowing to political pressure from the newly Republican Congress, had turned away from the tenor of its early antifascist messages, which had heavily featured New Deal reforms, liberal pluralism on race relations, the Four Freedoms, the Atlantic Charter, and FDR himself. The agency grudgingly embraced more businesslike appeals drawn from advertising and public relations. Cowles led this effort to trim the sails of the domestic OWI, bringing in broadcasters and admen proficient at, as one historian has put it, "selling America to Americans." But even the new business-friendly domestic branch did not last long. Congress slashed its funding in 1943, and it was hobbled for the rest of the war. Joe Barnes's foreign branch fared better, but he found himself forced out in 1944, a casualty of the straitened environment for progressive opinion. The agency reverted to an unsubtle message of American power and benevolence. The idea was simple, OWI head Elmer Davis said. It was "that we are coming, that we are going to win, and that in the long run everybody will be better off because we won."[10]

As the just-win-the-war spirit spread, many began to see themselves as fighting for private and prosaic ends. Most soldiers, historians have found, fought for the men next to them, or simply to get home. The war correspondent John Hersey asked a group of Marines on Guadalcanal what they were fighting for. After an uncomfortable silence, one grunt said, "Jesus, what I'd give for a piece of blueberry pie." It was both an evasion of the question and the real answer. "Blueberry pie" stood for home, for family, for everyday life in a liberal, capitalist society in which public goals found expression in privatized idioms.[11]

Suspicious of explicitly ideological war aims and the whiff of authoritarian indoctrination they gave off, GIs tended to express their fight for "freedom" in more basic ways. Take, for instance, those sexualized cousins to blueberry pie, the "cheesecake" pinups tacked above bunks, painted on fuselages, and carried in pockets. Glamour shots of Rita Hayworth, Lana Turner, or Betty Grable—or snapshots of wives and girlfriends posed in emulation of those stars—revealed how soldiers fought not *for* ideals but to return *to* something. As one GI wrote to Grable, whose girl-next-door image made her the most popular star of the war years: "There we were out in those damn dirty trenches. Machine guns firing. Bombs dropping all around us. We would be exhausted, frightened, confused and sometimes hopeless about our situation. When suddenly someone would pull your picture out of his wallet. Or we'd see a decal of you on a plane and then we'd *know* what we were fighting for."[12]

Many Americans felt called to protect the state only because it protected their private concerns. More abstract war aims struggled to win the same emotional allegiance. In 1943, Norman Rockwell translated each of Roosevelt's Four Freedoms into tableaus of family, community, and religious life for the *Saturday Evening Post*. His familiar images of prayer, parenting, a Thanksgiving feast, and a workman exercising free speech charged broad ideals with the necessary sentiment to connect with a mass audience. The images were widely distributed, showing up on postage stamps, as war bond posters in shop windows, and on all manner of other paraphernalia, and finally gave the Four Freedoms the necessary charge to catch on.

By framing Roosevelt's political principles in "terms everyone can understand," Rockwell changed them into fables of domestic life. With their appeal to idealized white, Christian families and communities living in classless harmony, they made domestic tranquility the sole ideology around which a majority of Americans could rally. They represented both an imaginary past and a hoped-for future that the nation might either re-create or achieve once it dispensed with the nasty business of another foolish foreign war. These sentimental tableaus had commercial analogues in the ad pages of the glossy magazines, where corporations took to framing the fight in terms of a postwar return to prosperity, with a new Kelvinator and a split-level ranch as the wages of victory. The war, historian John Morton Blum commented, "could signify only what the culture ordinarily endorsed."[13]

Fealty to private obligations did, ironically, serve to bind Americans more closely to the state. In fact, an invigorated federal government was one of the war's greatest outcomes. Global conflict supercharged the New Deal and laid the groundwork for the national security state of the Cold War era. War bond drives, morale campaigns by government and business, calls to national service in factories or on the front lines, and celebrations of the GI as the consummate citizen all worked best when they invoked the terms of public sacrifice for private ideals. The result was a paradoxical but potent patriotism that welded individualism to nationalism. Most Americans acquiesced to a sudden, unprecedented bump in federal authority because it protected home, family, consumer goods, and ordinary self-interest—the "American Way of Life."[14]

Support for a postwar organization fluttered a bit in mid-1944, buffeted by the furrowed-brow drift of the national mood, but it never cratered, holding at around 70 percent in the polls. Only 10 to 15 percent of the population clung to the old "isolationist" beliefs of the immediate prewar years, with the rest either undecided or not paying attention. The success of *One World* certainly contributed to this, but the larger internationalist movement was also finally finding its footing. In 1944, many of the competing peace groups united under the umbrella organization of Americans United for World Organization. Several national Protestant denominations—the Methodists, Baptists, and Congregationalists—launched drives for world organization inspired by their message of brotherhood and peace. All winter and spring, ministers across the country gave sermons in support of international cooperation and urged their parishioners to write letters to elected officials. In Congress, lawmakers found themselves deluged with mail advocating for global collaboration in the name of Christ. In April, more than 1,200 Protestant clergy signed a petition reiterating Willkie's earlier call for the immediate formation of a United Nations council as the germ of a new world body.[15]

In late summer Darryl Zanuck, still working on a film treatment of Willkie's book, released *Wilson*, an extravagant portrait of the Progressive president that had been in the works for more than two years. The studio head had a lot riding on the two internationalist epics. "Unless these two pictures are successful from every standpoint," he told a reporter, "I'll never make another film without Betty Grable." The Wilson biopic—"The Most Important Event in 50 Years of Motion Picture Entertainment," Twentieth Century–Fox announced—came festooned with a raft of period songs, a soft-focus portrayal of the dour and rigid former professor, and a melodramatic retelling of the League's betrayal at the hands of the Senate in 1919. Pitting Wilson against Henry Cabot Lodge hardly seemed a recipe for box office gold, but Hollywood stardust worked its usual spell and millions lined up to see what *Time* called Zanuck's "colorful, worshipful sermon on internationalism." Runaway production costs left the sentimental political epic in the red, but it won five Oscars. Perhaps Americans would not let Wilson's dream go down to defeat again.[16]

Near unanimity, however, disguised emerging impatience with the more visionary ideas for world cooperation. A bipartisan undercurrent of nationalism coursing beneath events began to surface, putting Willkie's hopes in jeopardy. Former isolationists on both sides of the aisle, now rebranded as zealous defenders of national sovereignty, were the loudest dissenters. Senator Burton Wheeler, Democrat of Montana, would later liken the UN Charter to a bid to "legalize tyranny." Robert Taft, Republican senator from Ohio, warned against any postwar organization that would commit Americans to shipping aid to "President Whoozis of Worlditania." Such a future, he said, appealed only to "the do-gooders who regard it as the manifest destiny of America to confer the benefits of the New Deal on every Hottentot."[17]

Many Republicans held more moderate views but were still concerned that internationalist initiatives might endanger US national interests. The prominent Senate foreign policy expert Arthur Vandenberg, a former noninterventionist, still feared a "wild-eyed internationalist dream of a world State," but by mid-1944 he had begun to look for a compromise that would simply guarantee that "the United States should not be forced into a future war" by a world body. Another Senate Republican, Alexander Wiley, approached negotiations over postwar cooperation "with no desire other than to safeguard the interests of my country first, last, and always, and, through so doing, to advance the interests of all other like-minded nations."[18]

At the same time, some prominent liberal internationalists found that their idealism had begun to curdle. The theologian Reinhold Niebuhr, later hailed for his fatalistic realism in the Cold War years, argued that Willkie and other "children of light" naïvely assumed that the technical universalism brought on by flight and radio would inevitably lead to world political union, underestimating the particularism on which national feeling fed. World political union would only arise when humanity itself had truly superseded the power politics practiced by the "children of darkness" and founded an actual "world community." That time was not now, Niebuhr felt, and it might never arrive.[19]

Walter Lippmann had also begun to sour on Willkie-style globalism. He admired the Hoosier, having served as an informal adviser to his first campaign. He had praised *One World,* too, but now found himself increasingly dubious about Willkie's ideas. In 1943 and 1944, he would later remember, he wrote two books, *U.S. Foreign Policy* and *U.S. War Aims,* in an "open attempt to get away from the One World doctrine." The idealists, he argued, were victims of their own illusions. Their universalism could easily become an expansive globalism that might encourage nations to intervene anywhere in the name of self-determination everywhere. "The constitution of the world society should not be based on the assumption that everything is everybody's business," Lippmann argued. "We must not write into the constitution of the world society a license to universal intervention." The United States, he argued, should pursue a limited, rigorously realistic policy of great power self-interest and alliance. He agreed with Willkie that this alliance should include the Soviet Union. It had to—peace was not possible without Soviet participation. But postwar diplomacy had to be based on the hard coin of military power, spheres of influence, national interest, and rigorous alliances, not deliberative democracy in a world body. Internationalism had to have as its foundation cooperation between the Great Powers, not between all nations.[20]

Other erstwhile allies, including the Luces, peeled off as well. Just months after greeting Willkie as a "global Abraham Lincoln" on the return from his trip, Clare Boothe Luce took a seat as a Republican representative in Congress. Looking to score points with her right-leaning colleagues, she launched an attack on Henry Wallace, remarking on the House floor that his "global thinking" was, "no matter how you slice it, still globaloney." She had not been elected, she declared, "to preside over the liquidation of America's best interests, either at home or abroad. The sky's the limit of those interests."[21]

By 1944, both Clare and Henry Luce had grown impatient with Willkie's pronounced tilt to the left. Wisconsinites, *Time* commented after the primary, "clearly voted no confidence in global good will and a foreign policy of generalities." The problem, Henry mused another time, was not that Willkie was "too idealistic, but, rather, that his idealism is not quite on the right beam." Having already laid out his vision of an expansive internationalism that made American interest the source of global peace back in 1941, he was beginning to see that Willkie did not mean to help usher in his "American Century." "His crusade," Luce complained, "is not correctly lined up with the historical realities."[22]

Relations with the Soviet Union were increasingly at the heart of the "historical realities" that troubled Willkie's critics. Harold Stassen, one of his competitors for the Republican nomination, faulted *One World* for "an overemphasis of the wrongs of the British colonial administration and an understatement of the evils of communism." Willkie was not blind to the Soviet problem, but recent events had put his attempts to forge better relations with Stalin in jeopardy. In Moscow, he had lightly pressed the premier on "the Polish question," asking for clarification on his plans for the future of Poland and the treatment of Polish exiles in the Soviet Union. Stalin had been evasive, and Willkie had not wanted to push too hard. Then, in April 1943, the Nazis alleged that back in 1940 the Soviets had executed 22,000 Polish prisoners of war. The atrocity was not proven until years later, but the charges roiled the already choppy waters of American and British relations with the Soviets.[23]

In *One World* Willkie had cautioned that Stalin had not yet "announced to a worried world Russia's specific aspirations with reference to eastern Europe." He edged out a bit further with an early 1944 *New York Times* piece called "Don't Stir Distrust of Russia." Despite an overall tone of solicitousness toward the Soviets—"probably the most powerful ally that we have ever had"—he repeated his warning. One of "the most pressing questions in everybody's mind," he wrote, was what "Russia intends to do about the political integrity of small states around her borders—Finland, Poland, the Baltic and Balkan states." He urged Americans to work to persuade the Soviets to "accept and give the guarantees of a general organization, in which she and we are both members, rather than to seek her own protection by political and military control over adjoining territories."[24]

This earned him a rebuke in *Pravda,* where he was denounced as a "political gambler" whose "strange tricks" would only help the Fascists. Willkie's detractors at home had a field day, playing it up as evidence of his foolishness in courting Stalin. Distressed by the attack, Willkie still attempted to play it cool. In a back-channel message to Stalin, passed on by Archibald Clark Kerr, the British ambassador he had befriended in Moscow, he joked that a few more articles like that were likely to get him elected president. A few weeks later Clark Kerr wrote him with an update. Stalin had felt the *Times* piece needed an official reply, but he had no wish to hurt Willkie personally and would not attack him again in public. He liked Willkie, but did not want him—as a Republican—to be president.[25]

The *Times* article convinced nascent cold warriors that Willkie was unreliable. The Luces, in particular, further distanced themselves

from him. Early in 1944, Henry Luce backed away from personal support for Willkie's candidacy and gave his publications permission to criticize him. Years later, with the benefit of more than a little self-satisfied
hindsight, Clare Boothe Luce would remark that she had tried to set
Willkie on the path to righteousness. She had, she said, urged him "to
stop drinking, lose forty pounds, and adopt a more realistic understanding of the Communists' announced plan to conquer the world."
Once outspoken supporters of US-Soviet rapprochement, the Luces and
many of their allies were swerving to the right. Meanwhile, in Hollywood, Darryl Zanuck, tinkering with the script for his *One World* film,
downplayed Willkie's attempts to head off confrontations with Stalin.
The story now centered on an Indiana farm family, depicted as friends of
Willkie, who had grown disturbed by the Soviet threat. What had been a
quasi-documentary take on the borderless world became a melodrama
about an imperiled American family.[26]

As the initial wartime openness of 1942 and 1943 faded, the elements of Cold War nationalist liberalism were assembling. The potent
brew would not cohere for some time, but the ingredients—one part
sour Niebuhr, one part hard-boiled Lippmann, and one part stirred-up
Luces—were out on the counter. This did not bode well for Willkie-style
idealism. To think in terms of "one world" was a mistake, the anticommunist journalist Eugene Lyons remarked in early 1945. In fact, "the
slogan '*two* worlds' is closer to the dominant facts of our day."[27]

The narrowing drift of public opinion was also beginning to shape
postwar planning. In the United States, official attempts to design a successor to the League of Nations had been under way off and on since the
earliest months of the war. They had taken place in secret, inside the State
Department, in committees charged with finding workable frameworks
for the political, economic, and social functions of an international organization. The planners, led by Cordell Hull and his deputy, Sumner
Welles, argued over the details but agreed on fundamentals. Motivated
by commitment to an embryonic version of the "nationalist globalism"
that would eventually underwrite Cold War liberalism, the world framers

wanted to dispel the old "isolationist" spirit that fueled the nonintervention campaign of 1940 and 1941, but also to temper universalist zeal. They worked to guide the world planning efforts into more predictable channels, where the sovereignty of nations, particularly that of the major powers, would not be unduly hampered. Assuming that the United States would, and should, take the lead in spreading liberal capitalist democracy by way of "free trade," they hoped to coax the British away from their imperial trade preferences toward a more open system that would ultimately profit American business. Their framework for world governance called for a multilateralism that carefully preserved room for the United States to act unilaterally when necessary. They did seek some kind of workable rapport with the Soviet Union, but did not want to bend too far. With a suspicious Congress and the consequences of Wilson's failure always in mind, the planners shied away from a world body that would spread power too evenly among too many small nations, command its own global police force, or infringe on American sovereignty.[28]

The planners had entertained a number of models along these lines. They had argued among themselves and with the British over several schemes, including plans favored by Welles and Churchill for an organization divided into regional zones overseen by the big Allied powers. By late 1943 they began to come around to Hull's preferred version: a more unified, tripartite structure that featured an international criminal court, a general assembly where all nations could be heard, and an executive body where the four large powers—the United States, the United Kingdom, the Soviet Union, and China—joined by a rotating group of three other nations would make the decisions that counted. The organization would have no police powers; member nations would lend their own military forces for peacekeeping missions. But each of the permanent members of the executive body—later to be called the Security Council—would have a veto over any plan to commit forces in a conflict. Many details remained unresolved, but the quasi-democratic form of the eventual United Nations was taking shape.

The president insisted that the substance of these negotiations remain secret. He allowed Welles to write and speak in favor of an expansive postwar peace, but Roosevelt himself kept quiet about the details—to which, preoccupied by the war, he paid less attention until early 1944.

Hints of his inclinations emerged, but to the public his views remained vague. His primary conviction was that Great Powers start wars, so any lasting peace required yoking those nations together in a web of mutual obligations through a world organization. But that also meant putting the Great Powers in charge of any such organization. Planning for a world body should start with the leaders of the major "United Nations" who were fighting and collaborating to win the war, not a true world council of the sort that Willkie favored.[29]

As far back as 1941, there had been hints that American policy would make compromises with imperial privilege and Great Power politics. Off-hand comments the president had made about restoring France's colonial possessions in 1942 suggested he might modify his basic anticolonial convictions in order to keep his European allies happy. As Willkie's foreign policy adviser Raymond Buell wrote to him that year, Roosevelt was "moving toward a big-power hegemony, dividing up the world into spheres of influence." The executive committee of the new world organization, FDR remarked to British foreign secretary Anthony Eden in 1943, would make "all the important decisions." The general assembly would meet once a year or so, to allow the small states to "blow off steam."[30]

Indeed, the president had taken to calling Britain and America "policemen" or "sheriffs," bound to keep the world's peace. Later he would pin badges on the Soviet Union—which he and Willkie agreed was the most crucial player—and, over British objections, on China as well. The Four Policemen, as he settled into calling them, would run things in the postwar world, overseeing regional spheres of influence and working together to ensure global peace. When Hull brought him the plans for world organization in 1944, he was well primed to embrace their hierarchical structure.[31]

The new world body would not be a "superstate" or a world government. The president was "after workable minimums, not impossible maximums," Forrest Davis of the *Saturday Evening Post* reported in May 1944, in the first article to make FDR's Big Four thinking public. His efforts, Roosevelt told reporters not long after, would be dedicated to ensuring peace "without taking away the independence of the United States in any shape, manner, or form." He made it clear he was determined to keep any world body from "bartering away"—as the popular saying went—American sovereignty. In reality, the pragmatic Roosevelt had never considered a more democratic form for world governance. But to many, even the president appeared to have acquiesced to the general tenor of the times.[32]

Reactions to this emerging consensus diverged. Republicans and former isolationists who now styled themselves nationalists worried about the influence of the Soviet Union but comforted themselves with the narrowing ambit of the possible world organization. On the left dismay mounted. Even Sumner Welles, who had done so much to shepherd the State Department planning efforts, viewed the proceedings with distaste. Cruelly cashiered from his government post in the summer of 1943 after rumors about his sexuality began circulating in Washington, by 1944 Welles had emerged as an independent voice for a more democratic peace, calling for the kind of expanded world council Willkie had previously demanded. His book *The Time for Decision* did well—besting even Lippmann in sales—but the confidential councils from which he had been expelled took little heed.

Some might have expected Willkie to be pleased, his failed election campaign notwithstanding. The world, led by the United States, seemed to be headed toward his great goal. All the pieces were falling into place for a new framework for global governance. But in fact he felt a mounting unease. A bellicose nationalism on right and left, accumulating worries about the Soviets, and the gradual retreat from a fully democratic plan for the world organization had left Willkie feeling unsure about the future. In the months after his Wisconsin defeat, as he considered how to mobilize his leverage over the upcoming presidential contest, he struggled with how to renew his call for an expansive, anti-imperial peace and make it stick.

That summer, seeking to galvanize independent voters and influence the Republican Party platform, Willkie—at Mike Cowles's urging—wrote a series of seven newspaper articles on domestic and international issues. Six papers from coast to coast published the articles, and thousands of other newspapers, big and small, reprinted them. Willkie distilled them into a liberal-leaning platform draft (which Republican officials predictably ignored). The first attacked states' rights and defended the intelligent use of federal power in a "modern complex industrial society." The next promoted civil rights, including an anti-lynching law. Others spoke up for expanded social security and labor rights, embraced a measure of federal economic intervention to stoke the fires of "responsible enterprise," and reiterated his belief in low tariffs and free trade.[33]

In the final article he tried to take on the surge of nationalism, challenging his fellow citizens to retire the distinction between home and abroad. "Our small American farms, our huge American factories," he wrote, "have close bonds with what is produced in the Andes and the hills of Szechuan, with the complex trade mechanisms of London, with the cargoes that sail from Bombay and Oslo and Melbourne. Whatever we do *at home* constitutes foreign policy. And whatever we do *abroad* constitutes domestic policy. That is the great, new political fact." Then he reiterated his call for a "Council of the United Nations" to ensure political representation for smaller nations, which, he said, were determined not to let "three or four great powers to continue to dictate their destiny." Ultimately, he argued, this would be in the national interest. All the talk about protecting American sovereignty missed the point. In an interconnected world, sovereignty was "not something to be hoarded, but something to be used."[34]

This was also the thrust of a remarkable piece he wrote for *Foreign Affairs* in April. The nature of one world, he argued in "Our Sovereignty: Shall We Use It?," was such that freedom and independence no longer meant going it alone. Clinging to a nationalist foreign policy actually meant losing freedom, he reasoned, for it allowed "other nations to make decisions affecting vital American interests at *their* convenience and when *they* choose." The emerging system of nations was no different from city infrastructure, he argued. Each car and building operated independently, but the system as a whole required traffic lights and fire departments. "Common support of a common fire department," he wrote, "does not affect the individual titles of ownership to individual properties." And it was "the red and green lights," he reasoned, "that give us freedom to use our automobiles."[35]

The point was clear: accepting interdependence was the best way to safeguard American independence. Membership in a robust, democratic world organization would empower rather than circumscribe American freedom, he argued, trying to heed John Chamberlain's advice and appeal to Americans *as* Americans. "To my mind, mutuality of responsibility and service represents more real freedom, in the sense of freedom from wars and economic disaster, than can be gained through adherence to all the sterile formulas of exclusive national sovereignty written into all the books of international law ever published." A new era in human governance was on its way, Willkie contended, one in which extensive internationalist agreement would now protect and enable the flourishing of national life. The United States, he said, could be a leader in world cooperation. "To use this leadership . . . will not be to weaken the sovereign power of the American people; it will be to widen it and make it more real."[36]

The *Foreign Affairs* essay was the most sophisticated argument Willkie ever made for his cause. Dispassionate and clinical by his standards, it was nonetheless heartfelt. He was shouting into the rising wind of national self-interest, but he continued to insist that getting the peace terms precisely right was crucial for the world—and for America itself. "Only occasionally does it happen that one issue arises which is so controlling that every other issue is subsidiary to it, and this is it," he told Samuel Grafton of the *New York Post*. "But it is not enough for a man to repeat the right words about world collaboration. He has to be on fire with it. He has to feel, in his belly, that this is the door which will open outward to an expansion of American activity and prosperity. You cannot be wrong on this issue and right on any other."[37]

For Willkie the fate of colonialism felt especially urgent. He had done more than anyone to push the problem of empire into the public square, but negotiations over what might actually happen to colonies and mandates rarely made headlines. Those debates unfolded in secret, alongside the discussions shaping a future world body, and pitted the British against the Americans. Before he lost his State Department position, Welles had taken the lead for the United States, arguing in the spirit of the Atlantic Charter that "the liberation of peoples should be the main principle"

underpinning American policy. He took a clue from some of his State Department colleagues who worked with their ears to the ground abroad and, like Willkie, recognized that the war had changed the calculus on race and empire. The Allies, one State Department report suggested in 1942, must "face the fact that the survival of the very democracy which they are fighting to defend demands the *spread* of democracy and the spread of democracy means the end of imperialism."[38]

The president shared his friend Welles's distaste for imperialism. He had often expressed visceral disgust at British imperial administration, often retelling the story of his stop in the British colony of Gambia on the way to Casablanca to meet Churchill in early 1943, during his first airplane flight abroad. Struck by just a glimpse of the conditions Willkie had immersed himself in the previous fall, the president was shocked. "It's just plain exploitation of those people," he said at one point, remembering the poverty he had seen. The people of Bathurst (now Banjul), Gambia's capital, he remarked on another occasion, were "treated worse than livestock." Imperialists had "robbed this continent of billions" and the ultimate result would be more bloody wars. What would he do about it? How would Roosevelt and Welles translate their distaste into policy?[39]

Welles's initial solution to imperial injustice was to transform colonies and mandated areas into "trusteeships." Former dependencies would move toward independence under the oversight of the new world body. Roosevelt found early support for this policy from China and the Soviet Union, but unsurprisingly the idea ran headlong into British intransigence and soon bogged down, as both sides wrangled over how far the Atlantic Charter's promise of "self-government" should go in replacing the old mandate system. For the Americans, self-government meant eventual independence. For Whitehall, "self-government" would have to mean something short of full independence. Nothing, Churchill warned FDR and Stalin at their meeting in Tehran in late 1943, "would be taken away from England without a war." "Self-government" was vague enough, they felt, to keep a busybody world parliament at bay and to permit remote or indirect quasi-colonial control by way of promises of eventual membership in the Commonwealth or proxy governments of the sort Willkie had witnessed in the Middle East.[40]

The British viewed American anti-imperialism as hypocritical. British officials loved to goad Americans about their own empire. Would Alaska or Hawai'i be made into a trusteeship? they gleefully asked. They suspected the whole thing was just a power grab. "Independence is a political catchword which has no meaning apart from economics," one Colonial Office official remarked. "The Americans are quite ready to make their dependencies politically 'independent' while economically bound hand and foot to them and see no inconsistency in this."[41]

They were not wrong. Much official American anti-imperialism served to benefit American liberal capitalist democracy. Welles himself saw the trusteeship idea as a way to open dependent areas to American trade and to offer fruitful sources of raw materials and markets for American industry and business. His trusteeship idea hewed to the evolutionary logic of most Western thinking about the global periphery. The primary problem, for Welles and Roosevelt, was not that the people of the colonies remained unfree, but that the European powers had not fulfilled their responsibilities in leading their dependents up the ladder of civilization. Trusteeships would not replace mandate-style paternalism, but instead aimed to improve its performance via a more robust regime of supervision and inspection. An American-led world body, US planners felt, would be a better steward of colonial fortunes than the exploitative European powers.[42]

Trusteeship, while likely an improvement on the old mandate system, was unlikely to please many of the anticolonial nationalists Willkie had met, and even fell short of his own call for "the orderly but scheduled abolition" of empire. Roosevelt and Welles both believed in ultimate independence, but they were less than clear about the timetable. Some places, like India and the Philippines, would be ready soon. Others might not be ready for a hundred years, and some, Welles and other officials agreed, might need "more than a thousand years." Welles, for all his anticolonial conviction, had conventional ideas about racial hierarchy. "The Negroes are in the lowest rank of human beings," he suggested, and "the colored races" were on the whole "unfit for self-government." He also intended to exempt Puerto Rico and Hawai'i from his own international trusteeship plan, viewing these as subject to the Monroe Doctrine and somehow not equivalent to European colonies.[43]

Most Americans—particularly elite opinion makers—did not seek to upend the colonial status quo. Lippmann, in principle no friend of empire, warned that Americans should not follow Willkie in fixating on global freedom and should instead concentrate more on creating a framework for "collective security within which weak peoples can safely learn the difficult art of governing themselves." The banker Thomas Lamont appreciated Willkie's global barnstorming for justice but saw no benefit in a rush toward self-government. It would only harm American interests if Britain were compelled "to abandon Gibraltar, Suez, Ceylon, and various other outposts of empire that for all these generations have served as the strategic points for the safeguarding of our own world commerce."[44]

Many Americans simply were not interested. Few polling outfits paid much attention to imperialism, but a later poll, taken in 1946, found that 50 percent of those asked were "not familiar with the term." Of the 48 percent who said they knew what it meant, 17 percent thought it referred to one-person rule of an emperor or monarch and 12 percent identified it with the traditional idea of "territorial expansion," while a small group understood it in its more informal guises: 6 percent said it meant one nation imposing its will or government on another and 3 percent believed it involved "economic gains or exploitation of others." Only 6 percent of those who said they knew what empire was thought that the United States was "imperialistic"; 26 percent saw Britain that way, 7 percent labeled France an empire, and, reflecting the looming Cold War, 30 percent understood the Soviet Union to be imperialistic. Americans, it appeared, were uncertain about imperialism, and many were either unaware or not much troubled by the idea that their own country might be an empire.[45]

Given the overlapping ambivalences toward a trustee system, it's not surprising that Secretary Hull deemed the plan overly idealistic. After Welles was dismissed, Hull trimmed sail and proposed that the trusteeship structure only be applied to present mandates and liberated Axis dependencies. Even this raised opposition, this time from a new source: the US military. Navy planners told the president that the United States needed undisturbed sway over conquered Japanese island territories and other strategic Pacific holdings already held as mandated areas.

Not unlike the Soviets on their western borders with Europe, American planners imagined a defensive chain across the Pacific, and they insisted that the islands be kept out of any scheme that might lead to a loss of US control.[46]

Roosevelt resisted the proposed "empire of bases" in the Pacific that Truman would eventually accept, but he wavered elsewhere, gradually acknowledging that the British and French would reclaim most of their colonies after the war. Right up until his death, in April 1945, he insisted in conversation that he intended to ensure future independence for the European colonies, but the powerful need to placate his allies won out in practice. He even pulled back on the Atlantic Charter, remarking in late 1944 that while he believed in its principles, it was just a press release, not a state paper.[47]

At the world organization planning meetings at Dumbarton Oaks in late 1944 the trusteeship problem was tabled, but at the Yalta talks in February 1945, and at the founding UN conference in San Francisco a few months later, US planners came up with a series of compromises that secured the concept of trusteeship but removed its teeth. First, they decreed, territories could enter into trusteeship only by voluntary consent of the states that controlled them. Then they devised two categories of trusteeships: nonstrategic and strategic. The first would report to the General Assembly; the second, like the Pacific Islands coveted by US admirals, would fall under the auspices of the Security Council, where any member could veto action it didn't like concerning a strategic trust territory. The UN would end the mandate system but preserve its imperial paternalism.

In a last, tortuous round of negotiation, the Americans and British split the difference over the language they had been fighting about since the signing of the Atlantic Charter. British negotiators won "self-government" rather than "independence" as the eventual goal of international oversight in sections of the UN Charter dealing with colonized nations, while the United States secured "independence" as the goal in the provisions dealing with trusteeships. The results placated the British and the French (added to the Security Council at Whitehall's request) but satisfied few critics of empire—least of all the foiled freedom petitioners of 1919. The debates had been a "cruel buoying of the hopes of subjugated and oppressed peoples from one end of the earth to the other," the African American newspaper the *Pittsburgh Courier* lamented. "All the words about trusteeship add up simply to saying that each of the three powers is going to do as it pleases, whether the other people of the world like it or not." Mandates expert Rayford Logan was even more caustic: the UN Charter was "a tragic joke."[48]

As the trusteeship debates reached their climax in late 1944, it is not clear if Willkie knew exactly what was happening behind closed doors at the State Department. He was busy setting out the terms on which Roosevelt or Dewey could win his endorsement. In two articles for *Collier's* he took aim at both the Republican and Democratic platforms, finding inadequacies on both sides in the arenas of internationalism, empire, and racial inequality. He repeated his call for the United States to use its sovereignty rather than hoard it. Both parties failed, by his reckoning, to see the foolishness of making a peace that allowed the United States and every other nation to maintain traditional sovereignty in a world with no meaningful difference between the foreign and domestic. This was nowhere more evident than in the area of race. The war, he wrote, returning to the arguments of *One World,* had revealed "colonial, subject, and minority peoples everywhere" desperate for American ideals of freedom, even as black Americans were themselves disenfranchised. One can almost hear Willkie straining in his prose, sensing that his moment was slipping away. "This is the great quest of our time," he implored. "To future historians it may well overshadow all other aspects of the present conflict." The future of international collaboration—and thus of the world's survival—depended on the United States dispatching the "ugly discrimination" that continued to underpin the national experiment and the world system.[49]

Willkie's reluctance to endorse Dewey finalized his exile from the Republican Party. The party bosses barely even bothered to include their previous presidential nominee in the convention in late June, offering him no formal role or input, only a pass to sit on the stage and watch. He declined the obvious snub, but before long rumors of a more intriguing invitation circulated. Ever since the Lend-Lease debates, when Willkie had helped get the bill through Congress, there had been whispers that Roosevelt was on the verge of appointing him to a government position. The president and Willkie had always enjoyed each other's company, even if their relationship had soured a bit after the unpleasant confrontation at the end of the trip. FDR even went out of his way to defend his former rival to skeptical New Dealers, once rebuking his close aide Harry Hopkins for an offhand insult of Willkie. "Don't you ever say anything like that around here again," speechwriter Robert Sherwood remembered FDR saying. "Don't even think it. You of all people ought to know that we might not have had Lend Lease or Selective Service or a lot of other things if it hadn't been for Wendell Willkie. He was a godsend to this country when we needed him most."[50]

Throughout 1942 and 1943, many Americans wrote to the president urging that Willkie be named to this or that top post. FDR had supposedly considered him as a candidate for secretary of state but changed his mind after their strained White House meeting. Perhaps the president realized that Willkie did not have the patience or discretion for a traditional diplomatic role, but that did not stop him from trying to figure out how he might harness his popularity. By 1944, Roosevelt was said to be considering him for secretary of the navy or a position overseeing the political reconstruction of Germany after the war. Floated also was the role that seemed most fitting: US representative to the fledgling United Nations once it was launched. Prior to the July Democratic convention, the president even sent Secretary of the Interior Harold Ickes up to New York to sound out Willkie as a potential running mate. This was the sort of thing that had long been gossiped about, but now that party insiders were keen to drop Henry Wallace from the ticket—much to the dismay of many in the liberal-left wing—the president thought Willkie might appeal to all sides. Willkie was intrigued but feared looking like an opportunistic office-seeker. Cowles warned that he'd be turning on the Republican friends who had worked for him in 1940. He stalled for time, wondering if the Democrats would even accept the idea, and a few days later FDR turned to Truman instead.[51]

Willkie had also pondered a far more dramatic change of affiliation. What was needed, he had become convinced, was a third party. His influence inside the Republican Party was mostly gone, destroyed by his defeat in Wisconsin and the enmity of the "ex-isolationists, re-christened nationalists." The president, meanwhile, felt hamstrung by the powerful bloc of conservative southern Democrats in Congress. They had always bent New Deal legislation toward safeguarding white supremacy, and now they were even beginning to peel away from the president himself. A new party could unite the left wings of both parties and solidify a new postwar liberal majority. For some months Willkie had considered breaking away from the Republicans, even going so far as to consider a run for mayor of New York City on New York's Liberal Party line in 1945. While that was on the boil, he mentioned his third-party idea to former Pennsylvania governor Gifford Pinchot, who had worked to organize the Progressive Party, the so-called Bull Moose Party of Theodore Roosevelt, back in 1912. Pinchot was enthused—and soon got word of Willkie's vision to FDR.[52]

The president seized upon the idea. "I agree with him one hundred percent and the time is now," FDR told his aide and friend Samuel Rosenman. "From the liberals of both parties," the president enthused, "Willkie and I together can form a new, really liberal party in America." In the midst of the intrigue surrounding the vice presidency he sent Rosenman to New York to talk this new scheme over with Willkie. Their secret meeting, in a suite at the St. Regis Hotel, was a dicey affair. Willkie was so nervous about press leaks that he left the room when a waiter brought in lunch. He was also wary of FDR himself—could this be an elaborate political game, designed to secure some advantage Willkie could not quite discern? But Rosenman assured him the president wanted to team up, and wanted to talk it over as soon as possible, even if they could not start in earnest until after the election. Willkie told Rosenman he was game, but that any further discussion had to wait for the votes to be counted, when it could no longer appear that the offer was intended to win his endorsement. Keeping gossip at bay was critical.[53]

Several weeks of frustration followed the meeting, as Willkie watched the third-party plan slip away. The president, unwilling to wait until November, wrote Willkie on July 13, asking to meet sooner. "I want to talk with you about the future," he wrote evasively. Willkie drafted a careful reply, holding to his original position—"I hope that you understand that I make this suggestion because you in a great way, and I in a small one, have the trust and confidence of people who might see in the most innocent meeting between us at this time, some betrayal of the principles which each of us hold so deeply"—but he never sent the letter. News of FDR's attempt to set up a meeting—although not the purpose of the rendezvous—had found its way into the papers, and Willkie became angry, suspicious that the White House had leaked it.[54]

The president redoubled the affront by claiming, at a news conference, that he had never extended an invitation. Willkie sent word through a back channel that he was no longer interested in the meeting. This elicited another letter from Roosevelt, this one apologetic and abashed, claiming that amid the bustle of travel he'd forgotten that he'd sent the initial invitation. He did not know how the leak of a "purely personal note between you and me" happened, and hoped they could still meet. Three days later this letter, too, appeared in the newspapers. "I've been lied to for the last time," Willkie exclaimed to a friend. In public, however, he struck a gracious tone. He said that he "would much prefer that no such conference occur until after the election. But if the President of the United States wishes to see me I shall of course comply." FDR made several more attempts, but Willkie, unsure of the president's intentions and figuring that he would have time to renew the possibilities after the election, kept his distance.[55]

But there would be no meeting after the election, or ever again. Friends and relatives who had seen Willkie that summer thought he looked unwell, and on a trip out to Rushville in late August he found himself winded and weak, his chest tightening, unable to open the door to the train's diner car. In truth Willkie had always been courting a collapse. He worked too hard, ate too much, smoked too much, drank too much, exercised too little. He saw a doctor in Indianapolis but refused to go into the hospital—he didn't want to be written off as a beaten man with a weak heart. He tried to rest on the way back to New York on September 6, but he had to be helped from the train at Penn Station. He took a strong dose of sedatives to dull the pain and was taken to Lenox Hill Hospital, where reporters were told that he had a stomach problem and needed rest.[56]

For a month and two days, as the world celebrated the liberation of Paris and Allied armies surged toward Germany, while the future United Nations was being hatched at Dumbarton Oaks, Willkie was bedridden. He suffered a series of small heart attacks, but then seemed to improve. He read books, wrote letters, and met with a few select reporters, although he still refused to say whether he would endorse either Dewey or Roosevelt. He simply hadn't decided, he told Roscoe Drummond of the *Christian Science Monitor.* He worked on the final galleys of *An American Program,* a short book gathering up his recent magazine articles and the seven newspaper pieces from the spring. He wrote to Walter White about a book on race in the United States they hoped to write together. He would "escape" his bed soon, he told his friend, and they could get together for a few cocktails to discuss the idea.[57]

On October 4 Willkie caught a throat infection and went steeply downhill. On October 7, the day *An American Program* went into stores and the Dumbarton Oaks proceedings wrapped up, the hospital announced to an astonished public that Willkie was in critical condition. That night he had three heart attacks in quick succession—making it thirteen he'd survived since his hospitalization. He seemed to rally at one point in the night—even taking a warm scotch and soda as a stimulant around 1:00 a.m.—but the fourteenth heart attack was too much. He died at 2:20 in the morning on Sunday, October 8, with Edith by his side. Lem Jones, Willkie's right-hand man, came out to find a solemn group of reporters waiting in the lobby. "It's all over," he said through tears. "He went very fast."[58]

The news came too late for the Sunday morning papers, but it went out over the radio that morning. Many were stunned by the suddenness of Willkie's passing. People who never met him, one family friend reported, told her they walked the street that night, unable to sleep, trying to come to grips with the loss. Thousands wrote letters or telegrams to the family, and stunned tributes poured in from around the world. They came from President Roosevelt, from Winston Churchill, from the leaders and everyday citizens of the nations he had visited in 1942, and many other lands besides. "His advocacy of people's equity and of reciprocity," the Sian Branch of the People's Foreign Relations Association declared, remembering Willkie's visit to the front near their city in 1942, "would have had an important bearing on the future world political situation." They recognized how rare his voice had been. "Mister Willkie," J. J. Singh of the Indian League of America cabled, "was one of the few leading Americans who understood the necessity for an internationalism freedom [sic] of imperialism."[59]

The tributes came from public figures right and left—from Herbert Hoover to the labor radical Harry Bridges, from journalists who followed him, from ministers and priests in the pulpit, and from the Hollywood executive still working to turn One World into a movie. "Little people all over the world today are mourning the passing of your Dad," Darryl Zanuck wrote to Willkie's son, Philip. "He more truthfully represented them than did any other American. He will be remembered by free men everywhere as long as there are free men in the world."[60]

People wrote to Edith in droves. E. B. Jordan of Dallas cabled his condolences: "I am a common man and I love him because he loved me. I mourn his passing deeply." Oscar Lange of Chicago wrote that America had "lost a great and unselfish leader," and the world "lost a champion of a new age." The largely African American porters at Penn Station, the redcaps, who had gotten to know Willkie well in his many comings and goings from New York, wired to acclaim him as "the most courageous champion in recent times of all minority groups particularly members of the Negro race . . . 15 million souls share your irreparable loss."[61]

Sixty thousand people shuffled solemnly through Fifth Avenue Presbyterian Church on October 10 to see his body lying in state; 2,500 guests packed the church at the next day's formal services, while 35,000 more clustered in the streets outside listening in on loudspeakers. The crowds were notable for their unusual mixture of people: there were soldiers and sailors, even the working-class Americans Willkie had struggled to reach. In her newspaper column Eleanor Roosevelt noted the many African Americans standing among the silent bunches of people. One elderly black man arrived with a copy of One World under his arm, a Willkie family friend remembered. "He was our friend," the man said simply.[62]

The War Department offered Willkie a burial with honors at Arlington National Cemetery, but Edith decided he would go to Indiana instead. A week later there was a small service at East Hill Cemetery in

Rushville, where his grave would eventually be marked by a twelve-foot stone cross and a great granite book at its base engraved with quotes from his speeches and *One World*. Willkie was only fifty-two when he died. His ideas outlived him, but their influence—and his legacy—awaited the unpredictable judgment of history.

Conclusion

O N THE WAY BACK to Washington, flying east from the founding conference of the United Nations in San Francisco, President Harry Truman stopped over in his home state of Missouri. Eager to convey the great stakes of the new organization, he didn't wait for his return to the capital to give a major public speech on the negotiations just concluded in San Francisco. In an address at Kansas City's Municipal Auditorium on June 28, 1945, Truman announced he would put the United Nations Charter before the US Senate for ratification in a matter of days, and he urged America to be the first nation to approve the new world body. That this was even possible in a country that had refused the League of Nations, he understood, was due to the countless men and women who had worked to transform public opinion.

Two names stood out. Truman had honored Woodrow Wilson in his closing remarks at San Francisco two days earlier, and Franklin Roosevelt, whose death two months earlier had left the nation in mourning and catapulted Truman, an unexpected last-minute choice for running mate during the 1944 campaign, to the presidency. The tragic patriarch of the League and the recently departed author of the Atlantic Charter were the expected heroes of the moment. But in Kansas City another name came to mind as well. Truman's flight east from California to Missouri—five and half hours in the air, with one stop in Salt Lake City, as compared to his grandfather's three-month wagon trip from Missouri to Salt Lake in the nineteenth century—summoned the memory of a fellow midwesterner. "I am anxious to bring home to you," the president told his audience, "that the world is no longer county size, no longer state size, no longer nation size. It is one world, as Willkie said."[1]

By that time the name Willkie stood on its own as an offhand icon of the interconnected world. It was Willkie, the president implied, who had brought home to Americans how modern communications, airplanes, and total war had shrunk the globe. Willkie's planet-girdling trip had shown Americans a world unimaginable to their grandparents. More than any other single person, he had prepared them to shed familiar forms of national belonging and consider what it might feel like to really *live* the new worldliness heralded by the United Nations. "It will be just as easy for nations to get along in a republic of the world," Truman declared, "as it is for you to get along with the Republic of the United States."

Swept up in the moment, reveling in the accomplishments of San Francisco, Truman oversold the new world body and its likely impact. The reality of the United Nations was more prosaic and more compromised. As the columnist Edgar Ansel Mowrer noted in the *St. Louis Post-Dispatch,* the UN Charter had provided for "a loose vigilance committee," not Truman's "republic of the world." Cheered by the president's invocation of Willkie, Mowrer hoped the UN might evolve into a true international government through which member nations would police the world and preserve the peace.[2]

Willkie's name still stood for a more expansive ideal of world cooperation, but the scale of the globe would remain "nation-size." Midcentury dreams of making the world whole would share the same fate as all their predecessors across recorded history. However those dreams take shape, they rest on fashioning a convincing rapport between variety and unity. Whether these global aspirations arise from the divine rule of emperors, the deliberative ideals of international law, the restless energy of the proletariat, the invisible tendrils of market exchange, the connective bonds of technology, or the ineffable diffusion of a world spirit, they tend to turn on the same question. Empire, international federation, world government, socialist utopia, capitalist globalization, and planetary consciousness all confront a shared dilemma: Why should the local—with its seductive affiliations of self, place, or nation—subordinate itself to the universal? Why should many become one? The troubles faced in forcing or encouraging this grand rapprochement have brought all dreams of world unity to eventual grief.[3]

Wendell Willkie's vision proved no different. Just a few years after his globe-spanning trip, his bestselling book, and Truman's triumphal announcement, the ideas he symbolized found themselves defeated, disparaged, or ignored. Commentators then and since have viewed his campaign as idiosyncratic, ephemeral, and naive. Willkie's voyage, they have remarked, was a cursory jaunt through complex and contradictory lands more divided by culture, politics, and history than unified by war, radio waves, and flight. If his "one world" vision assumed inevitable technological progress, it was also easily discounted as speculative, its airy ideals undisturbed by specific plans for the relations of part to whole. A true product of the age of broadcasting, "one world" traded in a kind of generic universalism common to many midcentury social ideas (think systems theory and cybernetics, Jungian collective consciousness, or the fear of a homogenizing "mass culture") that papered over social divisions with the prospect of coming wholeness.[4]

Like so many idealistic globalisms before it, one-worldism came apart when confronted with opposition, crumbling under the weight of its own contradictions, retreating before the harder faiths of nationalism and power politics. And yet, for all its faults, the idea had staying power. A vision of a world united without empire would live on in the political margins and in the global periphery Willkie had toured in 1942, waiting for another moment ripe with dreams of peace, freedom, and unity.

Willkie was an unlikely figurehead for dreams of world order. Neither statesman nor philosopher nor revolutionary, he thrived in the pragmatic and popular arena of electioneering and public opinion polling, middlebrow magazines and radio networks, newsreels and syndicated columns. But as a political celebrity in the age of broadcasting, he was well suited to a symbolic role at a propitious moment in the long history of the worldly imagination. Published at the tail end of a decade of economic depression, when international trade had decelerated and world politics lurched toward anarchy—seemingly a time of global division—*One World* tapped into a widely held sense that technology and war drove an undercurrent of mounting global interdependence. Whether he recognized it or not, Willkie's popular internationalism took flight in the slipstream of a host of late nineteenth- and early twentieth-century cosmopolitan visions that saw international cooperation as inevitable.[5]

The very conditions of modern life, writers, artists, and philosophers had observed, collapsed the globe. Whatever the political or economic crisis of the moment, the cultural and scientific forces of newness, swept along by capitalist expansion, propelled bouts of what later theorists would call "time-space compression." The steamship, the telegraph, the telephone, the airplane, the stock market, the radio: they all shrank space and sped up time, bringing far-flung places and cultures into greater contact. For the first time in human history, for worldly Europeans and Americans at least, people could imagine living in what historian Stephen Kern described as the "vast extended present of simultaneity." These forces bound people together, but they appeared to unleash chaos and disintegration, too. National feeling surged, offering narratives of shared purpose and common destiny as balms for disruption. But nationalism marked territory with myths of blood and belonging, sparking competition for patches of soil on the map. Internationalism's answer to the primal pull of the imagined community was heady—rational planning and appeals to cooperation between states. Fashioned properly, internationalism could ride the spreading global networks of communication, finance, and transportation. In fact, it would have to, the internationalists said, or the future held only war and privation.[6]

World-circling journeys of the modern era shared a similar spirit of unbridled confidence. Brashly sure that technology could conquer distance and offer humans an untroubled circuit of the whole planet, adventurers setting off to go around the world between the 1780s and the 1920s were themselves internationalists—propelled by a faith in the modern ability to throw a harness around space and time. By 1942 however, when the *Gulliver* took off from Mitchel Field, a note of doubt had crept into the experience of circumnavigation. The perils of flight were part of it, but air travel was safer than it had ever been, and Richard Kight and his crew had inherited the confidence of an earlier generation in machines and human know-how.[7]

The doubt was more geopolitical than technological. Willkie discovered a "small and completely interdependent" globe, but he also found a planet divided by the failed attempts to unite it. The troubled tenure of the League of Nations hovered like a shroud over his trip. International cooperation, everyone knew, had not forestalled the rise of fascism, and Willkie came to see that it had also failed to break the sway of empire and racial hierarchy. Internationalists looked to corral nations with laws and logic, but they remained comparatively ambivalent about empire.[8]

Many internationalists were themselves imperialists who feared how nationalism would divide empires into many smaller polities and splinter the colonial system that spread "civilization." But World War II, like the Great War before it, was a war between empires, and the peace would have to address the imperial system that the earlier conflict had left in place. If the United Nations was to succeed where the League of Nations failed, it would have to tame nationalism and dispel the power of empire and race to divide the world. So in truth, the world Willkie encountered was far from one. Its apparent unity was an illusion of technological hubris that did not so much bring people together as force them to confront their internal divisions. One world was not already achieved but was precarious, even endangered.[9]

The doubt that accompanied Willkie around the world fed a sense of urgency upon his return. In the anxious rush of his final years he sought to forge an internationalism equal to the challenges posed by empire and nationalism. His hopes and fears were global; he could never forget the surging freedom dreams he encountered from Egypt to China. But in those two years his attention turned back to the United States, where the League of Nations had never even gotten off the ground. By the time of his death he feared that resurgent American nationalism would hamstring internationalism and license a continuation of empire. He had dedicated himself to leading the country between "narrow nationalism" and "international imperialism," but it looked as if the two perils had joined forces. The "ex-isolationists, rechristened nationalists" and liberals had found common cause, or at least a common enemy in his brand of one-world internationalism.[10]

Still, enthusiasm for international cooperation swelled as the war ground toward its end. In early 1945, just as fifty nations were preparing to gather in San Francisco to write the charter for the new United Nations, public approval for a world body had soared as high as 90 percent in some polls. Of course, the final shape of the UN—with the Four Policemen astride the Security Council, the compromised trusteeship system, no world police, and the veto—would surely have disappointed Willkie, as it did all those who had placed so much hope in the Atlantic Charter. How could someone fully support the UN, W. E. B. Du Bois asked, "when at least one-fourth of the inhabitants of the world have no part in it, no democratic rights?" The UN plan may have been "designed especially to curb aggression," Du Bois wrote in his 1945 book on race, empire, and the war, *Color and Democracy,* "but also to preserve imperial power and even extend and fortify it." Cut to fit its times, the new world body ended up little different from its predecessor. Not long after, the United States was moving to help its European allies reestablish colonial regimes in Asia and Africa, and shoring up its sphere of influence ahead of the looming Cold War.[11]

The return of nationalism, the turn away from "one-world" idealism, the steep descent into Cold War antagonism—all of it suggested that Willkie's influence had amounted to very little indeed. Had he lived, he might have come to agree with Du Bois that "our imperialisms at home" forestalled any dream of an egalitarian world.

A British visitor to the United States during the war, the writer Norman Angell, marveled at the Willkie phenomenon but warned against overestimating its power. *One World* may have been on display in "every Woolworth and drug store," but he guessed that it still reached only something like 10 percent of the population. Angell underestimated Willkie's full influence, but he was not wrong to caution that the Willkie boom exemplified American public opinion and "its extreme susceptibility to mass movements—to fashions in ideas which run through the whole nation, and then as suddenly subside."[12]

It would have been hard enough, even at the height of the age of broadcasting, to move an entire country, let alone one that was sharply divided, accustomed to wayward individualism, and preoccupied by wartime anxiety. Willkie came as close as anyone other than President Roosevelt to doing so, in part because he knew how hard it would be to put a jar over the lightning bug of popular support. "The great amorphous mass of public opinion," the diplomat Archibald Clark Kerr recalled Willkie saying when they met in Moscow, "was a capricious and incalculable thing. It tended to crystallize this way or that, and once it had crystallized no man, no body of men, could make it fluid again."[13]

By the time opinion had "crystallized" in the shape of the UN, Willkie's vision had been both realized and diluted. He had helped inspire the new world body, but it was one that preserved the privileges of sovereignty and empire. Nationalism had tamed internationalism once more. This bittersweet outcome reflected the contradictions he and his American audience embodied. In his trip and his book, and in the worldly persona he adopted, Willkie gave Americans the clearest, most widely seen picture of the actual *world* war. By "passing on an invitation" from "the peoples of the East" he asked Americans to confront the great dilemma of their times. American influence was not absolute, but contingent on the forces of global economic and political interdependence. With their dreams of freedom, sovereignty, and modernization, the anti-imperial nationalists were bidding to join the emerging world system—and to do it as much as possible on their own terms. Americans, he argued, should adapt themselves to that reality. He encouraged them to embrace the idea that freedom should be unilaterally extended around the globe, without regard for restrictions of "civilization" or color. Freedom was not to be hoarded, or delivered via tutelary conquest. What would it be like to feel for this new world, he asked, and to turn those feelings into actual concrete politics? And yet blindness about American empire and his own investments in American exceptionalism ran through Willkie's own writing. It is worth asking: had he lived, would his urgent call for interdependence have eventually placed him and his followers directly athwart the advance of American empire?

One World arrived at a crucial hinge moment, when a form of US empire measured in global economic, military, and cultural sway began to supersede hemispheric territorial conquest as the chief mode of American expansion. This emerging form of dominion—in which the United

States stepped up to rebuild, guide, and safeguard the world capitalist system—shared the global universalism that Willkie heralded, but pitched it instead as an avenue for the exercise of American power and influence. Willkie sensed the arrival of this new form of empire and objected to its overt precursors, like "dollar diplomacy." But his faith in "free trade" suggested that its full ramifications lay just beyond his field of vision. That Willkie could not fully untangle the dilemmas of US imperial culture as Walter White or W. E. B. Du Bois could do may not be surprising, but it did suggest just how hard it would be for most Americans to recognize and challenge this imperial mode of national power.[14]

This new American empire traded on the idea of "freedom"—the very virtue Willkie had championed. His "war of liberation" had to extend to all; that was the only way to truly make the world one. But freedom is a liquid and capacious sentiment, and its power can be put to work for any number of ends. The "Declaration of Interdependence" Willkie hoped for back in 1943 never appeared, and for many Americans freedom continued to mean national autonomy, not global community.

Americans, Pearl Buck wrote to Willkie in 1944, had been excited by his ideas, but some were daunted as much as inspired. They did not "really know what you are talking about," she lamented. "They hadn't been around the world. They don't know what ONE WORLD means, either the book or the idea. That they fear it means *something,* is proved by the enormous numbers who read the book. But a lot of people who read the book were frightened by it, because they didn't know enough not to be afraid. They wanted to return to one country—our own."[15]

In the coming years globalist fatigue would set in, as many Americans recoiled from worldly imagination that was not tied directly to national interests. "People have been badgered half out of their minds by the sense of a sort of 'global' responsibility," the writer James Agee complained with an air of skeptical ennui. They were in retreat from "the relentless daily obligation to stay aware of, hep to, worked-up over, guilty towards, active about, the sufferings of people at a great distance for whom one can do nothing whatever."[16]

In fact, the rise of a global US empire of influence ensured that Americans would involve themselves with the world more than ever before. But the nationalist resurgence and the dawning struggle with the

Soviets channeled the new openness away from reciprocity. In the atmosphere of unrivaled American power and Cold War fear, American exceptionalism displaced one-world interdependence as the taproot of a universalist vision, making "freedom" and "modernization" weapons in a global struggle for hegemony. Some embraced the worldliness the war had made possible, but many came to see the globe as a stage for the exercise of American influence. It became harder for Americans to imagine, as Willkie had hoped they would, how they might care for concerns beyond their national interest. In the years ahead, the United States would prop up a series of authoritarian governments in places— Egypt, Turkey, Iraq, Iran—that Willkie had visited. It would back Israel in its dispossession of the Palestinians and carry out a series of devastating Cold War proxy conflicts. By then the freewheeling persona Willkie had adopted abroad appeared less like a blueprint for a new US cosmopolitanism than like a precursor to the "ugly American" heedlessly running roughshod over the globe.[17]

Americans may have opted for "one country" over "one world," but it would be a mistake to dismiss the Willkie moment as a fad. Even if it was a momentary mass dalliance with worldliness, it pays to watch closely when popular phenomena run headlong into the domains of politics and affairs of state. It is precisely in those disruptive, ephemeral moments, when great questions of policy and philosophy emerge in electrified and distilled form in the minds of the many, that they truly come alive as fully realized dilemmas, becoming real and consequential for the public, not just merely for thinkers and policymakers. Ideas like "one world" never disappear altogether. Even Willkie underestimated how it was possible for "crystallized" public views to become "fluid" once more.

One historian has summed up history since 1945 as a story of "one world divisible"—a tale of Willkie's universal dream relentlessly undone, split first into two worlds by the Cold War, then three with the emergence of the nonaligned movement among decolonizing peoples, and then splintered even further with the hypernationalism, terrorism, inequality, and globalization that succeeded the revolutions of 1989.[18]

This unraveling left a new conventional wisdom in its wake. In the same spirit as Agee's globalist fatigue and Walter Lippmann's attempt to do away with the "One World doctrine," an official consensus took hold: interdependent internationalism, particularly if it sought to curb national sovereignty, was irredeemably naive. One-world internationalism—or "globaloney," as Clare Booth Luce termed it—was an illegitimate approach to foreign affairs, to be banished in favor of more technical modes of thinking attuned to the interplay of national interests. Roughly divided into "international relations" for theorists and "national security" for policy professionals, this new approach redefined the old descriptive roles of "realism" and "idealism" as the only available choices on a menu scrubbed of cooperative internationalist options. Great Power realism and crusading idealism each turned on debates over how US power should be defended, expanded, and unleashed around the world.[19]

The new conventional wisdom had several unsavory results. First, it undid Willkie's efforts to expose the global color line. Willkie stood on the shoulders of innumerable thinkers, from Walter White and W. E. B. Du Bois to the anticolonial nationalists he encountered abroad, whose discomfiting ideas struggled to find a welcome audience in the halls of power. He had briefly put their challenge to white supremacy before a wide audience; the new consensus effectively silenced this passionate challenge to the international dominion of race and empire.

Second, the postwar consensus unfairly dismissed Willkie's ideas as naive fantasies of global harmony. *One World* actually offered a geopolitical analysis of the world to come—one that distilled much of the liberal-left thinking of the day. Accepting "Anglo-American dominance" of western Europe, Willkie argued, was not the way to "control the future." Drifting into a standoff with the Russians would lead to another war. Clear-eyed cooperation with the Soviet Union, equal partnership with the Chinese Nationalists, and pushing the British and other European allies toward decolonization: this was the path to true peace and national security for the United States.[20]

It is tempting to wonder how Willkie would have reacted to the deepening tension between the two superpowers had he lived. Would he have eventually followed most of his fellow liberals into the Cold War camp? Or could he have found another way? Maybe he could have restarted the Willkie Clubs as internationalist societies dedicated to expanding the UN. Perhaps he and Roosevelt would have launched a robust liberal party that could have kept Stalin in "the club," forged a rapport with Mao's China, curbed red-baiting at home, and paved the way for a non-imperial America. Starry-eyed fantasy, perhaps, beset with moral and political dilemmas at every turn. Counterfactual speculation is like armchair time travel, a fruitless guessing game. We can't say what would have happened had Willkie lived. We can discern only what he imagined—and consider what his ideas unleashed.

Here is where the habitual dismissal of one-world idealism comes to matter. The prevailing consensus has both diminished and obscured Willkie's actual legacy. Even in death and disfavor, Willkie did not disappear entirely, but his true significance vanished under a deluge of Cold War–induced amnesia. This would have surprised his contemporaries. In the immediate aftermath of his death many believed that his name would never be forgotten. For a while that idea held, even if the Republicans tried to forget him immediately, avoiding even mentioning his name at their 1948 convention. In 1946 the human rights advocacy organization Freedom House—formed with Willkie and Eleanor Roosevelt as honorary co-chairs back in 1941—awarded the inaugural One World Award to the broadcaster Norman Corwin. The prize was a trip around the world, and the result of Corwin's journey was a thirteen-part CBS radio documentary called *One World Flight*. Corwin found Willkie and the one-world ideal admired everywhere but the "reservoir of good will" for the United States severely depleted and incipient Cold War tensions on the rise. His 1947 broadcast was widely praised, but the audience was smaller than expected.[21]

In 1948 a national poll named Willkie one of the most admired public figures of the twentieth century, but his fade from prominence was already under way. Consider the fate of the movie *One World*. As late as November 1945, Darryl Zanuck still hoped to get the picture made, but discussions with directors Elia Kazan and John Ford bogged down, and the project was eventually shelved. It felt "dated," Kazan commented, and Zanuck himself was leaning away from Willkiean idealism toward more conventional Cold War liberalism. Joe Barnes's 1952 biography of Willkie recalled his fights for internationalism and civil liberties but struggled to find a large readership when Barnes himself was coming under Mc-Carthyite fire for having been a Soviet expert in the 1930s and 1940s.[22]

Still, Willkie's name popped up in peculiar places over the next generation. Take this improbable passage from Truman Capote's *Breakfast at Tiffany's,* published in 1958 but set in 1943 and 1944. The iconic cosmopolitan ingénue Holly Golightly is musing about her ideal match: "If I were free to choose from everybody alive, just snap my fingers and say come here you," she says, she wouldn't pick Jose, her fiancé. "Nehru, he's nearer the mark. Wendell Willkie. I'd settle for Garbo any day. Why not?" The company Willkie keeps in her freethinking fantasy is oddly fitting: he's right there with a screen idol and an anticolonial nationalist, still a natural symbol of glamour and global wisdom.[23]

Before long, Willkie began to seem like a name from another time. The excitement surrounding his trip slipped from historical memory and the book seemed just an oddity of wartime life. He was dimly recalled by the public as an idealist and almost-president, and remembered primarily by political aficionados as the Republican who helped Roosevelt save democracy in 1940. But even as Willkie's own name faded, the idea of "one world" enjoyed a strange career. Willkie's vision was discarded at the highest levels of diplomacy and statecraft, but it lived on elsewhere. A full history of the idea's long tail lies beyond the boundaries of this story, but even the outlines are suggestive.

"One world" echoed most forcefully in the world society in miniature of the United Nations. The slogan became a kind of rallying cry among the international lawyers, human rights advocates, and experts in global governance who flocked to the UN and its partner institutions in the postwar years. The UN may not have been perfect at its birth, they argued, but it was a workable framework, one through which a true global public might be nurtured and a more ideal world union achieved. The UN itself was, as the titles of two books of the time announced, still "one world" in the making.

The philosopher Ralph Barton Perry dedicated his book by that name to the memory of Willkie—"the First Private Citizen of that One

World Which Having Discovered for Himself He Disclosed to His Fellow-Americans." There were two "one worlds," Perry argued, both of which Willkie had described for his compatriots. "There is that oneness of the world which has already come to pass—a oneness of contact and interdependence brought about mainly by scientific and technological changes; and there is that oneness of the world which has yet to be achieved by organization and institutions. The first unity sets the stage for the second in making it both necessary and possible." At that point the UN could fulfill its vast potential: "Contact and interdependence create a problem which if not solved results in destruction; but which if solved will result in constructive good surpassing any which mankind has yet achieved."[24]

Nine days after the Senate ratified the UN Charter, the United States dropped the first of two atomic bombs on Japan. Paired with the grim revelations from the Nazi death camps, Hiroshima and Nagasaki cast a pall over the coming peace. In subsequent years the bomb would have multiple and paradoxical effects: at first it would stoke the tension between the United States and the Soviets, but then it helped to harden the Cold War freeze, locking each side into the standoff of "mutually assured destruction." The bomb severely strained the newborn UN, but it also ratcheted up the stakes of world cooperation and drove a resurgence in universalism. For a few years after the war, organizations pushing for a full world government—like the United World Federalists—surged in membership, joining forces with older internationalists, pacifists, religious organizations, women's groups, and nuclear disarmament advocates in recoiling from the possibility of nuclear catastrophe.[25]

In 1948, the first world citizen appeared. A former actor and bomber pilot named Garry Davis renounced his US citizenship and pitched a tent on the grounds of the UN's temporary Paris headquarters, declaring his intention to live as a stateless person. "A curious phrase beat faintly inside my mind," he later recalled, "a phrase which seemed to echo from nation to nation and in the minds of men around the globe. 'One world or none,' wrote Wendell Willkie; 'One world or none,' reaffirmed Bertrand Russell and Albert Schweitzer; 'One world or none,' repeated Gandhi and Einstein." The Cold War, Davis said, would lead to the "annihilation of civilization" unless enough people followed his lead and dared to "practice 'one world.'" Rushing the podium of the UN

General Assembly on November 19, 1948, he launched into an unauthorized speech. "Pass the word to the people," he yelled as security guards dragged him out, "one government for one world!" Hailed by everyone from Jean-Paul Sartre to Albert Einstein, Davis was widely ridiculed in the country of his birth. He spent most of a decade bouncing around Europe and India, publicizing his cause. Without papers other than his own homemade "World Passport," he had to stay on the move. Finally he found himself in an Italian internment camp for stateless persons. The prison library, to his great amusement, boasted a copy of *One World,* but in order to leave the camp he was forced to apply to emigrate back to the United States and renounce his world citizenship.[26]

Davis's actions have been written off as a gimmick, but the dark fears he heralded were widely shared. They had been most effectively brought home to the people of the world by the nuclear scientists themselves, who gave their 1946 report on the perils of the bomb the doomladen title that Davis misattributed to Willkie: *One World or None.* Willkie had never put it quite that way—he died ten months before Hiroshima—but this ominous expansion of his catchphrase made its way onto banners and letterhead and newspaper advertisements signed by an impressive list of intellectuals, scientists, artists, writers, and musicians. World government, one such appeal went, was the only way "war can be averted and the peace and plenty for humanity which we all desire, be made possible . . . The choice is indeed between one world or none."[27]

This movement aroused great passion but met the same fate as its namesake. With little support from officials in Europe and America, peace advocates turned to the global periphery for moral and political support. Leaders like Léopold Senghor of Senegal and Jawaharlal Nehru of India took up the world federalist cause. "Did I believe in One World?" Mahatma Gandhi asked on the eve of Indian independence. "Of course I believe in One World. And how can I possibly do otherwise?" Upon Gandhi's death in 1948, one of the world federalist organizations announced that the iconic anticolonialist had "died as the presumptive first president of One World."[28]

While the *One World or None* report painted a grim picture of the nuclear future, others repurposed "one world" as a slogan of decolonization and racial justice. Even as the term faded in the United States and

Europe, it prospered elsewhere, becoming a slogan of the nonaligned movement, which sought to thread the needle between the two Cold War powers and chart a path forward for decolonization efforts in the "Third World." Du Bois had Manuel Mansart, the hero of his 1961 historical novel, *Worlds of Color,* take a global tour in 1936, traveling through Europe, the Soviet Union, Japan, and China. During his trip, Mansart "began to have a conception of the world as one unified dwelling place," a realization that transforms his view of politics. "Not since I girdled the globe," Du Bois as Mansart testified, "not since I conceived of One World instead of increasing congeries of new peoples and nations, infinitely dividing and subdividing until nationalism becomes a virulent cancer that threatens to kill humanity, did I realize that unity in variety is the true end of this world and also I can see that the world is ripe or ripening for such union."[29]

It was Holly Golightly's Nehru who was most taken with the "unity in variety" at the heart of the one-world idea. When the Indian nationalist leader first read *One World,* back in 1944, he wrote to his daughter that he found it exhilarating. Even as Americans were beginning to turn away from one-worldism, Nehru discerned in Willkie's book a vision that was capacious enough for the ambitions of millions. Considering the author's background, he wrote, it was a remarkable book. "The concept of one world hanging together, all inter-linked, is still quite difficult enough for most people, in the East or West, to grasp. . . . Yet I think this is the basic idea of our present-day world and unless we imbibe it, our other ideas are apt to be airy and without reality." "World commonwealth" succeeded Indian independence as Nehru's chief political goal. Abjuring the Cold War standoff and calling for freedom and peace, he argued that the Third World could become the model for a true global society. "It is for this One World that free India will work," Nehru declared in 1946. He joined other internationalists in looking to strengthen the UN and make it a platform for decolonization. "We talk of world government and One World and millions yearn for it," he said in a major radio address in 1948, after independence. "I have no doubt in my mind that world government must and will come, for there is no other remedy for the world's sickness."[30]

Nehru's world commonwealth never arrived, but the United Nations, despite its limitations, did eventually help the nonaligned movement push onto the world stage. Using the General Assembly as a public arena for their grievances, the anti-imperial generation saw out the age of European colonialism. Not all freedom dreams ended happily, as many of the new states of Africa and Asia found themselves hamstrung by the aftermath of imperial plunder and mired in debt to former colonial masters or the American-led institutions of the World Bank or International Monetary Fund (created in the same postwar moment that made the UN). Beset by war and corruption, struggling to fully emerge from decades of conquest, the anti-imperial generation did not always live up to Willkie's hopes or Nehru's ideals. Some leaders proved adept at revolt but less skilled at governance. Many fell back on nationalism to preserve their power or strayed from the nonaligned path to form an alliance of convenience with the United States or the Soviets. Some fell victim to US covert action, as a series of CIA-backed coups unseated leaders who were seen as too close to Moscow. Radical factions urged land reform or other programs that hoped to flatten out postcolonial inequalities, but they were largely sidelined or suppressed. Despite this history, decolonization was where "one world" had its greatest impact. The idea outlived Willkie to become one of the global idioms by which freedom was actually won by "the peoples of the East" who had given him such an indispensable education back in 1942.

By the latter third of the twentieth century, the notion of "one world" as Gandhi or Nehru or Du Bois had known it began to fade. With formal decolonization under way, the UN hobbled by Cold War intrigue, and the United States and Soviets fighting a series of bloody proxy wars in the Third World, the phrase fell off the lips of all but the most committed partisans of world government. And yet it did not die. The idea returned once more not as an instrument of politics but as a talisman of the great promise and peril unleashed by space flight, ecological crisis, and global economic interdependency.

Willkie, it turned out, had offered a preview of the era of globalization. The world maps he had imagined—free of the "splotches of color" that signified nations—revealed the international giving way to the unbounded global. They depicted the planet, in a proto-environmental sense, as one whole earth. They anticipated the era in which humans would actually see the planet itself, in images transmitted from spacecraft in orbit. For most people that opportunity arrived in December 1968, when Apollo 8 rounded the moon and the astronauts captured an image of the earth hovering above the lunar horizon. *Earthrise,* as the image came to be known, was the first of several Apollo images of the planet suspended in the vast blackness of space. They immediately became icons of a renewed cosmopolitan idealism that gestured back to Willkie's era and beyond, echoing the universal imagination of global thinkers from Seneca to Kant to Wilson. One of the Apollo 8 crew, Frank Borman, summed up what would soon become a kind of globalist cliché: "When you're finally up at the moon looking back at the earth, all those differences and nationalistic traits are pretty well going to blend and you're going to get a concept that maybe this is really one world and why the hell can't we learn to live together like decent people."[31]

Earthrise and its ilk inspired a widespread sense of humility about humanity's place on the planet. The images helped usher in a new "whole earth" sensibility that coursed through the 1960s counterculture. They did their part to fuel the rise of the modern environmentalist movement and a new round of nuclear disarmament agitation. This spirit made its way into all manner of idealistic expressions of global fellowship in the years since—think, for instance, of the Western vogue for so-called world music—most of which devolved into vague calls for unity: "One world is enough for all of us" went the refrain in Sting's "One World (Not Three)" on his 1986 live album *Bring on the Night.* But if the image of the planet floating in the void conjured up age-old dreams of world community, it also revived imperial fantasies in a new guise.[32]

The "whole earth" movement was soon equaled, and even subsumed, by the era of globalization. Planetary imagery became the default branding iconography for any corporation eager to demonstrate its ability to navigate the flows of information, commerce, finance, and people unleashed by deregulated global capitalism in the wake of the oil shocks and economic crises of the 1970s. Over the next three decades, a new global orthodoxy established itself. What global governance had failed to do, boosters of the new market-based interdependence crowed, global capitalism was accomplishing with ease. Take down trade barriers, they argued, exercising their own brand of globalist cliché; let the law of the market work its self-propelled magic, and a rising tide will lift all boats. The Cold War was over—the West had won—and global capitalism, energized by the dispersed network of digital technology, was leveling barriers to opportunity everywhere. The world was not so much one, the columnist Thomas Friedman declared, as it was flat.[33]

In this latest incarnation, "one world" abruptly became global marketing kitsch, an offhand way to signify vague unity, worldly inclusivity, or the capacious reach of one's business interests. The conceit is now everywhere around us. One World is American Airlines' international airline alliance brand. OneWorld is a fast-fashion line featuring "ethnic" prints. One World is a publishing imprint dedicated to global literature. The tourist attraction at the top of the new World Trade Center in lower Manhattan is, of course, the One World Observatory. An ideal that began in the air age has been updated for the Wi-Fi age, and now signifies easy and carefree participation in a panoply of world cultures, each accessible by way of a flight, a screen, or a just-in-time supply chain.

But "one world" also returned as a threat. For some, globalization simply meant Americanization. The latest instrument of the informal US empire Willkie had been unable to fully confront in its early years, the spread of American corporate power and popular culture now threatened to subsume local cultures worldwide. Some, however, detected an even more all-encompassing power at work. *One World, Ready or Not* was William Greider's 1997 exposé of free trade, financial markets, and global capital exchange. A great machine "that reaps as it destroys," "one world" for Greider meant multinational corporations, borderless finance, and statistically flat job growth. Willkie's interdependence, free trade, and responsible enterprise had metastasized into "the manic logic of global capitalism," dooming local industry and community, driving inequality to new heights, and birthing a new financial and corporate elite.[34]

Willkie was largely forgotten, Greider remarked, and so was his boundless optimism about egalitarian global interdependence. Outside the rarefied triumphalist air of CNBC, Davos, and university economics departments, "'one world' now evokes a different, more ambivalent set of emotions among Americans," he wrote, "especially among those whose livelihoods are threatened by the implications." The United States still stood at the head of the global economy, "but the essence of what is forming now is an economic system of interdependence designed to ignore the prerogatives of nations, even the most powerful ones." This system spurred new prosperity in some quarters of the developing world, and Greider even supposed, improbably, that it might yet undo the fiction of Western white supremacy, ironically fulfilling one aspect of Willkie's vision through its sheer leveling power. But it also lodged inequality and political instability everywhere across the networked globe. Nationalism had once undone "one world," and now a berserk "one world" returned to take its vengeance on the illusions of the nation-state. "The global economy," Greider wrote, "divides every society into new camps of conflicting economic interests. It undermines every nation's ability to maintain social cohesion. It mocks the assumption of shared political values that supposedly unite people in the nation state."[35]

The perils of global interconnection only deepened in the ensuing years, as climate change highlighted planetary fragility and stateless terrorism eroded whatever lingering utopian sentiments the internet had once engendered. Another book titled *One World* appeared soon after the millennium, seeking to provide an "ethics of globalization." The book's author, philosopher Peter Singer, made no mention of Willkie, but he could take as obvious what his predecessor had to argue for: that the peoples of the planet are inescapably joined in a web of communications, market transactions, greenhouse gases, and interlocking political alliances and resentments. But the world's problems were too intertwined for the nation-state to solve. What was needed, Singer reasoned, was a "global ethic." The perils of "one world" demanded a true sense of global responsibility that "should not stop at, or give great significance to, national boundaries."[36]

Singer argued that the rusty institutions of global governance needed an overhaul. New environmental and labor standards would curb the excesses of capitalism, and a reinvigorated international jurisprudence should supersede national laws. Only then would humanity be prepared for "the coming era of a single world community." Singer detailed a host of needed renovations to the architecture of global community, but the fact that his one-worldist vision appeared in the rarefied air of a series of endowed lectures at Yale University, rather than in the popular magazines, network radio broadcasts, and bestsellers that carried Willkie's message, suggests the reduced fortunes of globalist idealism at the turn of the millennium.[37]

The terrorist attacks of September 11, 2001, were another herald of a shrinking, interconnected world—American global power had helped unleash a bitter and sadistic brand of borderless jihad. Blind to their country's postwar empire, many Americans responded by retreating once more into belligerent nationalism. Embracing a view of the globe riven by a "clash of civilizations," they drew on language that echoed the old visions of evolutionary hierarchy and racial difference to shape geopolitical strategy. The US government ignored or commandeered the UN and other institutions of global governance and strode willfully into just what Al Qaeda (and later Daesh) were looking to provoke: a series of cataclysmic wars in what Willkie had once called "that vast and ancient portion of the globe which stretches from North Africa around the eastern end of the world's oldest sea and up to Baghdad on the road to China."[38]

US officials have renamed that swath of the greater Middle East—once the source of so much hope for Willkie—the "Arc of Instability." But Willkie's words from sixty-five years ago still apply: it is once again "the area in which our war will be won or lost." For almost two decades now, neither the Taliban, Al Qaeda, Daesh, nor any other jihadist insurgency has proven much of a match for US armies, Special Forces, or drones on the battlefield. But in the wreckage left behind—in Afghanistan, in Pakistan, in Iraq, in Libya, in Syria, and beyond—military triumph has proven hollow. The region has again become the "great social laboratory" Willkie found on his journey in 1942, "where ideas and loyalties are being tested." Can anyone doubt that the experiments have had disastrous results—for those countries, for the United States, and for any vision of world order?

For a while, amid the smoke and blood of the "war on terror," Americans could distract themselves from the ongoing spread of globalization. But in 2008, when the global economy, propped up by a tangle of inscrutable debt, stumbled and went into decline, the hazards of economic interdependence and market fundamentalism came home to roost. Greider's fears proved prescient, but almost nobody was prepared for what was coming next.

For the political establishment a kind of ersatz globalism still reigned, unshakable even in the face of economic meltdown. It was a far cry from Singer's ethical heights or even Willkie's brash idealism, but when Barack Obama took the oath of office in the aftermath of the financial crisis, he did not hesitate to invoke a worldly calling. Even in the face of economic collapse and terrorism, he felt sure he spoke for his fellow citizens, who knew "that the old hatreds shall someday pass; that the lines of tribe shall soon dissolve; that as the world grows smaller, our common humanity shall reveal itself; and that America must play its role in ushering in a new era of peace."[39]

Seven years later, after millions of Americans had lost their homes and jobs, economic "recovery" accompanied pernicious inequality, and a host of global dreams—from the Arab Spring and the European Union to the "war on terror"—had begun to unravel. Among the turmoil, another political outsider, like Willkie a former Democrat from the New York business world, launched a bid for the Republican presidential nomination. His message stood in stark opposition to Willkie's internationalism or Obama's lofty optimism. "Americanism, not globalism," Donald Trump bellowed at the Republican National Convention in 2016, "will be our credo."[40]

Elected with seemingly little mandate, Trump did not hesitate to speak for what Willkie would have called "narrow nationalism." Taking up a rhetorical cudgel on behalf of those Americans left behind by globalization, his inaugural address painted a dark picture of shuttered factories, broken schools, poverty in the "inner cities," and gangs and crime and drugs everywhere. "This American carnage," he said, would "stop now." Turning toward the rest of the world, Trump chose his words deliberately, trying to turn back the clock. "We are one nation," he declared, "we share one heart, one home, one glorious destiny." The "one nation" would stand alone and face the interconnected planet in the name of an extreme, fascist-sympathizing, nationalist group from another era. "We assembled here today are issuing a new decree to be heard in every city, in every foreign capital, and in every hall of power," Trump announced. "From this day forward, a new vision will govern our land. From this moment on, it's going to be America first."[41]

The very idea of "one world" had long been a shibboleth on the American right, and over the years various inheritors of the America First mantle decried official liberal internationalism and one-worldism alike as harbingers of a tyrannical slide toward a world superstate. Despite the fact that the United Nations was actually checked by US nationalism, and viewed by most Americans as a glorified debating society, conspiracy-minded observers on the right saw it as a nascent universal world power, bent on eroding American national sovereignty. Now Trump brought that strain of globalist fearmongering into the White House and stated it as national policy.[42]

In office, Trump has proven less than consistent, showing mostly rhetorical fealty to the right-wing populism that catapulted him into office. His leadership may in the end reflect only the Republican Party's full embrace of an orthodoxy of tax cuts and subsidy for big business. But his support for an insurgent revolt against globalization and his willingness to embrace white nationalism have altered the political landscape on a host of issues from trade to immigration. In practice, Trump's foreign policy has been erratic, swinging between skepticism toward the US military's global reach and a quick-to-bristle nationalism that stands ready to abandon the mythic mantle of isolationism for militaristic swagger in defense of American power. Yet the baleful echo from the dark years of 1940 and 1941, when the country swung between war and descent into homegrown fascism, suggests the United States has embarked on a new political and cultural era.

As with any germinating reality, this new era portends both tragedy and possibility. Trump's ascendance has unleashed the white nationalism that has always underpinned the American experiment. But it also marks the final end of Cold War complacency about American benevolence. In the existential struggle Willkie had tried to prevent (a fixation on external threats fitfully extended by the "war on terror"), the United States "contained" not only communism but also a full reckoning with the power of race and empire in its own history. Now that reckoning seems to be rushing in everywhere. If Trump's rise threatens to undo the multilateral postwar order, as both liberals and conservatives have lamented, it also lays bare the imperial power underpinning that postwar compact.[43]

Perhaps this is an opportunity for the country, a moment not unlike the one Willkie discovered during his hopeful "one world" jaunt. Three-quarters of a century ago, Willkie asked Americans to give up their innocence, their sense that they could stand apart from the world and its troubles. True interdependence would displace the paternalist right to lead a benighted world, and American democratic ideals—honored too often in the breach—could be perfected, shared, and transformed into a new worldly spirit. Time had its way with these one-world dreams—and today we need to think in terms of the many worlds living on one fragile earth—but as the illusions of empire fade Americans may find that they face a renewed version of the very dilemma Willkie laid out for them all those years ago: How can we live in the world without needing to dominate it?

NOTES

ACKNOWLEDGMENTS

INDEX

Notes

ABBREVIATIONS

AFHRA   Air Force Historical Research Agency, Maxwell Air Force Base,
               Montgomery, Alabama
Barnard   Ellsworth Barnard, *Wendell Willkie: Fighter for Freedom* (Marquette:
               Northern Michigan University Press, 1966)
Barnes   Joseph Barnes, *Willkie* (New York: Simon and Schuster, 1952)
Barnes Columbia Joseph Barnes Papers, Columbia University Rare Book and Manu-
               script Library, New York
Barnes LOC   Joseph Barnes Papers, Manuscript Division, Library of Congress,
               Washington, DC
BNA   British National Archives, Kew Gardens, London
FDR Papers   Franklin Delano Roosevelt, Papers as President: The President's
               Secretary Files, 1933–1945, Franklin D. Roosevelt Library, Hyde Park,
               NY
FRUS   *Foreign Relations of the United States*
MFAR   Archive of the Ministry of Foreign Affairs of Russia, Moscow
NACP   National Archives, College Park, MD
Neal   Steve Neal, *Dark Horse: A Biography of Wendell Willkie* (Garden City,
               NY: Doubleday, 1984)
Van Doren Papers Irita Van Doren Papers, Manuscript Division, Library of Congress,
               Washington, DC
Willkie, *AAP* Wendell Willkie, *An American Program* (New York: Simon and
               Schuster, 1944)
Willkie, *OW*   Wendell Willkie, *One World* (New York: Simon and Schuster, 1943)
Willkie Papers Wendell Willkie Papers, Lilly Library, Indiana University,
               Bloomington

INTRODUCTION

1. Elizabeth Barnes to Aunt Anna, Aug. 26, 1942, in box 11, folder: Correspondence, 1942, Barnes Columbia.

2. Willkie, *OW,* 202.

3. Ralph Ellison, *Invisible Man* (New York: Random House, 1952), 581.

4. Timothy Snyder, *Bloodlands: Europe between Hitler and Stalin* (New York: Basic Books, 2010); Tom Brokaw, *The Greatest Generation* (New York: Random House, 1997). See also the sources on the World War II home front in Chapter 11, note 14.

5. John Dower, *War without Mercy: Race and Power in the Pacific War* (New York: Pantheon, 1986); Thomas Doherty, *Projections of War: Hollywood, America, and World War II* (New York: Columbia Univ. Press, 1993); Benjamin Alpers, *Dictators, Democracy, and American Public Culture: Envisioning the Totalitarian Enemy, 1920s–1950s* (Chapel Hill: Univ. of North Carolina Press, 2003), 129–219; Mary L. Dudziak, *War-Time: An Idea, Its History, Its Consequences* (New York: Oxford Univ. Press, 2012). On the Atlantic Charter, see Carol Anderson, *Eyes off the Prize: The United Nations and the African American Struggle for Human Rights, 1944–1955* (New York: Cambridge Univ. Press, 2003), 16–17, and sources in Chapter 3, note 52.

6. Willkie, *OW,* 180 and ix.

7. See Mark Greif, *The Age of the Crisis of Man: Thought and Fiction in America, 1933–1973* (Princeton: Princeton Univ. Press, 2015).

8. Frank Gervasi, "Willkie at the Front," *Collier's,* Oct. 24, 1942, 58.

9. On Willkie's memory of Roosevelt's quote, see Alexander Werth, *The Year of Stalingrad* (New York: Knopf, 1946), 263; "Conference," *New Yorker,* Sept. 22, 1944, 15. On political celebrity, see Charles L. Ponce de Leon, *Self-Exposure: Human Interest Journalism and the Emergence of Celebrity in America, 1890–1940* (Chapel Hill: Univ. of North Carolina Press, 2001), 172–205.

10. Michele Hilmes, *Only Connect: A Cultural History of Broadcasting in the United States,* 4th ed. (Boston: Wadsworth, 2014); James L. Baughman, *The Republic of Mass Culture: Journalism, Filmmaking, and Broadcasting in America since 1941,* 3rd ed. (Baltimore, MD: Johns Hopkins Univ. Press, 2005); Paul Starr, *The Creation of the Media: Political Origins of Modern Communications* (New York: Basic Books, 2004), 233–402; Michael Kammen, *American Culture, American Tastes: Social Change and the 20th Century* (New York: Knopf, 1999), 47–189; James L. Baughman, *Henry R. Luce and the Rise of the American News Media* (Baltimore, MD: Johns Hopkins Univ. Press, 2001).

11. George Orwell, "Wells, Hitler, and the World State," in *All Art Is Propaganda: Critical Essays,* ed. George Packer (New York: Mariner Books, 2009), 150.

12. Lloyd Gardner, "FDR and the 'Colonial Question,'" in *FDR's World: War, Peace, and Legacies,* ed. David B. Woolner, Warren F. Kimball, and David Reynolds (New York: Palgrave Macmillan, 2008), 128–129.

13. Gardner, "FDR and the 'Colonial Question,'" 133; Stephen Wertheim, "Tomorrow, the World: The Birth of U.S. Global Supremacy in World War II," PhD diss., Columbia University, 2015. For different takes on the "empire of liberty," compare Anthony Bogues, *Empire of Liberty: Power, Desire, and Freedom* (Hanover, NH:

Dartmouth College Press, 2010) and Gordon Wood, *Empire of Liberty: A History of the Early Republic* (New York: Oxford Univ. Press, 2011).

14. Warren F. Kimball, *The Juggler: Franklin Roosevelt as Wartime Statesman* (Princeton: Princeton Univ. Press, 1991), 186–187.

15. Lynn Hunt, *Writing History in the Global Era* (New York: Norton, 2014); Prasenjit Duara, "Transnationalism and the Challenge to National Histories," in *Rethinking American History in a Global Age,* ed. Thomas Bender (Berkeley: Univ. of California Press, 2002), 65–71; Peter N. Stearns, *Globalization in World History* (New York: Routledge, 2010); Barry K. Gills and William R. Thompson, *Globalization and Global History* (New York: Routledge, 2006).

CHAPTER 1 ⚭ TAKING FLIGHT

1. On flight details see Willkie, *OW*; Richard T. Kight, "Willkie Flight," n.d., reel A3009, frames 638–652, AFHRA; Intelligence Service, U.S. Army Air Forces, "Summary of Interview with Major R. T. Kight, Air Corps," Nov. 12, 1942, in reel A3009, frames 653–659, AFHRA; Intelligence Division, Air Transport Command, "Report of Interrogation in General George's War Room, Oct. 16, 1942, Willkie Trip, Aug. 27–Oct. 14, 1942, B-24 (Gulliver)," in reel A3009, frames 661–714, AFHRA; Patrick M. Stinson, *Around-the-World Flights: A History* (Jefferson, NC: McFarland, 2011), 148–155.

2. Jenifer Van Vleck, *Empire of the Air: Aviation and the American Ascendancy* (Cambridge, MA: Harvard Univ. Press, 2013); Oliver La Farge, *The Eagle in the Egg* (Cambridge, MA: Riverside Press, 1949).

3. Daniel Rust, *Flying across America: The Airline Passenger Experience* (Norman: Univ. of Oklahoma Press, 2009), 125, 87–131; Van Vleck, *Empire of the Air,* 89–130. On Gann see "What Was It Like to Fly?," in *America by Air,* Smithsonian National Air and Space Museum, 2007, http://airandspace.si.edu/exhibitions/america-by-air /online/innovation/innovation14.cfm; Warren Kimball, *Forged in War: Roosevelt, Churchill, and the Second World War* (New York: Morrow, 1997), 184.

4. Maurice Hindus et al. to Willkie, June 24, 1942, and Willkie to Hindus et al., July 6, 1942, in folder: Trip to Russia and Mideast, June 21, 1941–Jan. 26, 1943, box 114, Willkie Papers.

5. Willkie to FDR, July 29, 1942, in Correspondence, box 68, Willkie Papers; Walter White to FDR, May 4, 1942, in Accession #001439-009-0001, Part 14: Race Relations in the International Arena, 1940–1955, India, General, 1942, Mar.–May, NAACP Papers, Library of Congress; Barnes, 290; Manu Bhagavan, *The Peacemakers: India and the Quest for One World* (Noida: Harper Collins India, 2012), 25–28; M. S. Venkatarami and B. K. Shrivastava, *Quit India: The American Response to the 1942 Struggle* (New Delhi: Vikas, 1979), 317–320.

6. FDR to Willkie, Aug. 3, 1942, in Correspondence, box 68, Willkie Papers; FDR to General Marshall, July 31, 1942, in box 173, folder 10: Wendell Willkie, 9/40–9/42, Series 5, FDR Papers; Barnard, 347–348; FDR to Joseph Stalin, Aug. 22, 1942, in box 173, folder 10: Wendell Willkie, 9/40–9/42, Series 5, PSF 1933–1945, FDR Papers; FDR to General Arnold, Aug. 8, 1942, and H. H. Arnold to FDR, Aug. 10,

1942, both in box 173, folder 10: Wendell Willkie, 9/40–9/42, Series 5, PSF 1933–1945, FDR Papers. See also Secretary of State to Ambassador Standley, Aug. 24, 1942, in Department of State, *FRUS*, 1942, China (Washington, DC: Department of State, 1956), 141–142.

7. Willkie, *OW,* 103; Barnard, 348; Alexander Werth, *The Year of Stalingrad* (New York: Knopf, 1947), 263.

8. Gardner Cowles, *Mike Looks Back: The Memoirs of Gardner Cowles* (New York: Gardner Cowles, 1985), 71.

9. W. H. Lawrence, "Willkie May Visit Russia, Near East," *New York Times,* Aug. 8, 1942, 1; W. H. Lawrence, "Willkie to Start Abroad in 3 Weeks," *New York Times,* Aug. 21, 1942, 14; "Mr. Willkie's Mission," *New York Times,* Aug. 21, 1942, 18; "Willkie to Spread War Output Facts," *New York Times,* Aug. 22, 1942, 6.

10. Joseph Barnes to Willkie, Aug. 19, 1942, in folder: Trip to China and United China Relief, May 1942–Aug. 1942, box 114, Willkie Papers.

11. Neal, 232; "Mrs. Willkie Has Final Say, but Husband's Plan Stands," *New York Times*, Aug. 20, 1942, 40.

12. Biographies of Willkie: Barnes; Barnard; Neal. Also useful are David Levering Lewis, "The Implausible Wendell Willkie," in *Profiles in Leadership: Historians on the Elusive Quality of Greatness,* ed. Walter Isaacson (New York: Norton, 2010), 229–260; Philip Beidler, "Remembering Wendell Willkie's *One World,*" *Canadian Review of American Studies* 24, no. 2 (1994): 87–104; James H. Madison, ed., *Wendell Willkie: Hoosier Internationalist* (Bloomington: Indiana Univ. Press, 1992). Bill Severn, *Toward One World: The Life of Wendell Willkie* (New York: Ives, Washburn, 1967) is suggestive, but carries no account of its sources. Mary Earhart Dillon, *Wendell Willkie, 1892–1944* (Philadelphia: J. B. Lippincott, 1952) is useful for its skepticism about Willkie, but both Barnard and Neal have doubted its accuracy. David Levering Lewis, *The Improbable Wendell Willkie* (New York: Norton, 2018) appeared too late for full inclusion in these notes.

13. Barnard, 11–14; Barnes, 5–8; Neal, 1–2.

14. Barnes, 5–7; Barnard, 8–16.

15. Quote in Barnes, 22; Barnard, 15–16; Neal, 2–3.

16. Quote in Barnard, 14–15; Barnes, 22–24; Barnard, 9–15, Neal, 3.

17. Barnard, 16–19.

18. Quote in Barnard, 29; Barnard, 21–22, 28–30; Neal, 4; Barnes, 25–27.

19. Neal, 7; Barnes, 24; Barnard, 30–31.

20. Barnard, 19–20; Neal, 2; Barnes, 20–23.

21. Quotes in Neal, 5, and Barnard, 36; Neal, 8–12; Barnard, 31–38.

22. Quote in Barnes, 28; Neal, 12; Barnard, 42–43. See also Alden Hatch, *Young Willkie* (New York: Harcourt, Brace, 1944), 189–196.

23. Quote in Barnard, 46; Neal, 13–15; Barnard, 44–46; Barnes, 28–29.

24. Quote in Barnard, 52; Neal, 14–16; Barnes, 30–31.

25. Kight, "Willkie Flight," frame 638; Intelligence Division, "Report of Interrogation," frame 661; Stinson, *Around-the-World Flights,* 149–150; Barnard, 349.

26. "Willkie for Puerto Rico Statehood," *New York Times,* Nov. 4, 1940, 13. Fajardo: César J. Ayala, *American Sugar Kingdom: The Plantation Economy of the Spanish*

Caribbean, 1898–1934 (Chapel Hill: Univ. of North Carolina Press, 1999), 113–114, 226; April Merleaux, *Sugar and Civilization: American Empire and the Cultural Politics of Sweetness* (Chapel Hill: Univ. of North Carolina Press, 2015), 36–40. See also Samuel Zipp, "Dilemmas of World-Wide Thinking: Popular Geographies and the Problem of Empire in Wendell Willkie's Search for *One World*," *Modern American History* 1, no. 3 (2018): 295–319.

27. Willkie, *OW,* 202; "One-World Pledge Urged by Willkie," *New York Times,* July 5, 1943, 6; Jackson Lears, *Rebirth of a Nation: The Making of Modern America, 1877–1920* (New York: Harper Collins, 2009); James Livingston, *Pragmatism and the Political Economy of Cultural Revolution, 1850–1940* (Chapel Hill: Univ. of North Carolina Press, 1994); Jeffrey P. Sklansky, *The Soul's Economy: Market Society and Selfhood in American Thought, 1820–1920* (Chapel Hill: Univ. of North Carolina Press, 2002); William Leach, *Land of Desire: Merchants, Power and the Rise of a New American Culture* (New York: Vintage, 1993).

28. By population, see Daniel Immerwahr, "The Greater United States: Territory and Empire in U.S. History," *Diplomatic History* 40, no. 3 (2016): 376.

29. Christopher McKnight Nichols, *Promise and Peril: America at the Dawn of a Global Age* (Cambridge, MA: Harvard Univ. Press, 2011); Neil Smith, *American Empire: Roosevelt's Geographer and the Prelude to Globalization* (Berkeley: Univ. of California Press, 2003); Alan Dawley, *Changing the World: American Progressives in War and Revolution* (Princeton: Princeton Univ. Press, 2003). For a dissenting view: Frank Ninkovich, *Global Dawn: The Cultural Foundations of American Internationalism, 1865–1890* (Cambridge, MA: Harvard Univ. Press, 2009).

30. Grant quoted in Ussama Makdisi, *Faith Misplaced: The Broken Promise of U.S.-Arab Relations, 1820–2001* (New York: Basic Books, 2010), 165. See also Nichols, *Promise and Power,* 54–57; Thomas F. Gossett, *Race: The History of an Idea* (New York: Oxford Univ. Press, 1997), 328–329; Gail Bederman, *Manliness and Civilization: A Cultural History of Gender and Race in the United States, 1880–1917* (Chicago: Univ. of Chicago Press, 1995); Matthew Frye Jacobson, *Whiteness of a Different Color: European Immigrants and the Alchemy of Race* (Cambridge, MA: Harvard Univ. Press, 1998); Kristin Hoganson, *Fighting for American Manhood: How Gender Politics Provoked the Spanish-American and Philippine-American Wars* (New Haven: Yale Univ. Press, 2000); Matthew Pratt Guterl, *The Color of Race in America, 1900–1940* (Cambridge, MA: Harvard Univ. Press, 2001); Matthew Frye Jacobson, *Barbarian Virtues: The United States Encounters Foreign Peoples at Home and Abroad, 1876–1917* (New York: Hill and Wang, 2001); Amy Kaplan, *The Anarchy of Empire in the Making of U.S. Culture* (Cambridge, MA: Harvard Univ. Press, 2002); Paul Kramer, *The Blood of Government: Race, Empire, the United States, and the Philippines* (Chapel Hill: Univ. of North Carolina Press, 2006); Marilyn Lake and Henry Reynolds, *Drawing the Global Color Line: White Men's Countries and the International Challenge of Racial Equality* (New York: Cambridge Univ. Press, 2008), 95–113. On "civilization": Bruce Mazlish, *Civilization and Its Contents* (Stanford: Stanford Univ. Press, 2004).

31. Eric Foner, *The Story of American Freedom* (New York: Norton, 1998).

32. See Barnes, 29.

CHAPTER 2 ✂ POWER AND THE PRESIDENCY

1. Barnes, 32–42; Barnard, 57–77; Neal, 14–24.

2. Barnes, 54–59.

3. Barnes, 36, 51, 79; Barnard, 78–84; Neal, 25–28; Mark H. Leff, "Strange Bedfellows: The Utility Magnate as Politician," in *Wendell Willkie: Hoosier Internationalist,* ed. James H. Madison (Bloomington: Indiana Univ. Press), 22–46.

4. John Dos Passos, *U.S.A.* (Boston: Houghton Mifflin, 1936; repr., New York: Library of America, 1996), 1210. See also Neal, 26; Barnard, 79; Barnes, 51–53.

5. Barnes, 54–56; Barnard, 100; Neal, 28.

6. Steven M. Neuse, *David M. Lilienthal: The Journey of an American Liberal* (Knoxville: Univ. of Tennessee Press, 1996), 68–101; Barnes, 60–63; Barnard, 84–88.

7. Neuse, *David M. Lilienthal,* 72–123; Barnard, 84–124; Barnes, 60–148; Neal, 28–36; Amity Shlaes, *The Forgotten Man: A New History of the Great Depression* (New York: Harper Collins, 2007), 182–192, 236–239, 280–282, 301–305, 345–351.

8. Katharine Brush, "Personal Impressions, Wendell L. Willkie," *Washington Post,* Jan. 1, 1943, S5; Bill Cunningham, "Willkie Differs with World Blue-Printers," *Seattle Times,* April 15, 1943; Walter White, *A Man Called White: The Autobiography of Walter White* (New York: Viking, 1948), 203. Barnard, 36, 125–141; Barnes, 100–101, 160–161.

9. Flanner: Barnes, 98; Barnes, 97–101; Barnard, 130–136.

10. Neal, 38.

11. Raymond Buell, "Willkie Campaign Memoir," n.d., 66, in box 46, folder 14, Raymond Buell Papers, Manuscripts Division, Library of Congress; Shirer: Neal, 38. See also Barbara Bellows, *A Talent for Living: Josephine Pinckney and the Charleston Literary Tradition* (Baton Rouge: Louisiana State Univ. Press, 2006), 164–176.

12. Neal, 37–38; Buell, "Willkie Campaign Memoir," 64–66.

13. Barnes, Untitled Manuscript, 1966, p. 3, in box 38, folder: Irita Van Doren, Barnes Columbia; Neal, 38–44; Barnard, 136–137; Barnes, 98, 156; Shlaes, *Forgotten Man,* 327–329; Richard Kluger, *The Paper: The Life and Death of the New York Herald Tribune* (New York: Knopf, 1986), 322–329; Charles Peters, *Five Days in Philadelphia: 1940, Wendell Willkie, and the Political Convention That Freed FDR to Win World War II* (New York: PublicAffairs, 2005), 32–35; Joan Shelley Rubin, *The Making of Middlebrow Culture* (Chapel Hill: Univ. of North Carolina Press, 1992), 34–92.

14. Ellsworth Barnard to Joseph Barnes, Oct. 6, 1952, in box 39, folder: Wendell Willkie, Barnes Columbia.

15. Leona E. Kidwell to Editor, *Washington Post,* Sept. 20, 1942, B6.

16. Brush, S5; Barnard, 137–141; Buell, "Willkie Campaign Memoir," 64–66.

17. Gordon Hamilton, "Wendell Willkie of C & S," *Current History* 51, no. 6 (1940): 59.

18. Damon Runyon, "Our 'Hi-Neighbor' President," publication and date unknown, clip in box 14, Barnes LOC; Pearson: Peters, *Five Days in Philadelphia,* 24. Jeremy C. Young, *The Age of Charisma: Leaders, Followers, and Emotions in American Society, 1870-1940* (New York: Cambridge Univ. Press, 2017), 220–272;

David Greenberg, *Republic of Spin: An Inside History of the American Presidency* (New York: Norton, 2016), 187–198.

19. Peters, *Five Days in Philadelphia,* 23, 36. Pegler: Barnes, 11.

20. Neal, 45–65; Barnard, 142–152; Barnes, 149–160; Peters, *Five Days in Philadelphia,* 22–41; Leff, "Strange Bedfellows," 36–43; Alan Brinkley, *The Publisher: Henry Luce and His American Century* (New York: Random House, 2010), 253; Ross Gregory, "Seeking the Presidency: Willkie as Politician," in *Wendell Willkie: Hoosier Internationalist,* ed. James H. Madison (Bloomington: Indiana Univ. Press), 49–55; Warren Moscow, *Roosevelt and Willkie* (Englewood Cliffs, NJ: Prentice Hall, 1968), 1–54.

21. Neal, 74; Barnard, 152–163; Neal, 66–79; Barnes, 160–169; Peters, *Five Days in Philadelphia,* 42–56; Brinkley, *Publisher: Henry Luce,* 253–256; Shlaes, *Forgotten Man,* 366–371; Gregory, "Seeking the Presidency," 55–57; Moscow, *Roosevelt and Willkie,* 54–70.

22. Runyon: Peters, *Five Days in Philadelphia,* 65; Neal, 80–121; Barnard, 164–190; Barnes, 170–187; Peters, *Five Days in Philadelphia,* 57–115; Gregory, "Seeking the Presidency," 57–59; Moscow, *Roosevelt and Willkie,* 89–107.

23. Neal, 122–180; Barnard, 191–268; Barnes, 180–210; Peters, *Five Days in Philadelphia,* 154–179; Shlaes, *Forgotten Man,* 373–383; Gregory, "Seeking the Presidency," 59–65; Moscow, *Roosevelt and Willkie,* 132–183.

24. Barnes, 203; Neal, 138–141; Barnes, 201–204.

25. Barnes, 206–209; Neal, 154–155, 164–165; Moscow, *Roosevelt and Willkie,* 147.

26. See Neal, 158–161; Peters, *Five Days in Philadelphia,* 177–179; Barnes, 207–210; Barnard, 248–268.

27. Barnard, 291.

28. White, *Man Called White,* 204.

29. Peters, *Five Days in Philadelphia*; Moscow, *Roosevelt and Willkie*; Richard Moe, *Roosevelt's Second Act: The Election of 1940 and the Politics of War* (New York: Oxford Univ. Press, 2013); Michael Fullilove, *Rendezvous with Destiny: How Franklin D. Roosevelt and Five Extraordinary Men Took America into the War and into the World* (New York: Penguin Press, 2013), 153–198; Susan Dunn, *1940: FDR, Willkie, Lindbergh, Hitler—the Election amid the Storm* (New Haven: Yale Univ. Press, 2013); David Kaiser, *No End Save Victory: How FDR Led the Nation into War* (New York: Basic Books, 2014); Nicholas Wapshott, *The Sphinx: Franklin Roosevelt, the Isolationists, and the Road to World War II* (New York: Norton, 2014).

30. Justus D. Doenecke, *Storm on the Horizon: The Challenge to American Intervention, 1939–1941* (Lanham, MD: Rowman and Littlefield, 2000), 163; Neal, 211–212; Barnard, 301–303; Barnes, 258–260. Lindbergh: Jenifer Van Vleck, *Empire of the Air: Aviation and the American Ascendancy* (Cambridge, MA: Harvard Univ. Press, 2013), 42–52; Dunn, *1940;* Thomas Kessner, *The Flight of the Century: Charles Lindbergh and the Rise of American Aviation* (New York: Oxford Univ. Press, 2010). On "isolationism": Doenecke, *Storm*; Nichols, *Promise and Peril: America at the Dawn of a Global Age* (Cambridge, MA: Harvard Univ. Press, 2011); and Brooke L. Blower, "From Isolation to Neutrality: A New Framework for Understanding American Political Culture, 1919–1941," *Diplomatic History* 38, no. 2 (2014): 345–376.

31. Neal, 211–212; Barnard, 296–302; Willkie, "Americans Stop Being Afraid!," *Collier's*, May 10, 1941. Letters to Willkie from America Firsters: folder: Correspondence 1941–April 1942, box 115, Willkie Papers.

32. Ben M. Smith to Roosevelt, June 1, 1941, President's Official File, Index #4040, box 2, folder Jan.–June 1941, FDR Papers.

33. Journey to Africa: Kight, "Willkie Flight," n.d., reel A3009, frames 638–640, AFHRA; Intelligence Division, Air Transport Command, "Report of Interrogation . . . ," reel A3009, frames 661–662, AFHRA; Patrick M. Stinson, *Around-the-World Flights: A History* (Jefferson, NC: McFarland, 2011), 150–151.

34. Accra and Kano: Swinton to Cranborne, Oct. 24, 1942, in PREM4/27, file 1, Prime Minister's Office Papers, BNA; Barnes to Elizabeth Barnes, Sept. 1, 1942, in folder: Correspondence, 1942, W. Willkie Tour, box 11, Barnes Columbia; Carol Anderson, *Bourgeois Radicals: The NAACP and the Struggle for Colonial Liberation, 1941–1960* (New York: Cambridge Univ. Press, 2015), 11.

35. Gardner Cowles, speech to the Exeter Alumni Association, Dec. 2, 1942, 7–8, in box 11, folder: Special Correspondence, Willkie, Wendell, 1943, Van Doren Papers. Prep school Anglophilia: Hugh Wilford, *America's Great Game: The CIA's Arabists and the Shaping of the Modern Middle East* (New York: Basic Books, 2013), 10. Pan Am: Van Vleck, 144. ATC and US empire: Andrew Friedman, "US Empire, World War 2 and the Racialising of Labour," *Race and Class* 58, no. 4 (2017): 23–38.

36. Barnes to Elizabeth Barnes, Sept. 1, 1942, 2–3. Also Joseph Barnes, ed., *Empire in the East* (New York: Doubleday, 1934).

37. Barnes to Elizabeth Barnes, Sept. 1, 1942, 2–3, and Barnes to Willkie, Apr. 10, 1944, in folder: Wendell Willkie, box 5, Barnes Columbia; Barnes to Mike Cowles, Sept. 5, 1944, in box 12, Correspondence, 1944, Barnes Columbia.

CHAPTER 3 ✂ EGYPT IS SAVED

1. Willkie, *OW,* 2–3; Kight, "Willkie Flight," n.d., reel A3009, frame 640, AFHRA; Intelligence Division, "Report of Interrogation . . . ," reel A3009, frame 662, AFHRA; Patrick M. Stinson, *Around-the-World Flights: A History* (Jefferson, NC: McFarland, 2011), 151.

2. "Willkie Lands at Cairo to Start Mission," *Atlanta Constitution,* Sept. 3, 1942, 5; "Willkie Welcomed at Cairo Airport," *Los Angeles Times,* Sept. 3, 1942, A; "Willkie Is in Egypt; Tired after Trip," *New York Times,* Sept. 3, 1942, 1.

3. Frank Gervasi, "Willkie at the Front," *Collier's,* Oct. 24, 1942, 58; Willkie, *OW,* 3.

4. Gervasi, "Willkie at the Front," 58, 60; "A Great American," *Egyptian Mail,* Sept. 4, 1942, 2.

5. "Addresses American Troops," *New York Times,* Sept. 4, 1942, 3; Gervasi, "Willkie at the Front," 60.

6. "Willkie Offers Self as Proof of U.S. Harmony in War," *Atlanta Constitution,* Sept. 4, 1942, 3; "'Give 'Em Hell,' Willkie Urges Troops in Egypt," *Los Angeles Times,* Sept. 4, 1942, 2; "Willkie in Egypt Says 'Give 'Em Hell,'" *New York Times,* Sept. 4, 1942, 3; "Traveler's Tale," *Time,* Sept. 14, 1942, 21; Gervasi, "Willkie at the Front," 60; Neal, 234.

7. Gervasi, "Willkie at the Front," 60.

8. See "Now at 50, He Urges Us to Wake Up and Stay Awake," *P.M.*, Feb. 15, 1942, 11; Neal, 181–207; Barnard, 269–294; Barnes, 239–262.

9. Barnard, 281, 284; Neal, 201; "Statement of Wendell Willkie Before Senate Foreign Relations Committee, Feb. 11, 1941," in box 107, Willkie Papers.

10. Charles L. Ponce de Leon, *Self-Exposure: Human-Interest Journalism and the Emergence of Celebrity in America, 1890–1940* (Chapel Hill: Univ. of North Carolina Press, 2002); Sarah E. Igo, *The Averaged American: Surveys, Citizens, and the Making of a Mass Public* (Cambridge, MA: Harvard Univ. Press, 2007); Bruce Lenthall, *Radio's America: The Great Depression and the Rise of Modern Mass Culture* (Chicago: Univ. of Chicago Press, 2007); Jason Loviglio, *Radio's Intimate Public: Network Broadcasting and Mass-Mediated Democracy* (Minneapolis: Univ. of Minnesota Press, 2005); Douglas B. Craig, *Fireside Politics: Radio and Political Culture in the United States, 1920–1940* (Baltimore: Johns Hopkins Univ. Press, 2000); Susan J. Douglas, *Listening In: Radio and the American Imagination* (New York: Times Books, 1999), 22–39. Gallup poll: Neal, 219.

11. Barnes, 244–245.

12. Glenda Sluga, *Internationalism in the Age of Nationalism* (Philadelphia: Univ. of Pennsylvania Press, 2013); Mark Mazower, *Governing the World: The History of an Idea* (New York: Penguin, 2012); Emily S. Rosenberg, "Transnational Currents in a Shrinking World," in *A World Connecting, 1870–1945,* ed. Emily S. Rosenberg, 815–996 (Cambridge, MA: Harvard Univ. Press, 2012).

13. Sluga, *Internationalism,* 1–44; Mazower, *Governing the World,* 1–115.

14. Alan Dawley, *Changing the World: American Progressives in War and Revolution* (Princeton: Princeton Univ. Press, 2003), 26–27; Christopher McKnight Nichols, *Promise and Peril: America at the Dawn of a Global Age* (Cambridge, MA: Harvard Univ. Press, 2011), 1–228.

15. Dawley, *Changing the World,* 75–256; Nichols, *Promise and Peril,* 252–272; Sluga, *Internationalism,* 4–5; Mazower, *Governing the World,* 114–153; Erez Manela, *The Wilsonian Moment: Self Determination and the International Origins of Anticolonial Nationalism* (New York: Oxford Univ. Press, 2007), 3–54; Jay Winter, *Dreams of Peace and Freedom: Utopian Moments in the 20th Century* (New Haven: Yale Univ. Press, 2006), 48–74; Neil Smith, *American Empire: Roosevelt's Geographer and the Prelude to Globalization* (Berkeley: Univ. of California Press, 2003), 113–180; Frank Ninkovich, *The Wilsonian Century: U.S. Foreign Policy since 1900* (Chicago: Univ. of Chicago Press, 1999), 48–77; Thomas J. Knock, *To End All Wars: Woodrow Wilson and the Quest for a New World Order* (New York: Oxford Univ. Press, 1992).

16. Nichols, *Promise and Peril,* 257–352; Brooke L. Blower, "From Isolation to Neutrality: A New Framework for Understanding American Political Culture, 1919–1941," *Diplomatic History* 38, no. 2 (2014): 345–376; Emily S. Rosenberg, *Spreading the American Dream: American Economic and Cultural Expansion, 1890–1945* (New York: Oxford Univ. Press, 1982); Emily S. Rosenberg, *Financial Missionaries to the World: The Politics and Culture of Dollar Diplomacy, 1900–1930* (Cambridge, MA: Harvard Univ. Press, 1999); Robert Divine, *Second Chance: The Triumph of Internationalism in America during World War II* (New York: Atheneum, 1967), 20–21.

17. Dawley, *Changing the World,* 259–338; Mazower, *Governing the World,* 154–213; Sluga, *Internationalism,* 45–78; Divine, *Second Chance,* 6–28; Andrew Arsan, Su Sin Lewis, and Anne-Isabelle Richard, "The Roots of Global Civil Society and the Interwar Moment," *Journal of Global History* 7, no. 2 (2012): 157–165; Daniel Gorman, *The Emergence of International Society in the 1920s* (New York: Cambridge Univ. Press, 2012).

18. Divine, *Second Chance,* 23–34; Dawley, *Changing the World,* 346–347; Mazower, *Governing the World,* 187–193; Sluga, *Internationalism,* 76–81; Elizabeth Borgwardt, *A New Deal for the World: America's Vision for Human Rights* (Cambridge, MA: Harvard Univ. Press, 2005), 152–156.

19. Divine, *Second Chance,* 27–183; Borgwardt, *New Deal for the World,* 1–87; John Fousek, *To Lead the Free World: American Nationalism and the Cultural Roots of the Cold War* (Chapel Hill: Univ. of North Carolina Press, 2000); Christopher D. O'Sullivan, *Sumner Welles, Postwar Planning, and the Quest for a New World Order, 1937–1943* (New York: Columbia Univ. Press, 2008); Alan Brinkley, *The Publisher: Henry Luce and His American Century* (New York: Random House, 2010), 260–273; Frank Ninkovich, *The Diplomacy of Ideas: U.S. Foreign Policy and Cultural Relations, 1938–1950* (New York: Cambridge Univ. Press, 1981); John Morton Blum, *V Was for Victory: Politics and American Culture during World War II* (New York: Harcourt Brace Jovanovich, 1976), 255–292; Henry R. Luce, "The American Century," reprinted in *Diplomatic History* 23, no. 2 (1999): 159–171. Also: *Prefaces to Peace: A Symposium* (New York: cooperatively published by Simon and Schuster; Doubleday, Doran; Reynal and Hitchcock; and Columbia Univ. Press, 1943). African-American internationalism: Carol Anderson, *Bourgeois Radicals: The NAACP and the Struggle for Colonial Liberation, 1941–1960* (New York: Cambridge Univ. Press, 2015); Eric Porter, *The Problem of the Future World: W. E. B. Du Bois and the Race Concept at Midcentury* (Durham, NC: Duke Univ. Press, 2010); Carol Anderson, *Eyes off the Prize: The United Nations and the African-American Struggle for Human Rights, 1944–1955* (New York: Cambridge Univ. Press, 2003); Penny M. Von Eschen, *Race against Empire: Black Americans and Anticolonialism, 1937–1957* (Ithaca, NY: Cornell Univ. Press, 1997); Brenda Plummer, *A Rising Wind: Black Americans and U.S. Foreign Affairs, 1935–1960* (Chapel Hill: Univ. of North Carolina Press, 1996).

20. Stephen Wertheim, "Tomorrow, the World: The Birth of U.S. Global Supremacy in World War II" (Ph.D. diss., Columbia University, 2015); Frank Costigliola, *Roosevelt's Lost Alliances: How Personal Politics Helped Start the Cold War* (Princeton: Princeton Univ. Press, 2012); David B. Woolner, Warren F. Kimball, and David Reynolds, eds., *FDR's World: War, Peace, and Legacies* (New York: Palgrave Macmillan, 2008); Warren F. Kimball, *The Juggler: Franklin Roosevelt as Wartime Statesman* (Princeton: Princeton Univ. Press, 1991).

21. Divine, *Second Chance,* 236; Neal, 320.

22. Barnes, 291.

23. Alexander Kirk to Secretary of State, Sept. 17, 1942, Subject: Visit to Egypt of Mr. Wendell Willkie, 3–4, no. 96, in box 16, 032, Willkie, Wendell, Decimal Files: 1940–44, State Department Files, Record Group 59, NACP; Christopher

O'Sullivan, *FDR and the End of Empire: The Origins of American Power in the Middle East* (New York: Palgrave Macmillan, 2012), 49–68.

24. "Principal Factors Relating to Egypt," Aug. 19, 1942, 2, in box 15, folder: Wendell Willkie, World Trip 1942, Middle East, Van Doren Papers; "Egypt's King Receives Willkie on Holy Day," *Washington Post,* Sept. 5, 1942, B5; "Willkie Visit to King Ignores Garb Rules," *New York Times,* Sept. 5, 1942, 4.

25. Willkie, *OW,* 3.

26. "Willkie Visit to King Ignores Garb Rules," 4; Willkie, *OW,* 4.

27. Willkie, *OW,* 4; Nial J. A. Barr, *Pendulum of War: The Three Battles of Alamein* (London: Random House, 2005).

28. Willkie, *OW,* 4–8; Gardner Cowles, *Mike Looks Back: The Memoirs of Gardner Cowles* (New York: Gardner Cowles, 1985), 72.

29. Gardner Cowles, speech to the Exeter Alumni Association, Dec. 2, 1942, 7, in box 11, folder: Special Correspondence, Willkie, Wendell, 1943, Van Doren Papers; Willkie, *OW,* 9–10; Benjamin Alpers, *Dictators, Democracy, and American Public Culture: Envisioning the Totalitarian Enemy, 1920s–1950s* (Chapel Hill: Univ. of North Carolina Press, 2003), 157–187.

30. Willkie, *OW,* 9.

31. Barnard, 350–351; Gervasi, "Willkie at the Front," 60; Cowles, *Mike Looks Back,* 72.

32. Willkie, *OW,* 10–12; Barnard, 350; Neal, 236; Gervasi, "Willkie at the Front," 60.

33. Edward Kennedy, "Willkie Finds Nazis' Threat Eased in Egypt," *Washington Post,* Sept. 7, 1942, 3; A. C. Sedgwick, "Willkie Terms Blow Dealt Rommel 'Perhaps a Turning Point in War,'" *New York Times,* Sept. 7, 1942, 3. See also Kirk to Secretary of State, Sept. 17, 1942, 5, no. 96, in box 16, 032, Willkie, Wendell, Decimal Files: 1940–44, State Department Files, Record Group 59, NACP; Gervasi, "Willkie at the Front," 61; Barnard, 350–351; Neal, 236–237; Willkie, *OW,* 10–12; Lewis H. Brereton, *The Brereton Diaries: The War in the Air in the Pacific, Middle East, and Europe, October 3, 1941–May 8, 1945* (New York: Morrow, 1946), 152.

34. Willkie, *OW,* 15.

35. Barnes, 296–297.

36. On Egyptian history: Manela, *Wilsonian Moment,* 66–68; James Gelvin, *The Modern Middle East,* 3rd ed. (New York: Oxford Univ. Press, 2011), 150–157; Robert Tignor, *Egypt: A Short History* (Princeton: Princeton Univ. Press, 2009); Anne Alexander, *Nasser* (London: Haus Publishing, 2005); Timothy Mitchell, *Rule of Experts: Egypt, Techno-Politics, Modernity* (Berkeley: Univ. of California Press, 2002); Selma Botman, *Egypt from Independence to Revolution, 1919–1952* (Syracuse, NY: Syracuse Univ. Press, 1991); Timothy Mitchell, *Colonising Egypt* (Berkeley: Univ. of California Press, 1991); P. J. Vatikiotis, *The History of Modern Egypt: From Muhammad Ali to Mubarak,* 4th ed. (Baltimore, MD: Johns Hopkins Univ. Press, 1991); Afaf Lutfi Al-Sayyid Marsot, *A Short History of Modern Egypt* (New York: Cambridge Univ. Press, 1985); Jean Lugol, *Egypt and World War II: The Anti-Axis Campaigns in the Middle East* (Cairo: Société Orientale de Publicité, 1945). Quote is from Alexander, *Nasser,* 5.

37. Marilyn Lake and Henry Reynolds, *Drawing the Global Color Line: White Men's Countries and the International Challenge of Racial Equality* (New York: Cambridge

Univ. Press, 2008), 11; Robert Vitalis, *White World Order, Black Power Politics: The Birth of American International Relations* (Ithaca, NY: Cornell Univ. Press, 2015), 1–84.

38. Anticolonialists were far from unified. They argued over whether self-determination would result in traditional nation-building or some new kind of postcolonial, egalitarian community beyond the nation-state. Adom Getachew, *Worldmaking after Empire: The Rise and Fall of Self-Determination* (Princeton: Princeton Univ. Press, 2019); Manu Goswami, "Imaginary Futures and Colonial Internationalisms," *American Historical Review* 117, no. 5 (2012): 1461–1485; Pankaj Mishra, *From the Ruins of Empire: The Revolt against the West and the Remaking of Asia* (New York: Picador, 2012); Cemil Aydin, *The Politics of Anti-Westernism in Asia: Visions of World Order in Pan-Islamic and Pan-Asian Thought* (New York: Columbia Univ. Press, 2007).

39. Lake and Reynolds, *Drawing the Global Color Line.*

40. Mazower, *Governing the World,* 77; Sluga, *Internationalism,* 3, 20–30.

41. Mazower, *Governing the World,* 81; Paul Kramer, *The Blood of Government: Race, Empire, the United States, and the Philippines* (Chapel Hill: Univ. of North Carolina Press, 2006); Mark Cocker, *Rivers of Blood, Rivers of Gold: Europe's Conflict with Tribal Peoples* (London: Pimlico, 1998). Racial imperialism and European fascism: Aimé Césaire, *Discourse on Colonialism* (1972; New York: Monthly Review Press, 2000), 36, 41; Hannah Arendt, *The Origins of Totalitarianism* (New York: Harcourt, 1968), 123–304.

42. Knock, *To End All Wars,* 10–11.

43. Mishra, *From the Ruins of Empire,* 184–215; Manela, *Wilsonian Moment,* 3–34, 68–75, 141–157, 177–226; Mazower, *Governing the World,* 162–164; Sluga, *Internationalism,* 51–55; Lake and Reynolds, *Drawing the Global Color Line,* 284–309; Botman, *Egypt from Independence to Revolution,* 25–29; Tignor, *Egypt: A Short History,* 238–242; David Levering Lewis, *W. E. B. Du Bois: The Fight for Equality and the American Century, 1919–1963* (New York: Henry Holt, 2000), 59–60; Adriane Lentz-Smith, *Freedom Struggles: African Americans and World War I* (Cambridge, MA: Harvard Univ. Press, 2009). Cairo newspaper: Manela, *Wilsonian Moment,* 152–153. US consul: Manela, *Wilsonian Moment,* 75.

44. Manela, *Wilsonian Moment,* 215.

45. Nancy Cott, "Revisiting the Transatlantic 1920s: Vincent Sheean v. Malcolm Cowley," *American Historical Review* 118, no. 1 (2013): 46–75. See also Vincent Sheean, *Personal History* (1934; Secaucus, NJ: Citadel Press, 1986). On Willkie's middlebrow internationalism, see Samuel Zipp, "When Wendell Willkie Went Visiting: Between Interdependency and Exceptionalism in the Public Feeling for *One World,*" *American Literary History* 26, no. 3 (2014): 484–510.

46. Michael G. Thompson, *For God and Globe: Christian Internationalism in the United States between the Great War and the Cold War* (Ithaca, NY: Cornell Univ. Press, 2015), 4. David Hollinger, *Protestants Abroad: How Missionaries Tried to Change the World but Changed America* (Princeton: Princeton Univ. Press 2017); Peter Conn, *Pearl Buck: A Cultural Biography* (New York: Cambridge Univ. Press, 1996).

47. Walter White, *A Man Called White: The Autobiography of Walter White* (New York: Viking, 1948), 198; Harvard Sitkoff, "Willkie as Liberal: Civil Liberties and Civil Rights," in *Wendell Willkie: Hoosier Internationalist,* ed. James H. Madison (Bloomington: Indiana Univ. Press, 1992), 71–87; Brian J. Distelberg, "'Citizenship in the World of the Movie': African-Americans, Jews, and the Movies in War and Peace, 1941–1951," unpublished manuscript in author's possession. These influences were compounded by the counsel he received from the international relations theorist Raymond Buell, who saw the roots of "complex interdependency" in a world system based on racial exploitation. See Vitalis, *White World Order,* 11, 57, 90.

48. Anderson, *Bourgeois Radicals;* Porter, *The Problem of the Future World*; Von Eschen, *Race against Empire;* Anderson, *Eyes off the Prize;* Plummer, *A Rising Wind.* Locke: Vitalis, *White World Order,* 122.

49. Willkie, "Common Aspirations," July 20, 1942, in box 108, Willkie Papers. See also Willkie, "The Case for the Minorities," *Saturday Evening Post,* June 27, 1942, and for his careful condemnation of Japanese American internment, Neal, 271.

50. Lake and Reynolds, *Drawing the Global Color Line,* 335–356; Wendy Wall, *Inventing the "American Way": The Politics of Consensus from the New Deal to the Civil Rights Movement* (New York: Oxford Univ. Press, 2008), 63–159; Nikhil Pal Singh, *Black Is a Country: Race and the Unfinished Struggle for Democracy* (Cambridge, MA: Harvard Univ. Press, 2004), 103–130; Matthew Frye Jacobson, *Whiteness of a Different Color: European Immigrants and the Alchemy of Race* (Cambridge, MA: Harvard Univ. Press, 1998), 246–273; Lee D. Baker, *From Savage to Negro: Anthropology and the Construction of Race, 1896–1954* (Berkeley: Univ. of California Press, 1998); Gary Gerstle, *American Crucible: Race and Nation in the Twentieth Century* (Princeton: Princeton Univ. Press, 2001), 187–237; Naoko Shibusawa, "Ideology, Culture, and the Cold War," in *The Oxford Handbook of the Cold War,* ed. Richard H. Immerman and Petra Goedde (New York: Oxford Univ. Press, 2013).

51. Welles: Wm. Roger Louis, *Imperialism at Bay: The United States and the Decolonization of the British Empire, 1941–1945* (New York: Oxford Univ. Press, 1978), 154–155; O'Sullivan, *Sumner Welles,* 137–179. Lippmann: Lake and Reynolds, *Drawing the Global Color Line,* 340.

52. Borgwardt, *New Deal for the World,* 303–304; Costigliola, *Roosevelt's Lost Alliances,* 127–138; Warren Kimball, *Forged in War: Roosevelt, Churchill, and the Second World War* (New York: Morrow, 1997), 97–104; Douglas Brinkley and David R. Facey-Crowther, *The Atlantic Charter* (New York: St. Martin's Press, 1994).

53. Marsot, *Short History of Modern Egypt,* 82–98; Botman, *Egypt from Independence to Revolution,* 29–42, 56–57; Tignor, *Egypt: A Short History,* 243–254. Nasser: Alexander, *Nasser,* 8. Nehru: Mishra, *From the Ruins of Empire,* 267.

54. See "Principal Factors Relating to Egypt," Aug. 19, 1942, 2, in box 15, folder: Wendell Willkie, World Trip 1942, Middle East, Van Doren Papers. February 1942: Alexander, *Nasser,* 21–22; Botman, *Egypt from Independence to Revolution,* 44–46; Marsot, *Short History of Modern Egypt,* 100–101; Vatikiotis, *History of Modern Egypt,* 342, 345–352; Tignor, *Egypt: A Short History,* 254; O'Sullivan, *FDR and the End of Empire,* 54–55.

55. Alexander, *Nasser,* 21–24; Vatikiotis, *History of Modern Egypt,* 342–357; Botman, *Egypt from Independence to Revolution,* 42–47, 152–154; Marsot, *Short History of Modern Egypt,* 99–101. Axis radio broadcasts: Transcripts, Sept. 3, 1942, 1–4, in box 15, folder: Wendell Willkie, World Trip 1942, Middle East, Van Doren Papers; Kirk to State, Sept. 17, 1942, 7, no. 96, in box 16, 032, Willkie, Wendell, Decimal Files: 1940–44, State Department Files, Record Group 59, NACP; Jeffrey Herf, *Nazi Propaganda for the Arab World* (New Haven: Yale Univ. Press, 2009).

56. O'Sullivan, *FDR and the End of Empire,* 56–58; R. B. Landis to Willkie, Aug. 31, 1942, in Willkie Correspondence, Official, 1929–1944, box 95, Willkie Papers. On British-American tensions in Africa, see Swinton to Cranborne, Oct. 24, 1942, in PREM4/27, File 1, Prime Minister's Office Papers, BNA; James T. Sparrow, "Ruins of Empire: Tracking the Image of Britain at the Dawn of the American Century," in *Boundaries of the State in U.S. History,* ed. James T. Sparrow, William J. Novak, and Stephen W. Sawyer (Chicago: Univ. of Chicago Press, 2015), 101–126. Kirk: Noel F. Busch, "Ambassador Kirk," *Life,* Aug. 13, 1945, 80–92.

57. "Between Two Walls," *Time,* Sept. 14, 1942, 36–40.

58. Transcripts, Sept. 3, 1942, 1–4, in box 15, folder: Wendell Willkie, World Trip 1942, Middle East, Van Doren Papers; Erez Manela, "Goodwill and Bad: Rethinking U.S.-Egyptian Contacts in the Interwar Years," *Middle Eastern Studies* 38, no. 1 (2002): 71–88.

59. George Abdo Marzoog to Willkie, Sept. 3, 1942, in Willkie Correspondence, Official, 1929–1944, box 95, Willkie Papers.

60. Willkie, *OW,* 15.

CHAPTER 4 ∞ A GREAT SOCIAL LABORATORY

1. Robert L. Daniel, "The United States and the Turkish Republic before World War II: The Cultural Dimension," *Middle East Journal* 21, no. 1 (1967): 53.

2. Laurence Steinhardt to Secretary of State, Sept. 14, 1942, Subject: Visit of the Honorable Wendell Willkie to Ankara, Sept. 7–10, 1942, 1–2, no. 98, in box 16, 032, Willkie, Wendell, Decimal Files: 1940–44, State Department Files, Record Group 59, NACP; "Points East," *Time,* Sept. 28, 1942, 28; Neal, 237–238; Willkie, *OW,* 45.

3. "Turks Will Be Cool to Willkie, Say Nazis," *Los Angeles Times,* Sept. 7, 1942, 2; Steinhardt to State, Sept. 13, 1942, 1–2, no. 63, in box 16, 032, Willkie, Wendell, Decimal Files: 1940–44, State Department Files, Record Group 59, NACP; Steinhardt to State, Sept. 14, 1942, 2–3, no. 98, NACP; "Willkie Reaches Ankara," *New York Times,* Sept. 8, 1942, 10; "Willkie Reveals Allies Wrecked 100 of Rommel's 290 First Line Tanks," *New York Times,* Sept. 8, 1942, 3; Neal, 238; Barnard, 351–352.

4. Steinhardt to State, Sept. 14, 1942, enclosure no. 1, "Press Conference . . . ," 3–4; "Turkey," August 19, 1942, 1–2, in box 15, folder: Wendell Willkie, World Trip 1942, Middle East, Van Doren Papers.

5. Steinhardt to State, Sept. 11, 1942, 7, no. 61, in box 16, 032, Willkie, Wendell, Decimal Files: 1940–44, State Department Files, Record Group 59, NACP. Turkish history: Yusuf Turan Çetiner, *Turkey and the West: From Neutrality to Commitment* (Lanham, MD: Univ. Press of America, 2015); Charles King, *Midnight at the Pera*

Palace: The Birth of Modern Istanbul (New York: Norton, 2014); William Hale, *Turkish Foreign Policy since 1774,* 3rd ed. (London: Routledge, 2013), 31–77; Valentine M. Moghadam, *Modernizing Women: Gender and Social Change in the Middle East,* 3rd ed. (Boulder: Lynne Rienner, 2013); Carter Vaughn Findley, *Turkey, Islam, Nationalism, and Modernity: A History, 1789–2007* (New Haven: Yale Univ. Press, 2010), 247–304; Erik J. Zürcher, *Turkey: A Modern History,* rev. ed. (London: I. B. Tauris, 1997), 97–230; Serif Mardin, "Religion and Secularism in Turkey," in *The Modern Middle East,* ed. Albert Hourani, Philip S. Khoury, and Mary C. Wilson, 347–374 (Berkeley: Univ. of California Press, 1993); Selim Deringil, *Turkish Foreign Policy during the Second World War: An Active Neutrality* (Cambridge: Cambridge Univ. Press, 1989). Nadi quoted in King, *Midnight at the Pera Palace,* 256; Ernest Jackh, *The Rising Crescent: Turkey Yesterday, Today, and Tomorrow* (New York: Farrar and Rinehart, 1944), 32.

6. Mardin, "Religion and Secularism," 366; King, *Midnight at the Pera Palace,* 126, 190–191; Findley, *Turkey, Islam, Nationalism, and Modernity,* 256–258.

7. Moghadam, *Modernizing Women,* 53; Findley, *Turkey, Islam, Nationalism, and Modernity,* 247–262, 270–276; Deringil, *Turkish Foreign Policy,* 17, 30.

8. Ahmed Emin Yalman, *Turkey in My Time* (Norman: Univ. of Oklahoma Press, 1956), 200.

9. Willkie, *OW,* 43.

10. Italian diplomat: Deringil, *Turkish Foreign Policy,* 135. Zürcher, *Turkey: A Modern History,* 210–213; Deringil, *Turkish Foreign Policy,* 1–144; Hale, *Turkish Foreign Policy,* 56–77; Çetiner, *Turkey and the West,* 1–122.

11. Nicholas Tamkin, *Britain, Turkey, and the Soviet Union, 1940–1945: Strategy, Diplomacy, and Intelligence in the Eastern Mediterranean* (London: Palgrave Macmillan, 2009), 51–75; Deringil, *Turkish Foreign Policy,* 40.

12. Tamkin, *Britain, Turkey, and the Soviet Union,* 73–75; Hale, *Turkish Foreign Policy,* 60, 68, 75–77; Deringil, *Turkish Foreign Policy,* 92–143; State Department, "Turkey," August 19, 1942, 1–2.

13. Willkie, *OW,* 46; Willkie to FDR, Sept. 10, 1942, in box 173, folder 10: Wendell Willkie, 9/40–9/42, Series 5, FDR Papers; "Operation in Turkey," *Time,* Oct. 5, 1942, 31.

14. Steinhardt to State, Sept. 11, 1942, 2–7, no. 61, NACP; Ray Brock, "Turkey Heartened by Willkie's Visit," *New York Times,* Sept. 11, 1942, 4. See also "Willkie Takes President's Message to Turkish Leaders," *Los Angeles Times,* Sept. 10, 1942, 3; "Willkie Assured Turkey Will Stay Aloof from Axis," *Washington Post,* Sept. 10, 1942, 9; "Assurances Given Willkie in Turkey," *New York Times,* Sept. 10, 1942, 6; "Mr. Willkie's Stay in Ankara," *Eastern Times* (Beirut), Sept. 10, 1942, 1; "Saracoglu and Willkie Meet," *New York Times,* Sept. 11, 1942, 4; Neal, 238–239.

15. Willkie, *OW,* 46; Deringil, *Turkish Foreign Policy,* 50–56; Edward Weisband, *Turkish Foreign Policy, 1943–1945: Small State Diplomacy and Great Power Politics* (Princeton: Princeton Univ. Press, 1973), 46–52.

16. Willkie, *OW,* 44; Deringil, *Turkish Foreign Policy,* 136.

17. Daniel, "United States and the Turkish Republic," 52–53; Perin Gurel, "Turkey and the United States after World War I: National Memory, Local Categories, and Provincializing the Transnational," *American Quarterly* 67, no. 2 (2015): 360;

Matthew F. Jacobs, *Imagining the Middle East: The Building of an American Foreign Policy, 1918–1967* (Chapel Hill: Univ. of North Carolina Press, 2011), 8, 59–63, 68–71.

18. Willkie, *OW,* 45.

19. Willkie, *OW,* 38–39, 41–42.

20. Willkie to FDR, Sept. 10, 1942, 1; Willkie, *OW,* 41.

21. Willkie, *OW,* 45–47.

22. Willkie, *OW,* 48.

23. Willkie, *OW,* 48–49, 37.

24. Steinhardt to State, Sept. 14, 1942, enclosure no. 2, 1–8, no. 98, NACP.

25. Steinhardt to State, Sept. 14, 1942, enclosure no. 2, 4, no. 98, NACP. See also Steinhardt to State Department, Aug. 27, 1942, 1–2, no. 46, in box 16, 032, Willkie, Wendell, Decimal Files: 1940–44, State Department Files, Record Group 59, NACP; Steinhardt to Secretary of State, Sept. 7, 1942, in box 15, folder: Wendell Willkie, World Trip 1942, Middle East, Van Doren Papers.

CHAPTER 5 ✿ THE IMPERIAL DILEMMA

1. Mark Mazower, *Governing the World* (New York: Penguin, 2012), 167–169. Mandate system: Susan Pedersen, *The Guardians: The League of Nations and the Crisis of Empire* (New York: Oxford Univ. Press, 2015); Mazower, *Governing the World,* 154–173; Erez Manela, *The Wilsonian Moment* (New York: Oxford Univ. Press, 2007); Glenda Sluga, *Internationalism in the Age of Nationalism* (Philadelphia: Univ. of Pennsylvania Press, 2013), 51–53, 91–92; Marilyn Lake and Henry Reynolds, *Drawing the Global Color Line* (New York: Cambridge Univ. Press, 2008), 294–295.

2. William Gwynn to Secretary of State, Sept. 7, 1942, no. 55, and William Gwynn to Secretary of State, Sept. 18, 1942, no. 97, both in box 16, 032, Willkie, Wendell, Decimal Files: 1940–44, State Department Files, Record Group 59, NACP; Sir Edward Spears, *Fulfilment of a Mission: The Spears Mission to Syria and Lebanon, 1941–1944* (London: Archon Books, 1977), 169.

3. "Syria and Lebanon," n.d., 1–5, in box 15, folder: Wendell Willkie, World Trip 1942, Middle East, Van Doren Papers.

4. "Points East," *Time,* Sept. 28, 1942, 28; "Plane Output Tops Axis, Willkie Says," *New York Times,* Sept. 12, 1942, 4.

5. Spears, *Fulfilment of a Mission,* 169–170.

6. Samir Kassir, *Beirut* (Berkeley: Univ. of California Press, 2010), 264–265.

7. Naqqash: Kais M. Firro, *Inventing Lebanon: Nationalism and the State under the Mandate* (London: I. B. Tauris, 2003), 177–179, 190–200; William Harris, *Lebanon: A History, 600–2011* (New York: Oxford Univ. Press, 2012), 196–197; Eyal Zisser, *Lebanon: The Challenge of Independence* (London: I. B. Tauris, 2000), 36–40. Gwynn to State, Sept. 21, 1942, section 2, 1–2, no. 81, in box 16, 032, Willkie, Wendell, Decimal Files: 1940–44, State Department Files, Record Group 59, NACP.

8. See Zisser, *Lebanon,* 1–3, 11–13; Firro, *Inventing Lebanon,* 99–100. Gwynn to State, Oct. 1, 1942, in Walter L. Browne, ed., *The Political History of Lebanon, 1920–1950,* vol. 2, *Documents on French Mandate and World War II, 1936–1943* (Salisbury, NC: Documentary Publications, 1977), 366–368.

9. Lebanon's history: Zisser, *Lebanon*, 1–7; Firro, *Inventing Lebanon*, 15–41; Harris, *Lebanon: A History*, 3–26, 147–192; Jennifer Dueck, *The Claims of Culture at Empire's End: Syria and Lebanon under French Rule* (Oxford: Oxford Univ. Press, 2010); Elizabeth Thompson, *Colonial Citizens: Republican Rights, Paternal Privilege, and Gender in French Syria and Lebanon* (New York: Columbia Univ. Press, 2000); Meir Zamir, *Lebanon's Quest: The Road to Statehood, 1926–1939* (London: I. B. Tauris, 1997); Charles Winslow, *Lebanon: War and Politics in a Fragmented Society* (New York: Routledge, 1996).

10. Ussama Makdisi, *Faith Misplaced: The Broken Promise of U.S.-Arab Relations: 1820–2001* (New York: Basic Books, 2010), 128; Harris, *Lebanon: A History*, 173–174.

11. Makdisi, *Faith Misplaced*, 132–152; Dueck, *Claims of Culture*, 15–16; Thompson, *Colonial Citizens*, 39–43; Winslow, *Lebanon: War and Politics*, 56–57; Matthew F. Jacobs, *Imagining the Middle East: The Building of an American Foreign Policy, 1918–1967* (Chapel Hill: Univ. of North Carolina Press, 2011), 97–104, 141–145; Douglas Little, *American Orientalism: The United States and the Middle East since 1945* (Chapel Hill: Univ. of North Carolina Press, 2002), 159–160; Karl E. Meyer and Shareen Blair Brysac, *Kingmakers: The Invention of the Modern Middle East* (New York: Norton, 2008).

12. Dueck, *Claims of Culture*, 16–24; Firro, *Inventing Lebanon*, 9–70; Harris, *Lebanon: A History*, 173–190; Thompson, *Colonial Citizens*, 10–13; Winslow, *Lebanon: War and Politics*, 57–70; Zisser, *Lebanon*, 1–13; Zamir, *Lebanon's Quest*, 240–243; Kassir, *Beirut*, 256–267; Makdisi, *Faith Misplaced*, 154; Wadad Makdisi Cortas, *A World I Loved: The Story of an Arab Woman* (New York: Nation Books, 2009), 104–105.

13. Spears, *Fulfilment of a Mission*, 208; Kassir, *Beirut*, 301–304.

14. Thompson, *Colonial Citizens*; Dueck, *Claims of Culture*.

15. Harris, *Lebanon: A History*, 184–192; Zamir, *Lebanon's Quest*, 243–247; Zisser, *Lebanon*, 12–40; Firro, *Inventing Lebanon*, 195–200.

16. Gwynn to State, Sept. 21, 1942, section 2, 4, no. 81, NACP; Gwynn to State, Oct. 3, 1942, 3–5, no. 108, in box 17, 032, Willkie, Wendell, Decimal Files: 1940–44, State Department Files, Record Group 59, NACP; Willkie *OW*, 24; Wadsworth to Secretary of State, in *FRUS, 1942*, vol. 4, *The Near East and Africa* (Washington, DC: U.S. Government Printing Office, 1963), 671.

17. A. B. Gaunson, *The Anglo-French Clash in Lebanon and Syria, 1940–45* (New York: St. Martin's Press, 1987), 184; Christopher D. O'Sullivan, *FDR and the End of Empire: The Origins of American Power in the Middle East* (New York: Palgrave MacMillan, 2012), 131–145; Walter L. Browne, ed., *The Political History of Lebanon*, vol. 2, *Documents on French Mandate and World War II, 1936–1943*; Jean Lacouture, *De Gaulle: The Rebel, 1890–1944* (New York: Norton, 1990); Charles de Gaulle, *The Complete War Memoirs of Charles de Gaulle, 1940–1946* (New York: Da Capo, 1967); David Schoenbrun, *The Three Lives of Charles de Gaulle* (New York: Atheneum, 1967); O'Sullivan, *FDR and the End of Empire*; "Syria and Lebanon," n.d., 3, in box 15, Van Doren Papers; Gwynn to State, Sept. 21, 1942, section 2, 2–3.

18. Willkie, *OW*, 23–24; "Points East," *Time*, Sept. 28, 1942, 28–29; De Gaulle, *Complete War Memoirs*, 335; Gardner Cowles, *Mike Looks Back: The Memoirs of Gardner Cowles* (New York: Gardner Cowles, 1985), 73. See also Neal, 240–241;

Lacouture, *De Gaulle: The Rebel,* 365, Gaunson, *Anglo-French Clash,* 97; Schoen-brun, *Three Lives of Charles de Gaulle,* 135–151; O'Sullivan, *FDR and the End of Empire,* 127–131, 134–139; Gwynn to State, Sept. 21, 1942, section 3, 1, no. 81, NACP.

19. Schoenbrun, *Three Lives of Charles de Gaulle,* 135–151; O'Sullivan, *FDR and the End of Empire,* 127–131, 134–139.

20. De Gaulle, *Complete War Memoirs,* 335.

21. Cowles, *Mike Looks Back,* 73–75.

22. Lowell Pinkerton to Department of State, Sept. 21, 1942, 1, no. 73, in box 16, 032, Willkie, Wendell, Decimal Files: 1940–44, State Department Files, Record Group 59, NACP. *Filastin:* "Syrian Recognition to Be Discussed," *Palestine Post,* Sept. 17, 1942, 3; Rashid Khalidi, "The Formation of Palestinian Identity: The Critical Years, 1917–1923," in *Rethinking Nationalism in the Arab Middle East,* ed. James Jankowski and Israel Gershoni (New York: Columbia Univ. Press, 1997).

23. Barnes, 298; Benny Morris, *Righteous Victims: A History of the Zionist-Arab Conflict, 1881–1999* (New York: Knopf, 1999), 146–147, 167–175; Tom Segev, *One Palestine, Complete: Jews and Arabs under the British Mandate* (New York: Metropolitan Books, 2000), 416; Ronald W. Zweig, *Britain and Palestine during the Second World War* (London: Boydell Press for the Royal Historical Society, 1986).

24. Arab Revolt: Morris, *Righteous Victims,* 121–160; Segev, *One Palestine,* 295–445. Mandate Palestine: Ilan Pappe, *A History of Modern Palestine: One Land, Two Peoples* (Cambridge: Cambridge Univ. Press, 2004), 105–122; Rashid Khalidi, *The Iron Cage: The Story of the Palestinian Struggle for Statehood* (Boston: Beacon Press, 2006), 105–124; Weldon Matthews, *Confronting an Empire, Constructing a Nation: Arab Nationalists and Popular Politics in Mandate Palestine* (London: I. B. Tauris, 2006), 233–264; James L. Gelvin, *The Israel-Palestine Conflict: One Hundred Years of War,* 3rd ed. (New York: Cambridge Univ. Press, 2014), 103–115.

25. Gelvin, *Israel-Palestine Conflict,* 118–120; Khalidi, *Iron Cage,* 114–117; Segev, *One Palestine,* 436–443; Morris, *Righteous Victims,* 157–160.

26. Barnes, 298; Willkie, *OW,* 24–25; "Visits Wailing Wall," *New York Times,* Sept. 12, 1942, 4; "'Those Who Give Most Will Get Most': Wendell Willkie in Jerusalem," *Palestine Post,* Sept. 14, 1942, 1. MacMichael: Segev, *One Palestine,* 416, 465. See also Khalidi, *Iron Cage,* 51.

27. Segev, *One Palestine,* 5.

28. Morris, *Righteous Victims,* 67–120; Khalidi, *Iron Cage,* 31–64; Pappe, *History of Modern Palestine,* 72–105; Gelvin, *Israel-Palestine Conflict,* 76–91. British attitudes: Segev, *One Palestine,* 1–10.

29. Gelvin, *Israel-Palestine Conflict,* 120–123; Pappe, *History of Modern Palestine,* 116–120; Segev, *One Palestine,* 447–467; Morris, *Righteous Victims,* 162–173; Zweig, *Britain and Palestine,* 1–5; O'Sullivan, *FDR and the End of Empire,* 105–110.

30. Gelvin, *Israel-Palestine Conflict,* 120–122; Morris, *Righteous Victims,* 165–166; Segev, *One Palestine,* 452, 463–464.

31. Segev, *One Palestine,* 442.

32. Zweig, *Britain and Palestine,* 163–168.

33. "What Foreign Correspondents Think of Willkie," *Look,* Oct. 5, 1943, 32; Cheryl Heckler, *An Accidental Journalist: The Adventures of Edmund Stevens, 1934–1945* (Columbia: Univ. of Missouri Press, 2007), 214–215; Neal, 241; Barnard, 352–353.

34. Pinkerton to State, 2; "Points East," *Time,* Sept. 28, 1942; Willkie, *OW,* 25. Al-Hadis: Matthews, *Confronting an Empire,* 71, 89; and "Palestine Personalities," Palestinian Academic Society for the Study of International Affairs, web directory, http://www.passia.org/personalities, accessed November 14, 2015. Shertok: Gabriel Sheffer, *Moshe Sharett: Biography of a Political Moderate* (New York: Oxford Univ. Press, 1996).

35. "Points East," *Time,* Sept. 28, 1942; Neal, 241; Heckler, *Accidental Journalist,* 214–215; Barnes, 298.

36. Segev, *One Palestine,* 376; Morris, *Righteous Victims,* 91.

37. Gelvin, *Israel-Palestine Conflict,* 33–75; James L. Gelvin, *The Modern Middle East: A History,* 3rd ed. (New York: Oxford Univ. Press, 2011), 208–216. Herzl: Gelvin, *Israel-Palestine Conflict,* 51, 6.

38. Khalidi, "Formation of Palestinian Identity," 184–186; Gelvin, *Israel-Palestine Conflict,* 92–116; Pappe, *History of Modern Palestine,* 109–120; Musa Budeiri, "The Palestinians: Tensions between Nationalist and Religious Identities," and Zachary Lockman, "Arab Workers and Arab Nationalism in Palestine: A View from Below," both in *Rethinking Nationalism in the Arab Middle East,* ed. James Jankowski and Israel Gershoni, 191–206, 249–272 (New York: Columbia Univ. Press, 1997).

39. Gelvin, *Israel-Palestine Conflict,* 99–103; Khalidi, *Iron Cage,* 31–104; Matthews, *Confronting an Empire,* 9–43, 75–170; Gelvin, *Modern Middle East,* 221–223; Pappe, *History of Modern Palestine,* 86–87.

40. Gelvin, *Israel-Palestine Conflict,* 51; Morris, *Righteous Victims,* 91; Segev, *One Palestine,* 434; Sheffer, *Moshe Sharett,* 104–134. Intra-Zionist divides: Pappe, *History of Modern Palestine,* 87–94, 108–109; Gelvin, *Israel-Palestine Conflict,* 71–74; Khalidi, *Iron Cage,* 9–22; Yehuda Bauer, *From Diplomacy to Resistance: A History of Jewish Palestine, 1939–1945* (Philadelphia: Jewish Publication Society of America, 1970).

41. Willkie, *OW,* 25; Irving Fineman, *Woman of Valor: The Life of Henrietta Szold, 1860–1945* (New York: Simon and Schuster, 1961), 413–415; Michael Oren, *Power, Faith, and Fantasy: America in the Middle East, 1776 to the Present* (New York: Norton, 2007), 434–436.

42. Willkie, *OW,* 26; Neal, 241.

43. Willkie, *OW,* 25–26; Fineman, *Woman of Valor,* 413.

44. Oren, *Power, Faith, and Fantasy,* 420–432; Makdisi, *Faith Misplaced,* 180; Little, *American Orientalism,* 14–17; Hugh Wilford, *America's Great Game: The CIA's Secret Arabists and the Shaping of the Modern Middle East* (New York: Basic Books, 2013), 56–62; Michelle Mart, *Eye on Israel: How America Came to View Israel as an Ally* (Albany: State Univ. of New York Press, 2006), 41–42; Jacobs, *Imagining the Middle East,* 200–206; O'Sullivan, *FDR and the End of Empire,* 112; *FRUS, 1942,* vol. 4, *The Near East and Africa* (Washington, DC: U.S. Government Printing Office, 1963), 538–558.

45. Roosevelt to Secretary of State, July 7, 1942, in *FRUS, 1942,* vol. 4, 543–544; Oren, *Power, Faith, and Fantasy,* 442–445; O'Sullivan, *FDR and the End of Empire,* 105–120; Makdisi, *Faith Misplaced,* 178–180; Morris, *Righteous Victims,* 164–173; Jacobs, *Imagining the Middle East,* 206–208.

46. Mart, *Eye on Israel,* 4.

47. Mart, *Eye on Israel,* 1–64. On *National Geographic*: Little, *American Orientalism,* 18–19.

48. Mart, *Eye on Israel,* 55 (and more generally 53–64); Little, *American Orientalism,* 24.

49. Wendell Willkie, "The Case for the Minorities," *Saturday Evening Post,* June 27, 1942; Sarah Gualtieri, *Between Arab and White: Race and Ethnicity in the Early Syrian American Diaspora* (Berkeley: Univ. of California Press, 2009).

50. Oren, *Power, Faith, and Fantasy,* 462–464.

51. Little, *American Orientalism,* 17–24.

52. "Willkie's Message on Balfour Day," *Palestine Post,* Nov. 5, 1942, 3; Willkie, *OW,* 26.

53. See "Principal Factors Relating to Palestine," Aug. 19, 1942, 2, in box 15, Van Doren Papers.

CHAPTER 6 ☣ HOW EAST AND WEST WILL MEET

1. Richard T. Kight, "Willkie Flight," n.d., reel A3009, frame 641, AFHRA; Intelligence Division, Air Transport Command, "Report of Interrogation . . . ," in reel A3009, frame 663, AFHRA; Patrick M. Stinson, *Around-the-World Flights: A History* (Jefferson, NC: McFarland, 2011), 151–152; "Points East," *Time,* Sept. 28, 1942, 29.

2. "Iraq Greets American Visitor," *Palestine Post,* Sept. 14, 1942, 3; "Willkie Flies to Baghdad," *New York Times,* Sept. 13, 1942, 6. Details of Willkie visit to Baghdad: W. S. Farrell to Secretary of State, Sept. 14, 1942, no. 65, and Farrell to State, Sept. 23, 1942, no. 103, both in box 16, 032, Willkie, Wendell, Decimal Files: 1940–44, State Department Files, Record Group 59, NACP; Farrell to State, Sept. 24, 1942, no. 105 in box 17, 032, Willkie, Wendell, Decimal Files: 1940–44, Record Group 59, State Department Files, NACP. Clippings of *Iraq Times,* Sept. 12 and 14, 1942, in H. F. Bartlett to Edward Stanley, British Overseas Press Service, Oct. 20, 1942, in box 15, Folder Wendell Willkie, World Trip 1942, Middle East, Van Doren Papers; Gardner Cowles Jr., *Mike Looks Back: The Memoirs of Gardner Cowles* (New York: Gardner Cowles, 1985).

3. See "Principal Factors Relating to Iraq," n.d., in box 15, Folder Wendell Willkie, World Trip 1942, Middle East, Van Doren Papers. See also Christopher D. O'Sullivan, *FDR and the End of Empire: The Origins of American Power in the Middle East* (New York: Palgrave, 2012), 29–36.

4. See Adeed Dawisha, *Iraq: A Political History from Independence to Occupation* (Princeton: Princeton Univ. Press, 2009); Toby Dodge, *Inventing Iraq: The Failure of Nation Building and a History Denied* (New York: Columbia Univ. Press, 2003); Charles Tripp, *A History of Iraq,* 2nd ed. (New York: Cambridge Univ. Press, 2002). Churchill: O'Sullivan, *FDR and the End of Empire,* 27.

5. Dawisha, *Iraq: A Political History,* 149; Willkie, *OW,* 32.

6. O'Sullivan, *FDR and the End of Empire,* 38–39.

7. Salman al-Shaikh Daoud, "The Envoy of the American People; The Arab's Share of Freedom and Independence," *Al-Hawadith,* Sept. 13, 1942, n.p., translation in Farrell to Secretary of State, Sept. 24, 1942, 3–4, no. 105, NACP.

8. *Al-Shahab* quoted in Farrell to Secretary of State, Sept. 24, 1942, 3, no. 105, NACP; Anonymous to Willkie, n.d., c. Sept. 12, 1942, in Correspondence 1929–1944, box 95, Willkie Papers. Also M. Thompson to M. Peterson, Sept. 17, 1942, no. 5774, FO371/31338, Foreign Office Papers, BNA.

9. Willkie, *OW,* 32; Willkie, "Nine Months After," *Washington Post,* July 7, 1943, 1, 2.

10. Dawisha, *Iraq: A Political History,* 148–171; Tripp, *History of Iraq,* 108–147.

11. "Mr. Willkie's Message to Iraq," *Iraq Times,* Sept. 14, 1942, 1; "Willkie 'at Home' in Middle East," *Palestine Post,* Sept. 15, 1942, 3.

12. Cowles, *Mike Looks Back,* 77.

13. Willkie, *OW,* 33.

14. "A Baghdad Diary," *Iraq Times,* Sept. 14, 1942, 2; Farrell to State, Sept. 14, 1942, 1–2; Edmund Stevens, "Mr. Willkie Captures Baghdad amid Setting of Arabian Nights," *Christian Science Monitor,* Sept. 16, 1942, 1; "What Foreign Correspondents Think of Willkie," *Look,* Oct. 5, 1943, 32.

15. Farrell to State, Sept. 14, 1942, 1–2, no. 65, and Sept. 23, 1942, 4, no. 103, NACP.

16. Melani McAlister, *Epic Encounters: Culture, Media, and U.S. Interests in the Middle East, 1945–2000* (Berkeley: Univ. of California Press, 2001); Douglas Little, *American Orientalism: The United States and the Middle East since 1945* (Chapel Hill: Univ. of North Carolina Press, 2002), 1–76; Michael B. Oren, *Power, Faith and Fantasy: America in the Middle East, 1776 to the Present* (New York: Norton, 2007); Ussama Makdisi, *Faith Misplaced: The Broken Promise of U.S.-Arab Relations: 1820–2001* (New York: Basic Books, 2010).

17. "Mr. Roosevelt's Envoy in Iraq," *Iraq Times,* Sept. 14, 1942; Willkie, Statement, Sept. 14, 1942, Folder Wendell Willkie, World Tour, 1942, box 14, Van Doren Papers; "Willkie Harks Back to the Arabian Nights Days," *Palestine Post,* Sept. 16, 1942, 3.

18. Cowles, *Mike Looks Back,* 77–78.

19. Willkie, *OW,* 33–34; "Willkiana," *New Yorker,* Dec. 26, 1942, n.p., in box 11, Wendell Willkie Tour folder, Barnes Columbia.

20. Susan Nance, *How the Arabian Nights Inspired the American Dream, 1790–1935* (Chapel Hill: Univ. of North Carolina Press, 2009); Kristin Hoganson, *Consumer's Imperium: The Global Production of American Domesticity, 1865–1920* (Chapel Hill: Univ. of North Carolina Press, 2007); McAlister, *Epic Encounters;* Little, *American Orientalism,* 9–42.

21. Yuriko Yamanaka and Tetsuo Nishio, eds., *The Arabian Nights and Orientalism* (London: I. B. Tauris, 2006); Nance, *Arabian Nights;* Paul McMichael Nurse, *Eastern Dreams: How the Arabian Nights Came to the World* (Toronto: Viking Canada, 2010); Marina Warner, *Stranger Magic: Charmed States and the Arabian Nights* (Cambridge, MA: Harvard Univ. Press, 2012).

22. "Mr. Willkie's Message to Iraq," *Iraq Times,* Sept. 14, 1942; "Willkie Finds Unity in the Middle East," *New York Times,* Sept. 15, 1942, 3; "Willkie Moved by Iraq Farewell," *Los Angeles Times*, Sept. 15, 1942, 5.

CHAPTER 7 ❧ FIRST FLIGHT

1. Edmund Stevens, "Willkie Takes Shah of Iran on First Air Ride," *Christian Science Monitor,* Sept. 18, 1942, 1, 6.

2. Abbas Milani, *The Shah* (New York: Palgrave Macmillan, 2011), 134–135; Ian Munro, "Willkie Takes Leave of Iran," *Palestine Post,* Sept. 18, 1942, 3; "Takes Shah for Ride in Plane," *New York Times,* Sept. 18, 1942, 3; "Willkiana," *New Yorker,* Dec. 26, 1942; Intelligence Division, Air Transport Command, "Report of Interrogation . . . ," reel A3009, frame 664, AFHRA.

3. "Willkie Delivers Kiss at Tehran as Ordered," *Washington Post,* Sept. 16, 1942, 3; Louis Dreyfus to Secretary of State, Sept. 24, 1942, 2, no. 104, in box 16, 032, Willkie, Wendell, Decimal Files: 1940–44, State Department Files, Record Group 59, NACP; Kight, "Willkie Flight," n.d., reel A3009, frame 641, AFHRA; Intelligence Division, Air Transport Command, "Report of Interrogation . . . ," reel A3009, frames 663–664, AFHRA; "Willkie Is Welcomed by Dreyfus at Teheran," *Atlanta Constitution,* Sept. 15, 1942, 11.

4. Louis Dreyfus to Secretary of State, Sept. 18, 1942, no. 71, in box 16, 032, Willkie, Wendell, Decimal Files: 1940–44, State Department Files, Record Group 59, NACP; "Willkie Has Talk with Iran's Premier," *New York Times,* Sept. 16, 1942, 15.

5. "Willkie Writes Autographs in Iran on Dollars," *New York Herald Tribune,* Sept. 16, 1942; "Mr. Willkie Charms the Iranians," *Palestine Post,* Sept. 17, 1942, 3; Gardner Cowles, *Mike Looks Back: The Memoirs of Gardner Cowles* (New York: Gardner Cowles, 1985), 78.

6. Nikki Keddie, *Modern Iran: Roots and Results of Revolution* (New Haven: Yale Univ. Press, 2003), 1–72; James Gelvin, *The Modern Middle East,* 3rd ed. (New York: Oxford Univ. Press, 2011), 150–157; Behrooz Moazami, *State, Religion, and Revolution in Iran, 1796 to the Present* (New York: Palgrave Macmillan, 2013), 11–54.

7. See Ali M. Ansari, *Modern Iran since 1921: The Pahlavis and After* (London: Pearson, 2003), 20–24; Keddie, *Modern Iran,* 73–80; Milani, *The Shah,* 15–22; Gelvin, *Modern Middle East,* 204.

8. Reza Shah: Gelvin, *Modern Middle East,* 204–207; Ansari, *Modern Iran,* 24–74; Keddie, *Modern Iran,* 80–104; Milani, *The Shah,* 19–27, 53–59; Mohammad Gholi Majd, *Great Britain and Reza Shah: The Plunder of Iran, 1921–1941* (Gainesville: Univ. Press of Florida, 2001); Amin Banani, *The Modernization of Iran: 1921–1941* (Stanford, CA: Stanford Univ. Press, 1961). Iranian nationalism: Afshin Marashi, "Paradigms of Iranian Nationalism: History, Theory, and Historiography," in *Rethinking Iranian Nationalism and Modernity,* ed. Kamran Scott Aghaie and Afshin Marashi (Austin: Univ. of Texas Press, 2014); Majid Sharifi, *Imagining Iran: The Tragedy of Subaltern Nationalism* (Lanham, MD: Lexington Books, 2013); Afshin Marashi, *Nationalizing Iran: Culture, Power, and the State, 1870–1940* (Seattle: Univ. of Washington Press, 2008); Firoozeh Kashani-Sabet, *Frontier*

Fictions: Shaping the Iranian Nation, 1804–1946 (Princeton: Princeton Univ. Press, 1999); Moazami, *State, Religion, and Revolution in Iran,* 93–116; Ansari, *Modern Iran,* 1–20.

9. Third power strategy: Mark Hamilton Lytle, *The Origins of the Iranian-American Alliance, 1941–1953* (New York: Holmes and Meier, 1987); Mansour Bonakdarian, "Great Expectations: U.S.-Iranian Relations, 1911–1951," in *U.S.-Middle East Historical Encounters: A Critical Survey,* ed. Abbas Amanat and Magnus T. Bernhardsson (Gainesville: Univ. Press of Florida, 2007), 122. End of Reza Shah: Gelvin, *Modern Middle East,* 294; Ansari, *Modern Iran,* 82–84; Keddie, *Modern Iran,* 105–107; Milani, *The Shah,* 67–88.

10. "Iran," n.d., in folder Wendell Willkie, World Trip 1942, Middle East, box 15, Van Doren Papers. Turmoil post–Reza Shah: Sharifi, *Imagining Iran,* 93–95; Milani, *The Shah,* 82–110; Keddie, *Modern Iran,* 106–110; Moazami, *State, Religion, and Revolution in Iran,* 44–48; Gholam Reza Afkhami, *The Life and Times of the Shah* (Berkeley: Univ. of California Press, 2009), 61–85.

11. Milani, *The Shah,* 102–103; Sharifi, *Imagining Iran,* 93; Lytle, *Origins of the Iranian-American Alliance,* 29; Moazami, *State, Religion, and Revolution in Iran,* 48.

12. Milani, *The Shah,* 135.

13. Dreyfus to State, Sept. 18, 1942, 1–4, no. 71, NACP; "Willkie Has a Talk with Iran's Premier," *New York Times,* Sept. 16, 1942, 15.

14. Lytle, *Origins of the Iranian-American Alliance,* 27–32; O'Sullivan, *FDR and the End of Empire,* 72, 85.

15. Willkie speech: Dreyfus to State, Sept. 24, 1942, enclosure no. 8, no. 104, NACP; "Willkie Lunches with Iran's Ruler on Anniversary," *Washington Post,* Sept. 17, 1942, 7; "Willkie, Guest of Iran Ruler, Tells Aims of His World Trip," *Los Angeles Times,* Sept. 17, 1942, 2; "Willkie Dines at Celebration of Iran Ruler," *Atlanta Constitution,* Sept. 17, 1942, 7. See also R. Bullard to Foreign Office, Sept. 17, 1942, no. 5561, in FO371/31418, Foreign Office Papers, BNA.

16. "'Those Who Give Most Will Get Most': Wendell Willkie in Jerusalem," *Palestine Post,* Sept. 14, 1942, 1; Proteus, "Changing Scene," *Palestine Post,* Sept. 15, 1942, 4.

17. Sam Brewer, "Allied Defense Strengthened," *Los Angeles Times,* Sept. 15, 1942, 5; "Mr. Willkie's Persuasion," *Christian Science Monitor,* Sept. 16, 1942, 22.

18. "Willkie Sells U.S. Victory to Middle East," *Life,* Sept. 28, 1942, 29–31.

19. O'Sullivan, *FDR and the End of Empire,* 80; Lytle, *Origins of the Iranian-American Alliance,* 31.

20. Lytle, *Origins of the Iranian-American Alliance,* 16–81; O'Sullivan, *FDR and the End of Empire,* 69–87.

21. O'Sullivan, *FDR and the End of Empire,* 71–72.

22. O'Sullivan, *FDR and the End of Empire,* 83.

23. O'Sullivan, *FDR and the End of Empire,* 71; Lytle, *Origins of the Iranian-American Alliance,* xvii–xviii.

24. Lytle, *Origins of the Iranian-American Alliance,* 192–213; James F. Goode, *The United States and Iran: In the Shadow of Mussadiq* (New York: St. Martin's Press, 1997); Keddie, *Modern Iran,* 123–131; Ansari, *Modern Iran,* 106–124; Sharifi, *Imagining Iran,* 96–106.

25. See articles from *Iran, Keihan, Mardom,* and *Bahar,* collected in Dreyfus to State, Sept. 24, 1942, enclosures nos. 2, 3, 4, 5, and 6, no. 104, NACP. See also Bonakdarian, "Great Expectations," 135.

26. *Filastin:* Munro, "Willkie Takes Leave of Iran," 3.

27. Dreyfus to State, Sept. 24, 1942, enclosure no. 2, no. 104, NACP.

28. Dreyfus to State, Sept. 24, 1942, enclosure no. 4, no. 104, NACP.

29. Willkie, *OW,* 34.

30. O'Sullivan, *FDR and the End of Empire,* 134.

31. Willkie, *OW,* 37.

32. Dreyfus to State, Sept. 24, 1942, enclosure no. 9, no. 104, NACP.

33. Kight, "Willkie Flight," frame 642, AFHRA; Intelligence Division, "Report of Interrogation . . . ," frame 664, AFHRA; Patrick M. Stinson, *Around-the-World Flights: A History* (Jefferson, NC: McFarland, 2011), 152.

CHAPTER 8 ⚙ WORKING WITH RUSSIA

1. Walter Graebner, *Round Trip to Russia* (Philadelphia: J. B. Lippincott, 1943), 51; Alexander Werth, *Russia at War, 1941–1945* (New York: E. P. Dutton, 1964), 484.

2. Ronald Grigor Suny, *The Soviet Experiment: Russia, the USSR, and the Successor States,* 2nd ed. (New York: Oxford Univ. Press, 2011), 336–362; Nikita Lomagin, "The Soviet Union in the Second World War," in *A Companion to Russian History,* ed. Abbott Gleason (London: Blackwell, 2009), 386–413; John Barber and Mark Harrison, "Patriotic War, 1941–1945," in *The Cambridge History of Russia,* vol. 3, ed. Ronald Grigor Suny (Cambridge: Cambridge Univ. Press, 2006), 217–242; Geoffrey Roberts, *Stalin's Wars: From World War to Cold War, 1939–1953* (New Haven: Yale Univ. Press, 2006); Nicholas V. Riasanovsky and Mark D. Steinberg, *A History of Russia,* 7th ed. (New York: Oxford Univ. Press, 2005), 501–516; Amir Weiner, *Making Sense of War: The Second World War and the Fate of the Bolshevik Revolution* (Princeton: Princeton Univ. Press, 2001); William C. Fuller Jr., "The Great Fatherland War and Late Stalinism, 1941–1953," in *Russia: A History,* ed. Gregory L. Freeze (New York: Oxford Univ. Press, 1997), 319–346; John Barber and Mark Harrison, *The Soviet Home Front, 1941–1945* (London: Longman, 1991); Susan J. Linz, ed., *The Impact of World War II on the Soviet Union* (Totowa, NJ: Rowman and Allanheld, 1981).

3. Richard T. Kight, "Willkie Flight," n.d., reel A3009, frame 642, AFHRA; Intelligence Division, Air Transport Command, "Report of Interrogation . . . ," reel A3009, frame 664, AFHRA; Patrick M. Stinson, *Around-the-World Flights: A History* (Jefferson, NC: McFarland, 2011), 152; Willkie, *OW,* 50.

4. See William H. Standley (with Arthur A. Ageton), *Admiral Ambassador to Russia* (Chicago: Henry Regnery, 1955), 265–269; Kight, "Willkie Flight," frame 642, AFHRA; William Standley to Secretary of State, Sept. 17, 1942, no. 69, in box 16, 032, Willkie, Wendell, Decimal Files: 1940–44, State Department Files, Record Group 59, NACP; "Willkie in Russia, Greeted by Envoys," *New York Times,* Sept. 18, 1942, 3; "Willkie in Kuibyshev, Feasted on Sturgeon," New York *Daily News,* Sept. 18, 1942, 16.

5. Standley, *Admiral Ambassador to Russia,* 270; Maurice Hindus, *Mother Russia* (Garden City, NY: Doubleday, Doran, 1943), 123–124; Willkie, *OW,* 51; Graebner, *Round Trip to Russia,* 115–117; Henry C. Cassidy, *Moscow Dateline, 1941–1943* (Boston: Houghton Mifflin, 1943), 261; Larry Lesueur, *Twelve Months That Changed the World* (New York: Knopf, 1943), 307–310; Eddy Gilmore, "Willkie Is Just Another Tourist to Russians," *Chicago Tribune,* Sept. 22, 1942, 7; "No Crowds Gather," *New York Times,* Sept. 22, 1942, 6; John Evans, "Moscow Full of Conjectures about Willkie's Visit," *Christian Science Monitor,* Sept. 22, 1942, 8.

6. Standley, *Admiral Ambassador to Russia,* 354, 265–294; Alexander Werth, *The Year of Stalingrad* (New York: Knopf, 1947), 262–265. Vodka: William O'Neill, *A Better World: Stalinism and the American Intellectuals* (New York: Simon and Schuster, 1982), 151.

7. Willkie, *OW,* 70; Standley to Secretary of State, Sept. 22, 1942, no. 82; Standley to State, Sept. 25, 1942, no. 87; Standley to State, Sept. 29, 1942, no. 91, all in box 16, 032, Willkie, Wendell, Decimal Files: 1940–44, State Department Files, Record Group 59, NACP; "Mr. Willkie in Kuibyshev," in Bagallay to Eden, Sept. 20, 1942, 1–2, in FO371/33033, file 5388, Foreign Office Papers, BNA; F. Molotchkov, "Willkie's Stay in Moscow," Sept. 22, 1942, 1–2, in fond 06, inventory 4, file 239, paper folder 22, 13.04.1942–25.12.1942, MFAR. (Available at *SSSR i Soiuzniki: dokumenty Arkhiva MID Rossii o vneshnei politike i diplomatii vedushchikh derzhav antigitlerovskoi koalitsii* [The USSR and the Allies: documents from the archive of the Russian Ministry of Foreign Affairs (MID) on foreign policy and diplomacy of the leading states of the anti-Hitler Coalition], http://www.agk.mid.ru, accessed April 18, 2016.) Department of State, *FRUS, 1942,* vol. 3, *Europe* (Washington, DC: Department of State, 1961), 637–640; "Willkie Questions Russian Workers," *New York Times,* Sept. 19, 1942, 3; "Greeted by High Officials," *New York Times,* Sept. 21, 1942, 3; "Willkie Sees Trophies," *New York Times,* Sept. 23, 1942, 8; "Museum Gives Willkie Red Army Preview," *Washington Post,* Sept. 23, 1942, 18; "Talks with Many Workers," *New York Times,* Sept. 24, 1942, 1. Leningrad: Lomagin, "Soviet Union in the Second World War," 400; Barber and Harrison, *Soviet Home Front,* 27, 54, 65, 67.

8. H. Bostock in Bagallay to Eden, Sept. 20, 1942, 3, in FO371/33033, file 5388, Foreign Office Papers, BNA; "Russian Ballerina Kissed by Willkie," *New York Times,* Sept. 20, 1942, 2; "Willkie Delays Usually Prompt Bolshoi Curtain," *Washington Post,* Sept. 20, 1942, 6; "Wendell Willkie Stops Show at Soviet Ballet Performance," *Los Angeles Times,* Sept. 20, 1942, 3; Henry Shapiro, "Mr. Willkie in Kuibyshev," *Palestine Post,* Sept. 20, 1942, 1.

9. Georgiy Zarubin, "Transcript of Willkie's Stay in Kuibyshev," Sept. 22, 1942, 4, in fond 06, inventory 4, file 239, paper folder 22, 13.04.1942–25.12.1942, MFAR. See also Cassidy, *Moscow Dateline,* 257; Leonard Lyons, "Broadway Gazette," *Washington Post,* Oct. 27, 1942, B8; Standley, *Admiral Ambassador to Russia,* 272; Dept. of State, *FRUS, 1942,* vol. 3, *Europe,* 638.

10. Willkie, *OW,* 54; Michael David-Fox, *Showcasing the Great Experiment: Cultural Diplomacy and Western Visitors to the Soviet Union, 1921–1941* (New York: Oxford Univ. Press, 2012), 116.

11. Willkie, *OW,* 60–61; "Mr. Willkie Inspects Soviet Factories," *Palestine Post,* Sept. 22, 1942, 1; "Willkie in Moscow for a Week's Stay," *New York Times,* Sept. 21, 1942, 3.

12. Standley, *Admiral Ambassador to Russia,* 276.

13. Zarubin, "Transcript," 5 and 3, MFAR; M. M. Potrubach, "Conversation with Willkie in the Car . . . ," Sept. 18, 1942, 1, in fond 06, inventory 4, file 239, paper folder 22, 13.04.1942–25.12.1942, MFAR.

14. Zarubin, "Transcript," 6, MFAR; Standley, *Admiral Ambassador to Russia,* 275–276.

15. Zarubin, "Transcript," 1–4, MFAR; Standley, *Admiral Ambassador to Russia,* 271; Dept. of State, *FRUS, 1942,* vol. 3, *Europe,* 638. Factories: Suny, *Soviet Experiment,* 347–349; Lomagin, "Soviet Union in the Second World War," 396–397; Fuller, "The Great Fatherland War," 330; Barber and Harrison, "Patriotic War," 233–234; Barber and Harrison, *Soviet Home Front,* 127–132.

16. Willkie, *OW,* 64–68; Zarubin, "Transcript," 2.

17. Dept. of State, *FRUS, 1942,* vol. 3, *Europe,* 631. "Class enemies": David-Fox, *Showcasing the Great Experiment,* 247–285.

18. David Engerman, *Modernization from the Other Shore: American Intellectuals and the Romance of Russian Development* (Cambridge, MA: Harvard Univ. Press, 2003), 255; David-Fox, *Showcasing the Great Experiment,* 9; Ronald Suny, "Reading Russia and the Soviet Union in the Twentieth Century," in *The Cambridge History of Russia,* vol. 3, ed. Ronald Grigor Suny (Cambridge: Cambridge Univ. Press, 2006), 28–32; Stephen Kotkin, "Modern Times: The Soviet Union and the Interwar Conjuncture," *Kritika* 2, no. 1 (2001): 111–164; Stephen Kotkin, *Magnetic Mountain: Stalinism as a Civilization* (Berkeley: Univ. of California Press, 1995).

19. Engerman, *Modernization,* 153–154.

20. Engerman, *Modernization,* 187–188; David-Fox, *Showcasing the Great Experiment,* 133–138.

21. Engerman, *Modernization,* 171, 215.

22. Willkie, *OW,* 70; Willkie, "We Must Work with Russia," *New York Times,* Jan. 17, 1943, 5, 25.

23. Ralph B. Levering, *American Opinion and the Russian Alliance, 1939–1945* (Chapel Hill: Univ. of North Carolina Press, 1976), 117, 94–145; Ronald Smelser and Edward J. Davies II, *The Myth of the Eastern Front: The Nazi-Soviet War in American Popular Culture* (New York: Cambridge Univ. Press, 2008), 7–38.

24. See Benjamin Alpers, *Dictators, Democracy, and American Public Culture: Envisioning the Totalitarian Enemy, 1920s–1950s* (Chapel Hill: Univ. of North Carolina Press, 2003), 235–237; Engerman, *Modernization,* 275–276; Suny, *Soviet Experiment,* 354; Lomagin, "Soviet Union in the Second World War," 399, 401–404; Barber and Harrison, *Soviet Home Front,* 207–209; Milovan Djilas, *Conversations with Stalin* (1962; London: Penguin Classics, 2014), 33.

25. William Taubman, *Stalin's American Policy: From Entente to Détente to Cold War* (New York: Norton, 1982), 38.

26. Standley, *Admiral Ambassador to Russia,* 276; Dept. of State, *FRUS, 1942,* vol. 3, *Europe,* 646.

27. Levering, *American Opinion,* 104; M. Todd Bennett, *One World, Big Screen: Hollywood, the Allies, and World War II* (Chapel Hill: Univ. of North Carolina Press, 2012), 169–216.

28. *Fortune,* Nov. 1942, 239. *Life* and Russia: Levering, *American Opinion,* 114–115.

29. F. Molotchkov, "Willkie's Stay in Moscow," Sept. 23, 1942, 1–2, in fond 06, inventory 4, file 239, paper folder 22, 13.04.1942–25.12.1942, MFAR; "Willkie Supports Second Front Plea," *New York Times,* Sept. 22, 1942, 6.

30. Cassidy, *Moscow Dateline,* 260; Graebner, *Round Trip to Russia,* 114–117; Werth, *Russia at War,* 485; Werth, *Year of Stalingrad,* 262; Lesueur, *Twelve Months,* 309.

31. Willkie, *OW,* 55; Gardner Cowles, *Mike Looks Back: The Memoirs of Gardner Cowles* (New York: Gardner Cowles, 1985), 80; Cassidy, *Moscow Dateline,* 263; James Brown, *Russia Fights* (New York: Charles Scribner's Sons, 1943), 174; Leland Stowe, "Willkie Watches Reds Battle Nazis," *Los Angeles Times,* Sept. 26, 1942, 3; Ralph Parker, "Willkie Watches Battle in Rzhev," *New York Times,* Sept. 26, 1942, 4; Willkie, "What I Learned about the Nazis from Stalin," *Look,* Dec. 1, 1942, 13; F. Molotchkov, "Trip to the Front," Sept. 25, 1942, 1–3, in fond 06, inventory 4, file 239, paper folder 22, 13.04.1942–25.12.1942, MFAR.

32. Cowles, *Mike Looks Back,* 80.

33. Willkie, "What I Learned," 13; Willkie, *OW,* 57.

34. Willkie, *OW,* 55–59; Cowles, *Mike Looks Back,* 81.

35. Willkie, *OW,* 58–59; Suny, *Soviet Experiment,* 360; Lomagin, "Soviet Union in the Second World War," 402–404; Barber and Harrison, "Patriotic War," 229–234.

36. "Interview with Major R. T. Kight, A. C.," Oct. 23, 1942, 7, in Presidential Secretary Files, 1933–1945, Series 5, box 173, folder 11, Willkie, Wendell, Oct. 1942–Oct. 1944, FDR Papers; Werth, *Russia at War,* 477; Werth, *Year of Stalingrad,* 270, 274; Derek Watson, "Molotov, the Making of the Grand Alliance, and the Second Front, 1939–1942," *Europe-Asia Studies* 54, no. 1 (2002): 51–85.

37. Ilya Ehrenburg, *The War: 1941–1945* (Cleveland, OH: World Publishing, 1964), 79; "Willkie in Moscow for a Week's Stay," *New York Times,* Sept. 21, 1942, 3.

38. "Willkie in Moscow for a Week's Stay," 3.

39. Dept. of State, *FRUS, 1942,* vol. 3, *Europe,* 463; Standley, *Admiral Ambassador to Russia,* 271–282; Dept. of State, *FRUS, 1942,* vol. 3, *Europe,* 465–466; Graebner, *Round Trip to Russia,* 186; Ehrenburg, *War: 1941–1945,* 79; Brown, *Russia Fights,* 164; Barnard, 355–366.

40. Konstantin Simonov, *Raznye dni voyny: Dnevnik pisatelya* [Various days of the war: a writer's diary] (Moscow: Grifon M, 2005), 157–160.

41. Willkie, *OW,* 76–80; Simonov, *Raznye dni voyny,* 157–160; Ehrenburg, *War: 1941–1945,* 79.

42. V. M. Molotov, Diary, "Transcript of Conversation with Willkie and Standley," Sept. 21, 1942, 1–5, in fond 06, inventory 4, file 236, paper folder 22–13.04.1942–25.12.1942, MFAR; Standley to State, Sept. 23, 1942, no. 85, in box 16, 032, Willkie, Wendell, Decimal Files: 1940–44, State Department Files, Record Group 59, NACP; Standley, *Admiral Ambassador to Russia,* 279–280; Djilas, *Conversations with Stalin,* 20.

43. Standley, *Admiral Ambassador to Russia,* 280–285; Dept. of State, *FRUS, 1942,* vol. 3, *Europe,* 640–641; Cassidy, *Moscow Dateline,* 267.

44. "Willkie and Stalin," *New York Times,* Sept. 25, 1942, 20; Suny, *Soviet Experiment,* xvi–xx, 235–315; Lynne Viola, "Stalinism in the 1930s," in *A Companion to Russian History,* ed. Abbott Gleason (London: Blackwell, 2009), 368–385; David R. Shearer, "Stalinism, 1928–1940," and Yoram Gorlizki and Oleg Khlevniuk, "Stalin and His Circle," both in *The Cambridge History of Russia,* vol. 3: *The Twentieth Century,* ed. Ronald Grigor Suny (Cambridge: Cambridge Univ. Press, 2006),192–216 and 243–267; essays by David L. Hoffman (1–8), Ronald Grigor Suny (13–36), Moshe Lewin (39–62), Sheila Fitzpatrick (161–178), Jochen Hellbeck (181–210), and Amir Weiner (239–274) in *Stalinism,* ed. David L. Hoffman (London: Blackwell, 2003); Sheila Fitzpatrick, *Everyday Stalinism: Ordinary Life in Extraordinary Times* (New York: Oxford Univ. Press, 1999); Kotkin, *Magnetic Mountain.*

45. "Agrarian despotism": Moshe Lewin in Viola, "Stalinism in the 1930s," 380. Frank Costigliola, *Roosevelt's Lost Alliances: How Personal Politics Helped Start the Cold War* (Princeton: Princeton Univ. Press, 2012); Melvyn Leffler, *For the Soul of Mankind: The United States, the Soviet Union, and the Cold War* (New York: Hill and Wang, 2007), 20–37; Geoffrey Roberts, *Stalin's Wars: From World War to Cold War, 1939–1953* (New Haven: Yale Univ. Press, 2006), 165–192, 254–346; Robert Dallek, *Franklin D. Roosevelt and American Foreign Policy, 1932–1945* (New York: Oxford Univ. Press, 1995), 533–534, 542–543; Warren Kimball, *The Juggler: Franklin Roosevelt as Wartime Statesman* (Princeton: Princeton Univ. Press, 1991).

46. Cowles, *Mike Looks Back,* 81.

47. See Graebner, *Round Trip to Russia,* 119–121; Willkie, *OW,* 83–84.

48. See Graebner, *Round Trip to Russia,* 121; Taubman, *Stalin's American Policy,* 38–39.

49. See Willkie, *OW,* 80–84; Graebner, *Round Trip to Russia,* 121; Willkie, "Describes Soviet Premier," *New York Times,* Sept. 29, 1942, 5.

50. V. Pavlov, "Transcript of Comrade J. V. Stalin's Conversation with Willkie, Sept. 23, 1942," Sept. 28, 1942, 1–8, available from Center for Military-Political Studies, Moscow, Russia, and at http://www.eurasian-defence.ru/?q=node/22886; Standley to State, Sept. 26, 1942, no. 88, in box 16, 032, Willkie, Wendell, Decimal Files: 1940–44, State Department Files, Record Group 59, NACP; "Willkie Confers with Stalin for Two Hours at Kremlin," *Los Angeles Times,* Sept. 24, 1942, 3; "Stalin Receives Willkie for Talk Lasting 2 Hours," *New York Times,* Sept. 24, 1942, 1.

51. Pavlov, "Transcript," 1–3; Graebner, *Round Trip to Russia,* 122; Dept. of State, *FRUS, 1942,* vol. 3, *Europe,* 629.

52. Pavlov, "Transcript," 4–5.

53. Pavlov, "Transcript," 6–8; Graebner, *Round Trip to Russia,* 121.

54. Cowles, *Mike Looks Back,* 83. The letter returned to the United States with Willkie, who gave it to Irita Van Doren, who kept it for posterity. See box 11, Van Doren Papers. There were a number of competing versions of the letter story retailed over the years, from Cowles's laundry bag story to columnist Drew Pearson's version, in which the travelers lost the letter and only found it in the laundry *after* the meeting with Stalin. See Drew Pearson, *Diaries, 1949–1959,* ed. Tyler Abell (New York: Holt, Rinehart and Winston, 1974), 387. In 1946, perhaps in an attempt to burnish the image of "the boss," Barnes would write to the journalist Roscoe Drummond that Willkie had not forgotten the letter at all; instead, he was "smart enough to know that

his name and face were better introduction than any necessarily formal letter from the President." See Barnes to Roscoe Drummond, July 1, 1946, in box 39, folder: Wendell Willkie, Barnes Columbia.

55. Ralph Parker, "More Aid to Soviet Vital, Says Willkie," *New York Times,* Sept. 27, 1942, 1, 3; "Willkie Says Soviet People Disappointed," *Christian Science Monitor,* Sept. 24, 1942, 7; "Willkie Feels Red Coolness," *Los Angeles Times,* Sept. 25, 1942, A; Eddy Gilmore, "Red Resentment Worries Willkie," *Washington Post,* Sept. 25, 1942, 1.

56. Ernest Lindley, untitled, *Washington Post,* Sept. 27, 1942, B7; "Enough Rope," *New York Daily Mirror,* Nov. 13, 1942, 29; Anne O'Hare McCormick, "Mr. Willkie Opens an International Debate," *New York Times,* Sept. 28, 1942, 16; Arthur Krock, "Effects of Willkie Statement in the Capital," *New York Times,* Sept. 29, 1942, 22; "Public Prodding," *Washington Post,* Nov. 29, 1942, 10; "He Declares Urgent Need for Second Front," *New York Times,* Sept. 29, 1942, 5; Barnet Nover, "Russia's Plight: Mr. Willkie Lifts a Curtain," *Washington Post,* Sept. 29, 1942, 11; Ernest Lindley, "Public Prodding," *Washington Post,* Sept. 30, 1942, 7; Neal, 248–249; Levering, *American Opinion,* 89–91.

57. Dallek, *Franklin D. Roosevelt and American Foreign Policy,* 360; "Army-Navy Journal Warns on Willkie," *New York Times,* Oct. 4, 1942, 11; Edwin L. James, "Second Front Debate Reaches Thorny Stage," *New York Times,* Oct. 4, 1942, B3; "Willkie Hopes Stalin Note Will Spur Allies," *Washington Post,* Oct. 6, 1942, 2; "Stalin Says Aid from Allies So Far Is 'Little Effective,'" *New York Times,* Oct. 5, 1942, 1; Cassidy, *Moscow Dateline,* 269–283.

58. "Roosevelt Hasn't Read Willkie Statements," *Atlanta Constitution,* Oct. 7, 1942, 7; W. H. Lawrence, "President Brushes Aside Willkie's Second Front Plea," *New York Times,* Oct. 7, 1942, 1; Raymond Daniell, "Churchill Blocks Second Front Debate," *New York Times,* Oct. 7, 1942, 10; J. Reilly O'Sullivan, "Says What He 'Damn Pleases,' Willkie Avers," *Atlanta Constitution,* Oct. 8, 1942, 14. See also Barnard, 360–362; Barnes, 300.

59. "Statements on Asia and Second Front Were Ordered by Him, President Asserts," *Christian Science Monitor,* Oct. 9, 1942, 1; "Roosevelt Mum on Status of Willkie," *Washington Post,* Oct. 10, 1942, 7; "Silent on Willkie Mission," *New York Times,* Oct. 10, 1942, 4.

60. Barnard, 359.

61. Kremlin dinner: Brown, *Russia Fights,* 171–172; Cassidy, *Moscow Dateline,* 265–267; Costigliola, *Roosevelt's Lost Alliances,* 299–300; Barnes, 301–303; Neal, 249–250; Drew Pearson, "Washington Merry-Go-Round," *Washington Post,* December 11, 1942; Dept. of State, *FRUS, 1942,* vol. 3, *Europe,* 642–645; Standley, *Admiral Ambassador to Russia,* 287–289; Cowles, *Mike Looks Back,* 82–83; "Willkie Is Toasted by Stalin as Guest at Kremlin Dinner," *New York Times,* Sept. 28, 1942, 1; "Stalin Jests with Guests," *New York Times,* Sept. 28, 1942, 1.

62. Missing planes: Barnes, 301; Dept. of State, *FRUS, 1942,* vol. 3, *Europe,* 643.

63. Standley, *Admiral Ambassador to Russia,* 294; Taubman, *Stalin's American Policy,* 56–59; Brown, *Russia Fights,* 163–164. More balanced accounts: Alpers, *Dictators, Democracy, and American Public Culture,* 237–238, and Levering, *American Opinion,* 89–91.

64. "Willkie and the Bear," *Time,* Oct. 5, 1942, 30. See also Costigliola, *Roosevelt's Lost Alliances,* 299–300.

65. Willkie, *OW,* 52. Barnes on purges: Joseph Barnes, "The Great Bolshevik Cleansing," *Foreign Affairs,* April 1939, 556–568.

66. Clark Kerr to Foreign Office, Sept. 27, 1942, in 371/33033, File 4943, Foreign Office Papers, BNA; British Embassy to Eden, Jan. 14, 1943, 2, in 954/19B, File 469, Foreign Office Papers, BNA.

67. Costigliola, *Roosevelt's Lost Alliances;* Valentin Berezhkov, *History in the Making: Memoirs of World War II Diplomacy* (Moscow: Progress Publishers, 1983), 191–192; Ehrenburg, *War: 1941–1945,* 124.

68. Graebner, *Round Trip to Russia,* 123; Lesueur, *Twelve Months,* 312; Brown, *Russia Fights,* 177; Leland Stowe to *Chicago News,* Sept. 27, 1942, 1–3, in box 15, Van Doren Papers; Ralph Parker, "Willkie Helps Bridge Russian-American Gap," *New York Times,* Sept. 27, 1942, B4; "Willkie Received 'Good Press' in Soviet Union," *Washington Post,* Sept. 28, 1942, 2.

CHAPTER 9 ⚇ THE CHINA MYSTIQUE

1. "Willkie's Journey," *Washington Post,* Sept. 28, 1942, 6; Clifford A. Bowman to Editors, *New York Herald Tribune,* Sept. 28, 1942.

2. See Russell Davenport to Willkie, n.d., and Irita Van Doren to Willkie, n.d., in box 95, folder: Correspondence, Jan.–Sept. 1942, Official, Willkie Papers.

3. "Willkie's Journey," 6.

4. Gardner Cowles, *Mike Looks Back: The Memoirs of Gardner Cowles* (New York: Gardner Cowles, 1985), 93–94; Neal, 250–251.

5. Barnes, 299.

6. Richard T. Kight, "Willkie Flight," n.d., reel A3009, frames 644–646, AFHRA; Intelligence Division, Air Transport Command, "Report of Interrogation . . . ," reel A3009, frames 664–665, 674, AFHRA.

7. Willkie, *OW,* 117. See also C. E. Gauss to Secretary of State, Oct. 8, 1942, no. 124, in box 17, 032, Willkie, Wendell, Decimal Files: 1940–44, State Department Files, Record Group 59, NACP.

8. Patrick M. Stinson, *Around-the-World Flights: A History* (Jefferson, NC: McFarland, 2011), 153; Cowles, *Mike Looks Back,* 86.

9. "Willkie Is Greeted in China's Capital," *New York Times,* Sept. 30, 1942, 10; "Authorities in Chinese Capital Say His Trip Is Taking Longer than Expected," *New York Times,* Oct. 1, 1942, 9; "Chungking Bedecked to Greet Willkie," *New York Times,* Oct. 2, 1942, 5; "Chungking Acclaim Welcomes Willkie," *New York Times,* Oct. 3, 1942, 1, 3.

10. Kight, "Willkie Flight," frame 646, AFHRA; Intelligence Division, Air Transport Command, "Report of Interrogation . . . ," reel A3009, frames 674, 677, AFHRA; Karl Eskelund, "Chungking's Gala Reception for Mr. Willkie," *Palestine Post,* Oct. 2, 1942, 1; "Willkie Evades Jap Scout Plane, Reaches Chungking," *Atlanta Constitution,* Oct. 3, 1942, 14; "Given Tremendous Welcome on Arrival in China's Capital," *Washington Post,* Oct. 3, 1942, 2; "Mr. Willkie Is Given Most Hearty

Welcome Here," *National Herald* (Chongqing), Oct. 3, 1942, 1; Untitled, Foreign News, *Time*, Oct. 12, 1942, 28.

11. Willkie, *OW,* 127–128; Barnes, 305; H. J. Seymour to Anthony Eden, Oct. 29, 1942, File 7414, FO 371/31723, Foreign Office Papers, BNA.

12. Barbara Tuchman, *Stilwell and the American Experience in China* (New York: Macmillan, 1970), 424.

13. John S. Service, "Memorandum for the Ambassador," Nov. 14, 1942, 1–3, in Gauss to State, Nov. 17, 1942, no. 126, in box 17, 032, Willkie, Wendell, Decimal Files: 1940–44, State Department Files, Record Group 59, NACP; Joseph W. Esherick, ed., *Lost Chance in China: The World War II Dispatches of John S. Service* (New York: Random House, 1974), 276.

14. Tuchman, *Stilwell,* 425; Joseph Stilwell, with Theodore H. White, *The Stilwell Papers* (New York: William Sloane Associates, 1948), 156; "Attack Everywhere, Willkie Says," *Atlanta Constitution,* Oct. 4, 1942, 4A; Lee McIsaac, "The City as Nation: Creating a Wartime Capital in Wartime Chongqing," in *Remaking the Chinese City: Modernity and National Identity, 1900–1950,* ed. Joseph W. Esherick (Honolulu: Univ. of Hawai'i Press, 1999), 174–191; Matthew T. Combs, "Chongqing 1943: People's Livelihood, Price Control, and State Legitimacy," in *1943: China at the Crossroads,* ed. Joseph W. Esherick and Matthew T. Combs (Ithaca, NY: Cornell Univ. Press, 2015), 282–322.

15. "Wendell Willkie Arrives in China at Chungking, 1942," film 62200, in 342-AFNR-1700, in Record Group 32, Records of Air Force Commands, Activities, and Organizations, National Archives Motion Pictures Division, NACP; Part 6 of United News Reel, "U.S. Pacific War Heroes Decorated, etc.," film 38926, in 208-UN-21, in Record Group 208, Records of the Office of War Information, 1928–1951, in National Archives Motion Pictures Division, NACP. "Willkie Gets a Hot Towel, an Old Chinese Custom," *New York Times,* Oct. 3, 1942, 3; "Willkie Averts Hunger by Discarding Chopsticks," *New York Times,* Oct. 4, 1942, 7; "Willkie Wields Chopsticks," *Atlanta Constitution,* Oct. 5, 1942, 2. "Chinese Industry Pleases Willkie; He Kisses Orphan," *Washington Post,* Oct. 5, 1942, 1, 2.

16. John N. Hart, "Wendell Willkie in China: The Birth of the GOP-KMT Alliance," 13–14, typescript in Fairbank Collection, Harvard-Yenching Library, Harvard University, Cambridge, MA; "Willkie Visits Cultural Center of Chungking," *National Herald* (Chungking), Oct. 6, 1942, 1; "Speaks Only for Himself, Willkie Says," *Washington Post,* Oct. 8, 1942, 3; "Willkie Concludes Talks with Chiang," *New York Times,* Oct. 8, 1942, 3; Barnard, 366.

17. Hart, "Wendell Willkie in China," 14–15; John Paton Davies, *China Hand: An Autobiography* (Philadelphia: Univ. of Pennsylvania Press, 2012), 95; John Carter Vincent, Report, n.d., in President's Secretary's File, box 173, folder, Willkie, Wendell: Oct. 1942–1944, FDR Papers; Graham Peck, *Two Kinds of Time* (Boston: Houghton Mifflin, 1950), 303–304.

18. Hart, "Wendell Willkie in China," 3, 9; "Extract: From transcript of a conversation between the USSR ambassador to China, A. S. Panyushkin and Mme. Sun Yat-Sen on 9/X-42," n.d., in fond 129, inventory 26, file 11, paper folder 144, 09/01/1942–31/12/1942, MFAR (available at *SSSR i Soiuzniki: Dokumenty Arkhiva MID Rossii o*

vneshnei politike i diplomatii vedushchikh derzhav antigitlerovskoi koalitsii [The USSR and the Allies: Documents from the archive of the Russian Ministry of Foreign Affairs (MID) on foreign policy and diplomacy of the leading states of the anti-Hitler coalition], http://www.agk.mid.ru); Davies, *China Hand,* 96; Peck, *Two Kinds of Time,* 433; Gauss to State, Oct. 8, 1942, in *FRUS, 1942, China* (Washington, DC: Department of State, 1956), 161–165.

19. "Chungking Acclaim Welcomes Willkie," *New York Times,* Oct. 3, 1942, 1, 3.

20. Joseph W. Esherick "Prologue: China and the World in 1943," in *1943: China at the Crossroads,* ed. Joseph W. Esherick and Matthew T. Combs (Ithaca, NY: Cornell Univ. Press, 2015), 1–40; Rana Mitter, *Forgotten Ally: China's World War II, 1937–1945* (Boston: Houghton Mifflin Harcourt, 2013); Odd Arne Westad, *Restless Empire: China and the World since 1750* (New York: Basic Books, 2012), 247–284; Jay Taylor, *The Generalissimo: Chiang Kai-shek and the Struggle for Modern China* (Cambridge, MA: Harvard Univ. Press, 2009), 141–295; Hans J. Van de Ven, *War and Nationalism in China, 1925–1945* (London: Routledge, 2003); Henrietta Harrison, *China: Inventing the Nation* (London: Arnold, 2001), 207–225; Jonathan D. Spence, *The Search for Modern China,* 2nd ed. (New York: Norton, 1999), 419–458; Youli Sun, *China and the Origins of the Pacific War, 1931–1941* (New York: St. Martin's Press, 1993); Lloyd E. Eastman, "Nationalist China during the Sino-Japanese War 1937–1945," in *The Cambridge History of Modern China,* vol. 13, *Republican China 1912–1949, Part 2,* ed. John K. Fairbank and Albert Feuerwerker (Cambridge: Cambridge Univ. Press, 1986), 547–608.

21. Michael Schaller, *The United States and China: Into the Twenty-First Century* (New York: Oxford Univ. Press, 2015), 60–76; Gordon H. Chang, *Fateful Ties: A History of America's Preoccupation with China* (Cambridge, MA: Harvard Univ. Press, 2015), 168–171; Michael Schaller, "FDR and the 'China Question,'" in *FDR's World: War, Peace, and Legacies,* ed. David B. Woolner, Warren F. Kimball, and David Reynolds (New York: Palgrave Macmillan, 2008), 145–174; Warren I. Cohen, *America's Response to China: A History of Sino-American Relations,* 4th ed. (New York: Columbia Univ. Press, 2000), 105–134; Van de Ven, *War and Nationalism in China,* 1–63.

22. Taylor, *Generalissimo,* 214.

23. Stilwell, *Stilwell Papers,* 156–159; Stilwell to Diary, Oct. 6, 1942 and Oct. 7, 1942, Stilwell Diaries, 80.

24. Taylor, *Generalissimo,* 213; Kight, "Willkie Flight," frame 646, AFHRA. See also "Interview with Major R. T. Kight, A. C.," Oct. 23, 1942, 10–11, in Presidential Secretary Files, 1933–1945, Series 5, box 173, folder 11, Willkie, Wendell, Oct. 1942–Oct. 1944, FDR Papers.

25. Stilwell to Diary, December 16, 1942, Stilwell Diaries, 95.

26. Willkie, *OW,* 141–144; Tuchman, *Stilwell,* 429–436; Taylor, *Generalissimo,* 218–220; Mitter, *Forgotten Ally,* 300–301; Schaller, *United States and China,* 66–75; Claire Lee Chennault, *Way of a Fighter: The Memoirs of Claire Lee Chennault,* ed. Robert Hotz (New York: G. P. Putnam's Sons, 1949).

27. Willkie, *OW,* 139.

28. Willkie, *OW,* 131–132; "Telling Mr. Willkie: China Is Building a Country under Duress," *Ta Kung Pao,* Oct. 4, 1942, 2; Qin Xiyaoi, ed., *Zong tong Jiang gong da shi chang pian chu gao* [Preliminary draft of President Chiang's chronological biography], vol. 5 (Taipei: Chungchang Cultural and Educational Foundation, 1978), 2045–2047.

29. Gauss to State, Oct. 8, 1942, enclosure 6, 2, no. 124, NACP; *All We Are and All We Have* (New York: Chinese News Service, 1942), 38–40, in box 14, folder Wendell Willkie, World Trip, 1942, China, Van Doren Papers; Willkie, *OW,* 133–134.

30. Ho Chi Minh, "On Reading of Wendell Willkie's Reception in China," in "Seven Prison Poems," trans. Steve Bradbury, *Manoa* 7, no. 2 (1995): 67.

31. Peck, *Two Kinds of Time,* 69.

32. Willkie, *OW,* 136–137; Cowles, *Mike Looks Back,* 86.

33. Peck, *Two Kinds of Time,* 412–416.

34. "Willkie in China: The Story of a Historic Visit," in China Information Committee, *China at War,* vol. 9, no. 5 (Nov. 1942): 25–26, in box 114, folder: Trip to China and UCR, Sept.–Oct. 1942, Willkie Papers; Service, "Memorandum . . . ," 3, in Gauss to State, Nov. 17, 1942, no. 126, NACP; "Willkie and the Torches," *Time,* Oct. 19, 1942, 37–38; J. Reilly O'Sullivan, "2 Jap Efforts to Kill Willkie in China Fail," *Washington Post,* Oct. 10, 1942, 1; Harrison Forman, "Japanese Shoot Twice at Willkie," *New York Times,* Oct. 10, 1942, 4; "Station Shelled before Arrival," *New York Times,* Oct. 10, 1942, 4; Willkie, *OW,* 147–149.

35. Willkie, *OW,* 149; Cowles, *Mike Looks Back,* 87; Neal, 257; Tuchman, *Stilwell,* 427; Peck, *Two Kinds of Time,* 430; Henry R. Luce, "China to the Mountains," *Life,* June 30, 1941.

36. William Fenn to Willkie, Oct. 8, 1942, in box 114, folder: Trip to China and UCR, Sept.–Oct. 1942, Willkie Papers; Willkie, *OW,* 150–156.

37. Willkie, *OW,* 137–138.

38. Barnes, 307; Willkie, *OW,* 135.

39. Taylor, *Generalissimo,* 595; Westad, *Restless Empire,* 162–170, 195–198, 253–284; Willkie, *OW,* 134–135.

40. Stilwell, *Stilwell Papers,* 156.

41. Chang, *Fateful Ties,* 1, 40–46; T. Christopher Jespersen, *American Images of China, 1931–1949* (Stanford, CA: Stanford Univ. Press, 1996), 4.

42. Jespersen, *American Images,* 2–3, 73; Chang, *Fateful Ties,* 68, 84, 103–106; Robert G. Lee, *Orientals: Asian Americans in Popular Culture* (Philadelphia: Temple Univ. Press, 1999), 1–144; Mari Yoshihara, *Embracing the East: White Women and American Orientalism* (New York: Oxford Univ. Press, 2003), 1–11; James Bradley, *The China Mirage: The Hidden History of American Disaster in Asia* (New York: Little, Brown, 2015); Kristin Hoganson, *Consumer's Imperium: The Global Production of American Domesticity, 1865–1920* (Chapel Hill: Univ. of North Carolina Press, 2007); Karen J. Leong, *The China Mystique: Pearl Buck, Anna May Wong, Mayling Soong, and the Transformation of American Orientalism* (Berkeley: Univ. of California Press, 2005); Christina Klein, *Cold War Orientalism: Asia in the Middlebrow Imagination, 1945–1961* (Berkeley: Univ. of California Press, 2003), 1–49.

43. Chang, *Fateful Ties,* 49–146; Jespersen, *American Images,* 1–10.

44. See Jespersen, *American Images,* xv–xix, 2, 36, 50, 65; Chang, *Fateful Ties,* 164; Leong, *China Mystique,* 1–11; Bradley, *China Mirage,* 85–168.

45. Jespersen, *American Images,* 67; "He Who Has Reason," *Time,* Oct. 5, 1942; Chang, *Fateful Ties,* 164–167; Bradley, *China Mirage,* 111–115; Alan Brinkley, *The Publisher: Henry Luce and His American Century* (New York: Random House, 2010), 273–281, 293–300; Robert E. Herzstein, *Henry R. Luce,* Time, *and the American Crusade in Asia* (New York: Cambridge Univ. Press, 2005), 1–48; James L. Baughman, *Henry R. Luce and the Rise of the American News Media* (Baltimore, MD: Johns Hopkins Univ. Press, 2001), 129–156.

46. Jespersen, *American Images,* 36.

47. Yoshihara, *Embracing the East,* 169; Jespersen, *American Images,* 26, 147; M. Todd Bennett, *One World, Big Screen: Hollywood, the Allies, and World War II* (Chapel Hill: Univ. of North Carolina Press, 2012), 217–255.

48. Yoshihara, *Embracing the East,* 149–169; Leong, *China Mystique,* 12–56; Chang, *Fateful Ties,* 146–150; Bradley, *China Mirage,* 116–117, 130–131, 175; Peter Conn, *Pearl Buck: A Cultural Biography* (New York: Cambridge Univ. Press, 1996).

49. Jespersen, *American Images,* 45–58; Chang, *Fateful Ties,* 164–165; Bradley, *China Mirage,* 232–237.

50. Laura Tyson Li, *Madame Chiang Kai-shek: China's Eternal First Lady* (New York: Atlantic Monthly Press, 2006), 153; Willkie, *OW,* 135, 126.

51. "Willkie Pleads for Offensives on Every Front," *Chicago Tribune,* Oct. 4, 1942, 14; "Mr. Willkie's Response," in Generalissimo Chiang Kai-Shek, "A Friend From Distant Lands," in *All We Are and All We Have: Speeches and Messages Since Pearl Harbor* (New York: Chinese News Service, 1942), 39, in box 14, folder Wendell Willkie, World Trip, 1942, China, Van Doren Papers; Willkie, *OW,* 118–121.

52. Tyson Li, *Madame Chiang Kai-shek,* 152; Hannah Pakula, *The Last Empress: Madame Chiang Kai-shek and the Birth of Modern China* (New York: Simon and Schuster, 2009).

53. Jespersen, *American Images,* 92.

54. Grace C. Huang, "Madame Chiang's Visit to America," in *1943: China at the Crossroads,* ed. Joseph W. Esherick and Matthew T. Combs (Ithaca, NY: Cornell Univ. Press, 2015), 41–74; Jespersen, *American Images,* 82–107; Chang, *Fateful Ties,* 175; Leong, *China Mystique,* 106–154.

55. Cowles, *Mike Looks Back,* 88; Pakula, *Last Empress,* 405; Tyson Li, *Madame Chiang Kai-shek,* 182.

56. Compare "Mme. Chiang Kai-shek Entertains Roosevelt's Envoy at Tea Party," *National Herald,* Oct. 5, 1942, 1; J. Reilly O'Sullivan, "Chinese Industry Pleases Willkie; He Kisses Orphan," *Washington Post,* Oct. 5, 1942, 1, 2; Harrison Forman, "Willkie to 'Howl' for a Free World," *New York Times,* Oct. 5, 1942, 3; "Willkie Lauds China Efficiency," *Los Angeles Times,* Oct. 5, 1942, 2.

57. Cowles, *Mike Looks Back,* 88–89; Drew Pearson, *Diaries, 1949–1959,* ed. Tyler Abell (New York: Holt, Rinehart and Winston, 1974), 388.

58. Pearson, *Diaries,* 387–388; Pakula, *Last Empress,* 434; Barnard, 369; Neal, 255–256.

59. "Mme. Chiang Kai-Shek Entertains Roosevelt's Envoy at Tea Party," *National Herald,* 1, 2; Forman, "Willkie to 'Howl' for a Free World," 3; "Willkie 'Symbol of Free Nations,' Madame Chiang Tells Notables," *Atlanta Constitution,* Oct. 4, 1942, 2; "Mme. Chiang Has Willkie to Tea; He Kisses a Girl," *Chicago Tribune,* Oct. 5, 1942, 6.

60. Willkie, *OW,* 140; Tuchman, *Stilwell,* 427–428.

61. Albert Feuerwerker, "The Foreign Presence in China," in *The Cambridge History of China,* ed. John K. Fairbank, vol. 12, *Republican China, 1912–1949, Part 1* (Cambridge: Cambridge Univ. Press, 1983), 128–207; Westad, *Restless Empire,* 173–176; Harrison, *China,* 61–65; Chang, *Fateful Ties,* 35–40.

62. Westad, *Restless Empire,* 176.

63. Erez Manela, *The Wilsonian Moment: Self-Determination and the International Origins of Anticolonial Nationalism* (New York: Oxford Univ. Press, 2007), 216.

64. Mitter, *Forgotten Ally,* 245; Taylor, *Generalissimo,* 194–196.

65. "Text of Translation of Editorials of Leading Newspapers in Chungking for Oct. 3, 1942," n.d., 2, in box 14, folder Wendell Willkie, World Tour 1942, China, Van Doren Papers.

66. Chinese News Service, "Willkie in China, as Reported by Voice of China, October 5 to October 14, 1942," Oct. 7, 1942, 3, in box 15, folder Wendell Willkie, World Tour 1942, China, Van Doren Papers; Chinese Faculty to Willkie, Oct. 5, 1942, box 14, folder Wendell Willkie, World Tour 1942, China, Van Doren Papers; "Faculty Members of Four Schools Greet Mr. Willkie," *National Herald,* Oct. 6, 1942, 4.

67. Hai to Willkie, Sept. 28, 1942, in box 14, folder Wendell Willkie, World Tour, China, 1942, Van Doren Papers; Willkie, *OW,* 129–130.

68. "Memorandum to Mr. Willkie Presented by People's Organizations in Sian," n.d., 2, translation in bound manuscript, "The English Translation of Memorandum and Newspaper Editorials in Welcome of Mr. Wendell Willkie. Si-an, China," n.d., in box 14, folder Wendell Willkie, World Tour 1942, China, Van Doren Papers.

69. "Text of Translation of Editorials of Leading Newspapers in Chungking for Oct. 3, 1942," n.d., 2 (4), in box 14, folder Wendell Willkie, World Tour 1942, China, Van Doren Papers; T. V. Soong, "Organizing the New World Order for Victory and Peace," Oct. 10, 1942, n.p., in box 14, folder Wendell Willkie, World Tour, China, 1942, Van Doren Papers.

70. H. H. Kung to Willkie, "A Memorandum to the Honorable Wendell L. Willkie," Oct. 6, 1942, in box 11, folder: Correspondence, 1942, W. Willkie Tour, Barnes Columbia.

71. Gauss to State, Oct. 8, 1942, enclosure no. 3, 5, no. 124, NACP; H. L. Seymour to Anthony Eden, Oct. 13, 1942, File 7656, FO 371/31723, Foreign Office Papers, BNA.

72. Chinese News Service, "Willkie in China . . . ," Oct. 12, 1942, 3, in box 15, folder Wendell Willkie, World Tour 1942, China, Van Doren Papers; Gauss to State, Oct. 8, 1942, enclosure no. 5, 1, no. 124, NACP.

73. "Statement by Wendell L. Willkie, Chungking, Oct. 7, 1942," in box 108, Willkie Papers; Harrison Forman, "Global Offensive Urged by Willkie," *New York Times,* Oct. 7, 1942, 1; Joseph G. Harrison, "U.S. Supporting Willkie Demands for World in Which All Men Are Free," *Christian Science Monitor,* Oct. 7, 1942, 1; "Willkie

Vigorously Demands 'All-Out Offensive Everywhere,'" *Los Angeles Times,* Oct. 7, 1942, A; "Mr. Willkie Sees End of Empires," *Palestine Post,* Oct. 7, 1942, 1; "Offensive Called For, Willkie Says Will Dedicate His Life to Free World," *Charleston Evening Post,* Oct. 7, 1942, 1; "Fight Back with All Forces to Secure Freedom," *Ta Kung Pao,* Oct. 8, 1942, 2.

CHAPTER 10 ⚙ A REPORT TO THE PEOPLE

1. "Prime Minister's Survey," *Times* (London), Nov. 11, 1942, 4; "The Widening Prospect," *Times* (London), Nov. 11, 1942, 5; "'Great Design' in Africa," *Times* (London), Nov. 11, 1942, 8; Winston Churchill, "The Bright Gleam of Victory" speech, Nov. 10, 1942, audio at International Churchill Society, https://www.win stonchurchill.org/resources/speeches/1941-1945-war-leader/alamein-the-end-of-the -beginning.

2. Willkie, *OW,* 92.

3. Willkie, *OW,* 97–98.

4. Willkie, *OW,* 89.

5. Kight, "Willkie Flight," n.d., reel A3009, frames 647–648, AFHRA; Intelligence Division, Air Transport Command, "Report of Interrogation . . . ," reel A3009, frames 666–667, AFHRA; Bert Andrews, "Willkie Promises to Give People a 'Full, Frank' Report on Trip," *New York Herald Tribune,* Oct. 14, 1942, 1, 4.

6. "Willkie Evolves a Plain Vanilla Foreign Policy for Republicans," *Life,* Oct. 19, 1942, 36; Joseph G. Harrison, "U.S. Supporting Willkie Demands for World in Which All Men Are Free," *Christian Science Monitor,* Oct. 7, 1942, 1; "Thank You, Mr. Willkie," *Christian Science Monitor,* Oct. 7, 1942, 24; "Mr. Willkie Reports," *Minneapolis Morning Tribune,* Oct. 8, 1942, in box 123, Willkie Papers.

7. "Willkie Rankles Rankin," *New York Times,* Oct. 8, 1942, 3; "They Can Keep Him," *Chicago Tribune,* Oct. 9, 1942, 14; "Willkie in the Fog," New York *Daily News,* Nov. 11, 1942, in box 123, Willkie Papers.

8. "Unvarnished Wisdom," *Dallas Morning News,* Oct. 8, 1942, in box 123, Willkie Papers; "Statements to 'New Masses' from Prominent Americans: What the War Means to the Negro," *New Masses,* Oct. 20, 1942, 22.

9. "Willkie Flying to Capital Today; President Asked Quick Report," *New York Times,* Oct. 14, 1942, 1; Joyce Chaplin, *Round about the Earth: Circumnavigation from Magellan to Orbit* (New York: Simon and Schuster, 2012); "Gulliver's Traveler," *Time,* Oct. 26, 1942, 22; "Willkie Demands Global Thinking," *New York Times,* Nov. 7, 1942, 7.

10. "Around the World with Willkie," *Christian Science Monitor,* Oct. 27, 1942, 22; "Raymond Clapper—Broadcast, Oct. 8, 1942," 5–7, in box 108, folder Raymond Clapper Broadcast, 10/8/42, Willkie Papers; "The World Is Our Business," *New York Times,* Oct. 18, 1942, E8.

11. Grafton quoted in "Toward World Unity," *Time,* Oct. 19, 1942, 19.

12. "Notes and Comment," *New Yorker,* Oct. 3, 1942; Henry McLemore, "The Lighter Side," *Los Angeles Times,* Oct. 13, 1942, 18.

13. Raymond Buell to Willkie, Oct. 17, 1942, in box 11, Willkie Papers; Mrs. J. D. Gardner to Editor, *Dallas Morning News,* Oct. 13, 1942, in box 123, Willkie Papers; Lars Halstad to Editor, *Chicago Tribune,* Oct. 22, 1942, 14.

14. "Mr. Willkie's Two Roles," *New York Times,* Oct. 8, 1942, 26.

15. Mabel Wyeth to Editor, *New York Herald Tribune,* Oct. 13, 1942; Frank G. Fowler to Willkie, Oct. 20, 1942, in box 28, Willkie Papers.

16. Arthur Krock, "Interest in Willkie Keen," *New York Times,* Oct. 14, 1942, 3; "When Indiana Goes Visiting," *New York Times,* Oct. 11, 1942, E8.

17. Robert A. Divine, *Second Chance: The Triumph of Internationalism in America during World War II* (New York: Atheneum, 1967), 62, 31. Andrew Preston, *Sword of the Spirit, Shield of the Faith: Religion in American War and Diplomacy* (New York: Norton, 2012), 365–409.

18. Divine, *Second Chance,* 22–23.

19. Divine, *Second Chance,* 39, 68–69.

20. Divine, *Second Chance,* 69; Ahmed Emin Yalman, *Turkey in My Time* (Norman: Univ. of Oklahoma Press, 1956), 192.

21. See Hadley Cantril and Mildred Strunk, eds., *Public Opinion, 1935–1946* (Princeton: Princeton Univ. Press, 1951), 1057.

22. Divine, *Second Chance,* 103. Glenda Sluga, *Internationalism in the Age of Nationalism* (Philadelphia: Univ. of Pennsylvania Press, 2013), 79–117.

23. Divine, *Second Chance,* 70–71.

24. Department of State, *FRUS, 1942, China* (Washington, DC: Department of State, 1956), 268–418; Qin Xiyaoi, ed., *Zong tong Jiang gong da shi chang pian chu gao* [Preliminary draft of President Chiang's chronological biography], vol. 5 (Taipei: Chungchang Cultural and Educational Foundation, 1978), 2049–2050; "Willkie's Four Findings," *New York Times,* Oct. 11, 1942, E1; Joseph C. Harsch, "New Allied Front: Freedom in Far East," *Christian Science Monitor,* Oct. 14, 1942, 10; "Toward a Free Orient," *Christian Science Monitor,* Oct. 16, 1942, 1; Selden Menefee, "China's New Sovereignty," *Washington Post,* Oct. 17, 1942, 9; "Gulliver's Return," *New York Times,* Oct. 18, 1942, E1; "Says Willkie Heartened China," *New York Times,* Oct. 20, 1942, 5.

25. "An Open Letter from the Editors of *Life* to the People of England," *Life,* Oct. 12, 1942, 34.

26. "Willkie on Way to Answer 'Flippancies,'" *Washington Post,* Oct. 13, 1942, 1; Barnard, 374–375; Neal, 259.

27. Mary Earhart Dillon, *Wendell Willkie, 1892–1944* (Philadelphia: J. B. Lippincott, 1952), 288; Barnard, 375; Neal, 260; "Draft Notes for Conversation with President Roosevelt. Oct. 14, 1942," 6, in box 14, Van Doren Papers.

28. "Draft Notes for Conversation with President Roosevelt. Oct. 14, 1942," 1–5.

29. "Draft Notes for Conversation with President Roosevelt. Oct. 14, 1942," 2, 4.

30. Edward T. Folliard, "Willkie Again Calls for Second Front," *Washington Post,* Oct. 15, 1942, 1, 6. See also W. H. Lawrence, "Willkie Reports, Then Renews Call for Second Front," *New York Times,* Oct. 15, 1942, 1, 7.

31. "Willkie Returns to Farm Work," *Los Angeles Times,* Oct. 18, 1942, 16; Neal, 260; Barnard, 377–378; Barnes, 310.

32. Mark Sullivan, "A Post-War Vision," *Washington Post,* Oct. 30, 1942, 9.

33. Frank Kingdon, "Introduction," in *Wendell L. Willkie's Report to the People, Oct. 26, 1942,* 5, in box 108, Willkie Papers.

34. *Wendell L. Willkie's Report to the People,* 7–9.

35. *Wendell L. Willkie's Report to the People,* 8–11.

36. *Wendell L. Willkie's Report to the People,* 13.

37. See William Allen White, "Willkie Rocks Political Scene," *Indianapolis Star,* Oct. 30, 1942, in box 123, Willkie Papers; William Shirer, "The Propaganda Front," *Washington Post,* Oct. 25, 1942, B7; "Memorandum of Telephone Conversation between Mr. Wendell Willkie and Mr. Davis on January 8, 1943," attached to Forrest Davis to Adolf A. Berle, January 10, 1943, no. 1-1043, in box 17, 032, Willkie, Wendell, Decimal Files: 1940–44, State Department Files, Record Group 59, NACP; Gardner Cowles to Willkie, January 15, 1943, in box 18, Willkie Papers; Wm. Roger Louis, *Imperialism at Bay: The United States and the Decolonization of the British Empire, 1941–1945* (New York: Oxford Univ. Press, 1978), 177–180, 230–232, 242–258, 360–362; Penny Von Eschen, *Race against Empire* (Ithaca, NY: Cornell Univ. Press, 1997), 25–28; Carol Anderson, *Bourgeois Radicals: The NAACP and the Struggle for Colonial Liberation, 1941–1960* (New York: Cambridge Univ. Press, 2015), 14–22.

38. Louis, *Imperialism at Bay,* 130, 8–26.

39. Louis, *Imperialism at Bay,* 121–133.

40. "Mr. Willkie's Report," *Daily Oregonian,* Oct. 28, 1942, 10; "The World Charter," *New York Times,* Nov. 1, 1942, E10; "Atlantic Charter Covers World," *Los Angeles Times,* Oct. 28, 1942, 1; "Charter Refers to 'All Peoples,'" *New York Times,* Oct. 28, 1942, 4; "Willkie Demands Global Thinking," *New York Times,* Nov. 7, 1942, 7.

41. Manu Bhagavan, *The Peacemakers: India and the Quest for One World* (Noida: Harper Collins India, 2012), 1–40; M. S. Venkataramani and B. K. Shrivastava, *Quit India: The American Response to the 1942 Struggle* (New Delhi: Vikas, 1979); M. S. Venkataramani and B. K. Shrivastava, *Roosevelt, Gandhi, Churchill: America and the Last Phase of India's Freedom Struggle* (New Delhi: Radiant, 1983), 1–54.

42. Venkataramani and Shrivastava, *Quit India,* 1–60; Nico Slate, *Colored Cosmopolitanism: The Shared Struggle for Freedom in the United States and India* (Cambridge, MA: Harvard Univ. Press, 2012), 125–160.

43. Venkataramani and Shrivastava, *Quit India,* 249–315.

44. "Willkie Grieves Indians," *New York Times,* Sept. 21, 1942, 3; Norris Haselton to Secretary of State, Oct. 3, 1942, no. 93, in box 16, 032, Willkie, Wendell, Decimal Files: 1940–44, State Department Files, Record Group 59, NACP; Darrell Berrigan, "U.S. Asked to Intervene," *Palestine Post,* Oct. 9, 1942, 1; "Suggests Inquiry by Willkie," *New York Times,* Oct. 9, 1942, 4; "Mr. Willkie Invited to India," *Times of India,* Oct. 9, 1942, 7; Haselton to Secretary of State, Oct. 9, 1942, no. 102, in box 16, 032, Willkie, Wendell, Decimal Files: 1940–44, State Department Files, Record Group 59, NACP; "Hindus Ask Willkie to Visit India," *New York Times,* Oct. 10, 1942, 4; Venkataramani and Shrivastava, *Quit India,* 316–340; Kenton J. Clymer, *Quest for Freedom: The United States and India's Independence* (New York: Columbia Univ. Press, 1995), 102–107.

45. *Wendell L. Willkie's Report to the People,* 13–14.

46. Mark Mazower, *Governing the World: The History of an Idea* (New York: Penguin Press, 2012), 131–135; Mazower, *No Enchanted Palace: The End of Empire and the Ideological Origins of the United Nations* (Princeton: Princeton Univ. Press, 2009), 28–65; Saul Dubow, "Smuts, the United Nations, and the Rhetoric of Race and Rights," *Journal of Contemporary History* 43, no. 1 (2008): 64–66.

47. Jan Christian Smuts, "The British Colonial Empire," *Life,* Dec. 28, 1942, 11–15. See also Louis, *Imperialism at Bay,* 219, and Andrew Baker, *Constructing a Post-War Order: The Rise of U.S. Hegemony and the Origins of the Cold War* (London: I. B. Tauris, 2011), 66–71. Logan: Robert Vitalis, *White World Order, Black Power Politics: The Birth of American International Relations* (Ithaca, NY: Cornell Univ. Press, 2015), 111.

48. *Wendell L. Willkie's Report to the People,* 14.

49. *Wendell L. Willkie's Report to the People,* 19–21.

50. "Quick Aid Urged," *New York Times,* Oct. 27, 1942, 1; Barnes, 311. See *Wendell L. Willkie's Report to the People,* 23–31; "The Press on Willkie," *Louisville Courier-Journal,* Oct. 30, 1942, and other clippings in box 123, Willkie Papers.

51. "A Great Speech," *Minneapolis Tribune,* Oct. 28, 1942, in box 123, Willkie Papers; Mrs. O. L. Ewing to Roosevelt, Oct. 27, 1942, in box 2, folder Oct. 1942, Index #4040, President's Official File, FDR Library; "A Battle Cry for Freedom," *Christian Century,* Nov. 4, 1942, 1343–1345.

52. Roscoe Drummond, "Willkie's Appraisal of War Rated as High Statesmanship," *Christian Science Monitor,* Oct. 27, 1942, 9.

53. *Wendell L. Willkie's Report to the People,* 30; Shirley Baum to Roosevelt, Oct. 28, 1942, in box 2, folder Oct. 1942, index #4040, President's Official File, FDR Library; Virgil MacMickle to Willkie, Oct. 28, 1942, in box 50, Willkie Papers.

54. "A Battle Cry for Freedom," 1343; Anne O'Hare McCormick, "A Discoverer of the New World in the East," *New York Times,* Oct. 28, 1942, 22.

55. MacMickle to Willkie, Oct. 28, 1942; Clare Boothe Luce to Willkie, Oct. 27, 1942, in box 48, Willkie Papers.

56. A. M. Wendell Malliet, "World Fronts," *New York Amsterdam News,* Nov. 14, 1942, 8.

57. Dorothy Thompson, "Mr. Willkie's Speech," *New York Herald Tribune,* Oct. 28, 1942, clipping in box 123, Willkie Papers; Sullivan, "A Post-War Vision," 9.

58. "Mr. Willkie's Report," *New York Times,* Oct. 27, 1942, 24; Walter Lippmann, "Mr. Willkie in Asia," *Washington Post,* Oct. 31, 1942, 9; "Imperialist Order," *Washington Post,* Nov. 20, 1942, 10; Robert Dallek, *Franklin D. Roosevelt and American Foreign Policy, 1932–1945* (New York: Oxford Univ. Press, 1995), 360.

59. Sullivan, "A Post-War Vision," 9; "Globe Trotting U.S. Do-Gooders Hit by Tydings," *Chicago Tribune,* Nov. 2, 1942, 21; Paul Mallon, "Realism Must Be Peace Basis," *Los Angeles Examiner,* Nov. 19, 1942; M. H. Jacobs, "World Listening Post," *Houston Post,* Nov. 27, 1942, clippings in box 123, Willkie Papers.

60. "Mr. Willkie's Report," *Times* (London), Oct. 28, 1942; Negley Farson, "What's All This Talk of Giving Up the Empire?," *Daily Mail,* Oct. 28, 1942, clippings in W. J. Gallman to Secretary of State, Dec. 12, 1942, no. L/4, in box 3859, 811.44, Willkie,

Wendell Decimal Files, State Department Files, Record Group 59, NACP; "Empire Views Stir British," *New York Times,* Oct. 28, 1942, 4.

61. Sir Edward Grigg, "Our Colonial Empire," *Times* (London), Nov. 22, 1942, clipping in Gallman to State, Dec. 12, 1942, no. L/4, NACP; Louis, *Imperialism at Bay,* 203–204.

62. Foreign Office to Washington, Oct. 22, 1942, no. 6418, in FO954/29B, File 609, Foreign Office Papers, BNA; Viscount Halifax to Foreign Office, Oct. 23, 1942, 1–2, no. 5249, in FO 954/29B, File 611, Foreign Office Papers, BNA; Halifax to Foreign Office, Nov. 18, 1942, no. 5647, in FO954/29B, File 665, Foreign Office Papers, BNA; Halifax to Foreign Office, Oct. 31, 1942, no. 5369, in FO954/29B, File 639, Foreign Office Papers, BNA.

63. Winston Churchill to Eden, Oct. 27, 1942, 1–2, in PREM4/27, File 1, Prime Minister's Office Papers, BNA; Arnold Toynbee to Viscount Halifax, Oct. 29, 1942, 1–2, and Toynbee to Halifax, Oct. 28, 1942, 1–4, both in PREM4/27, File 1, Prime Minister's Office Papers, BNA; Isaiah Berlin to Foreign Office, "Interview with Mr. Wendell Willkie," March 13, 1944, in PREM4/27, File 1, Prime Minister's Office Papers, BNA; Louis, *Imperialism at Bay,* 14; Halifax to Foreign Office, Nov. 1, 1942, no. 5386, in FO954/29B, File 642, Foreign Office Papers, BNA; Viscount Halifax to Foreign Office, Oct. 27, 1942, no. 5299 in FO954/29B, File 624, Foreign Office Papers, BNA; Anthony Eden, "Extract from Foreign Secretary's Minute, P.M./42/241 of 27th October, 1942," Oct. 27, 1942, in PREM4/27, File 1, Prime Minister's Office Papers, BNA.

64. Churchill to Willkie, Dec. 3, 1942, in Foreign Office to Washington, Dec. 3, 1942, no. 7563, in FO954/29B, File 679, Foreign Office Papers, BNA; Halifax to Foreign Office, Dec. 7, 1941, no. 5939, in PREM 4/27, File 1, in Prime Minister's Office Papers, BNA; Halifax to Foreign Office, Dec. 12, 1942, no. 6043, in FO954/29B, File 685, Foreign Office Papers, BNA; "Jamaicans Want Willkie to Visit," *New York Times,* Nov. 4, 1942, 6; Venkataramani and Shrivastava, *Roosevelt, Gandhi, Churchill,* 71.

65. Wendell Willkie, "Economic Freedom for the World," Nov. 16, 1942, 9–14, in box 17, Van Doren Papers; "Willkie Demands Frank Discussion of War Aims," *New York Times,* Nov. 17, 1942, 1.

66. Willkie, "Economic Freedom for the World," 1.

67. Barnard, 391–400; Barnes, 311–312; Neal, 262; Steven Casey, *Cautious Crusade: Franklin D. Roosevelt, American Public Opinion, and the War against Nazi Germany* (New York: Oxford Univ. Press, 2001), xxvi, 112–118.

68. Davis to Berle, Jan. 10, 1943, 1.

CHAPTER 11 ⬧ ONE WORLD BARNSTORMING

1. Mrs. H. H. Kight to Willkie, July 14, 1943, in box 41, Willkie Papers.

2. Publishing history: Barnes, 315–316; Robert A. Divine, *Second Chance: The Triumph of Internationalism in America during World War II* (New York: Atheneum, 1967), 105; Howard Cook, "Publisher's Plans," *New York Herald Tribune Book News,* April 16, 1943; "The Willkie," *New Yorker,* May 15, 1943, 14; Harry Hansen, "Eve

Curie Now Completely in Tune with American Life," *Chicago Tribune,* May 16, 1943, D12; Simon and Schuster, press releases and ads, 1943, in box 115, Promotional Material folder and Miscellaneous folder, Willkie Papers.

3. Frank S. Adams, "Rationing Cuts down Greatest Book Sales in History," *New York Times,* Aug. 8, 1943, BR4; Leon Shimkin to Gardner Cowles, April 29, 1943, and Gardner Cowles Jr. Memo: Influence of Willkie's Book on Voters, July 23, 1943, both in Willkie, Wendell—One World folder, Gardner Cowles Jr. Papers, Cowles Library, Drake University, Des Moines, Iowa; David Welky, *Everything Was Better in America: Print Culture in the Great Depression* (Urbana: Univ. of Illinois Press, 2008).

4. Gardner Cowles Jr. to Wendell Willkie, June 14, 1943, in box 18, Willkie Papers; Simon and Schuster memo, "Newspapers that have purchased serialization rights to Wendell Willkie's 'One World' as of June 28, 1943" (n.d.), box 115, Miscellaneous folder, Willkie Papers; letters between Darryl Zanuck and Willkie collected in box 115, folder: Correspondence, July–August 1943, and folder: Correspondence, January–April 1944, Willkie Papers; George F. Custen, *Twentieth Century Fox: Darryl F. Zanuck and the Culture of Hollywood* (New York: Basic Books, 1997), 269–270.

5. "Publisher's Note," in Willkie, *AAP*; "Words at War," radio adaptation of *One World,* by Richard McDonagh, July 1, 1943, in box 115, folder: Writings—Radio Adaptation, Willkie Papers; Allan M. Winkler, *Home Front U.S.A.: America during World War II* (Arlington Heights, IL: Harlan Davidson, 1986), 35.

6. "The Willkie," 14.

7. Daniel Immerwahr, "The Books of the Century, 1940–1949," www.booksofthecentury.com.

8. Willkie, *OW,* 202.

9. "Cecelia Ager Meets: Wendell Willkie, Who Has His Eye on 1944," *P.M.,* Nov. 16, 1942, 7.

10. Barnes, 321–324; Barnard, 400–405; Neal, 267–270.

11. Marquis Childs, "Willkie: Crusader for Peace," *Look,* March 9, 1943; FDR to Willkie, March 6, 1943, in President's Personal File, Index #7023, FDR Papers; Barnes, 311.

12. Writings and speeches in boxes 108 and 109, Willkie Papers.

13. Barnard, 411–412; Neal, 262–264; Barnes, 312–314.

14. John Morton Blum, *V Was for Victory: Politics and American Culture during World War II* (New York: Harcourt Brace Jovanovich, 1976); Paul Boyer, *By the Bomb's Early Light: American Thought and Culture at the Dawn of the Atomic Age* (New York: Pantheon, 1985); Winkler, *Home Front U.S.A.;* Ernest Mandel, *The Meaning of the Second World War* (London: Verso, 1986); Paul Fussell, *Wartime: Understanding and Behavior in the Second World War* (New York: Oxford Univ. Press, 1989); Michael C. C. Adams, *The Best War Ever: America and World War II* (Baltimore, MD: Johns Hopkins Univ. Press, 1993); Michael Sherry, *In the Shadow of War: The United States since the 1930s* (New Haven: Yale Univ. Press, 1995), 64–120; George Roeder Jr., *The Censored War: American Visual Experience during World War II* (New Haven: Yale Univ. Press, 1995); Lewis A. Erenberg and Susan Hirsch, eds.,

The War in American Culture: Society and Consciousness during World War II (Chicago: Univ. of Chicago Press, 1996); John W. Jeffries, *Wartime America: The World War II Home Front* (Chicago: Ivan R. Dee, 1996); David Kennedy, *Freedom from Fear: The American People in Depression and War, 1929–1945* (New York: Oxford Univ. Press, 1999), 746–797; Ronald Takaki, *Double Victory: A Multicultural History of America in World War II* (New York: Little, Brown, 2000); Robert Westbrook, *Why We Fought: Forging American Obligations in World War II* (Washington, DC: Smithsonian Books, 2004); James T. Sparrow, *Warfare State: World War II Americans and the Age of Big Government* (New York: Oxford Univ. Press, 2011); M. Todd Bennett, *One World, Big Screen: Hollywood, the Allies, and World War II* (Chapel Hill: Univ. of North Carolina Press, 2012).

15. See the well-sourced Wikipedia page, https://en.wikipedia.org/wiki/World_War_II_casualties; Rana Mitter, *Forgotten Ally: China's World War II, 1937–1945* (Boston: Houghton Mifflin Harcourt, 2013), 5, 381; William C. Fuller Jr., "The Great Fatherland War and Late Stalinism, 1941–1953," in *Russia: A History,* ed. Gregory L. Freeze (New York: Oxford Univ. Press, 1997), 334; Nikita Lomagin, "The Soviet Union in the Second World War," in *A Companion to Russian History,* ed. Abbott Gleason (London: Blackwell, 2009), 409. US war propaganda: Jeffries, *Wartime America,* 188; Blum, *V Was for Victory,* 16.

16. Kennedy, *Freedom from Fear,* 747–748, 778.

17. Blum, *V Was for Victory,* 97.

18. Sparrow, *Warfare State,* 90; Bennett, *One World, Big Screen,* 89–135.

19. Blum, *V Was for Victory,* 118.

20. Blum, *V Was for Victory,* 231, 234; Kennedy, *Freedom from Fear,* 782–783; Ira Katznelson, *Fear Itself: The New Deal and the Origins of Our Time* (New York: Liveright, 2013), 378–379.

21. Sparrow, *Warfare State,* 11–14.

22. Willkie to Mrs. H. H. Kight, April 26, 1943, in box 41, Willkie Papers.

23. Elizabeth Borgwardt, *A New Deal for the World: America's Vision for Human Rights* (Cambridge, MA: Harvard Univ. Press, 2005), 76–85, quote on 79.

24. Divine, *Second Chance,* 85; Oscar Cox to Harry L. Hopkins, March 17, 1943, and Jerome S. Bruner, "Presenting Post-war Planning to the Public," both in book 7, box 328, folder: Postwar Planning 1943, Harry Hopkins Papers, Robert Sherwood Collection, FDR Library.

25. Divine, *Second Chance,* 96.

26. Carl Thompson, *Travel Writing* (New York: Routledge, 2011), 5; Samuel Zipp, "When Wendell Willkie Went Visiting: Between Interdependence and Exceptionalism in the Public Feeling for *One World,*" *American Literary History* 26, no. 3 (2014): 484–510.

27. "Notes and Comment," *New Yorker,* Oct. 21, 1944.

28. Barnes, 314.

29. H. G. Wells to Willkie, Oct. 30, 1943 in box 86, Willkie Papers; Norman Ian MacKenzie and Jeanne MacKenzie, *H. G. Wells: A Biography* (New York: Simon and Schuster, 1973), 424–425; Or Rosenboim, *The Emergence of Globalism: Visions of*

World Order in Britain and the United States, 1939–1950 (Princeton: Princeton Univ. Press, 2017), 212–216. Willkie, *OW,* 196.

30. Willkie, *OW,* 202, 2; Alan K. Henrikson, "FDR and the 'World-Wide Arena,'" in *FDR's World: War, Peace, and Legacies,* ed. David B. Woolner, Warren F. Kimball, and David Reynolds (New York: Palgrave Macmillan, 2008), 35–62; Alan K. Henrikson, "The Map as an 'Idea': The Role of Cartographic Imagery during the Second World War," *American Cartographer* 2, no. 1 (1975): 19–53; Susan Schulten, *The Geographical Imagination in America, 1880–1950* (Chicago: Univ. of Chicago Press, 2001), 1–14, 204–238; Andrew Baker, *Constructing a Post-War Order: The Rise of U.S. Hegemony and the Origins of the Cold War* (London: I. B. Tauris, 2011); Jenifer Van Vleck, *Empire of the Air: Aviation and the American Ascendancy* (Cambridge, MA: Harvard Univ. Press, 2013); Timothy Barney, *Mapping the Cold War: Cartography and the Framing of America's International Power* (Chapel Hill: Univ. of North Carolina Press, 2015), 25–60; William Rankin, *After the Map: Cartography, Navigation, and the Transformation of Territory in the Twentieth Century* (Chicago: Univ. of Chicago Press, 2016), 70–80.

31. Willkie, "The Next Step Toward the World We Want," Nov. 17, 1943, 5–6, in box 18, Van Doren Papers; "Airways to Peace: An Exhibition of Geography for the Future," *Bulletin of the Museum of Modern Art* 1, no. 11 (August 1943): 20; Van Vleck, *Empire of the Air,* 116–117; Fred Turner, *The Democratic Surround: Multimedia and American Liberalism from World War II to the Psychedelic Sixties* (Chicago: Univ. of Chicago Press, 2013), 3–5, 82, 102–113.

32. Willkie, *OW,* 203; Samuel Zipp, "Dilemmas of World-Wide Thinking: Popular Geographies and the Problem of Empire in Wendell Willkie's Search for *One World,*" *Modern American History* 1, no. 3 (2018): 295–319.

33. Willkie, *OW,* 165–166, 172–174, 180.

34. Willkie, *OW,* 177–179; Dan Plesch, "How the United Nations Beat Hitler and Prepared the Peace," *Global Society* 22, no. 1 (2008): 137–158; Mark Mazower, *Governing the World: The History of an Idea* (New York: Penguin Press, 2012), 191–213; Divine, *Second Chance,* 98–136.

35. Willkie, *OW,* 157–158.

36. Willkie, *OW,* 158–159.

37. Willkie, *OW,* 166.

38. Willkie, *OW,* 190.

39. Willkie, *OW,* 191.

40. Takaki, *Double Victory;* Kennedy, *Freedom from Fear,* 760–776; Richard J. Breitman and Allan J. Lichtman, *FDR and the Jews* (Cambridge, MA: Harvard Univ. Press, 2013).

41. Walter White to Willkie, July 14, 1943, and "Race Hatred," July 24, 1943, both in box 109, Willkie Papers; Domenic Capeci, "The Detroit Rioters of 1943: A Reinterpretation," *Michigan Historical Review* 16, no. 1 (1990): 49–72; Barbara Savage, *Broadcasting Freedom: Radio, War, and the Politics of Race, 1938–1948* (Chapel Hill: Univ. of North Carolina Press, 1999), 177–180.

42. Max Lerner, "Willkie's World," *P.M.,* April 8, 1943, 2; also Earl Browder, "The Education of Wendell Willkie," *Daily Worker,* April 18, 1943, 6–7, and Walton

Hamilton, "Wendell Willkie Learns to Listen," *The Progressive,* May 10, 1943, 5. US empire: Emily Rosenberg, *Spreading the American Dream: American Economic and Cultural Expansion, 1890–1945* (New York: Hill and Wang, 1982); Penny M. Von Eschen, *Race against Empire: Black Americans and Anticolonialism, 1937–1957* (Ithaca, NY: Cornell Univ. Press, 1997); Thomas Bender, *A Nation among Nations: America's Place in World History* (New York: Hill and Wang, 2006), 182–245; Smith, *American Empire;* Richard J. Immerman, *Empire for Liberty: A History of American Imperialism from Benjamin Franklin to Paul Wolfowitz* (Princeton: Princeton Univ. Press, 2010), 128–179; Daniel Immerwahr, "The Greater United States: Territory and Empire in U.S. History," *Diplomatic History* 40, no. 3 (2016): 373–391; Paul A. Kramer, "Power and Connection: Imperial Histories of the United States in the World," *American Historical Review* 116, no. 5 (2011): 1348–1391; Charles S. Maier, *Among Empires: American Ascendancy and Its Predecessors* (Cambridge, MA: Harvard Univ. Press, 2006); Jane Burbank and Frederick Cooper, *Empires in World History: Power and the Politics of Difference* (Princeton: Princeton Univ. Press, 2010), 321–329, 447–452; Julian Go, *Patterns of Empire: The British and American Empires, 1688 to the Present* (New York: Cambridge Univ. Press, 2011).

43. Willkie, *OW,* 111; "Willkie Pleads for Offensives on Every Front," *Chicago Tribune,* Oct. 4, 1942, 14; Harrison Forman, "Offensive in Asia Urged by Willkie," *New York Times,* Oct. 4, 1942, 6; "Up to People to Define Purposes, Says Willkie," *Los Angeles Times,* Nov. 26, 1942, 6; "Scores Foreign Policy," *New York Times,* Dec. 2, 1942, 2; Emily Rosenberg, *Financial Missionaries to the World: The Politics and Culture of Dollar Diplomacy, 1900–1930* (Durham, NC: Duke Univ. Press, 2004).

44. Willkie, *OW,* 190, 159–160.

45. Zipp, "Dilemmas of World-Wide Thinking."

46. R. J. Malley to Willkie, Oct. 20, 1942, in box 51, Willkie Papers; Willkie, *OW,* 185.

47. John Franklin Carter in Robert Vitalis, *White World Order, Black Power Politics: The Birth of American International Relations* (Ithaca, NY: Cornell Univ. Press, 2015), 79.

48. William Prescott Allen to Willkie, Oct. 19, 1942, Willkie to Allen, Oct. 27, 1942, both in box 2, Willkie Papers; George H. Winters to Secretary of State, Oct. 26, 1942, no. 113, and Ambassador George Messersmith to Philip Bonsal, Nov. 2, 1942, no. 127, both in box 17, 032, Willkie, Wendell, Decimal Files: 1940–44, State Department Files, Record Group 59, NACP; John Robert Badger, "Number One U.S. Colony," *Chicago Defender,* Sept. 4, 1943, 15.

49. Mabel Wyeth to Editor, *New York Herald Tribune,* Oct. 13, 1942; Clifford Bowman to Editor, *New York Herald Tribune,* Sept. 28, 1942; "When Indiana Goes Visiting," *New York Times,* Oct. 11, 1942, E8; Carrie Tirado Bramen, *American Niceness: A Cultural History* (Cambridge, MA: Harvard Univ. Press, 2017); Christina Klein, *Cold War Orientalism: Asia in the Middlebrow Imagination, 1945–1961* (Berkeley: Univ. of California Press, 2003), 1–99.

50. William C. Rourk to Willkie, Nov. 3, 1942, in box 68, Willkie Papers; Marquis Childs, "The World and Wendell Willkie," *St. Louis Post-Dispatch,* April 11, 1943, 1D; Willkie, *OW,* 55, 92, 120.

51. Willkie, *OW,* 119, 19–20; "Cecelia Ager Meets: Wendell Willkie," 7.

52. Willkie, *OW,* 120–121.

53. David Ekbladh, *The Great American Mission: Modernization and the Construction of an American World Order* (Princeton: Princeton Univ. Press, 2010); Kiran Klaus Patel, *The New Deal: A Global History* (Princeton: Princeton Univ. Press, 2016), 285–300; Katznelson, *Fear Itself,* 51–57, 253–255; Nils Gilman, *Mandarins of the Future: Modernization Theory in Cold War America* (Baltimore, MD: Johns Hopkins Univ. Press, 2003); David Engerman, *Modernization from the Other Shore: American Intellectuals and the Romance of Russian Development* (Cambridge: Harvard Univ. Press, 2003). Mumford: Andrew Needham, *Power Lines: Phoenix and the Making of the Modern Southwest* (Princeton: Princeton Univ. Press, 2015), 248.

54. Ekbladh, *Great American Mission,* 8.

55. Willkie, *OW,* 172–173; Wendell Willkie, "Old Stencils," February 11, 1943, 3, in box 18, Van Doren Papers.

56. Hull: Mandel, *Meaning of the Second World War,* 16; Mazower, *Governing the World,* 38–48; Burbank and Cooper, *Empires in World History,* 19, 293–301, 306, 324, 447; Go, *Patterns of Empire,* 113–115, 212–213, 224–227; Quinn Slobodian, *Globalists: The End of Empire and the Birth of Neoliberalism* (Cambridge, MA: Harvard Univ. Press, 2018); Alfred Eckes and Thomas Zeiler, *Globalization and the American Century* (New York: Cambridge Univ. Press, 2003), 9–37; Oscar Handlin, "One World," in *The Distortion of America* (New Brunswick, NJ: Transaction, 1996), 20–39; Wm. Roger Louis, *Imperialism at Bay: The United States and the Decolonization of the British Empire, 1941–1945* (New York: Oxford Univ. Press, 1978), 24.

57. Bill Cunningham, "Willkie Differs with World Blue-Printers," *Seattle Times,* April 15, 1943; Willkie to John Chamberlain, March 4, 1944, in box 14, Willkie Papers.

58. John Chamberlain, "Books of the Times," *New York Times,* April 8, 1943, 21.

59. Willkie, *OW,* 22.

60. See digest of press responses in box 115, folder: Correspondence, Excerpts, July–August 1943, Willkie Papers; Rabbi Nathan Kaber, "Wendell L. Willkie's 'One World,'" May 15, 1943, 2, in box 15, folder: Correspondence, May–June 1943, Willkie Papers; K. M. Landis, "Willkie's World," *Chicago Sun,* April 21, 1943.

61. Ralph McGill, "One Word More," *Atlanta Constitution,* April 8, 1943; Walter Lippmann, "Wendell Willkie's Book," *New York Herald Tribune,* April 8, 1943; Reinhold Niebuhr, "Mr. Willkie's Two Odysseys," *The Nation,* April 24, 1943, 604–606.

62. Divine, *Second Chance,* 105; Guy L. Smith, "'One World': No Mush and Milk Utopia," *Knoxville Journal,* May 19, 1943, 1.

63. Cunningham, "Willkie Differs"; Cowles to Willkie, Sept. 1, 1943, in box 18, Willkie Papers.

64. Paul Mallon, "Willkie Goes Beyond Facts," *Birmingham News,* April 23, 1943; George R. Baldwin to Willkie, July 17, 1943, in box 4, Willkie Papers.

65. John N. Hart, "Wendell Willkie in China," 31, in Fairbank Collection, Harvard-Yenching Library, Harvard University, Cambridge, MA; "Prime Minister," April 19, 1943, in PREM4/26, file 6, Prime Minister's Office Papers, BNA.

66. Alexander Kirk to Secretary of State, June 15, 1943, no. 1104, and Kirk to State, June 23, 1943, no. 1121, in Central Files [Informational files on the Mediterranean-African region], entry NC 148 374, box 432, Record Group 208, Records of the Office of War Information, NACP; Maritia Koshaba Badal to Willkie, March 25, 1944, in box 4, Willkie Papers; "Translation of Editorial in 'Al-Akhbar' (July 20, 1943—Baghdad, Iraq)," in John Badeau to Willkie, July 21, 1943, box 4, Willkie Papers; G. H. Thompson to Foreign Office, July 23, 1943, no. 265 in FO624/33, file 531, Foreign Office Papers, BNA.

67. "One World," *Lexington Herald,* April 18, 1943, 4; Virgil Steed, "Background for Lasting World Peace Outlined in Willkie's 'One World,'" *Lexington Herald,* April 18, 1943.

68. Henry Steele Commager, "World Planners, Then and Now," *New York Times,* July 18, 1943, BR 1.

69. "America and the Future," June 26, 1943, 4–5, in box 109, Willkie Papers; "One-World Pledge Urged by Willkie," *New York Times,* July 5, 1943, 6.

70. Willkie, "Nine Months After, Cannot Postpone Decisions Now," *New York Times,* July 7, 1943, 1.

71. Divine, *Second Chance,* 134; Hadley Cantril and Mildred Strunk, eds., *Public Opinion, 1935–1946* (Princeton: Princeton Univ. Press, 1951), 907.

72. See Divine, *Second Chance,* 129–133; Neal, 283–284; Barnard, 419–420; Barnes, 340.

73. Divine, *Second Chance,* 150, 141–155; Patrick J. Hearden, *Architects of Globalism: Building a New World Order during World War II* (Fayetteville: Univ. of Arkansas Press, 2002), 162–164; Warren F. Kimball, *Forged in War: Roosevelt, Churchill, and the Second World War* (New York: William Morrow, 1997), 227–231; Robert Dallek, *Franklin D. Roosevelt and American Foreign Policy, 1932–1945,* 2nd ed. (New York: Oxford Univ. Press, 1995), 419–423; Warren F. Kimball, *The Juggler: Franklin Roosevelt as Wartime Statesman* (Princeton: Princeton Univ. Press, 1991), 93–96.

74. Willkie, "The Next Step towards the World We Want," 1–3.

75. Darryl Zanuck to Willkie, Oct. 27, 1943, in box 91, Willkie Papers.

76. Cantril and Strunk, eds., *Public Opinion,* 1043–1044.

77. Thomas W. Lamont, "What a Capitalist Reads," *Saturday Review of Literature,* Dec. 4, 1943, 14–15; Wendell Willkie, Address to the United Church Canvass Program, Columbia Broadcasting System, Dec. 11, 1943, 1, in box 110, Willkie Papers.

CHAPTER 12 ✧ THE NARROWS OF 1944

1. Walter White, "Willkie's Book and 1944," *Chicago Defender,* June 12, 1943, 15.

2. Barnes, 331–361; Barnard, 422–469; Neal, 277–307.

3. Neal, 289–290; Barnard, 430–433.

4. Barnes, 342; Wendell L. Willkie, "America's Purposes," Oct. 15, 1943, in box 17, Van Doren Papers.

5. Neal, 291; Barnes, 332.

6. Neal, 300.

7. Elmo Roper, *You and Your Leaders: Their Actions and Your Reactions, 1936–1956* (New York: William Morrow, 1957), 91–92; Barnes, 361.

8. Ronald Takaki, *Double Victory: A Multicultural History of America in World War II* (New York: Little, Brown, 2000), 170; John Morton Blum, *V Was for Victory: Politics and American Culture during World War II* (New York: Harcourt Brace Jovanovich, 1976), 46; John Dower, "Race, Language, and War in Two Cultures: World War II in Asia," in *The War in American Culture: Society and Consciousness during World War II,* ed. Lewis A. Erenberg and Susan Hirsch, 169–201 (Chicago: Univ. of Chicago Press, 1996).

9. James T. Sparrow, *Warfare State: World War II Americans and the Age of Big Government* (New York: Oxford Univ. Press, 2011), 45; Blum, *V Was for Victory,* 46.

10. See Wendy L. Wall, *Inventing the "American Way": The Politics of Consensus from the New Deal to the Civil Rights Movement* (New York: Oxford Univ. Press, 2008), 117; John W. Jeffries, *Wartime America: The World War II Home Front* (Chicago: Ivan R. Dee, 1996), 177; Justin Hart, *Empire of Ideas: The Origins of Public Diplomacy and the Transformation of U.S. Foreign Policy* (New York: Oxford Univ. Press, 2013), 71–106; Blum, *V Was for Victory,* 31–45; Sparrow, *Warfare State,* 74–77.

11. See Jeffries, *Wartime America,* 172; Paul Fussell, *Wartime: Understanding and Behavior in the Second World War* (New York: Oxford Univ. Press, 1989).

12. Robert Westbrook, *Why We Fought: Forging American Obligations in World War II* (Washington, DC: Smithsonian Books, 2004), 78–79; Ann Elizabeth Pfau, *Miss Yourlovin: GIs, Gender, and Domesticity during World War II* (New York: Columbia Univ. Press, 2008).

13. Jeffrey A. Engel, ed., *The Four Freedoms: Franklin D. Roosevelt and the Evolution of an American Idea* (New York: Oxford Univ. Press, 2016), 27; Blum, *V Was for Victory,* 89.

14. See Sparrow, *Warfare State,* 9–12, 48, 53–54, 76, 259; Wall, *Inventing the American Way.*

15. Robert A. Divine, *Second Chance: The Triumph of Internationalism in America during World War II* (New York: Atheneum, 1967), 182, 160–163.

16. See Divine, *Second Chance,* 170–171; John A. Thompson, *A Sense of Power: The Roots of America's Global Role* (Ithaca, NY: Cornell Univ. Press, 2015), 213.

17. See Divine, *Second Chance,* 312; Elizabeth Borgwardt, *A New Deal for the World: America's Vision for Human Rights* (Cambridge, MA: Harvard Univ. Press, 2005), 159.

18. Divine, *Second Chance,* 197, 260.

19. Divine, *Second Chance,* 175–176; Andrew Preston, *Sword of the Spirit, Shield of the Faith: Religion in American War and Diplomacy* (New York: Norton, 2012), 303–314; Reinhold Niebuhr, *The Children of Light and the Children of Darkness* (New York: Scribner's, 1944), 153–190.

20. See Divine, *Second Chance,* 178; Ronald Steel, *Walter Lippmann and the American Century* (Boston: Atlantic Monthly Press, 1980), 410, 404–412; David Milne, *Worldmaking: The Art and Science of American Diplomacy* (New York: Farrar,

Straus and Giroux, 2015), 168–216; Barton J. Bernstein, "Walter Lippmann and the Early Cold War," in *Cold War Critics,* ed. Thomas G. Paterson (Chicago: Quadrangle Books, 1971), 18–53.

21. Michael Veseth, *Globaloney: Unraveling the Myths of Globalization* (Lanham, MD: Rowman and Littlefield, 2005), 19.

22. Neal, 309, 290.

23. Harold E. Stassen, "Report on a Wakening World," *New York Times,* April 11, 1943, BR1; Timothy Snyder, *Bloodlands: Europe between Hitler and Stalin* (New York: Basic Books, 2010), 133–141, 287.

24. Willkie, *OW,* 176; Barnard, 445–446.

25. Barnes, 350–351; Neal, 297–298.

26. Neal, 290; John B. Wiseman, "Darryl Zanuck and the Failure of 'One World,' 1943–1945," *Historical Journal of Film, Radio, and Television* 7, no. 3 (1987): 283–284; Fred Stanley, "How 'One World' Will Be Filmed," *New York Times,* October 10, 1943, X3.

27. Abbott Gleason, *Totalitarianism: The Inner History of the Cold War* (New York: Oxford Univ. Press, 1995), 63–64.

28. John Fousek, *To Lead the Free World: American Nationalism and the Cultural Roots of the Cold War* (Chapel Hill: Univ. of North Carolina Press, 2000), 7. Postwar planning: Borgwardt, *New Deal for the World;* Divine, *Second Chance;* Thompson, *A Sense of Power;* Hart, *Empire of Ideas,* 60–70; Aiyaz Husain, *Mapping the End of Empire: American and British Strategic Visions in the Postwar World* (Cambridge, MA: Harvard Univ. Press, 2015); Stewart Patrick, *The Best Laid Plans: The Origins of American Multilateralism and the Dawn of the Cold War* (Lanham, MD: Rowman and Littlefield, 2009); Christopher D. O'Sullivan, *Sumner Welles, Postwar Planning, and the Quest for a New World Order, 1937–1943* (New York: Columbia Univ. Press, 2008); Patrick J. Hearden, *Architects of Globalism: Building a New World Order during World War II* (Fayetteville: Univ. of Arkansas Press, 2002).

29. Andrew Preston, "Franklin D. Roosevelt and America's Empire of Anti-Imperialism," in *Rhetorics of Empire: Imperial Discourse and the Language of Colonial Conflict after 1900,* ed. Martin Thomas and Richard Toye (Manchester, UK: Manchester Univ. Press, 2017), 75–90; Frank Costigliola, *Roosevelt's Lost Alliances: How Personal Politics Helped Start the Cold War* (Princeton: Princeton Univ. Press, 2012); David B. Woolner, Warren F. Kimball, and David Reynolds, eds., *FDR's World: War, Peace, and Legacies* (New York: Palgrave Macmillan, 2008); Kimball, *Forged in War: Roosevelt, Churchill, and the Second World War* (New York: Morrow, 1997); Robert Dallek, *Franklin D. Roosevelt and American Foreign Policy, 1932–1945,* 2nd ed. (New York: Oxford Univ. Press, 1995); Warren F. Kimball, *The Juggler: Franklin Roosevelt as Wartime Statesman* (Princeton: Princeton Univ. Press, 1991).

30. Raymond Buell to Willkie, November 17, 1942, in box 11, Willkie Papers; Hearden, *Architects of Globalism,* 156.

31. Warren F. Kimball, "The Sheriffs: FDR's Postwar World," and Lloyd Gardner, "FDR and the 'Colonial Question,'" in *FDR's World: War, Peace, and Legacies,* ed.

David B. Woolner, Warren F. Kimball, and David Reynolds (New York: Palgrave, 2008), 91–121 and 123–144.

32. Divine, *Second Chance,* 199, 185.

33. Barnard, 470–475; Barnes, 365–366; Neal, 311.

34. Willkie, *AAP,* 22, 23.

35. Willkie, "Our Sovereignty: Shall We Use It?," *Foreign Affairs* 22, no. 3 (April 1944): 349, 356, 354.

36. Willkie, "Our Sovereignty," 356, 361.

37. Neal, 283.

38. O'Sullivan, *Sumner Welles,* 149; Carol Anderson, *Bourgeois Radicals: The NAACP and the Struggle for Colonial Liberation, 1941–1960* (New York: Cambridge Univ. Press, 2015), 14. See also Husain, *Mapping the End of Empire,* 187–219; Borgwardt, *New Deal for the World,* 184–189; Hearden, *Architects of Globalism,* 97–118; Wm. Roger Louis, *Imperialism at Bay: The United States and the Decolonization of the British Empire, 1941–1945* (New York: Oxford Univ. Press, 1978).

39. Louis, *Imperialism at Bay,* 356, 226–227.

40. See Louis, *Imperialism at Bay,* 285, 131, 361.

41. Louis, *Imperialism at Bay,* 247.

42. O'Sullivan, *Sumner Welles,* 150; Preston, "Franklin D. Roosevelt and America's Empire of Anti-Imperialism," 83–86.

43. O'Sullivan, *Sumner Welles,* xvii, 164, 161.

44. Walter Lippmann, "Mr. Willkie and the Empire," *Washington Post,* November 3, 1942, 7; Thomas W. Lamont, "What a Capitalist Reads," *Saturday Review of Literature,* December 4, 1943, 14.

45. Hadley Cantril and Mildred Strunk, eds., *Public Opinion, 1935–1946* (Princeton: Princeton Univ. Press, 1951), 311.

46. Husain, *Mapping the End of Empire,* 166, 188–201; Hearden, *Architects of Globalism,* 117–118, 202–210; Louis, *Imperialism at Bay,* 351–377.

47. Divine, *Second Chance,* 259. See also Anderson, *Bourgeois Radicals,* 34–37.

48. Borgwardt, *New Deal for the World,* 186–191; Stephen Schlesinger, *Act of Creation: The Founding of the United Nations* (Boulder, CO: Westview Press, 2003), 233–236; Mary Ann Glendon, *A World Made New: Eleanor Roosevelt and the Universal Declaration of Human Rights* (New York: Random House, 2001), 12–16. *Courier:* Penny Von Eschen, *Race against Empire: Black Americans and Anticolonialism, 1937–1957* (Ithaca, NY: Cornell Univ. Press, 1997), 83. Logan: Carol Anderson, *Eyes off the Prize: The United Nations and the African-American Struggle for Human Rights, 1944–1955* (New York: Cambridge Univ. Press, 2003), 55.

49. Willkie, *AAP,* 48–49.

50. Robert E. Sherwood, *Roosevelt and Hopkins: An Intimate History* (New York: Harper, 1948), 635.

51. Positions for Willkie: folder: 1944–1945, box 2, index # 4040, President's Official File, FDR Papers; Barnes, 367–370; Barnard, 478–480; Neal, 313–319.

52. Willkie, *AAP,* 39; Neal, 316–317; Barnard, 480.

53. Samuel Rosenman, *Working with Roosevelt* (New York: Harper, 1952), 463–470; Barnes, 371–372; Neal, 317; Barnard, 480–481.

54. FDR to Willkie, July 13, 1944 in President's Personal File, index #7023, FDR Papers.

55. FDR to Willkie, Aug. 21, 1944 in President's Personal File, index #7023, FDR Papers; Barnes, 372–378; Neal, 318; Barnard, 481–485.

56. Neal, 321–323; Barnard, 494–499; Barnes, 384–386.

57. Neal, 322.

58. Neal, 323.

59. See Dagmar to Ruth, Oct. 23, 1944, 2, in box 95, folder: Correspondence, Official, 1944, Willkie Papers; "Statement by the President," Oct. 8, 1944, in box 2, folder 1944–1945, index #4040, President's Official File, FDR Papers; J. J. Singh to Edith Willkie, in box 11, folder: Willkie, Edith (Messages of Condolence), Van Doren Papers; Sian Branch of the People's Foreign Relations Association, in George Atcheson to Secretary of State, Nov. 16, 1944, no. 11-1644, in box 3859, 811.44, Willkie, Wendell, Decimal Files: 1940–44, State Department Files, Record Group 59, NACP. See also condolences in box 155, Willkie Papers; Barnes, 386; Neal, 323; Barnard, 498–499.

60. Darryl Zanuck to Philip Willkie, Oct. 9, 1944, in box 95, folder: Correspondence, Official, 1944, Willkie Papers.

61. E. B. Jordan to Edith Willkie; Oscar Lange to Edith Willkie; Pennsylvania Station Red Caps to Edith Willkie; all n.d., all in box 11, folder: Willkie, Edith (Messages of Condolence), Van Doren Papers.

62. Dagmar to Ruth, 2; Barnes, 386; Barnard, 499.

CONCLUSION

1. Harry S. Truman, "Remarks Upon Receiving An Honorary Degree from the University of Kansas City, June 28, 1945," in *Public Papers of the Presidents of the United States: Harry S. Truman,* vol. 1, *1945* (Washington, DC: Government Printing Office, 1961), 149–152; Bertram D. Hulen, "'We Must Lead Way to Peace of World,' President Warns," *New York Times,* June 29, 1945, 1.

2. Edgar Ansel Mowrer, "President Truman and the Republic of the World," reprinted in US Government Printing Office, *Congressional Record,* Proceedings and Debates of the 79th Congress, First Session, appendix, vol. 91, part 12, June 11, 1945, to Oct. 11, 1945, A3657–A3658.

3. See Jo-Anne Pemberton, *Global Metaphors: Modernity and the Quest for One World* (London: Pluto Press, 2001).

4. William S. Graebner, *The Age of Doubt: American Thought and Culture in the 1940s* (New York: Twayne, 1991), 69–100.

5. Harold James, *The End of Globalization: Lessons from the Great Depression* (Cambridge, MA: Harvard Univ. Press, 2001); Daniel Sargent, "Globalization's Paradox: Economic Interdependence and Global Governance," in *Outside In: The Transnational Circuitry of US History,* ed. Andrew Preston and Doug Rossinow (New York: Oxford Univ. Press, 2017), 36–54; Lynn Hunt, *Writing History in the Global Era* (New York: Norton, 2014), 44–77; David Armitage, "Is There a Pre-History of Globalization?," in *Foundations of Modern International Thought*

(New York: Cambridge Univ. Press, 2013), 33–45; Peter N. Stearns, *Globalization in World History* (New York: Routledge, 2010); Barry K. Gills and William R. Thompson, *Globalization and Global History* (New York: Routledge, 2006); Alfred Eckes and Thomas Zeiler, *Globalization and the American Century* (New York: Cambridge Univ. Press, 2003); Thomas Bender, ed., *Rethinking American History in a Global Age* (Berkeley: Univ. of California Press, 2002).

6. David Harvey, *The Condition of Postmodernity: An Enquiry into the Origins of Cultural Change* (London: Blackwell, 1991); Stephen Kern, *The Culture of Time and Space, 1880–1918* (Cambridge, MA: Harvard Univ. Press, 1983), 318; Emily S. Rosenberg, ed., *A World Connecting, 1870–1945* (Cambridge, MA: Harvard Univ. Press, 2012); Or Rosenboim, *The Emergence of Globalism: Visions of World Order in Britain and the United States, 1939–1950* (Princeton: Princeton Univ. Press, 2017); Glenda Sluga, *Internationalism in the Age of Nationalism* (Philadelphia: Univ. of Pennsylvania Press, 2013); Mark Mazower, *Governing the World: The History of an Idea* (New York: Penguin Press, 2012); Akira Iriye, *Cultural Internationalism and World Order* (Baltimore, MD: Johns Hopkins Univ. Press, 1997).

7. Joyce Chaplin, *Round about the Earth: Circumnavigation from Magellan to Orbit* (New York: Simon and Schuster, 2012).

8. Willkie, *OW*, 1.

9. Jane Burbank and Frederick Cooper, *Empires in World History: Power and the Politics of Difference* (Princeton: Princeton Univ. Press, 2010); Susan Pedersen, *The Guardians: The League of Nations and the Crisis of Empire* (New York: Oxford Univ. Press, 2015).

10. Willkie, *OW*, 202; Willkie, *AAP*, 39.

11. Robert A. Divine, *Second Chance: The Triumph of Internationalism in America during World War II* (New York: Atheneum, 1967), 252; David Levering Lewis, *W. E. B. Du Bois: The Fight for Equality and the American Century, 1919–1963* (New York: Henry Holt, 2000), 504; W. E. B. Du Bois, "Color and Democracy: Colonies and Peace," in *The Oxford W. E. B. Du Bois*, ed. Henry Louis Gates, Jr. (New York: Oxford Univ. Press, 2007), 246; Eric Porter, *The Problem of the Future World: W. E. B. Du Bois and the Race Concept at Midcentury* (Durham, NC: Duke Univ. Press, 2010), 63–102.

12. Norman Angell, "America's Favorite Book," *John O'London's Weekly*, Sept. 24, 1943, 249.

13. Archibald Clark Kerr to Foreign Office, Sept. 28, 1942, in CO968/45, file 14, Colonial Office Papers, BNA.

14. A. G. Hopkins, *American Empire: A Global History* (Princeton: Princeton Univ. Press, 2018); Aiyaz Husain, *Mapping the End of Empire: American and British Strategic Visions in the Postwar World* (Cambridge, MA: Harvard Univ. Press, 2015); John A. Thompson, *A Sense of Power: The Roots of America's Global Role* (Ithaca, NY: Cornell Univ. Press, 2015); Paul A. Kramer, "Power and Connection: Imperial Histories of the United States in the World," *American Historical Review* 116, no. 5 (2011): 1348–1391; Julian Go, *Patterns of Empire: The British and American Empires, 1688 to the Present* (New York: Cambridge Univ. Press, 2011), 133–165; Andrew Baker, *Constructing a Post-War Order: The Rise of U.S. Hegemony and the Origins of*

the Cold War (London: I. B. Tauris, 2011); Richard J. Immerman, *Empire for Liberty: A History of American Imperialism from Benjamin Franklin to Paul Wolfowitz* (Princeton: Princeton Univ. Press, 2010); Michael Hunt, *The American Ascendancy: How the United States Gained and Wielded Global Dominance* (Chapel Hill: Univ. of North Carolina Press, 2007); Charles S. Maier, *Among Empires: American Ascendancy and Its Predecessors* (Cambridge, MA: Harvard Univ. Press, 2006); Odd Arne Westad, *The Global Cold War: Third World Interventions and the Making of Our Times* (New York: Cambridge Univ. Press, 2005), 1–38; Neil Smith, *American Empire: Roosevelt's Geographer and the Prelude to Globalization* (Berkeley: Univ. of California Press, 2003); Thomas J. McCormick, *America's Half Century: United States Foreign Policy in the Cold War and After*, 2nd ed. (Baltimore, MD: Johns Hopkins Univ. Press, 1995). A dissenting view: Frank Ninkovich, *The Global Republic: America's Inadvertent Rise to World Power* (Chicago: Univ. of Chicago Press, 2014).

15. Pearl Buck to Willkie, April 8, 1944, 2, in box 11, Willkie Papers.

16. Mark Greif, *The Age of the Crisis of Man: Thought and Fiction in America, 1933–1973* (Princeton: Princeton Univ. Press, 2015), 77.

17. Westad, *Global Cold War,* 73–206.

18. David Reynolds, *One World Divisible: A Global History since 1945* (New York: Norton, 2000).

19. Hans Morgenthau, *Politics among Nations: The Struggle for Power and Peace* (New York: Knopf, 1948); Andrew Preston, "Monsters Everywhere: A Genealogy of National Security," *Diplomatic History* 38, no. 4 (2014): 477–500.

20. Willkie, *OW,* 105.

21. Michael C. Keith and Mary Ann Watson, eds., *Norman Corwin's One World Flight: The Lost Journal of Radio's Greatest Writer* (New York: Continuum, 2009).

22. Barnes, 386–389; Elmo Roper, *You and Your Leaders: Their Actions and Your Reactions, 1936–1956* (New York: William Morrow, 1957), 95; John B. Wiseman, "Darryl Zanuck and the Failure of 'One World,' 1943–1945," *Historical Journal of Film, Radio, and Television* 7, no. 3 (1987): 279–287.

23. Truman Capote, *Breakfast at Tiffany's* (New York: Random House, 1958), 82–83.

24. Ralph Barton Perry, *One World in the Making* (New York: Current Books, 1945), 13–14; William Carr, *One World in the Making: The United Nations* (Boston: Ginn, 1946). See Mark Philip Bradley, *The World Reimagined: Americans and Human Rights in the Twentieth Century* (New York: Cambridge Univ. Press, 2016), 19–69; Perrin Selcer, *The Postwar Origins of the Global Environment: How the United Nations Built Spaceship Earth* (New York: Columbia Univ. Press, 2018), 1–61.

25. Paul Boyer, *By the Bomb's Early Light: American Thought and Culture at the Dawn of the Atomic Age* (New York: Pantheon, 1985).

26. Graebner, *Age of Doubt,* 72–73; Lawrence S. Wittner, *One World or None: A History of the Nuclear Disarmament Movement through 1953* (Stanford: Stanford Univ. Press, 1993), 113–115; Garry Davis, *The World Is My Country* (New York: G. P. Putnam's Sons, 1961), 18–19, 58–62.

27. Dexter Masters and Katharine Masters, *One World or None: A Report to the Public on the Full Meaning of the Atomic Bomb* (New York: McGraw-Hill, 1946); Wittner, *One World or None,* 161.

28. Manu Bhagavan, *The Peacemakers: India and the Quest for One World* (Noida: Harper Collins India, 2012), 111; Wittner, *One World or None,* 166.

29. Robeson Taj Frazier, *The East Is Black: Cold War China in the Black Radical Imagination* (Durham, NC: Duke Univ. Press, 2015), 62, 69. See also C. L. R. James writing as J. R. Johnson, "The American People in 'One World,'" *New International* 10, no. 7 (July 1944); 225–230; J. R. Johnson, "The Late Wendell Willkie: The Politician Who Came Too Late," *New International* 8, no. 43 (October 1944): 3; Leah Victoria Khaghani, "'One World or None': Transnational Struggles against Imperialism in the American Century" (Ph.D. diss., Yale University, 2011).

30. Bhagavan, *Peacemakers,* 178n29; Wittner, *One World or None,* 307; Kenton J. Clymer, *Quest for Freedom: The United States and India's Independence* (New York: Columbia Univ. Press, 1995), 107; Mark Mazower, *No Enchanted Palace: The End of Empire and the Ideological Origins of the United Nations* (Princeton: Princeton Univ. Press, 2009), 149–189.

31. Denis Cosgrove, *Apollo's Eye: A Cartographic Genealogy of the Earth in the Western Imagination* (Baltimore, MD: Johns Hopkins Univ. Press, 2001), 258; William Rankin, *After the Map: Cartography, Navigation, and the Transformation of Territory in the Twentieth Century* (Chicago: Univ. of Chicago Press, 2016), 5–16; Ursula K. Heise, *Sense of Place and Sense of Planet: The Environmental Imagination of the Global* (New York, 2008), 3–4, 22–28; Selcer, *Postwar Origins of the Global Environment,* 1–8.

32. Sting, "One World (Not Three) / Love is the Seventh Wave (Live in Paris)," *Bring on the Night,* A&M Records, 1986.

33. Thomas L. Friedman, *The World Is Flat: A Brief History of the Twenty-First Century* (New York: Farrar, Straus and Giroux, 2005); Sargent, "Globalization's Paradox," 36–38, 46–51; Quinn Slobodian, *Globalists: The End of Empire and the Birth of Neoliberalism* (Cambridge, MA: Harvard Univ. Press, 2018).

34. William Greider, *One World, Ready or Not: The Manic Logic of Global Capitalism* (New York: Simon and Schuster, 1997), 9–20.

35. Greider, *One World, Ready or Not,* 17–18.

36. Peter Singer, *One World: The Ethics of Globalization* (New Haven, CT: Yale Univ. Press, 2002), 148; Emily Apter, "On Oneworldedness; Or Paranoia as a World System," *American Literary History* 18, no. 2 (2006): 365–399.

37. Singer, *One World,* 198.

38. Willkie, *OW,* 37.

39. See "Barack Obama's Inaugural Address," *New York Times,* Jan. 20, 2009.

40. Trump quoted in George Packer, "The Unconnected," *New Yorker,* Oct. 31, 2016, 61.

41. Trump inaugural address, Jan. 20, 2017, https://www.whitehouse.gov/briefings -statements/the-inaugural-address.

42. Selcer, *Postwar Origins of the Global Environment,* 44–59.

43. G. John Ikenberry, "The Plot against American Foreign Policy: Can the Liberal Order Survive?," *Foreign Affairs,* May–June 2017; Aziz Rana, "Goodbye, Cold War," *n+1,* no. 30 (Winter 2018): 20–29.

Acknowledgments

LIKE WILLKIE'S WORLD, this book seemed small in my mind, but, as these things do, it soon swelled right up and got out of hand. I could not have wrestled it into any comprehensible shape without the help, advice, encouragement, and critiques of many people who took an interest in this somewhat improbable project.

My ability to write with any success about internationalism, race, and empire has been shaped by the work of many international historians and historians of the United States and the world. Beyond the many works in the notes, I am indebted first, and above all, to Melani McAlister for her many years of insight and counsel. Thanks also on that score to Andrew Friedman, Adriane Lentz-Smith, Paul Kramer, Chris Nichols, George Blaustein, Brooke Blower, Andrew Preston, Andy Seal, Dara Orenstein, Andrew Johnstone, Michaela Hoenicke Moore, Hadji Bakara, Quinn Slobodian, Paul Murphy, Justin Reynolds, Andrew McNally, Jenifer Van Vleck, Naoko Shibusawa, and Daniel Immerwahr for their comments, critiques, and interest.

Many friends and colleagues at Brown and beyond have helped with comments, suggestions, resources, and support in any number of ways. Matt Guterl and Robert Self each read early sections of the book and helped me bash it into shape—I'm indebted to each of them for that and a great deal else. Thanks also go to Debbie Weinstein, Bob Lee, Ralph Rodriguez, Susan Smulyan, Rebecca Nedostup, Ethan Pollock, Brooke Lamperd, Nancy Cott, David Levering Lewis, Pete Coviello, Aaron Sachs, Alison Isenberg, Matt Lassiter, Jeff Cowie, Jean-Christophe Agnew, Matt Jacobson, Howard Brick, Weldon Matthews, Judith Smith, Barney Mergen, Catherine Kodat, Lawrence J. Friedman, Jay Taylor, Patrick Stinson, Larry Glickman, Alison Siegler, Sarah Phillips, Andrew Bell, Alex Starre, Frank Kelleter, Christian Lammert, Christoph Lindner, Babs Boter, Renee de Groot, Casey Blake, Michael Kimmage, Angus Burgin, Uwe Lübken, Britta Waldschmidt-Nelson, Mary Nolan, Daniel Geary, Brendon O'Connor, Emily Levine, Maren Roth, Timothy Barney, Bill Rankin, Brian Distelberg, Sandhya Shukla, Gordon Hutner, George Hutchinson, Michael Kramer, Chris Suh, and the anonymous reviewers for Harvard University Press.

This book involved research drawn from three different continents in many languages. I relied on others to help me with much of this work. In Beirut, Racha Chkair and Joyce Aways helped Liz Wolfson find Arabic-language newspaper accounts of Willkie's journey. Elliott Urdang found sources in Russian and translated them for me. Wing Sze Ho translated Chinese sources. I could not have done this without all of them. Closer to home, I am most in debt to the staff of the Lilly Library at Indiana University, and in particular to Dave Frasier, Rebecca Cape, Erika Dowell, Sarah McElroy Mitchell, Jody Daryell Mitchell, and Isabel Planton, all of whom were patient, friendly, and helpful over the years. Dave, Sarah, and Erika, in particular, went out of their way to make this book possible. Also indispensable were Mark Stumme at the Cowles Library at Drake University, Kirsten Carter and Matt Hanson at the FDR Presidential Library, Lynn Gamma of the Air Force Historical Records Agency, David Langbart and Robert Thompson at the National Archives, and the staffs of the Columbia University Rare Books and Manuscripts Library, the Library of Congress, and the British National Archives.

Lizabeth Cohen, Nancy Cott, Robin Bernstein, Jim Kloppenberg, and David Armitage made it possible for me to spend a year at Harvard in the Charles Warren Center for Studies in American History and the

Department of History as I worked on the early stages of this book. Arthur Patton-Hock and Larissa Kennedy went out of their way to make the top floor of Emerson Hall a welcoming and conducive place for that work. This book, and little else of my life in American Studies and Urban Studies at Brown, could have happened without the effort, advice, and time of Jeff Cabral, Meredith Paine, and Carrie Cardoso.

Chris Spilker, Jess Sankey, and all the Spilker-Sankeys in between have been important sources of respite and inspiration for me these last few years. My great thanks to them, and to Pam and Eric Sankey for a week spent writing in their cabin on the road to Mt. Baker in the summer of 2016.

David Willkie welcomed me to Indiana, showed me around Elwood and Rushville, and provided generous encouragement in my journey to understand his grandfather. He introduced me to several people in Rushville, among them John McCane, Brian Sheehan, Paul Barada, and Mayor Mike Pavey, all of whom were generous with their time and long familiarity with the place Willkie felt most at home.

Isabelle Lewis made the great map of Willkie's journey, Ben Tyler scanned images, and Ann Sandhorst, Daniel Boland, Sarah Kubiak, Ed Carter, May Hong Haduong, Kristine Krueger, Matthew Lutts, Leonard Nelson, and Christian Martin arranged and granted permissions. Thanks to all. Every effort has been made to find the copyright holders of uncredited material. Any corrections are welcome, and will be addressed in future printings.

Zoe Pagnamenta took this book on and, with the help of Sarah Levitt and Alison Lewis, saw it through thick and thin. She also introduced me to Pete Beatty, who showed up at just the right moment. His summer of edits saved this book. Joyce Seltzer saw promise in this work when few others did, and guided it toward completion until her retirement in 2018. Joy de Menil took up where she left off, and dove right into the details, helping me to focus an unruly manuscript and find the story in the history. I am also in debt to their colleagues at Harvard University Press, Brian Distelberg, Kathi Drummy, Joy Deng, Stephanie Vyce, and Louise Robbins, and to John Donohue at Westchester Publishing Services, who helped behind the scenes to bring this book into the light.

I'd also like to thank my father, Steve Zipp, my sister, Holly Zipp, and my brother-in-law, Eric Bauer, for their patience with me over the years that this book always seemed to be just about finished. That goes doubly, triply, exponentially, for the heart of my one world, Ilona Miko. She read and responded to the opening sections of the book, listened as I tried to explain it all again and again, and brought her eye (and ear!) for clear and deliberate communication to bear on my recalcitrant elaborations. I've tested her patience more than once with this thing, but she remains steadfast. This book is for her.

Index

Abd al-Hadi, Awni, 105, 107
Abd al-Hadi, Ruhi, 105, 107
Abd al-Ilah, Prince of Iraq, 114, 119
Abd-al-Nasser, Gamal, 75
Acheson, Dean, 219
Addams, Jane, 59
African Americans, 10, 31–32; anticolo-
    nialism and, 223, 225; internationalists
    and, 215, 217; support of Willkie and, 10,
    43, 46, 230; war and undermining of
    racism (double V) and, 73, 225; Willkie's
    death and, 296; Willkie's support of civil
    rights of, 230, 244, 252–253, 291, 307
Agee, James, 305, 307
Age of broadcasting: Luce and Willkie's
    idealism, 134; "one world" idea and,
    300–301, 303–304; Russia and the
    United States and, 154; Willkie and, 9,
    11, 42, 57; Zionism and, 110
Air travel: conditions in 1940s, 15–17;
    Gulliver's "firsts" and, 212; shah of
    Iran's first flight, 126–127; shrinking
    globe and, 8, 16, 69, 222, 249, 251,
    301–302
Allen, William Prescott, 256
Altman, Dr. Aryeh, 105
America First Committee, 48–49, 244,
    264, 319
"American Century, The" (Luce), 61
American exceptionalism, 6, 14, 72, 137,
    139, 304, 306

Americanness, Willkie and, 58, 134–135,
    254, 261–262, 318
American Program, An (Willkie), 295
Americans United for World Organization,
    277
American University of Beirut, 92, 121
Angell, Norman, 303
Anglo-Iranian Oil Company, 129
Anticolonialism, 74–75, 103, 198–203, 223,
    228; anticolonial nationalism, 74,
    199–200, 307, 309; Willkie and, 240,
    256, 262, 271, 283, 307, 309
Anticommunism: China and, 186; Soviet
    Union and, 143, 151
Anti-imperialism, 14, 30; Churchill's
    Mansion House speech, Willkie, and
    postwar world, 207–209, 233–235;
    planning for postwar "trusteeship" of
    former dependencies, 286–291; race
    and, 31; West Africans and, 51–52;
    Willkie's commitment to, 230, 233–235;
    Willkie's "Report to the People" and,
    221–229
Anti-Semitism, 48, 103, 106, 108–111.
    See also Zionism / Zionists
Apollo 8, and changing perceptions of
    world, 314
Arab Higher Committee, 105, 107
Arab revolt (1936), 103, 105, 106–107
"Arc of Instability," Middle East as, 317
Armenian genocide, 85

Arnold, Hap, 18

Atatürk ("father of the Turks"). *See* Kemal, Mustafa

Atlanta Constitution, 263

Atlantic, 110

Atlantic Charter, and self-determination, 213; China and, 201–204; Egypt and, 67–68, 71, 75; Great Britain and, 133, 232, 287; Iran and, 133, 135–136, 138–140; Iraq and, 116–117, 121, 265; Lebanon and Syria and, 97–99; Palestine and, 100, 109, 112; planning for postwar "trusteeship" of former dependencies, 232, 286–287, 290; public opinion about, 274; Turkey and, 88; Welles on, 286; Willkie and, 140, 222–224, 229–234, 241, 245, 250–252, 262, 303; World War II goals and, 7–8, 11, 61–62, 74–75, 287

Attlee, Clement, 166, 232

Baath Party, 118

Badger, John Robert, 256

Baldwin, George R., 264

Balfour, Arthur, 102

Balfour Declaration, 102, 104, 108, 112

al-Barazi, Husni, 96

Barnard, Ellsworth, 40–41

Barnes, Joseph, 1, 19, 20, 51–52, 72, 275; biography of Willkie, 308–309; China and, 177, 190, 197; on Henrietta Willkie, 23; in Iran, 129; in Iraq, 122; on MacMichael, 100–101; *One World* and, 242; in Palestine, 104; in the Soviet Union, 140, 145, 155, 159, 160, 162, 165, 168, 169, 175; in Turkey, 86; on Willkie, 27, 32, 40, 41, 67, 272, 273

Ben-Gurion, David, 105–106, 107, 109

Bentham, Jeremy, 58

Beria, Lavrentiy, 168, 171

Berlin, Isaiah, 233

Bevans, Tom Torre, 236, 248

Beveridge, Albert, 30

Big Four. *See* Four Policemen

Big Money, The (Dos Passos), 36

Bilad al-Sham, 93, 102

Birmingham Age-Herald, 263

Black freedom struggle, global, 73, 225. *See also* African Americans; Civil rights movement, in the United States

Blum, John Morton, 276

Blum, Léon, 91

Boas, Franz, 74

Borman, Frank, 314

Bourke-White, Margaret, 153–154

Breakfast at Tiffany's (Capote), 309

Bridges, Harry, 296

Brock, Ray and Mary, 128

Brown, James, 170

Brush, Katharine, 38, 41

Bryan, William Jennings, 23, 32

Bryce, James, 69, 70

Buck, Pearl, 72–73, 192–194, 215, 225, 305

Buell, Raymond, 39, 213, 283

Capitalism: American anti-imperialism and, 288; China and, 191–192; Communism and the Soviet Union's economic growth, 143, 149–153; global capitalist system, 13–14, 62, 261, 299, 305, 314–315; Stalin's concerns about, 161, 171. *See also* Free trade policies

Capote, Truman, 309

Cassidy, Henry, 154–155, 167

Catroux, Georges, 91, 93

Catroux, Madame, 99–100

Chamberlain, John, 261–262, 263, 286

Chennault, Claire L., 182–184, 219

Chiang Kai-shek: in *One World,* 248; Willkie's China mystique and, 191–193; Willkie's trip and, 19, 20, 180, 184–190; World War II goals of, 181–184

Chiang Wei-kao, 188

Chicago Defender, 256

Chicago Sun, 263

Chicago Tribune, 211, 214, 231

Childs, Marquis, 241, 257

China: anticolonial imperialism and, 198–203; deaths in World War II, 243; India and, 220, 225; internationalism and postwar world order, 62, 174–175; Iran and, 127–128; Nationalist government (Guomindang) in, 175, 178–181, 182, 184–186, 188–190, 192–194, 195,

200, 202, 218, 225, 247, 307; as one of Four Policemen, 12, 62, 283; postwar planning and United Nations, 283; racism and, 185, 191–193, 199–201, 203; roots of Willkie's belief in China mystique, 190–192; trade issues and, 191–193, 254; treaty ports and, 199–200, 254; US pioneer narrative and, 257–259; Willkie and Mayling Soong, 196–198, 203; Willkie's Chongqing speech and, 203–206, 218–219; Willkie's journey to, 175–177; Willkie's preparation for global trip and, 18, 19; Willkie's visit to, and diplomacy, 174, 184–190; Willkie's visit to, and public reception, 177–181; World War II and, 175–177, 181–187, 192–193, 204, 207

China mystique, 190–195, 202; Mayling Soong as embodiment of, 196

Chinese-American Institute of Cultural Relations, 202

Chongqing speech, of Willkie, 203–206, 211–212, 218–219, 232

Christian Century, 229, 230

Christian Science Monitor, 104, 120, 134, 211, 212, 229, 295

Churchill, Winston, 45, 133; Atlantic Charter and, 7, 11, 61–62, 223–224; mandate system and, 90, 91, 97, 115; Mansion House speech of, 207–209, 233; position on British empire after World War II, 208, 287; postwar planning and, 282; reactions to Willkie's "Report to the People," 232–233; Soviet Union and second front issue, 166–167, 169; Stalin and, 161; trip to Moscow, 157, 166; Willkie meets with, 56; Willkie's internationalism and, 265

Civilization, race, empire, and hierarchy of, 30–31, 68–72, 74, 226–228, 232, 288, 302, 304; China and, 191–192, 199, 201, 258; Egypt and, 71–72; Iran and, 136, 139–140; Palestine and, 89–90, 102, 107, 110, 194; Soviet Union and, 150–151, 153, 194, 258; Turkey and, 80–82, 85, 194

Civil rights movement, in the United States, 72–74, 244; "double V" and, 73, 225; election of 1940 and, 47–48;

Willkie's commitment to, 230, 244, 252–253, 291, 307

Clapper, Raymond, 213

Clark Kerr, Archibald, 168, 169, 172, 280, 304

Climate change, 316–317

Cobden, Richard, 260

Cold War era, 278, 289, 310–312, 315; America First and, 244; "loss" of China and, 181; one world concept and, 14, 303, 306–308, 319; US foreign policy and, 306, 313; US nationalism and, 276, 281–282

Collier's, 9, 44, 54–55, 234, 291

Colonialism: Egypt and, 68; Great Britain and, 75, 225, 265; United Nations and platform for decolonization, 312–313; World War II as opportunity to end, 3, 11–12, 61, 73. *See also* Anticolonialism; Mandate system

Color and Democracy (Du Bois), 303

Commager, Henry Steele, 265

Commission to Study the Organization of Peace, 215

Commonwealth and Southern (utility holding company), 34–37

Commonwealth compromise, suggested for Great Britain, 227–228, 232, 287

Communism: and capitalism's shared faith in modernization and economic growth, 149–153; in China, 175, 178, 181, 185–186, 189–190; in the Soviet Union, 143, 162, 171, 280–281

Convergence theory, regarding the Soviet Union, 152–153

Cornwallis, Kinahan, 119

Cortas, Wadad Makdisi, 95

Corwin, Norman, 308

Cowles, Gardner "Mike" Jr., 1, 19–20, 27, 210, 284, 292; China and, 176, 188, 197; in Egypt, 64, 65; in Iran, 129; in Iraq, 114, 122; Lebanon and Syria and, 98–100; Office of War Information and, 1, 19, 99, 274; *One World* and, 242; in Palestine, 104; as publisher, 43, 110, 211, 229; in the Soviet Union, 145, 155, 162, 165, 168, 169; in Turkey, 86; on Willkie's internationalism, 174–175

Cowles, John, 44
Cowley, Malcolm, 264
Cripps, Stafford, 224, 225, 227

Daily Mail, 232
Daily Oregonian, 224
Dallas Morning News, 212
al-Daoud, Salman Shaikh, 116, 124
Darlan, Jean François, 235, 241
Davenport, Russell, 43, 174
Davies, John Paton, 180, 197–198
Davies, Joseph, 153
Davis, Forest, 235, 283
Davis, Gary, 310–311
Debs, Eugene V., 30
De Gaulle, Charles, 5, 90–92, 97–99, 100
Des Moines Register, 43
Dewey, Thomas E., 44, 241, 272, 273, 291, 295
Divine, Robert, 217
Dodge, Bayard, 92
"Dollar diplomacy," of the United States, 137, 254, 305
Dos Passos, John, 36
"Double victory," 73, 225
Dreiser, Theodore, 147
Dreyfus, Louis, 133, 135, 220
Drummond, Roscoe, 229, 295
Druze-Syrian Arab revolt (1925), 95
Du Bois, W. E. B., 61, 69–70, 71, 73, 303, 305, 307, 312, 313
Dulles, John Foster, 215
Duranty, Walter, 151

Eddy, Sherwood, 72
Eden, Anthony, 232, 267, 283
Egypt: British imperial system and, 66–68, 75–76; history of race and empire in, 68–69; United States and, 76–77, 306; Willkie's visit to, 53–56, 63–68, 75–77
Ehrenburg, Ilya, 158–159, 171
Eichelberger, Clark, 215
Eisenhower, Dwight D., 235
Election of 1940, 2, 3, 10, 19, 22; as beginning of Willkie's national influence, 47–49; civil rights issues and, 47–48; general election campaign,
17, 43–47, 213; other candidates for Republican nomination, 44; Willkie's growing interest in and talent for politics, 40–42; Willkie's internationalism as campaign issue, 43, 45–47; Willkie's loss to Roosevelt, 10, 46; Willkie's unofficial campaign for nomination, 42–44; World War II as backdrop of, 43, 45
Election of 1942 (mid-terms), 244–245
Election of 1944, 47, 55, 198, 211, 241, 245; Roosevelt's choice of Truman as running mate, 292, 298; Willkie and issue of endorsement of candidate, 273, 291, 293, 295; Willkie and Republican Party, 270–273, 291–292; Willkie and Roosevelt and third party, 292–294
Emotions, in politics, culture, and internationalism: one world concept and, 315–316; Orwell on, 11; Palestine and, 102, 137; World War II goals and, 275–276
"Empire of liberty," of Jefferson, 30
Empires: American, 12–13, 29–32, 191, 258, 288–290, 303–305, 315–317, 319–320; Dutch, 12, 43; European, 3, 5, 11, 12, 61, 76, 89, 252; French, 12, 43, 90–100; Japanese, 11; Jefferson's "empire of liberty," 12, 30; Soviet, 161. *See also* Anti-imperialism; Great Britain; Ottoman Empire
England. *See* Great Britain
Environmental movement, 314–315
Ewing, Mrs. O. L., 229
Exceptionalism, of all nations, 262. *See also* American exceptionalism
Extraterritoriality, China and, 199–200, 218

Fadiman, Clifton, 263
Failures, history of, 5
Fajardo Sugar Company, 27, 28
Farouk, king of Egypt, 63, 67–68, 75
Farrell, William S., 120
Farson, Negley, 232
Faysal I, king of Iraq, 94, 105, 115
Faysal II, king of Iraq, 118
Feminists. *See* Women

Filastin, 100, 105, 106, 112, 137

Fischer, Louis, 151

Flanner, Janet, 38

Foreign Affairs, 285–286

Fortune, 43, 153, 192, 216

"Four Fears," of Arabs, 139

Four Freedoms, of Roosevelt, 7, 62, 120, 139, 213, 245, 250, 274; Rockwell's paintings of, 275–276

Four Policemen, in postwar planning, 12, 62, 283, 303

Fowler, Frank, 214

France, and mandate system as *mission civilisatrice,* 90–100

Franklin, Benjamin, Willkie compared to, 214

Freedom House, 308

"Free enterprise," Willkie's' support of, 8, 32, 34, 36–37, 41, 149, 161, 243, 259, 261–262

Free trade policies, 30, 59, 60, 61, 315; *One World* and, 260–261; open-door trade with China and, 191–193, 254; spread of capitalist democracy and, 282; Willkie's support of, 211, 254, 260–262, 285, 305

Friedman, Thomas, 315

Fu'ad, king of Egypt, 75

al-Gailani, Rashid Ali, 114–115, 131

Gallup, George, 216

Gandhi, Mohandas, 200, 224, 225, 311, 313

Gann, Ernest, 16

Gardner, Mrs. J. D., 213

Gauss, Clarence, 180, 185, 220

Germany, deaths in World War II, 243

Gervasi, Frank, 54–55, 66

Gide, André, 147

Gilmore, Eddy, 17

Globalization, 306, 313–319; global capitalist system, 13, 62, 299, 305, 314–315; globalist fatigue and, 305–307; in history, 13–14; nationalists' concerns about the United Nations and ideal of, 277–281

Global mission, of Willkie, 2, 3, 301–302; in Egypt, 53–56, 63–68, 75–77; initial assessment of, 212–215; in Iran, 126–130,

131, 132–135, 137–140, 219; in Iraq, 113–114, 116–125, 219; in Palestine, 101–102, 103, 104–105, 107–108, 112; participants in trip, 15; post-trip meeting with Roosevelt, 208; preparation and planning for, 17–21; public interest in, 2–3; in Puerto Rico, 28–30, 49, 255; Roosevelt's goals for, 2, 3, 20; Roosevelt's warnings to Willkie about, 19; in Siberia, 209–210; trip from Puerto Rico to Africa, 49–52; in Turkey, 78–79, 80–81, 82, 83–87, 88, 216, 219; Willkie's fostering of global connection, 10–11, 14, 19, 128, 139, 217; Willkie's goals for, 3–4, 5–8, 141, 205; Willkie's meeting with Roosevelt after, 208, 219–221; World War II as backdrop of, generally, 50–52, 209. *See also* China; "Report to the People" of Willkie; Soviet Union, Willkie's visit to

Gölkap, Ziya, 78, 81

Good Earth, The (Buck), 193–194

Good Neighbor Policy, of the United States, 131, 254, 256

Graebner, Walter, 162, 172

Grafton, Samuel, 213, 214–215, 286

Grant, Madison, 31

Grant, Ulysses S., 178

Graves, John Temple, 263

Great Britain: Atlantic Charter and, 223; China and, 182; Churchill's defense of empire of, 208, 287; Commonwealth compromise suggested for, 227–228, 232, 287; distrust of Willkie's internationalism, 265; India and self-government issues, 224–228, 231, 233, 288; Iran and, 127, 129–130, 131, 132–133, 135–136, 137; Iraq and, 114–118, 120; Lebanon and Syria and, 90–92, 97–98, 100–110; as one of Four Policemen, 12, 62, 283; and planning for postwar "trusteeship" of former dependencies, 286–287; postwar planning and United Nations, 283; reactions to Willkie's "Report to the People," 232–233; United States and tolerance for imperialism of, 219–220; Willkie's 1941 trip to, 57, 67

Greider, William, 315–316, 317

Grigg, Edward, 232

Gulliver (Willkie's airplane): crew of, 1, 50; described, 1, 17; transportation "firsts" of, 212

Gunther, John, 72

Gwynn, William, 90, 92, 96–97

Halifax, Viscount, 232

Halstad, Lars, 213–214

Harwood, Henry, 66–67

Hashemites, 94, 102, 115

Al-Hawadith, 116

Hawai'i, 12, 205, 254, 288

Haykal, Muhammad Husayn, 71

Hersey, John, 275

Herzl, Theodor, 106, 107

Hindus, Maurice, 17

Historical watersheds, 4–5

Ho Chi Minh, 71, 185–186

Hoover, Herbert, 61, 296

Hopkins, Harry, 19, 292

Hull, Cordell, 20, 109, 133, 219, 223, 260–261, 267, 281–283, 289; Atlantic Charter and, 223; postwar planning and, 281, 282, 283, 289; trade and, 260, 261

al-Husayni, Hajj Amin, 103

Husayn, Sharif (Hashemite king), 94, 102

Hussein, Saddam, 118

Ickes, Harold, 42, 292

Immigration: attempts to limit, 31, 69, 319; China and, 192–193; Jews and Palestine, 101–105; self-government issues and, 69–70

Immigration Act (1924), in the United States, 192

Imperial gradualism, 226–228

Imperialism: imperial imagination of the United States, 30–32; international imperialism, 13, 266, 302; US tolerance of British, 219–220. *See also* Anti-imperialism; Empires

India: China and, 220, 225; self-government issues and Great Britain, 224–228, 231, 233, 288; Willkie's global trip and, 18

Inönü, Ismet, 80, 83, 84

Insull, Samuel, 35–36

Interdependence: interdependent internationalism, 10, 47, 88, 307; need for balance with independence, 32; Willkie on globe's, 3; Willkie's "declaration of," 265–266, 305; Willkie's idea of peace after World War II, 6–8, 11–14, 285–286

International imperialism, 13, 266, 302

Internationalism: anticolonial internationalism, 198–203; China and anticolonial, 198–203; conflict with nationalism, 261–263, 269, 302–303; and development of idea of United Nations, 266–268; growing support for, 215–218; historical development of, 58–59; interdependent internationalism, 10, 47, 88, 307; liberal internationalism, 219, 231, 236; postwar dismissal of, 306–308; race, empire, and "stage" of civilization, 68–72; supporters of, 215; Turkey and, 86–87; Willkie and election of 1944, 270–273; of Willkie, as 1940 campaign issue, 43, 45–47; Wilson and, 6; World War II, Willkie, and US role in world, 57–63

International nationalism, of China, 202

Iran: geopolitical importance of, 130; nationalism in, 130–132, 139; third power strategy of, 131, 137; United States and policy of "unselfishness," 126–127, 131, 132–140, 306; Willkie's visit to, 126–130, 131, 132–135, 137–140, 219

Iran (journal), 138

Iraq: mandate history and British in, 90, 94, 114–118, 120; military coup in 1958 and, 118; United States and, 117, 120–125, 306; Willkie's visit to, 113–114, 116–125, 219; World War II and, 114–118

Iraq Times, 119–120

Isolationism: America First Committee and, 48–49; "ex-isolationists," 293, 302; nationalism and, 6, 43, 284, 293; postwar planning and, 267, 276–278, 282; Republicans in 1940 and, 43–46; United States between world wars and, 60, 108–109, 139–140

Israel, 93, 105, 306. *See also* Zionism/Zionists

Istiqlal Party, 105, 107

Jackh, Ernest, 81

Japan: China and, 73, 175–176, 181–183, 185–189, 193, 199–200, 209; deaths in World War II, 243; issues of Pacific Theater after war, 274; race and, 71; Russia and, 69; Turkey and, 83

Japanese Americans, 244

Jefferson, Thomas, 12, 30

Jewish Agency, 104, 105, 106

Jews, rumors of subversion by, 244

Johnson-Reed Act (1924), 69

Jones, Lem, 295

Jordan, E. B., 296

Kemal, Mustafa, 79–82, 130

Kennan, George, 150, 171

Kern, Stephen, 301

Khan, Reza, shah of Iran, 127, 130–131

al-Khoury, Faris, 96, 97

Kight, Mrs. H. W., 237

Kight, Richard, 2, 112, 157, 301; on China, 182–183; as model for Willkie's internationalist, 245–246; *One World* and, 237; as pilot, 15, 16, 28, 49–50, 51, 113, 124, 125, 126, 140, 144, 175, 176, 177, 210; Siberia and, 210; in the Soviet Union, 157

Kingdon, Frank, 221

Kirk, Alexander, 54, 76, 90

Klotz, Alexis, 2, 49–50, 140, 176–177, 210

Krock, Arthur, 42, 214

Kung, H. H., 195, 202

Lamont, Thomas, 268, 289

Lampson, Miles, 75–76

Lange, Oscar, 296

Lattimore, Owen, 215

Lausanne, Treaty of, 80, 82, 88

League of Nations, 59–60, 70–71, 74–75, 298; idea of United Nations and, 61, 250, 281; mandate system and, 89, 94, 98, 108–109; public opinion and, 216–217; Smuts and, 227; Willkie's support of and disappointment about failure of, 7, 28, 32, 34, 41, 43, 203, 240, 248, 302

Lebanon and Syria: history of mandates and, 90–91, 93; Willkie in, 90–93, 96–97, 99–100

Lelyushenko, Dmitri, 156–157

Lend-Lease program, 56, 289, 291; Britain and, 18, 45; Egypt and, 63; Iran and, 129–130, 132; Iraq and, 116, 121; Russia and, 142, 155, 163–164, 219; Soviet Union and, 142, 163–164, 219; Turkey and, 84, 85

Lerner, Max, 215, 253–254, 256, 261, 262

Lewis, Sinclair, 33

Lexington Herald, 265

Liberal internationalism, 219, 231, 236

Liberalism: Cold War nationalist liberalism, 281–282; racial liberalism, 253, 264; in the United States, 149, 245; of Willkie, 32, 72, 308–309

Life, 1, 9, 43, 44, 61, 134–135, 136, 153–154, 162, 163, 172, 192, 194, 211, 218, 227

Lilienthal, David, 259–260

Lindley, Ernest, 166

Lippmann, Walter, 47, 61, 74, 231, 233, 263, 278–279, 284, 289, 307

Litvinov, Maxim, 20

Locke, Alain, 73

Lodge, Henry Cabot, 277

Logan, Rayford, 227, 291

Longworth, Alice Roosevelt, 42

Look, 1, 43, 44, 47, 110, 241

Los Angeles Times, 134

Luce, Clare Boothe, 230, 279, 280–281, 307; China and, 188, 196

Luce, Henry, 61, 215, 217; China and, 188, 192–194; Willkie and, 43, 62, 279, 280–281

Lyons, Eugene, 281

MacArthur, Douglas, 272, 273

MacMichael, Harold, 100–102, 104

MacMickle, Virgil, 230

Malaria, in Africa, 51

Malley, R. J., 255

Malliet, A. M. Wendell, 230

Mallon, Paul, 264

Mandate system, 89–90, 227, 232; postwar planning for "trusteeship" of former dependencies, 286–291. *See also* Iraq; Lebanon and Syria; Palestine mandate

Mansion House speech, of Churchill, 207–209, 233

Mao Zedong, 175, 181, 189, 308
Mardom, 138
Maronite Christians, 94–96
Marx, Karl, 260
Marzoog, George Abdo, 77
Mason, Grant, 15, 16, 51, 169
Mazower, Mark, 90, 227
McCormick, Anne O'Hare, 230, 267
McGill, Ralph, 263
McKinley, William, 260
Mead, Margaret, 74
Menemencioglu, Numan, 80, 82–83,
  84–85, 87
Middle East, as "Arc of Instability," 317.
  See also Mandate system; *specific*
  countries
Mikoyan, Anastas, 168
Milani, Abbas, 132
Minneapolis Morning Tribune, 211
Minneapolis Tribune, 229
Missionaries, 72, 77, 109, 120–121, 123,
  191–192, 251, 255
Mission to Moscow (Davies), 153
Modernity: air travel as symbol of, 15,
  48; American University of Beirut as
  symbol of, 121; China's evolution and,
  192, 199; concern about consequences
  of shrinking world and, 69; Soviet
  Union and socialism and, 143, 150–151;
  Turkey's neutrality in World War II
  and, 79; Tennessee Valley Authority as
  symbol of, 260
Modernization: China and, 179, 190,
  194–195, 247, 258; communism and
  capitalism's shared faith in, 143, 149–153;
  Iran and, 130–131; Middle East and,
  110; race and goals of World War II,
  74; Soviet Union and, 143, 149–150, 153, 161,
  209, 247, 258; Turkey and, 79, 80–81,
  85, 87–88; Willkie and American-led,
  34, 259–261, 304, 306
Molotov, Viacheslav, 159–160, 162, 165,
  167–169, 171, 174, 267
Monroe Doctrine, 12, 137, 254, 288
Montgomery, Bernard, 64–66, 77, 103
Moscow agreement (1943), 267–269, 270,
  280
Mossadeq, Mohammed, 137
Mowrer, Edgar Ansel, 299

Multilateralism / multilateralists, 59–62,
  216–217, 250, 282, 319
Mumford, Lewis, 259
Muratov (Siberian communist official),
  209–210
Murray, Wallace, 135
Muslims: in Iraq, 115; in Lebanon and
  Syria, 91, 93–94, 95–96, 111

NAACP, Willkie and, 73, 200, 252. *See also*
  White, Walter
Nadi, Yunus, 80
al-Nahhas, Mustafa, 63, 67–68, 75
Naqqash, Alfred, 92–93, 96
Narrow nationalism, 218, 245; Trump and,
  318; Willkie's warnings against, 13, 14,
  29, 49, 209, 266, 302
Nation, The, 273
National Geographic, 110–112
Nationalism: anticolonial nationalism, 74,
  199–200, 307, 309; anti-Semitism, Jews
  and, 106; conflict with internationalism, 261–263, 269, 302–303; in Egypt,
  139; free trade and, 260–261; in India,
  224–225; international nationalism, of
  China, 202; in Iran, 130–132, 139; in
  Iraq, 114–118, 120–125; lingers after
  isolationism, 235–236; nationalists'
  concerns about the United Nations and
  ideal of globalism, 277–281; postwar
  realities of, one world concept and,
  299–304; Trump and white nationalism, 319; in Turkey, 79, 81–82, 83, 86;
  Willkie's hopes for Palestine and, 112;
  Willkie's writing about sovereignty
  and, 284–286; after World War II, 317.
  See also Narrow nationalism
"Natives," Willkie on, 257–259
Nehru, Jawaharlal, 75, 198, 200, 224–225,
  309, 311–313
New Deal, 32, 34–37, 40, 42–43, 149;
  Willkie's pro-business conflict with, 45,
  60, 152, 244–245, 259, 276, 293
New Masses, 212
New Szechwan Daily, 202
New York Amsterdam News, 230
New York Daily Mirror, 166
New York *Daily News,* 211

New Yorker, 9, 213, 239, 263
New York Herald Tribune, 1, 17, 39–40, 42, 173–174, 214; Willkie's speech at forum of, 233–235
New York Post, 213, 229–230, 286
New York Times, 42, 84, 124, 128, 160, 212–214, 230–231, 241, 257, 280; Willkie's "Don't Stir Distrust of Russia" in, 280–281
New York Times Magazine, 241
Niebuhr, Reinhold, 263, 278, 281

Obama, Barack, 318
Office of Strategic Services (OSS), report on Iran, 136
Office of War Information (OWI), 1, 19–20, 99, 186, 259–260, 274–275
One World Award, 308
One world concept, of Willkie, 3, 9, 10, 14, 248, 262; globalization and, 313–318; Lerner and, 254; postwar realities of nationalism and political power, 269, 299–306; potential of United Nations and, 309–313; public opinion and, 315–316; shrinking globe and, 8, 222, 249, 251, 299–302. *See also* Internationalism
One World Flight (documentary), 308
"One World (Not Three)" (Sting), 314
"One world or none" expression, 310–312
One World, Ready or Not (Greider), 315–316
One World (Singer), 316–317
One World (Willkie), 234, 263–266, 303, 304–305, 307, 311, 312; American empire in, 253–257; China in, 183–184, 185, 194, 201; civil rights in, 252–253; critiques and reviews of, 238, 263–266, 278, 279–280; epilogue to, 266; film version of, proposed, 239, 281, 296, 308; Iraq in, 117, 122; open trade and modernization, 259–261; origins of idea for, 236; popularity of, 3, 237–239, 268, 277; race and empire in, 252–253; "reservoir of good will" for the United States in, 251–252; Soviet Union in, 148–149; Stalin in, 163; style of, 247–248; Turkey in, 85–86, 88; Willkie

and writing of, 40, 242; Willkie's vision of internationalism and, 239–240, 248–251, 263–266
"Open door" trade policy, China and, 191–192
Orientalism. *See* China mystique
Orwell, George, 10–11
Ottoman Empire: Egypt and, 68, 70; Lebanon and Syria and, 89, 91–95; Turkey and, 78, 81–82, 88

Pacifism/pacifists, 48, 61, 62, 70, 224, 244, 310
Pahlavi, Mohammad Reza, shah of Iran, 126–128, 131–132, 139
Palestine mandate: British opinions about, 110; history of Arabs and Zionists in, 100–109; history of mandates and, 90, 91, 93–94; *nakbah* catastrophe of 1948, 107; US opinions about, 110–112; Willkie in, 101–102, 103, 104–105, 107–108, 112
Palestine Post, 133
Pan American Airways, 15–16, 51
Passing of the Great Race, The (Grant), 31
Pearson, Drew, 42, 197
Peck, Graham, 186–187, 188, 194
Pegler, Westbrook, 42
Perkins, Frances, 197
Perry, Ralph Barton, 309–310
Philippines, 12, 70, 226, 255; "trusteeship" issues and, 205, 288
Pihl, Paul, 15
Pinchot, Gifford, 293
Pioneer myths, of the United States: China and, 191, 199; Palestine and, 110–112; Soviet Union and, 150, 257–259; Willkie and, 29, 155, 194, 257
P.M., 254
Pravda, 279
Problems of Lasting Peace, The (Hoover), 61
Progressive Party, 264, 293
Progressivism, 35, 59; Willkie and, 8, 32; Wilson and, 59, 277
Publishers Weekly, 238
Puerto Rico: "trusteeship" issues and, 12, 205, 256, 288; Willkie's 1942 visit to, 28–30, 49, 255; Willkie's work in, 26–27, 28

Qavam, Ahmad, 128, 131–132, 137
Queeny, Edgar M., 271

Racial discrimination: Buck as critic of, 72–73, 193; China and, 185, 191–193, 199–201, 203; Egypt and, 68–69; internationalists and, 68–72; Iraq and, 123–124, 136, 139–140; postwar planning and, 288; racial liberalism in the United States and, 253, 264; "scientific" racism, 192; Smuts and, 227–228; Soviet Union and, 150; US imperial ambitions and, 3, 30–32, 74, 291; World War II as opportunity to end, 3, 11, 73, 225. *See also* Civilization, race, empire, and hierarchy of
Rankin, John, 211
Reader's Digest, 43
Reid, Ogden and Helen Rogers, 40, 42–43
"Report to the People" of Willkie: India and self-government issues, 224–228; *One World* and, 251; reactions to, in Great Britain, 232–233; reactions to, in the United States, 229–231; US war aims and, 221–224, 228
Republican Party, 6, 8, 10, 60, 62, 235; election of 1940 and, 3, 19, 22, 40, 42–47; election of 1944 and, 211, 217, 245, 262, 266–268, 271–273, 292–293; mid-term elections of 1942 and, 241, 244–245
Robert College, 121
Robertson, Ben, 17
Robeson, Paul, 147, 212, 225
Rockwell, Norman, 275–276
Rommel, Erwin, 53, 55–56, 64, 65–66, 75, 80, 103, 106–107, 167, 207
Roosevelt, Eleanor, 215, 217, 296, 308
Roosevelt, Franklin D., 17, 39, 60, 217; Atlantic Charter and, 7, 11, 61–62, 116, 117, 121, 223–224; China and, 181, 183, 204, 205; convergence theory and, 152; Darlan and, 235, 241; death of, 298; dislike of imperialism, 287; election of 1940 and, 10, 45, 46; goals for Willkie's trip, 2, 3, 20; India and, 225; Iran and, 136; Lebanon and Syria and, 97, 100; Lend-Lease program and, 45, 56; possible government post for Willkie,

291–292; postwar planning and, 12, 61–62, 246, 267, 282–284, 288, 289–290; Stalin, the Soviet Union, and second front issues, 161, 162, 163, 164, 165, 166–167; Turkey and, 84, 86; Willkie's "Report to the People" and, 231; Willkie and letter to Stalin, 19–20, 159, 162, 165; on Willkie as "Private Citizen Number One," 9; Willkie's global trip preparation and, 18–20; Willkie's meeting with, after global trip, 208, 219–221, 241; Willkie's previous travels and, 17–18; Willkie's third party idea and, 293–294; Zionism and, 109. *See also* New Deal; Tennessee Valley Authority; World War II
Roosevelt, Theodore, 30, 31, 59, 61, 69, 70, 72, 293
Roper, Elmo, 273
Rosenman, Samuel, 293
Rourk, William C., 257
Runyon, Damon, 42, 44
Russia. *See* Soviet Union

al-Sadat, Anwar, 75
al-Said, Nuri, 113, 115–116, 117–118, 121–122, 248
Saracoglu, Sükrü, 80, 84
Saturday Evening Post, 9, 44, 111, 234, 235, 275, 283
Schneiderman, William, 241
"Scientific" racism, 192
Second front, in World War II: controversy around Willkie's support of, 167, 173, 175, 204, 208, 213, 219–220, 232, 235, 241; Soviet Union's concerns about, 142, 157–159, 165–167, 173; Turkey and, 80
Self-determination: Commonwealth compromise and, 227–228, 232, 287; Lippmann on, 278–279; Middle East and mandate system, 89, 95, 97, 117, 123–124, 258–259, 265, 287; Philippines and, 255; planning for postwar "trusteeship" of former dependencies, 286–291; race and, 69, 72, 85, 87, 288; United Nations' charter and, 290; Wilson and, 59–60, 68–69, 89, 121. *See also* Atlantic Charter, and self-determination

Senghor, Léopold, 311

"Separate spheres," Henrietta Willkie and doctrine of, 23

September 11, 2001 terrorist attacks, 317

Service, John Stewart, 178, 185, 194

Al-Shahab, 117

Shaw, George Bernard, 147

Sheean, Vincent, 72

Sheng Shicai, 176

Shertok, Moshe, 105, 107

Sherwood, Robert, 292

Shi'a Muslims, 93, 115

Shirer, William L., 39, 72, 223

Shotwell, James, 215

Siberia, 209–210

Simonov, Konstantin, 158–159

Singer, Peter, 316–317

Singh, J. J., 296

Smith, Gerald L. K., 244

Smith, Guy L., 264

Smuts, Jan, 70, 227–228

Socialism: in France, 91; New Deal and, 37; in the Soviet Union, 143, 148–151; Willkie and, 32

Soong, Mayling (Madame Chiang), 179, 180, 182, 192, 202; character of, 195–196; as embodiment of China Mystique, 196; family of, 195; Willkie and, 184, 196–198, 203

Soong, T. V., 20, 195, 200, 202

Sorokin, Pitirim, 152

Soviet Union: China and, 175–176, 189; concerns about postwar global alliance with, 279–281; Iran and, 127–130, 131, 132–133, 135–136, 137; as one of Four Policemen, 12, 62, 283; postwar planning and, 282, 283, 284, 289; state-driven economy of, 149–152; Turkish concerns about, 80, 82, 83, 84; World War II's impact on, 141–142, 144–146, 147, 153–155, 157–159, 168–169, 204, 243

Soviet Union, Willkie's visit to, 17, 18, 20; communism and capitalism's shared faith in modernization and economic growth, 143, 149–153; convergence theory and, 152–153; "cultural show" and exposure to Soviet life and industrialization, 142–143, 144–149, 154; flight to, 140–141; goals of international cooperation and, 141–143,

147–148, 170–172, 174–175; meetings with Stalin, 146, 159–165, 167–169; Soviet concerns about US aid and need for second front, 142, 157–159, 165–167, 173; trip to front, 155–157; US pioneer narrative and, 150, 257–259; US public opinion about the Soviet Union and, 150, 153–157

Sparrow, James, 245

Spears, Edward, 91–92, 95

Stalin, Joseph, 133, 250; character and personality of, 161, 171; industrialization and, 150–151, 161–162; meetings with Willkie, 146, 159–165, 167–169; in *One World,* 248; Willkie and Roosevelt's letter to, 19–20, 159, 162, 165; Willkie's global trip preparation and, 18, 19, 20. *See also* Soviet Union, Willkie's visit to

Standley, William, 144–145, 147, 148, 152–153, 158, 159–160, 167–168, 171, 220

Stassen, Harold, 272, 273, 279

State-driven economy, Soviet Union and, 149–152

Stevens, Edmund, 104, 120

Stilwell, Joseph "Vinegar Joe," 178–179, 180–184, 185, 188, 190–191, 194, 196, 198

Stimson, Henry, 235

Sting, 314

St. Louis Post-Dispatch, 299

Stormovik dive bomber plant, 144, 148, 154

Suez Canal, 68, 83, 102, 289

al-Sulh, Sami, 96

Sullivan, Mark, 231

Sulzberger, Arthur Hays, 212

Sunni Muslims, 93, 95, 96, 115

Sun Yat-sen, 108–111, 189–190, 195, 199, 218

Sykes-Picot Agreement, 94

Syria. *See* Lebanon and Syria

Szold, Henrietta, 107–108, 112

Taft, Robert, 44, 278

Ta Kung Pao, 200

Tan (Turkish paper), 88

Tennessee Valley Authority, 36–37, 259–260; Willkie's opposition to, 37, 40, 41, 149, 151

Thief of Baghdad, The (film), 123

This Week, 241

Thompson, Dorothy, 72, 231

Time, 43, 44, 61, 76, 84, 170–171, 192–194, 212, 277, 279

Time for Decision, The (Welles), 284

Times of London, 232

Tong, Hollington K., 176, 184

Toynbee, Arnold, 233

Treaty ports, in China, 199–200, 254

Trippe, Juan, 16

Truman, Harry: as Roosevelt's 1944 running mate, 292, 298; United Nations and, 298–300

Trump, Donald, 318–319

Turkey: competing Western narratives about, 79, 83; concerns about Russia in, 80, 82, 83, 84; internationalism and, 86–87; modernization in, 79, 80–81, 85, 87–88; nationalism in, 79, 81–82, 83, 86; United States and, 306; Willkie's visit to, 78–79, 80–81, 82, 83–87, 88, 216, 219

TVA: Democracy on the March (Lilienthal), 259–260

Twain, Mark, 30

Tydings, Millard, 231

Unilateralism/unilateralists, 59, 61–62, 184, 216–217, 282, 304

United China Relief (UCR), 72–73, 192, 194, 202

United Nations (allies during wartime), 84, 204, 250, 266

United Nations: development of idea of, 246–247, 250, 266–268, 276–277, 281–284; nationalist concerns about ideal of globalism, 277–281; Palestine and Zionism issues, 104; planning for "trusteeship" of former dependencies, 286–291; potential of one world concept and, 309–313; public opinion and, 303, 319; success dependent on managing nationalism and race, 302; Truman and, 298, 299

United States: Arab nationalism and, 117, 120–125; "dollar diplomacy" of, 137, 254, 305; as one of Four Policemen, 12, 62, 283; postwar planning and United Nations, 252, 283; postwar role of, envisioned in *One World,* 240; Willkie and "reservoir of good will" for, 220,

222, 251–252, 308; Willkie and World War II's meaning to, 56, 62–63; World War II and changing attitude toward federal authority, 242–245, 274–276; Zionism and, 110–112. *See also* Pioneer myths, of the United States

Universalism/universalists, 70, 278–279, 282, 300, 305–306, 310

U.S. Foreign Policy (Lippmann), 278

U.S. War Aims (Lippman), 278

Vandenberg, Arthur, 44, 278

Van Doren, Irita, 39–40, 72, 174; *One World* and, 236, 242

Versailles Treaty (1919): China and, 119, 202, 224; Egypt and, 67, 68, 71, 74, 76–77; Germany and, 164; Iran and, 130; Middle East and mandate system, 89, 93, 94, 105–106, 115; Wilson and internationalism, 59–60, 262

Voroshilov, Marshal, 168

Wagner, John, 50

Wallace, Henry, 61, 215, 217, 264, 279, 292

"War of liberation," World War II as, 7, 11, 117, 250, 305

Washington Post, 173, 179, 196

Welles, Sumner, 215; Atlantic Charter and, 223; civil rights and, 74; convergence theory and, 152; end of imperialism and, 211; postwar planning and, 281, 282, 284, 286–287, 288, 289; Zionism and, 109

Wells, H. G., 248

West, Rebecca, 39

"We the People" (Willkie), 43

Wheeler, Burton, 278

White, E. B., 248

White, Walter, 18, 47, 61, 73, 225, 252–253, 295, 305, 307

White, William Allen, 223

White nationalism, Trump and, 319

Whole earth movement, 314–315

Wiley, Alexander, 278

Willkie, Edith Wilk, 2, 20–21, 35, 38, 39, 221; marriage to Willkie, 27; Willkie's death and, 295–297

Willkie, Henrietta Trisch, 21, 22–23, 25–26

Willkie, Herman, 21–22, 23–24, 25–26, 32

Willkie, Philip, 20, 28, 49, 221, 296

Willkie, Wendell Lewis: belief in free enterprise as engine of opportunity, 36–37; birth name reversed by, 28; character and personality of, 2, 29, 34, 37–41, 161, 234, 257; charisma and influence of, 8–11; childhood and parents of, 21–26, 29; college and young adulthood of, 26–27; death of, 10, 294–297, 311; development of political, economic, and social ethics, 29–32; "friendships" with women, 39–40; hatred of injustice, 27, 28–29; legacy and influence of, 298–306, 308–309; marriage, 27; *New York Herald Tribune* forum speech of, 233–235; political and legal activities after global trip, 240–241; as popular medium for global connection, 39, 217; public opinion and, 57, 268; race and, 71–74; thoughts of starting third party, 292–294; trip to England in 1941, 57, 67; work as lawyer in Akron, Ohio, 33–34; work at utility holding company in New York, 34–37; World War I and, 27–28; writing about nationalism and sovereignty, 284–286

Wilson (film), 277

Wilson, Woodrow: China and, 199, 201, 203, 205; Egypt and, 68–69, 71; mandate system and, 89–90, 94; race and, 70–71; self-determination and, 121; trade and, 260; Truman honors, 298; Versailles Treaty and, 59–60, 74, 77, 89; Willkie's admiration for, 6, 27, 58, 72; Zionism and, 108. *See also* League of Nations

Women: internationalism and, 217; in Iraq, 120; as multilateralists, 59; peace movement and, 70, 215, 310; in the Soviet Union, 154, 156; "separate spheres" and, 23; in Turkey, 81, 86–87; World War II and, 243, 246; Zionism and, 107

Wong Pong Hai, 201

Worlds of Color (Du Bois), 312

World War I: American internationalism and, 59–60; Persia and, 130; Turkey and, 80, 85; Willkie and, 27–28, 156. *See also* Versailles Treaty (1919)

World War II, 207, 221, 310; as backdrop of 1940 election, 43, 45; as backdrop of global trip, 50–52, 209; as backdrop of stop in China, 175–177, 181–187, 192–193, 204; as backdrop of stop in Egypt, 1, 53–56, 63–68, 75, 77, 134, 173, 174; as backdrop of stop in Iran, 127–130, 131–136, 138–140; as backdrop of stop in Iraq, 114–118, 134; as backdrop of stop in Lebanon and Syria, 90–93; as backdrop of stop in Palestine, 134; changing American attitude toward and growth of federal authority, 242–245, 274–276; deaths in, 243; El Alamein and, 52, 64–66, 207, 244; GIs during and after, 245–246, 275–276; global nature of, 7; as hinge of the American Century, 5; impact on the Soviet Union, 141–142, 144–146, 147, 153–155, 159, 168–169; internationalist movement toward union of nations and, 215–216; Operation Torch and, 157, 167, 169, 207, 235; planning for postwar years, 12, 61–62, 246, 267, 276–278, 281–284, 286–291, 303; Tehran conference and, 133, 268–269, 287; Turkish neutrality and, 78–79, 82–85, 86, 173; as "war of liberation," 7, 11, 225, 250, 305; Willkie and future US role in world, 56, 57–63, 274; Willkie's idea of interdependence and peace after, 6–8, 11–14. *See also* Lend-Lease program; Second front, in World War II

Wyeth, Mabel, 214

Yalman, Ahmed Emin, 82, 216

Yang Yibo, 199

Yi Shih Pao, 201

Zaghlul, Saad, 68, 71, 94

Zanuck, Darryl, 239, 268, 277, 281, 296, 308

Zarubin, Georgiy, 147–148

Zhou Enlai, 189

Zionism/Zionists: in Europe and the Middle East, 94, 100–109; in the United States, 108–111